T0134107

MATHEMATICAL ASPECTS OF LOGIC PROGRAMMING SEMANTICS

Chapman & Hall/CRC
Studies in Informatics Series

SERIES EDITOR

G. Q. Zhang

Department of EECS
Case Western Reserve University
Cleveland, Ohio, U.S.A.

PUBLISHED TITLES

Stochastic Relations: Foundations for Markov Transition Systems
Ernst-Erich Doberkat

Conceptual Structures in Practice
Pascal Hitzler and Henrik Schärfe

Context-Aware Computing and Self-Managing Systems
Waltenegus Dargie

Introduction to Mathematics of Satisfiability
Victor W. Marek

Ubiquitous Multimedia Computing
Qing Li and Timothy K. Shih

Mathematical Aspects of Logic Programming Semantics
Pascal Hitzler and Anthony Seda

Chapman & Hall/CRC
Studies in Informatics Series

MATHEMATICAL ASPECTS OF LOGIC PROGRAMMING SEMANTICS

PASCAL HITZLER
KNO.E.SIS CENTER AT
WRIGHT STATE UNIVERSITY
DAYTON, OHIO, USA

ANTHONY SEDA
UNIVERSITY COLLEGE CORK
IRELAND

CRC Press
Taylor & Francis Group
Boca Raton London New York

CRC Press is an imprint of the
Taylor & Francis Group, an **informa** business
A CHAPMAN & HALL BOOK

CRC Press
Taylor & Francis Group
6000 Broken Sound Parkway NW, Suite 300
Boca Raton, FL 33487-2742

International Standard Book Number: 978-1-4398-2961-5 (Hardback)

Visit the Taylor & Francis Web site at
http://www.taylorandfrancis.com

and the CRC Press Web site at
http://www.crcpress.com

Dedication

To Anne, to Martine, and to the memory of Barbara and Ellen Lucille

Contents

List of Figures

List of Tables

Preface

This book presents a rigorous, comprehensive, modern, and detailed account of the mathematical methods and tools required for the semantic analysis of logic programs. It is, in part, the outcome of a fruitful research collaboration between the authors over the last decade or so and contains many of the results we obtained during that period. In addition, it discusses the work of many other authors and places it within the overall context of the subject matter. A major feature of the book is that it significantly extends the tools and methods from the order theory traditionally used in the subject to include non-traditional methods from mathematical analysis depending on topology, generalized distance functions, and their associated fixed-point theory. The need for such methods arises for several reasons. One reason is the non-monotonicity of some important semantic operators, associated with logic programs, when negation is included in the syntax of the underlying language, and another arises in the context of neural-symbolic integration, as discussed briefly in the next paragraph and in more detail in the Introduction. Furthermore, it is our belief that certain of our results, although here focused on logic programming, have much wider applicability and should prove useful in other parts of theoretical computer science not immediately related to logic programming. However, we do not discuss this issue in the book in detail and instead we give references to the literature at appropriate places in the text in order to aid readers interested in investigating this point more thoroughly.

All the well-known, important semantics in logic programming are developed in the book from a unified point of view using both order theory and the non-traditional methods just alluded to, and this provides an illustration of the main objectives of the book. In addition, the interrelationships between the various semantics are closely examined. Moreover, a significant amount of space is devoted to examining the integration of logic programming and connectionist systems (or neural networks) from the point of view of semantics. Indeed, in the wide sense of integrating discrete models of computation with continuous models, one can expect to employ a mix of mathematical tools of both a discrete and continuous nature, as illustrated by the particular choice of models we make here. Therefore, there is a need in the study of the semantics of logic programming (and in the study of general models of computation) for a self-contained and detailed exposition of the development of both conventional and non-conventional methods and techniques, as just explained, and their interaction. This book sets out to provide such an exposition, at

xvi   *Preface*

least in part, and is, we believe, unique in its content and coverage and fills a significant gap in the literature on theoretical computer science.

The book is mainly aimed at advanced undergraduate students, graduate students, and researchers interested in the interface between mathematics and computer science. It presents material from the early days of logic programming through to topics which are of current importance. It should be of special interest to those engaged in the foundations of logic programming, theoretical aspects of knowledge representation and reasoning, artificial intelligence, the integration of logic-based systems with other models of computation, logic in computer science, semantics of computation, and related topics. The book should also prove to be of interest to those engaged in domain theory and in applications of general topology to computer science. Indeed, it carries out for logic programming semantics, in a general model-building sense, something akin to what the well-known treatments of Abramsky and Jung [Abramsky and Jung, 1994] and Stoltenberg-Hansen et al. [Stoltenberg-Hansen et al., 1994] set out to do for the semantics of conventional programming languages.

We have inevitably built up a considerable debt of gratitude to a number of colleagues, collaborators, post-doctoral researchers, and post-graduate students during the course of conducting the research presented here. It is therefore a pleasure to record our thanks for insights, comments, and valuable discussions to all of them. They include Sebastian Bader, Federico Banti, Howard Blair, Eleanor Clifford, Artur S. d'Avila Garcez, Ben Goertzel, Barbara Hammer, Roland Heinze, Steffen Hölldobler, Achim Jung, Matthias Knorr, Ekaterina Komendantskaya, Vladimir Komendantsky, Ralph Kopperman, Markus Krötzsch, Kai-Uwe Kühnberger, Luis Lamb, Máire Lane, Jens Lehmann, Tobias Matzner, Turlough Neary, John Power, Sibylla Prieß-Crampe, Paulo Ribenboim, Bill Rounds, Sibylle Schwarz, Paweł Waszkiewicz, Matthias Wendt, Andreas Witzel, Damien Woods, and Guo-Qiang Zhang. In particular, we are grateful to Sebastian Bader for his contribution to Chapter 7, and indeed this chapter was written jointly with him.

Our acknowledgments and thanks are also due to a number of institutions and individuals for hosting us on a number of research projects and visits and to various funding agencies for making the latter possible.

In particular, Pascal Hitzler acknowledges the support of Science Foundation Ireland; the Boole Centre for Research at University College Cork; University College Cork itself; the Deutscher Akademischer Austauschdienst (DAAD); and Case Western Reserve University, Cleveland, Ohio. While conducting the research which led to the contents of this book, P. Hitzler changed affiliation several times, and he is grateful to University College Cork Ireland; the International Center on Computational Logic at Technical University Dresden; Case Western Reserve University, Cleveland, Ohio; the Institute for Applied Informatics and Formal Description Methods (AIFB) at the University of Karlsruhe; and the Kno.e.sis Center at Wright State University, Dayton, Ohio for providing excellent working environments.

It is a pleasure for Anthony Seda to thank Professor Steffen Hölldobler for providing excellent research facilities and hospitality on two visits to the Knowledge Representation and Reasoning Group at the Artificial Intelligence Institute of the Department of Computer Science, Technical University Dresden, and to thank Deutscher Akademischer Austauschdienst (DAAD) for support on those occasions. He also acknowledges research support provided by the Boole Centre for Research in Informatics, Science Foundation Ireland, and University College Cork and is also considerably indebted to University College Cork for the leave of absence needed to finish this work.

We also wish to thank several publishers for permission to reproduce parts of certain of our papers, as follows.

• Elsevier Science Publishers Ltd. for extracts from [Hitzler and Seda, 1999a], [Hitzler and Seda, 2002b], [Hitzler and Seda, 2003], [Hitzler et al., 2004], and [Seda, 2006].

• International Information Institute for extracts from [Lane and Seda, 2006], [Seda, 2002], and [Seda and Lane, 2005].

• IOS Press for permission to reprint the examples on Pages 111 and 112 from [Seda, 1997].

• Oxford University Press for extracts from [Seda and Hitzler, 2010].

• The Mathematics Department of Auburn University, USA for extracts from [Hitzler and Seda, 1999c] and [Seda and Hitzler, 1999b].

Finally, we are grateful to Kari A. Budyk, Iris Fahrer and especially to Randi Cohen, all of Taylor & Francis Group, for their sustained help and unfailing assistance at all stages in the preparation of the book for publication. In addition, we would like to express our thanks to Shashi Kumar at the LaTeX Help Desk for solving a number of problems concerned with typesetting and to the editorial support staff of Taylor & Francis Group for their careful reading of the manuscript. We are highly indebted to the referees also for their many helpful comments and suggestions, which led to a considerable broadening and extension of the scope of the book, and also to the inclusion of a number of important topics which otherwise would have been omitted. Last, but very far from least, we extend our heartfelt thanks to our wives, Anne and Martine, for their constant support and also for their endurance and forbearance in the face of countless hours spent by us in the preparation of the manuscript.

Pascal Hitzler

Anthony Seda

Dayton and Cork

Introduction

Logic programming is programming with logic. In essence, the idea is to use formal logic as a knowledge representation language with which to specify a problem and to view computation as the (automated) deduction of new knowledge from that given. The foundations of logic programming are usually based upon the seminal paper of Robert Kowalski [Kowalski, 1974], which built on John Alan Robinson's well-known paper [Robinson, 1965] wherein foundations were laid for the field of automated deduction using the resolution principle. These ideas gave rise, more or less simultaneously, to the programming language Prolog, first realized by Alain Colmerauer et al. in Marseilles in 1973, see [Colmerauer and Roussel, 1993]. In this computing paradigm, a knowledge base is given in the form of a logic program, which may be thought of as a conjunctive normal form of a formula in the first-order language $\mathcal{L}$ underlying the program as defined formally in Chapters 1 and 2. Then the program, or system, can be queried with conjunctions Q of partially instantiated atomic formulas, that is, with conjunctions of atomic formulas containing variables. The resulting answers produced by the system are substitutions θ for these variables by terms in $\mathcal{L}$ such that $Q\theta$ is a logical consequence of the knowledge base. The automated deduction performed by the system is usually based on a restricted form of resolution called *SLD(NF)-resolution*, see [Apt, 1997].

Since this early work, logic programming has become a major programming paradigm and has developed in a considerable number of different and diverse directions, including automated deduction (in the context, for example, of model checking), natural language processing, databases, knowledge representation and reasoning (including applications to the Semantic Web), cognitive robotics, and machine learning, to mention a few. Furthermore, the industrial applications using the underlying technologies, Prolog in the main, but also an increasing number of related systems, are growing steadily more numerous and more and more varied.[1]

---

[1]For some examples, the proceedings of the annual International Conference on Logic Programming (ICLP) provide a current view of the subject. The book [Bramer, 2010] contains an introduction to Prolog programming. A standard reference for the theory underlying Prolog programming is [Apt, 1997]. The reference [Apt and Wallace, 2007] contains much about constraint logic programming. See [De Raedt et al., 2008] for details of current work in (probabilistic) inductive logic programming. For information about disjunctive logic programming systems, see [Leone et al., 2006] and the website for the DLV project at http://www.dbai.tuwien.ac.at/proj/dlv/, and for information concerning the related system smodels, see [Simons et al., 2002] and the website http://www.tcs.hut.fi/Software/smodels/.

This book is concerned with the theory of logic programming languages or, in other words, with their syntax and their semantics, especially the latter. Very briefly, syntax in this context deals with formal grammar and automated deduction, as discussed earlier; semantics, as usual, is occupied with meaning. We will discuss semantics in more detail next. However, it should be observed straightaway that the semantics of logic programming languages is complicated in a way which is peculiar to them by the introduction of negation into their syntax. The manner in which one handles negation is important, and it is worth remarking that its development in logic programming has been much influenced by the development of negation in non-monotonic reasoning, a subject familiar in the field of artificial intelligence. Therefore, it will be helpful to say a little about negation in these terms before describing in detail the precise objectives of the book and its contents. This is because our treatment of negation and semantics, see Chapter 2, is partly guided by these considerations and also because negation and semantics are central themes of the book.

Non-monotonic reasoning came into existence as a result of the desire to capture certain aspects of human commonsense reasoning based on the observation that, in many situations occurring in everyday life, humans can reach conclusions under incomplete or uncertain knowledge. More formally, it is typically the case that more facts can be derived from given facts or knowledge when using commonsense reasoning than is the case when first-order logic is employed. This has the consequence that some conclusions already made may have to be withdrawn when more facts become known. By contrast, classical logics such as propositional or predicate logic are monotonic in that whenever a formula F is entailed by a theory or set of formulas Γ, then $\Gamma \cup \{G\}$ still entails F, for any formula G.

The non-monotonic aspect of commonsense reasoning, however, has turned out to be rather difficult to formalize in a satisfactory way. Early work in this area was mainly based on three entirely different approaches[2]: John McCarthy's circumscription, see [McCarthy, 1977, McCarthy, 1980]; Robert Moore's autoepistemic logic, see [Moore, 1984, Moore, 1985]; and Ray Reiter's default logic, see [Reiter, 1980]. In fact, Prolog naturally includes some features which can be viewed as being non-monotonic: if the system can prove that a certain fact A does *not* follow from a given knowledge base, or program, then A is considered to be false and hence $\neg A$ is considered to be true. However, by adding the fact A to the program, we can now prove A, and thus we have to retract the earlier conclusion $\neg A$. (Note that the negation occurring in $\neg A$ should not necessarily be taken here to be the negation encountered, say, in first-order logic, but rather it symbolizes *negation as (finite) failure* to prove A, as introduced in [Clark, 1978].)

---

[2]See [Gabbay et al., 1994] for an excellent account of some of the main approaches to non-monotonic reasoning including discussions of their advantages and drawbacks, and of the validity of the intuitions underlying non-monotonic reasoning. Introductory textbooks are [Antoniou, 1996, Berzati, 2007, Makinson, 2005].

For reasons of this sort, research into non-monotonic reasoning has influenced research into logic programming, and vice-versa, giving rise to important and fruitful ideas and research directions in both areas. In particular, such cross fertilization has led to the realization that logic programs, possibly augmented with some additional syntactic features, provide an excellent language for knowledge representation in the presence of non-monotonicity. In addition, such research has led to a number of implementations of non-monotonic-reasoning-based logic programming systems commonly known as *answer set programming* systems.[3]

Thus, the interaction between logic programming and non-monotonic reasoning is important. It is not, however, the main focus of our work. On the contrary, our main focal points are, in a nutshell, first, the detailed development of the mathematical tools and methods required to study the semantics of logic programs, and second, in order to illustrate these methods, the detailed development of the main semantics of logic programs per se. In addition, we give an application of the methods we present to study semantics in the context of neural-symbolic integration, as described in more detail shortly. Thus, we do not treat procedural matters and matters concerned with implementation in any depth, and indeed these issues are only touched on incidentally. We also do not discuss matters primarily concerned with non-monotonic reasoning other than in the context of their role in guiding our thinking in relation to negation in logic programs, as already noted. It will therefore be of value to say a little more about our precise objectives, and we do this next.

In common with most programming languages, the syntax of logic programming is comparatively easy to specify formally, whereas the semantics is much harder to deal with. Again, in common with other programming languages, there are several ways of giving logic programs a formal semantics. First, logic programs have, of course, a *procedural* or *operational* semantics, which describes and is described by their behaviour when executed on some (abstract) machine. Second, unlike imperative or functional programs, logic programs have a natural semantics, called their *declarative* semantics, which arises simply because a logic program is a consistent set of well-formed formulae and can be viewed as a theory. This semantics is usually captured by means of models, in the sense of mathematical logic, and will play a dominant role in our development. Indeed, a central problem in the theory is the question of selecting the "right" model for a program, namely, a model which reflects the intended meaning of the programmer and relates it to what the program can compute. It is here that ideas from non-monotonic reasoning play a fundamental role in determining the right models, including well-known ones such as the supported, stable, and well-founded models. Third, a standard and very important way of selecting the appropriate models for a logic program is to as-

---

[3]For a discussion of these matters, see [Lifschitz, 1999, Marek and Truszczyński, 1999, Baral, 2003]. For current developments in non-monotonic reasoning (versus logic programming), one may consult the proceedings series of the International Conferences on Logic Programming and Non-Monotonic Reasoning (LPNMR), for example.

sociate with the program one or more of a number of operators called *semantic operators*[4] defined on spaces of interpretations (or valuations) determined by the program. One then studies the fixed points of these operators, leading to the *fixed-point* semantics of the program in question. This latter semantics can roughly be equated with the *denotational* semantics of imperative and functional programs associated with the names of Dana Scott and Christopher Strachey because some, but not all, of the important semantic operators which have been introduced are Scott continuous in the sense of domain theory, or at least are monotonic. Moreover, fixed points play a fundamental role also in denotational semantics. Finally, there is a general requirement that all the semantics described previously should coincide or at least be closely related in some sense.[5]

Taking the observations just made a little further forward, we note that there are several interconnected strands to the programme of analyzing the fixed points of semantic operators, but three of the main ones are as follows. First, we consider a number of operators already well-known in the theory, in addition to introducing several more. In this step, we focus on ensuring that the operators we study, and their fixed points, correctly reflect the meaning of programs and their properties. Second, we investigate the properties of the operators themselves, especially in relation to whether or not they are Scott continuous and, if not, what properties they do possess. Scott continuity is a desirable feature for a semantic operator to have because it implies that the operator has a least fixed point. Furthermore, this least fixed point is often taken to be the fixed-point semantics of the program in question, and indeed, operators which are not Scott continuous may in general fail to have any fixed points at all. Third, we study the fixed-point theory of semantic operators in considerable generality. In fact, the failure of certain apparently reasonable semantic operators (already known to capture declarative semantics) to be Scott continuous often results from the introduction of negation, because the introduction of negation may render the operators in question to be non-monotonic and hence to fail to be Scott continuous, as we will see in Chapter 2.

The point just made is important because it is one of the reasons for introducing alternatives to order theory in studying fixed-point theory in relation to semantics and in establishing fixed-point theorems applicable to non-monotonic operators, see Chapter 4. Therefore, it will help to give some insight next into the non-traditional methods we introduce and develop, how they work in the context of negation, and especially how they work in finding models for logic programs with negation. Our point of view is to regard programs, and logic programs in particular, as (abstract) dynamical systems whose states change under program execution and whose state changes can be modelled by an operator T. Starting with some initial state, s_0, say, it is inter-

---

[4]This is a generic term which we use to cover all of a number of specific operators we will study, such as the T_P-operator, see Definition 2.2.1.

[5]See Theorem 2.2.3, for example, and [Lloyd, 1987] for details of how procedural semantics relates to declarative semantics.

esting to observe the behaviour of the sequence of iterates s_0, $T(s_0)$, $T^2(s_0)$, $T^3(s_0)$, ... of T on the state s_0. Suppose, for example, that s_0 is the nowhere defined partial function on the natural numbers, and T is the operator on the partial functions determined in the usual way by some well-defined recursive definition on the natural numbers, see [Stoltenberg-Hansen et al., 1994], for example. Then, typically, the sequence of iterates will form an ω-chain as defined in Chapter 1 and will converge in the Scott topology (defined in Chapter 3) to the supremum s of the chain; thus, we have $s = \lim T^n(s_0)$ in the Scott topology on the partial functions. Furthermore, T will typically be Scott continuous (see Chapter 3 again for the definition of Scott continuity) in the sense that $T(s) = T(\lim s_n) = \lim T(s_n)$ whenever s_n is a sequence converging to s in the Scott topology, that is, a sequence satisfying $\lim s_n = s$. If T is indeed Scott continuous, then it is now easy to deduce that $T(s) = s$ so that s is a fixed point, in fact, the least fixed point, of T. (These observations are the heart of the proof of Kleene's theorem, Theorem 1.1.9, which is sometimes viewed as the fundamental theorem in semantics. They are also quite close in form to the proof of the Banach contraction mapping theorem, Theorem 4.2.3, except that it is order rather than a contraction property which determines the convergence.) In such a situation, s is usually taken to be the meaning or semantics of the original recursive definition. Precisely the same sort of thing happens in relation to logic programming semantics in the case of logic programs P which do not contain negation or in other words are definite programs. Specifically, the iterates of the single-step operator (or immediate consequence operator)[6] T applied to the empty interpretation converge in the Scott topology to an interpretation M. This interpretation M is the (least) fixed point of T, captures well the declarative semantics for P, and relates well to the procedural semantics for P under SLD-resolution, see Theorem 2.2.3 and the discussion following it.

Following on from the comments just made in the previous paragraph is the interesting observation from our point of view, or the mathematical point of view, that the discussion just presented can quite easily be generalized: all that one needs is an abstract notion of convergence and an abstract notion of continuity. Such a setting is provided by the notion of convergence space, and in particular by convergence classes or equivalently by topological spaces, as defined in Chapter 3. These notions provide a general setting in which one can study semantics and in particular logic programming semantics for logic programs P which may or may not contain negation. The classical case of definite programs corresponds to taking the Scott topology, but we consider quite extensively another topology, called the Cantor topology by us, defined in Chapter 3, which is closely connected to negation, has connections with the Scott topology, and underlies important classes of programs which do involve negation such as acceptable programs and their generalizations, see Chapter 5. Indeed, a quite elementary property we use is given in Proposition 3.3.2

---

[6]See Chapter 2 for the definitions of these terms.

and in a rather general form by Theorem 5.4.2 and simply states that if P is any logic program, and I is an interpretation such that $T^n(I)$ converges in the Cantor topology to an interpretation M, then M is a model for P; if, further, T is continuous in the Cantor topology, then M is a fixed point of T (here, again, T denotes the single-step operator associated with P). Further comments on this result are to be found in Remark 3.3.3 and in the comments immediately following Remark 3.3.3. In particular, this fact is exploited on a number of occasions to find models in the presence of negation and in particular in studying acceptable programs, as just mentioned, and also in studying the perfect model for locally stratified programs in Chapter 6. Indeed, the working out of this observation together with some of its implications occupies a significant proportion of our time. In addition, because convergence is a key notion, our development of topology in Chapter 3 is based on it, although the main conclusions presented there are also given in other equivalent and familiar forms.

In practice, detecting whether sequences converge or whether operators have fixed points is most easily done by means of metrics and more general distance functions (generalized metrics) together with their associated fixed-point theorems, the latter perhaps being reminiscent of the Banach contraction mapping theorem, see Theorem 4.2.3. Furthermore, underlying the use of generalized metrics are topologies defined on spaces of interpretations, and we study these in Chapter 3 with a view to developing, in conjunction with Chapter 4, the mathematical analysis we apply later in Chapters 5 and 6 in studying acceptable programs and related semantics, as already mentioned, and in Chapter 7 in the context of artificial neural networks in relation to logic programming. This latter work concerns the problem of integrating different models of computation in an attempt to combine the best of each in a single system and understanding the semantics of the combined system. In our case, we consider the integration of logic programming, perhaps taken as representative of discrete systems, with connectionist systems, or neural networks, considered as continuous systems inspired by biological models of computation. A means of doing this is to compute semantic operators by means of neural networks. However, in the case of first-order (non-propositional) programs, it is necessary to employ approximation techniques (rather than exact computation) which depend on viewing spaces of interpretations as compact Hausdorff spaces, that is, to employ yet again methods from mathematical analysis. Such applications as these are another important reason for developing a quite extensive body of mathematics which provides alternative tools to those based on order theory in studying semantics. In fact, one of the main highlights, themes and motivating features of this book is the analysis we carry out of foundational structures of various sorts, with an eye to potential applications in the field of computational logic in general, as exemplified by our results in, for example, Chapter 7. Indeed, it seems probable that such methods and tools will prove useful in developing foundations in other areas where discrete and continuous models of computation are combined, quite apart from neural-symbolic integration. Such non-classical models of computation are of great interest generally in present times and may contain both continuous and discrete components, especially those inspired by physical phenomena. As such, their study will almost certainly require techniques appropriate to both their continuous elements and to their discrete elements and may well be of the sort developed here.

It should be noted that other authors have, to a greater or lesser extent, employed mathematical analysis in the context of logic programming semantics. Their work is complementary to what we present here, and we briefly discuss some of it and its relationship with ours next and in more detail in the body of the text. For example, some of the recent work of Howard Blair and several of his colleagues on logic programming semantics is much concerned with the interaction between the continuous and the discrete, and it makes use of ideas from dynamical systems, convergence spaces, and automata theory to model hybrid systems. We consider this work further in Chapter 3. We mention also the work of Sibylla Prieß-Crampe and Paulo Ribenboim on the role of generalized ultrametrics in fixed-point theory in the context of logic programmimg semantics. They discuss both single-valued and multivalued mappings in this context, and we consider their results in considerable detail in Chapter 4 and some of their applications in Chapter 5. In addition, we also include in Chapter 4 a discussion of recent work of Umberto Straccia, Manuel Ojeda-Aciego, and Carlos Damásio on multivalued mappings in the context of semantics and the relationship between their work and ours. Finally, we discuss in Chapter 4 also the extensive work of William Rounds and Guo-Qiang Zhang on the use of domain theory as a theoretical foundation for logic programming, both from the point of view of procedural aspects and from the point of view of semantics.

Summarizing the chapters, Chapter 1 contains, in fairly condensed form, the preliminaries from order theory, domain theory, and logic which we will employ throughout this book. In addition, we present two well-known fixed-point theorems, based on order, which are fundamental in applications to semantics. The next chapter, Chapter 2, introduces logic programs and the most important ways of assigning semantic operators and declarative semantics to them. The manner in which the material is presented is rather novel and employs the syntactic notion of level mapping, defined in Chapter 2. Indeed, we make several different applications of level mappings in our discussions, and they play a unifying role in several places in the course of developing our main themes. For example, their use in Chapter 2 provides a uniform and comprehensive treatment of all of the important different semantics known in the subject, including those associated with the supported, stable, and well-founded models mentioned earlier.[7] Sets of interpretations are important in that they are, among other things, the carrier sets for the various semantic

---

[7]The uniform characterizations by means of level mappings which will be given in Chapter 2 are due mainly to [Hitzler and Wendt, 2002].

operators we discuss. Such sets themselves may be endowed with various, useful structures. In Chapter 3, we illustrate the point just made by studying various topologies on spaces of interpretations, including the Scott topology and a topology called the Cantor topology, as already mentioned. The continuity of semantic operators in the Scott topology is examined in Chapter 3, but the treatment of their continuity in the Cantor topology is deferred until we reach Chapter 5, where the results are needed. In fact, as noted earlier, it is convergence in these topologies which is of main interest because it can be used to find models for logic programs as we show in Chapters 5 and 6, and thus, convergence is the dominant theme in our development of topology.

We take the theme of structures defined on spaces of interpretations yet further in Chapter 4 in presenting a detailed account of both various generalized distance functions defined on spaces of interpretations and their associated fixed-point theorems. These tools, some of which depend on level mappings again, are developed specifically for investigating semantic operators of logic programs with negation, but we believe that Chapter 4 is a self-contained account of results which are likely to have applications within computer science outside those areas considered here. In Chapter 5, we combine the developments of Chapters 2, 3, and 4 by applying the fixed-point theorems of Chapter 4 to the more important semantic operators introduced in Chapter 2. More specifically, we focus on classes of programs, which we call unique supported model classes, each of which has the property that all programs in that class have a unique supported model. An example of such a class is the class of acceptable programs well-known in termination analysis, but we examine other important unique supported model classes as well. These classes are interesting because it turns out that for each of the programs they contain, many of the main semantics studied in the earlier chapters coincide, and hence the meaning of each program in a unique supported model class is unambiguous relative to the most important semantics. In essence, we obtain these classes by applying to various semantic operators those fixed-point theorems of Chapter 4 which guarantee a unique fixed point, if there is a fixed point at all. The process involves working with successively more general semantic operators, especially Fitting-style operators, and examining their properties in relation to single-step operators and convergence of their iterates in the Cantor topology studied in Chapter 3. Indeed, the process culminates in a very general semantic operator T which subsumes many of those studied in the earlier chapters, and we estabish many of its important properties in Chapter 5. In particular, we examine in depth the continuity of T in the Cantor topology, thereby obtaining the corresponding results for single-step operators and Fitting-style operators. Finally, we note that the work we do in this chapter consolidates the uniform approach provided in Chapter 2, employing level mappings, to encompass the additional semantics we introduce in Chapter 5.

Turning now to Chapter 6, our objectives here are twofold. First, we revisit the stable model semantics and establish a close connection between the well-known Gelfond–Lifschitz operator GL_P and the fixpoint completion fix(P) for any normal logic program P by deriving the identity $\text{GL}_P(I) = T_{\text{fix}(P)}(I)$, for any two-valued interpretation I, see Theorem 6.1.4. This will make it a simple and routine matter to prove many facts about GL_P, and hence about the stable model, from properties of the single-step operator, including the derivation of continuity properties of GL_P. Our second objective in Chapter 6 is to revisit stratification and the perfect model and to present an iterative process for obtaining the perfect model for locally stratified normal logic programs. This approach involves careful control of negation in order to produce monotonic increasing sequences by means of non-monotonic operators and is interesting for the insight it gives into the structure of the perfect model. In Chapter 7, we apply the topological and analytical tools developed earlier in order to discuss logic programming in the context of dynamical systems and artificial neural networks with a view, in particular, to presenting a detailed account of these methods in the foundations of neural-symbolic integration. Specifically, in Chapter 7, we consider the computation by artificial neural networks of various semantic operators associated with normal logic programs. We view this as a means of integrating these two computing paradigms because both can be represented by functions: the semantic operator on the one hand and the I/O function of the neural network on the other. In fact, exact computation of semantic operators is only possible in the case of propositional normal logic programs. In the case of first-order programs, approximation methods are required, and this is where analytical and topological methods make their entrance. Indeed, it turns out that continuity of a semantic operator in the Cantor topology is a necessary and sufficient condition for this approximation process to work, see Theorem 7.5.3. This observation is yet further motivation for studying the Cantor topology, and hence Chapter 7 represents an important application of analytical ideas in logic programming semantics. In Chapter 8, we give a brief discussion of further possible applications of our results and future directions for research involving the methods and results of this book. In particular, we discuss possible future work in the context of the foundations of program semantics, quantitative domain theory, fixed-point theory, the Semantic Web, and neural-symbolic integration, among other things. In the Appendix, we bring together a summary of those facts from the theory of ordinals and general topology which will be needed at various points in our investigations, but are not developed in the main body of the text; its inclusion makes our treatment essentially self-contained. In particular, the results of Chapter 3 together with those of the Appendix give a treatment of the Scott topology in terms of convergence.

Finally, on a point of convention, we note that the symbol ■ will be employed as an end marker in two ways in the body of the text. First, it will be used to indicate the end of every proof. Second, it will be used on a few occasions to mark clearly the end of any statement (theorem, proposition, definition, remark, example, program, etc.), where the end of that statement might otherwise be unclear.

About the Authors

Pascal Hitzler is an assistant professor at the Kno.e.sis Center for Knowledge-Enabled Computing, which is an Ohio Center of Excellence at Wright State University in Dayton, Ohio, U.S.A. From 2004 to 2009, he was an assistant professor at the Institute for Applied Informatics and Formal Description Methods (AIFB) at the University of Karlsruhe in Germany, and from 2001 to 2004 he was a post-doctoral researcher at the Artificial Intelligence Institute at TU Dresden in Germany. In 2001 he obtained a PhD in mathematics from the National University of Ireland, University College Cork, Cork, Ireland, under the supervision of Anthony Seda, and in 1998 he obtained a Diplom (Masters degree equivalent) in mathematics from the University of Tübingen in Germany. His research record lists over 150 publications in such diverse areas as the Semantic Web, neural-symbolic integration, knowledge representation and reasoning, denotational semantics, and set-theoretic topology. He is editor-in-chief of the IOS Press journal *Semantic Web – Interoperability, Usability, Applicability* and the IOS Press book series *Studies on the Semantic Web*. He is vice-chair of the steering committee of the conference series on Web Reasoning and Rule Systems (RR) and the RR2010 PC co-chair. He is co-chair of the 2010 International Semantic Web Conference (ISWC) "Semantic Web In Use" and "Industry" tracks and co-chair of the 2011 Extended Semantic Web Conference (ESWC) "Reasoning" track. He is co-author of the W3C Recommendation *OWL 2 Primer*, of the first German introductory textbook to the Semantic Web, published by Springer-Verlag, and of the book *Foundations of Semantic Web Technologies* published by CRC Press, 2009. For more information, see http://www.pascal-hitzler.de.

Anthony Karel Seda is a senior lecturer in the Department of Mathematics, University College Cork, Cork, Ireland. He holds a BSc and a PhD in pure mathematics from the University of Wales, UK, and an MSc from the University of Warwick, UK, also in pure mathematics. His research record lists nearly 100 publications in areas ranging from measure theory and functional analysis to topology and fixed-point theory in computer science through to denotational semantics and the semantics of logic programs, including two books of which he is a co-editor. In addition, he has a wide range of teaching interests, including the research areas just listed. He is a member of several editorial boards of journals, including the editorial board, and associate editor for Europe, of the international journal *Information*; editorial board of the *International Journal of Advanced Intelligence*; and he was for ten years a member of the board of editors of the *Bulletin of the European Association for Theoretical Computer Science (EATCS)*, and also, for a number of years, was on the editorial board of *Asian Information-Science-Life: An International Journal.* He is a co-founder of the "Irish Conference on the Mathematical Foundations of Computer Science and Information Technology (MFCSIT)," a conference series the proceedings of which are published by Elsevier Science Publishers, and has strong connections with a considerable number of other conferences. These include the conference series "International Information Conference," usually held in Asia, and the "International Workshop on Formal Methods," usually held in Ireland. He is a co-founder of the Boole Centre for Research in Informatics (BCRI) at University College Cork, is a member of its executive committee, and leader of the "Theory of Computation" theme within BCRI. He has led various groups of researchers in the theory of computation and has supervised many Masters degree and PhD degree students to completion. More information can be found at the Web site http://euclid.ucc.ie/pages/staff/seda/tseda.htm

Chapter 1

Order and Logic

The study of the semantics of logic programs rests on a certain amount of order theory and logic, and it will be convenient to collect together here in this first chapter those basic facts we need throughout the book to accomplish this study.[1] At the same time, we establish some notation and terminology which is common to all the chapters.

1.1 Ordered Sets and Fixed-Point Theorems

We start by presenting the minimum amount that we need of the theory of ordered sets. In addition, we discuss certain important and well-known fixed-point theorems applying to functions defined on ordered sets. In fact, the first of these theorems has fundamental applications in the semantics of computation in general, as well as in logic programming semantics.

Let D be a set. Recall that a binary relation $\sqsubseteq$ on D is simply a subset $\sqsubseteq$ of $D \times D$. As usual, the symbol $\sqsubseteq$ will be written infix, and hence we write $x \sqsubseteq y$ rather than $(x, y) \in \sqsubseteq$, where $x, y \in D$. Furthermore, we write $x \sqsubset y$ if $x \sqsubseteq y$ and $x \neq y$. The relation $\sqsubseteq$ on D is called *reflexive* if, for all $x \in D$, we have $x \sqsubseteq x$; it is called *antisymmetric* if, for all $x, y \in D$, $x \sqsubseteq y$ and $y \sqsubseteq x$ imply $x = y$; and it is called *transitive* if, for all $x, y, z \in D$, $x \sqsubseteq y$ and $y \sqsubseteq z$ imply $x \sqsubseteq z$. We call $\sqsubseteq$ a *partial order* if $\sqsubseteq$ is reflexive, antisymmetric, and transitive, and in that case we call the pair $(D, \sqsubseteq)$, or simply D when $\sqsubseteq$ is understood, a *partially ordered set*, a *poset*, or sometimes a *partial order* by abuse of terminology. We may sometimes simply refer to a partially ordered set $(D, \sqsubseteq)$ as an *ordered set* and to the relation $\sqsubseteq$ as an *ordering* (on D).

Two elements x and y of a partially ordered set D are said to be *comparable* if either $x \sqsubseteq y$ or $y \sqsubseteq x$ holds; otherwise, x and y are called *incomparable*. A non-empty subset $A \subseteq D$ is said to be *totally ordered* by $\sqsubseteq$ or is called a *chain* if any two elements of A are comparable with respect to $\sqsubseteq$, that is, given $a, b \in A$, we have $a \sqsubseteq b$ or $b \sqsubseteq a$. A partial order $\sqsubseteq$ on D is called a *total order* if D itself is totally ordered by $\sqsubseteq$. We call A an *ω-chain* if A is an increasing sequence $a_0 \sqsubseteq a_1 \sqsubseteq a_2 \ldots$, where ω denotes the first limit ordinal.

---

[1]The text [Davey and Priestley, 2002] is a useful reference for the subject of ordered sets.

(We refer the reader to the Appendix for a brief discussion of the theory of ordinals.) We note that any ω-chain is, of course, a chain.

A non-empty subset A of a partially ordered set $(D, \sqsubseteq)$ is called *directed* if, for all $a, b \in A$, there is $c \in A$ with $a \sqsubseteq c$ and $b \sqsubseteq c$. An element b in an ordered set D is called an *upper bound* of a subset A of D if we have $a \sqsubseteq b$ for all $a \in A$ and is called a *least upper bound* or *supremum* of A if b is an upper bound of A satisfying $b \sqsubseteq b'$ for all upper bounds b' of A. Of course, by antisymmetry, the supremum, $\bigsqcup A$ or sup A, of A is unique if it exists. Similarly, one defines *lower bound* and the *greatest lower bound* or *infimum*, $\bigsqcap A$ or inf A, of a subset A of D. An element x of D is called *maximal* (*minimal*) if we do not have $x \sqsubset y$ ($y \sqsubset x$) for any element y of D. Given an ordering $\sqsubseteq$ on a set D, we define the *dual ordering* $\sqsubseteq^d$ on D by $x \sqsubseteq^d y$ if and only if $y \sqsubseteq x$. Lower bounds, greatest lower bounds, etc. in $\sqsubseteq$ correspond to upper bounds, least upper bounds, etc. in $\sqsubseteq^d$.

1.1.1 Definition Let $(D, \sqsubseteq)$ be a partially ordered set.

(1) We call $(D, \sqsubseteq)$ an ω-*complete partial order* or an ω-*cpo* if $\bigsqcup A$ exists in D for each ω-chain A in D, and D has an element $\bot$, called the *least element* or *bottom element*, satisfying $\bot \sqsubseteq x$ for all $x \in D$.

(2) We call $(D, \sqsubseteq)$ *chain complete* if every chain in D has a supremum.

(3) We call $(D, \sqsubseteq)$ a *complete partial order* or a *cpo* if $\bigsqcup A$ exists in D for each directed subset A of D, and D has a bottom element.

(4) We call $(D, \sqsubseteq)$ a *complete upper semi-lattice* if $\bigsqcup A$ exists in D for each directed subset A of D, and $\bigsqcap A$ exists for each subset A of D.

(5) We call $(D, \sqsubseteq)$ a *complete lattice* if $\bigsqcup A$ and $\bigsqcap A$ exist in D for every subset A of D.

Later on, we will encounter examples of each of these notions in the context of spaces of valuations. Notice that on taking $A = D$ in the previous definition, we see that a complete upper semi-lattice or a complete lattice always has a bottom element and that a complete lattice always has a *top element* or *greatest element*, that is, an element $\top$ satisfying $a \sqsubseteq \top$ for all $a \in D$.

There are various implications between the notions formulated in Definition 1.1.1, some of which are obvious. Indeed, as far as the various notions of completeness are concerned, each defined concept is apparently less general than its predecessor. For example, since any chain is a directed set, we see that any complete partial order is chain complete, and any chain-complete poset with a bottom element is an ω-complete partial order. However, the following fact, which we simply state, is less trivial.[2]

---

[2] For a discussion of chain completeness versus completeness (for directed sets), we refer the reader to [Markowsky, 1976]; see also [Abramsky and Jung, 1994, Proposition 2.1.15].

1.1.2 Proposition A partially ordered set $(D, \sqsubseteq)$ is a complete partial order if and only if it has a bottom element and is chain complete.

Many aspects of theoretical computer science depend on the notion of a partially ordered set. More structure is often required, however, than is provided simply by a partial order or even by a complete partial order or complete lattice. For example, one needs extra structure in order to model standard programming language constructs or to provide an abstract theory of computability, as well as having a satisfactory fixed-point theorem available. It is now widely recognized that Scott's theory of domains provides a satisfactory setting in which to attain all these objectives, and we will find it useful later on to view spaces of valuations as Scott domains. It will therefore be convenient to give next the definition of the term "(Scott) domain" in the form in which we will always use it. First, however, we need to define the notion of compact element.

1.1.3 Definition Let $(D \sqsubseteq)$ be a partially ordered set. We call an element $a \in D$ *compact* or *finite* if it satisfies the property that whenever A is directed and $a \sqsubseteq \bigsqcup A$, we have $a \sqsubseteq x$ for some $x \in A$. We denote the set of compact elements in D by D_c.

Notice that the bottom element in a complete partial order is always a compact element, and hence the set D_c is always non-empty in this case. The compact elements are fundamental in domain theory.

1.1.4 Definition A *Scott-Ershov domain*, *Scott domain*, or just *domain* $(D, \sqsubseteq)$ is a consistently complete algebraic complete partial order. Thus, the following statements hold.

(1) $(D, \sqsubseteq)$ is a complete partial order.

(2) For each $x \in D$, the set $\mathrm{approx}(x) = \{a \in D_c \mid a \sqsubseteq x\}$ is directed, and we have $x = \bigsqcup \mathrm{approx}(x)$ (the *algebraicity* of D).

(3) If the set $\{a, b\} \subseteq D_c$ is consistent (that is, there exists $x \in D$ such that $a \sqsubseteq x$ and $b \sqsubseteq x$), then $\bigsqcup\{a, b\}$ exists in D (the *consistent completeness* of D).

We next give some simple examples of the concepts defined above; note that (1) and (2) are special cases of Theorem 1.3.2.

1.1.5 Example (1) The power set $D = \mathcal{P}(\mathbb{N})$ of the set $\mathbb{N}$ of natural numbers is a complete lattice when ordered by set inclusion. In this ordering, D is also a domain in which the compact elements are the finite subsets of $\mathbb{N}$. Furthermore, the bottom element of D is the empty set $\emptyset$ and $\emptyset$ is also the only minimal element of D; the top element of D is $\mathbb{N}$ and $\mathbb{N}$ is the only maximal element of D.

(2) Let X be a non-empty set, and let D denote the set of all pairs (I^+, I^-), where I^+ and I^- are disjoint subsets of X. We define an ordering on D by $(I^+, I^-) \sqsubseteq (J^+, J^-)$ if and only if $I^+ \subseteq J^+$ and $I^- \subseteq J^-$. Then D is a domain in which the bottom element is the pair $(\emptyset, \emptyset)$, the compact elements of D are the pairs (I^+, I^-) in D in which I^+ and I^- are finite sets, and the maximal elements are the pairs (I^+, I^-) which satisfy $I^+ \cup I^- = X$. Note that D is not a complete lattice.

(3) Let D denote the set of all partial functions $f : \mathbb{N}^n \to \mathbb{N}$ ordered by graph inclusion, that is, $f \sqsubseteq g$ if and only if $\text{graph}(f) \subseteq \text{graph}(g)$, where f and g are partial functions. (Thus, $f \sqsubseteq g$ if and only if whenever $f(x)$ is defined, so is $g(x)$ and $f(x) = g(x)$.) Then D is a domain in which a partial function f is a compact element if and only if $\text{graph}(f)$ is a finite set and the bottom element is the empty function. Here, the maximal elements of D are the total functions. Again, D is not a complete lattice.

1.1.6 Remark Mathematically speaking, the denotational semantics, or mathematical semantics, approach to the theory of procedural and functional programming languages is highly involved with providing a satisfactory framework within which to model constructs made in conventional programming languages. Such frameworks must be closed under the formation of products, sums, and function spaces and therefore are, simply, Cartesian closed categories. One of the most successful Cartesian closed categories to have arisen out of these considerations is that of Scott domains,[3] as formulated in Definition 1.1.4. Moreover, most functions and operators encountered within domain theory are order continuous, see Definition 1.1.7, and therefore the most useful fixed-point theorem in domain theory is Theorem 1.1.9. On the other hand, as we shall see in the next chapter and subsequent chapters, a logic program has a well-defined and mathematically precise meaning inherent in its very nature, namely, its semantics as a first-order logical theory. In addition, certain important operators arising in logic programming are not monotonic in general due to the presence of negation, resulting in Theorems 1.1.9 and 1.1.10 often being inapplicable, and this has no direct parallel in conventional programming language semantics. For these reasons, the semantics of logic programming languages has developed rather differently from that of procedural programming languages. Nevertheless, we shall study domains in Chapter 4, in the context of fixed-point theory.[4]

If D is a set, A is a subset of D, and $f : D \to D$ is a function, then we denote the image set $\{f(a) \mid a \in A\}$ of A under f by $f(A)$. We also define

---

[3] See [Scott, 1982b].

[4] Our basic references to domain theory are the book [Stoltenberg-Hansen et al., 1994] and the book chapter [Abramsky and Jung, 1994], but the reader interested in domain theory may also care to consult the notes of G.D. Plotkin [Plotkin, 1983] and also the comprehensive treatment to be found in [Gierz et al., 2003].

iterates of a function $f : D \to D$ inductively as follows: $f^0(x) = x$, and $f^{n+1}(x) = f(f^n(x))$ for all $n \in \mathbb{N}$ and $x \in D$.

1.1.7 Definition A function $f : D \to E$ between posets D and E is called *monotonic* if, for all $a, b \in D$ with $a \sqsubseteq b$, we have $f(a) \sqsubseteq f(b)$. Furthermore, f is called *antitonic* if, for all $a, b \in D$ with $a \sqsubseteq b$, we have $f(b) \sqsubseteq f(a)$. If D and E are ω-complete partial orders, then a function $f : D \to E$ is called ω-*continuous* if it is monotonic and $\bigsqcup f(A) = f(\bigsqcup A)$ for each ω-chain A in D. Finally, if D and E are complete partial orders, then f is called (*order*) *continuous* if, again, it is monotonic and, for every directed subset A of D, we have $\bigsqcup f(A) = f(\bigsqcup A)$.

We note that if f is monotonic, then the image of any ω-chain under f is an ω-chain, and similarly the image of any directed set under f is itself a directed set. Therefore, the two suprema required in making the previous definition always exist. Indeed, it is easy to see that, equivalently,[5] one may define f to be continuous by requiring, for each directed set A, that $f(A)$ is a directed set and that $\bigsqcup f(A) = f(\bigsqcup A)$. In fact, if f is monotonic and A is directed, then it is easily checked that the inequality $\bigsqcup f(A) \sqsubseteq f(\bigsqcup A)$ always holds. Therefore, it follows that f is continuous if and only if it is monotonic and $f(\bigsqcup A) \sqsubseteq \bigsqcup f(A)$ whenever $A \subseteq D$ is directed. As a matter of fact, preservation of suprema of chains is enough in defining continuity as shown by the next result, which again we simply state.[6] We note finally that if a function f between complete partial orders is continuous, then it is clear that it is ω-continuous as a function between ω-complete partial orders.

1.1.8 Proposition A function $f : D \to E$ between complete partial orders is continuous if and only if it is monotonic and $\bigsqcup f(A) = f(\bigsqcup A)$ for each chain A in D.

We define *ordinal powers* of a monotonic function f on a complete partial order $(D, \sqsubseteq)$ inductively as follows: $f \uparrow 0 = \bot$, $f \uparrow (\alpha + 1) = f(f \uparrow \alpha)$ for any ordinal α, and $f \uparrow \alpha = \bigsqcup \{ f \uparrow \beta \mid \beta < \alpha \}$ if α is a limit ordinal. Noting that $(D, \sqsubseteq)$ is chain complete, being a complete partial order, it is straightforward using transfinite induction to see that $f \uparrow \beta \sqsubseteq f \uparrow \alpha$ whenever $\beta \leq \alpha$, and hence that ordinal powers of f are well-defined. More generally, the same comments apply to the ordinal powers $f^\alpha(x)$ for any $x \in D$ which satisfies $x \sqsubseteq f(x)$: we define $f^0(x) = x$, $f^{\alpha+1}(x) = f(f^\alpha(x))$ for any ordinal α, and $f^\alpha(x) = \bigsqcup \{ f^\beta(x) \mid \beta < \alpha \}$ if α is a limit ordinal.

A *fixed point* of a function $f : D \to D$ is an element $x \in D$ satisfying $f(x) = x$. A *pre-fixed point* of a function f on a poset $(D, \sqsubseteq)$ is an element $y \in D$ satisfying $f(y) \sqsubseteq y$. Finally, a *post-fixed point* of f is an element $y \in D$ satisfying $y \sqsubseteq f(y)$. The *least fixed point*, lfp(f), of f is a fixed point x of f

---

[5]This is the definition adopted in [Stoltenberg-Hansen et al., 1994].

[6]A discussion of the various ways of formulating the notion of continuity is to be found in [Markowsky, 1976].

satisfying the property: if y is a fixed point of f, then $x \sqsubseteq y$. *Least pre-fixed points* and *least post-fixed points* are defined similarly.

The following two theorems are fundamental in handling the semantics of logic programs.[7] Indeed, the first of them, which is frequently referred to as *the fixed-point theorem*, is fundamental in procedural and functional programming as well.[8]

1.1.9 Theorem (Kleene) Let $(D, \sqsubseteq)$ denote an ω-complete partial order and let $f : D \to D$ be ω-continuous. Then f has a least fixed point $x = f \uparrow \omega$ which is also its least pre-fixed point.

Proof: We sketch the proof of this well-known result.

The sequence $(f \uparrow n)_{n \in \mathbb{N}}$ is an ω-chain. It therefore has a supremum $f \uparrow \omega = x$, say. By ω-continuity, we have $x = f \uparrow \omega = \bigsqcup \{f \uparrow (n+1) \mid n \in \mathbb{N}\} = f(\bigsqcup \{f \uparrow n \mid n \in \mathbb{N}\}) = f(x)$, and so x is a fixed point of f. If y is a pre-fixed point of f, then $\bot \sqsubseteq y$, and, by monotonicity of f, we obtain $f \uparrow 1 = f(\bot) \sqsubseteq f(y) \sqsubseteq y$. Inductively, it follows that $f \uparrow n \sqsubseteq y$ for all $n \in \mathbb{N}$, and hence $x = f \uparrow \omega \sqsubseteq y$. So x is the least pre-fixed point of f and hence also its least fixed point. ∎

By our earlier observation that a continuous function is ω-continuous, this theorem applies, of course, to continuous functions on complete partial orders. Moreover, if the function is not ω-continuous, but is monotonic, the existence of a least fixed point can still be guaranteed, as we see next.[9]

1.1.10 Theorem (Knaster-Tarski) Let $(D, \sqsubseteq)$ denote a complete partial order, let $f : D \to D$ be monotonic, and let $x \in D$ be such that $x \sqsubseteq f(x)$. Then f has a least fixed point a above x, meaning $x \sqsubseteq a$, which is also the least pre-fixed point of f above x, and there exists a least ordinal α such that $a = f^\alpha(x)$. In particular, f has a least fixed point a which is also its least pre-fixed point.

Proof: Again, this theorem is well-known, and we just sketch its proof.

Let γ be an ordinal whose cardinality exceeds that of D, and form the set $\{f^\beta(x) \mid \beta \leq \gamma\}$. By cardinality considerations, there must be ordinals $\alpha < \beta \leq \gamma$ with $f^\alpha(x) = f^\beta(x)$, and we can assume without loss of generality that α is least with this property. Since $f^\alpha(x) \sqsubseteq f(f^\alpha(x)) \sqsubseteq f^\beta(x) = f^\alpha(x)$,

---

[7] Fixed points of certain operators associated with logic programs are of extreme importance in the semantics of logic programs, as we shall see in later chapters.

[8] A result similar to Kleene's theorem, in fact, equivalent to it, is the well-known theorem due to Tarski and Kantorovitch in which ω-chains are replaced by countable chains, see [Jachymski, 2001]. Indeed, the collection containing [Jachymski, 2001] is an excellent general reference to fixed-point theory. As noted in [Lloyd, 1987], the reference [Lassez et al., 1982] contains an interesting discussion of the history of fixed-point theorems on ordered sets.

[9] In attributing Theorem 1.1.10 to Knaster and Tarski, we are noting Proposition 1.1.2 and then following Jachymski in [Jachymski, 2001]. Theorem 1.1.9 is usually attributed to Kleene, since this theorem is an abstract formulation of the first recursion theorem, and we are consistent with [Jachymski, 2001] in this respect.

we obtain that $f^\alpha(x) = f(f^\alpha(x))$, and so $a = f^\alpha(x)$ is a fixed point of f. Clearly, we have $x \sqsubseteq a$. Furthermore, if b is any pre-fixed point of f with $x \sqsubseteq b$, then by monotonicity of f and the fact that $f(b) \sqsubseteq b$ we obtain $f^\beta(x) \sqsubseteq b$ for all ordinals β. Hence, $a \sqsubseteq b$, and so a is both the least pre-fixed point and the least fixed point of f above x.

To obtain the final conclusion, we simply set $x = \bot$ and note then that $x \sqsubseteq f(x)$. ∎

Note that, in particular, the least fixed point of f is equal to $f \uparrow \alpha$ for some ordinal α. We call the smallest ordinal α with this property the *closure ordinal* of f.

One other point to make in this context is that Kleene's theorem shows that ω-continuity ensures that in finding a fixed point the iteration will not continue beyond the first infinite ordinal ω. This contrasts with the Knaster-Tarski theorem, where it may be necessary to iterate beyond ω if one only has monotonicity of the operators in question. This is a significant point in relation to computability considerations and explains the importance of Kleene's theorem in the theory of computation.

1.2   First-Order Predicate Logic

We assume that the reader has a slight familiarity with first-order predicate logic, but for convenience we summarize next the elementary concepts of the subject, beginning by formally describing its syntax.[10]

1.2.1   Syntax of First-Order Predicate Logic

As usual, an *alphabet* $\mathcal{A}$ consists of the following classes[11] of symbols: a (possibly empty) collection of constant symbols $a, b, c, d, \ldots$; a non-empty collection of variable symbols $u, v, w, x, y, z, \ldots$; a (possibly empty) collection of function symbols $f, g, h, \ldots$; and a non-empty collection of predicate sym-

---

[10]Our approach to the syntax and semantics of first-order logic is standard and is to be found in any of the well-known texts on mathematical logic, see, for example, [Hodel, 1995, Mendelson, 1987]. For fuller details of logic in relation to logic programming, the reader may care to consult [Apt, 1997] or [Lloyd, 1987].

[11]Similarly, our use of classes in the definition of an alphabet is also standard in developing first-order logic and, in our case, is not intended to hint at foundational issues. In logic programming practice, the classes referred to, namely, those of constant, variable, function, and predicate symbols, will be finite sets. When working with the set ground$_J(P)$ defined in Chapter 2, J will usually (although not necessarily) denote the Herbrand preinterpretation, and then we will in effect be working with a set containing a possibly denumerable collection of elements (atoms, in fact).

bols[12] $p, q, r, \ldots$. In addition, we have the connectives $\neg, \wedge, \vee, \rightarrow$, and $\leftrightarrow$; the quantifiers $\forall$ and $\exists$; and the punctuation symbols "(", ")" and ",". The arity of a function symbol f or of a predicate symbol p is commonly denoted by $\#(f)$ or by $\#(p)$.

In the following four definitions, we assume that $\mathcal{A}$ denotes some fixed, but arbitrary, alphabet.

1.2.1 Definition We define a *term* (*over*) $\mathcal{A}$ inductively[13] as follows.

(1) Each constant symbol in $\mathcal{A}$ is a term.

(2) Each variable symbol in $\mathcal{A}$ is a term.

(3) If f is any n-ary function symbol in $\mathcal{A}$ and $t_1, \ldots, t_n$ are terms, then $f(t_1, \ldots, t_n)$ is a term.

A term is called *ground* if it contains no variable symbols.

1.2.2 Definition An *atom, atomic formula,* or *proposition* A (*over* $\mathcal{A}$) is an expression of the form $p(t_1, \ldots, t_n)$, where p is an n-ary predicate symbol in $\mathcal{A}$ and $t_1, \ldots, t_n$ are terms (over $\mathcal{A}$).

1.2.3 Definition A *literal* L is an atom A or the negation $\neg A$ of an atom A. Atoms A are sometimes called *positive* literals, and negated atoms $\neg A$ are sometimes called *negative* literals.

1.2.4 Definition A (*well-formed*) *formula* (*over* $\mathcal{A}$) is defined inductively as follows.

(1) Each atom is a well-formed formula.

(2) If F and G are well-formed formulae, then so are $\neg F$, $F \wedge G$, $F \vee G$, $F \rightarrow G$, and $F \leftrightarrow G$.

(3) If F is a well-formed formula and x is a variable symbol, then $\forall x F$ and $\exists x F$ are well-formed formulae also.

A well-formed formula is called *ground* if it contains no variable symbols. Thus, in particular, a *ground atom* is an atom containing no variable symbols.

Of course, brackets are needed in writing down well-formed formulae to avoid ambiguity. Their use can be minimized, however, by means of the customary precedence hierarchy (in descending order) in which $\neg, \forall, \exists$ have highest precedence, followed by that of $\vee$, followed next by the precedence of $\wedge$, and finally followed by $\rightarrow$ and $\leftrightarrow$ with the lowest precedence.

---

[12]Constant symbols, variable symbols, function symbols, and predicate symbols are sometimes referred to as simply constants, variables, functions, and predicates, respectively

[13]As usual, in giving inductive definitions of sets, we omit the explicit statement of the closure step and assume that what is being defined is the smallest set satisfying the basis and induction steps.

1.2.5 Definition The *first-order language* $\mathcal{L}$ given by an alphabet $\mathcal{A}$ consists of the set of all well-formed formulae determined by the symbols of $\mathcal{A}$. We refer to terms over $\mathcal{A}$ as terms *in* or *over* $\mathcal{L}$.

1.2.6 Example Suppose we are given an alphabet $\mathcal{A}$ containing constant symbols a and b; variable symbols x and y; a unary function symbol f and a binary function symbol g; and a unary predicate symbol p and a binary predicate symbol q. Then the following are examples of terms over $\mathcal{A}$: a, b, x, y, $f(a)$, $f(x)$, $g(a, f(b))$, $g(g(a, b), f(y))$, $f(g(x, b))$, ... In particular, we note that, for example, $f(a)$ and $g(a, f(b))$ are ground terms, whereas $f(g(x, b))$ is not.

Furthermore, the following are examples of well-formed formulae in the first-order language $\mathcal{L}$ determined by $\mathcal{A}$: $p(a)$, $q(a, g(b, b))$, $\neg p(x)$, $q(x, g(a, y))$, $q(x, g(a, y)) \vee (p(y) \wedge \neg p(x))$, $p(x) \leftarrow p(f(a)) \wedge q(f(b), g(x, f(y))) \wedge q(x, g(y, b))$, $p(x) \leftrightarrow q(f(x), g(x, x))$, $\forall x(p(x) \leftarrow p(a) \wedge \neg q(f(b), g(x, f(x))) \wedge q(x, g(x, b)))$. In particular, the last of these is in a form of great significance in logic programming. Moreover, $p(a)$ and $q(a, g(b, b))$, for example, are ground (atomic) formulas, whereas $\forall x \forall y (p(x) \leftarrow p(a) \wedge \neg q(f(b), g(x, f(y))) \wedge q(x, g(y, b)))$ is not ground.

1.2.2 Semantics of First-Order Predicate Logic

The definition formally describes the syntax of first-order predicate logic. We want now, briefly, to describe formally the semantics or meaning given to well-formed formulae. In doing this, we adopt the usual set-based approach from model theory, but with two caveats which direct us. The first is that we do need to handle more truth values than just the two conventional ones. The second is that we do not usually need to handle quantified formulae because, for purposes of the semantics of logic programs P, we usually consider the set ground(P), as defined in Chapter 2, instead of P itself, and elements of the former contain no variable symbols and no quantifiers. However, in order to proceed further it is necessary to discuss spaces of truth values, and we do this next.

In classical two-valued logic and almost always in mathematics it is usual to employ the set $\mathcal{TWO} = \{\mathbf{f}, \mathbf{t}\}$ of truth values *false* $\mathbf{f}$ and *true* $\mathbf{t}$. However, in many places in logic programming and in other areas of computing, it has been found advantageous to employ more truth values than these. Indeed, quite early on, Melvin Fitting argued in several places for the use in logic programming of Kleene's strong and weak three-valued logics, see [Fitting, 1985, Fitting and Ben-Jacob, 1990], for example, in which the truth set is $\mathcal{THREE} = \{\mathbf{u}, \mathbf{f}, \mathbf{t}\}$. Here, $\mathbf{f}$ denotes false and $\mathbf{t}$ denotes true, again, but $\mathbf{u}$ denotes a third truth value which may be thought of as representing *underdefined*, *none* (neither true nor false) or no information, or, in some contexts, *non-termination.*[14] These and other three-valued logics will be encountered in Chapter 2 and in many other places in Chapters 3, 5, 6, and 7.

Fitting also considered Belnap's four-valued logic[15] in which the truth set is $\mathcal{FOUR} = \{\mathbf{u}, \mathbf{f}, \mathbf{t}, \mathbf{b}\}$. Here, $\mathbf{b}$ denotes a fourth truth value intended to represent both true and false, *both* or *overdefined*, which, it can be argued, should be used to handle the conflicting information "both true and false" returned, perhaps, in a distributed logic programming system. On a point of notation, we remark that the listing of the elements in $\mathcal{TWO}$ corresponds to the truth ordering $\leq_t$, as defined in Section 1.3.2, and in the case of $\mathcal{THREE}$ and $\mathcal{FOUR}$ the listing is derived from the knowledge ordering $\leq_k$, see again Section 1.3.2, with incomparable elements listed alphabetically.

A fundamental concept throughout this work is that of valuation, or interpretation, and also that of model. Indeed, spaces of interpretations are one of the central concepts here when viewed as the carrier sets for various semantic operators determined by programs. We will usually work later on in the truth sets $\mathcal{TWO}$ and $\mathcal{THREE}$ and sometimes in $\mathcal{FOUR}$. Nevertheless, in formulating the concepts of valuation and interpretation, we will work quite generally, at no extra cost, and allow arbitrary sets of truth values and certain connectives defined on them. Thus, let $\mathcal{T}$ denote an arbitrary *set of truth values* or *truth set* containing at least two elements, one of which will be the distinguished value $\mathbf{t}$, denoting true. We assume further that certain binary *connectives*, namely, *conjunction* ($\wedge$) and *disjunction* ($\vee$) are given, together with a unary connective *negation* ($\neg$), as functions over $\mathcal{T}$. A third binary connective *implication* ($\leftarrow$) may also be given or it may be defined in terms of the other connectives, and the latter is the way we will usually handle implication. However, we will defer giving the definition of implication we want until we have dealt with orderings on truth sets, see Definition 1.3.3. A set $\mathcal{T}$ together with specified definitions of these connectives will be referred to as a *logic* and, when the definitions of the connectives are understood, will be denoted simply by the underlying truth set $\mathcal{T}$ without causing confusion. Quite often, the definitions of $\wedge$, $\vee$, and $\neg$ are given by means of a truth table, and this is the case for most of the logics we encounter here. For example, Table 1.1 specifies Belnap's logic as employed by Fitting and by us. It contains classical two-valued logic and Kleene's strong three-valued logic as *sublogics.*[16] Moreover, $\mathcal{FOUR}$ is a complete lattice, as we see later, and is therefore technically easy to work with. Indeed, these are some of the reasons why four-valued logic plays an important unifying role in the theory[17] and is

---

[14]The truth value $\mathbf{u}$ is sometimes denoted in the literature by $\mathbf{n}$, indicating *none.*

[15]We refer to [Belnap, 1977, Fitting, 1991, Fitting, 2002], but note that Fitting worked with a minor variant of the logic defined in [Belnap, 1977]; we work with this same variant of Belnap's definition.

[16]The term a sublogic $\mathcal{S}$ of a logic $\mathcal{T}$ means that $\mathcal{S}$ is a subset of the set $\mathcal{T}$ of truth values, and the connectives in $\mathcal{S}$ are restrictions to $\mathcal{S}$ of the corresponding connectives in $\mathcal{T}$.

[17]Fitting has shown the utility of $\mathcal{FOUR}$, when viewed as a bilattice, in giving a unified treatment of several aspects of logic programming, and we refer the reader to [Fitting, 2002] and the works cited therein for more details.

TABLE 1.1: Belnap's four-valued logic.

p	q	$\neg p$	$p \wedge q$	$p \vee q$
u	u	u	u	u
u	f	u	f	u
u	t	u	u	t
u	b	u	f	t
f	u	t	f	u
f	f	t	f	f
f	t	t	f	t
f	b	t	f	b
t	u	f	u	t
t	f	f	f	t
t	t	f	t	t
t	b	f	b	t
b	u	b	f	t
b	f	b	f	b
b	t	b	b	t
b	b	b	b	b

the main reason we work with it despite the fact that most of our applications are to $\mathcal{TWO}$ and $\mathcal{THREE}$. Notice that Kleene's weak three-valued logic also uses the truth set $\mathcal{THREE}$, but its connectives are defined by Table 5.1.[18]

The next two definitions are fundamental. In presenting the first of them, we will use the notation commonly employed in logic programming.

1.2.7 Definition Let $\mathcal{L}$ be a first-order language and let D be a non-empty set. A *preinterpretation* J for $\mathcal{L}$ with *domain D (of preinterpretation)* is an assignment $\cdot^J$ which satisfies the following: (1) $c^J \in D$ for each constant symbol c in $\mathcal{L}$, and (2) f^J is an n-ary function over D for each n-ary function symbol f in $\mathcal{L}$. A *J-variable assignment* is a (total) mapping, θ, say, from variable symbols to elements of D.

Given a preinterpretation J with domain D and a J-variable assignment θ, we can assign to each term t in $\mathcal{L}$ an element of D, called its *denotation* or *term assignment*, inductively as follows: $(t\theta)^J = \theta(t)$ if t is a variable symbol, $(t\theta)^J = t^J$ if t is a constant symbol, and $(t\theta)^J = f^J\left((t_1\theta)^J, \ldots, (t_n\theta)^J\right)$ if $t = f(t_1, \ldots, t_n)$ for some n-ary function symbol f and terms $t_1, \ldots, t_n$. For an atom $A = p(t_1, \ldots, t_n)$, say, in the language $\mathcal{L}$, we define $(A\theta)^J$ to be the symbol $p\left((t_1\theta)^J, \ldots, (t_n\theta)^J\right)$ and call this a *J-ground instance of the atom* $p(t_1, \ldots, t_n)$. We denote by $B_{\mathcal{L},J}$ the set of J-ground instances of atoms in $\mathcal{L}$.

---

[18] Indeed, disjunction and conjunction in Kleene's weak three-valued logic are given by $\vee_2$ and $\wedge_3$, respectively, in Table 5.1, see also [Fitting, 1994a].

Thus, $B_{\mathcal{L},J}$ is the set of all symbols $p(d_1, \ldots, d_n)$, where p is an n-ary predicate symbol in $\mathcal{L}$ and $d_1, \ldots, d_n \in D$. ∎

1.2.8 Definition Let $\mathcal{L}$ be a first-order language, let J be a preinterpretation for $\mathcal{L}$ with domain D, and let $\mathcal{T}$ be a logic. A *valuation* or *interpretation for $\mathcal{L}$ (based on J) with values in $\mathcal{T}$* is a mapping $v : B_{\mathcal{L},J} \to \mathcal{T}$. Let $v : B_{\mathcal{L},J} \to \mathcal{T}$ be a valuation and let θ be a J-variable assignment. Then v and θ determine, inductively, a well-defined truth value in $\mathcal{T}$ for any quantifier-free, well-formed formula F in $\mathcal{L}$ by means of the construction of F and the definitions of the connectives in $\mathcal{T}$. We say that v is a *model for F*, written $v \models F$, if v gives truth value $\mathbf{t}$ to F. We sometimes refer to valuations, interpretations, and models based on J as J-valuations, J-interpretations, and J-models.

In fact, if $\mathcal{T}$ is ordered as a complete lattice (and this issue will be considered shortly), then a valuation v gives unique truth value in $\mathcal{T}$, in the standard way, to any closed well-formed formula F in $\mathcal{L}$: universal quantification corresponds to the infimum of a set of truth values, and existential quantification corresponds to the supremum of a set of truth values. The term *closed* here has, of course, its normal meaning in mathematical logic, namely, that each variable symbol occurring in F falls within the scope of a quantifier. (By default, we allow the term closed to apply to formulae with no variable symbols and no quantifiers.) Once this observation is made, one can go on, in the standard way, to define at our present level of generality the terms *model*, *(un)satisfiable*, *valid*, and *logical consequence* when applied to sets of closed well-formed formulae.

1.3   Ordered Spaces of Valuations

Following Definition 1.2.8, we will generally denote the set of all valuations for $\mathcal{L}$ based on J with values in $\mathcal{T}$ by $I(B_{\mathcal{L},J}, \mathcal{T})$, and we will consider $I(B_{\mathcal{L},J}, \mathcal{T})$ as an ordered set. The orderings we have in mind are derived from orderings on $\mathcal{T}$, and the set $B_{\mathcal{L},J}$ plays no role in this. Therefore, to ease notation we will work with an arbitrary set X for the rest of this chapter. Thus, we regard a valuation or interpretation for the time being as simply a mapping $X \to \mathcal{T}$ and denote the set of all these by $I(X, \mathcal{T})$; typical elements of $I(X, \mathcal{T})$ will be denoted by u, v, etc. Later on, in applying the results of this section, we will of course take X to be a set of ground atoms or of J-ground instances of atoms, and no confusion will be caused. There is, however, a convention we need to establish concerning the terminology "valuation" versus "interpretation", as follows.

1.3.1 Remark Much of the theory of logic programming semantics is concerned with sets of valuations. It is important, therefore, to have convenient notation for valuations and to have ways of representing them, which both facilitate discussion and also allow easy passage backwards and forwards between the different representations employed. There are three ways of handling valuations, which are commonly used in the literature on the subject and which we adopt also. Having these three forms available will, in certain places, greatly increase readability and reduce technical difficulty.

First, when considering general structures such as orderings or topologies on $I(X, \mathcal{T})$, the easiest way is to think of valuations as mappings, and this we will usually do. Thus, in the main, our future use of the term *valuation* will refer to mappings whose domain is a set of atoms (or ground instances of atoms) and whose codomain is a set $\mathcal{T}$ of truth values.

Second, when $\mathcal{T}$ is a small set containing two, three, or four elements, say, it is convenient to identify a valuation with the (ordered) tuple of sets on which it takes the various truth values in $\mathcal{T}$, as discussed in Section 1.3.2. This is by far the most frequently used representation, and, in common with most authors, we will in future usually employ the term *interpretation* when thinking in these terms. Thus, as we progress, more and more we employ the terminology interpretation instead of valuation, use the standard notation I, K, etc. to denote interpretations, and adopt the notation described at the end of Section 2.1 for sets of interpretations.

Third, there is yet another representation frequently used for interpretations when $\mathcal{T}$ is the set $\mathcal{THREE}$, namely, signed sets as discussed in Section 1.3.3. This form is particularly expressive, as we shall see in Chapter 2, when one wants to discuss the truth value of conjunctions of literals in relation to $\mathcal{THREE}$.

1.3.1　Ordered Spaces of Valuations in General

Usually, the set $\mathcal{T}$ of truth values carries an order, $\leq$, in which $(\mathcal{T}, \leq)$ is perhaps a complete partial order, complete upper semi-lattice, complete lattice, or Scott domain, with bottom element $\bot$, say, or even a bilattice[19] when equipped with two compatible orderings. When $\mathcal{T}$ carries an ordering, $\leq$, we can define the corresponding pointwise ordering on $I(X, \mathcal{T})$, denoted by $\sqsubseteq$, in which $v_1 \sqsubseteq v_2$ if and only if $v_1(x) \leq v_2(x)$ for all $x \in X$.

It is routine to check that the ordering $\sqsubseteq$ is in fact a partial order if $\leq$ is one. Moreover, if $\mathcal{T}$ has a bottom element, $\bot$, then the valuation which maps each x in X to $\bot$ serves as a bottom element in $I(X, \mathcal{T})$, and we may denote this valuation simply by $\bot$ again, without causing confusion. Finally, if $(\mathcal{T}, \leq)$ is a Scott domain, we shall say that a valuation v in $I(X, \mathcal{T})$ is *finite* if $v(x)$ is

---

[19]A (complete) bilattice is a set D carrying two partial orders in each of which D is a (complete) lattice. In addition, the two orderings are required to interact with each other so as to obtain various distributive laws.

a compact element in $(\mathcal{T}, \leq)$ for each $x \in X$, and the set $\{x \in X \mid v(x) \neq \bot\}$ is finite.

The structural properties of $I(X, \mathcal{T})$ may be summarized in the following result.[20]

1.3.2 Theorem Let X be a non-empty set, let $(\mathcal{T}, \leq)$ be an ordered set of truth values with bottom element $\bot$, and let $I(X, \mathcal{T})$ be endowed with the pointwise ordering and bottom element just defined.

(a) If $(\mathcal{T}, \leq)$ is a partially ordered set, then so is $I(X, \mathcal{T})$.

(b) If $(\mathcal{T}, \leq)$ is an ω-complete partial order, then so is $I(X, \mathcal{T})$.

(c) If $(\mathcal{T}, \leq)$ is a complete partial order, then so is $I(X, \mathcal{T})$.

(d) If $(\mathcal{T}, \leq)$ is a complete upper semi-lattice, then so is $I(X, \mathcal{T})$.

(e) If $(\mathcal{T}, \leq)$ is a complete lattice, then so is $I(X, \mathcal{T})$.

(f) If $(\mathcal{T}, \leq)$ is a Scott domain, then so is $I(X, \mathcal{T})$. In this case, the compact elements of $I(X, \mathcal{T})$ are the finite valuations.

Proof: (a) As already noted, it is routine in this case to verify that the ordering on $I(X, \mathcal{T})$ is a partial ordering, with bottom element as already specified.

(b) The argument in this case is similar to the next and is omitted.

(c) If $M \subseteq I(X, \mathcal{T})$ is directed, then it is easy to check that, for each $x \in X$, the set $\{v(x) \mid v \in M\}$ is directed and hence has a supremum in $\mathcal{T}$. It is now clear that the valuation v_M defined on X by $v_M(x) = \bigsqcup\{v(x) \mid v \in M\}$ is the supremum, $\bigsqcup M$, of M in $I(X, \mathcal{T})$. Indeed, for any directed subset $M \subseteq I(X, \mathcal{T})$, $\bigsqcup M$ satisfies the following relationship: for each $x \in X$, $(\bigsqcup M)(x) = \bigsqcup(M(x))$, where $M(x)$ denotes the set $\{v(x) \mid v \in M\}$.

(d) By the argument used in (c), the supremum $\bigsqcup M$ exists for any directed subset M of $I(X, \mathcal{T})$. Also, for any subset M of $I(X, \mathcal{T})$, we have that $\bigsqcap M$ exists and is defined by $(\bigsqcap M)(x) = \bigsqcap(M(x))$ for each $x \in X$, where again $M(x)$ denotes the set $\{v(x) \mid v \in M\}$.

(e) It is clear from the argument in (c) that any subset M of $I(X, \mathcal{T})$ has a supremum in $I(X, \mathcal{T})$, and, from (d), M has an infimum in $I(X, \mathcal{T})$.

(f) We begin by showing that the finite valuations are compact elements. Suppose that v is a finite valuation and that $\{x \in X \mid v(x) \neq \bot\} = \{x_1, \ldots, x_n\}$. Suppose that $M = \{u_k \mid k \in K\}$ is a directed set of valuations in $I(X, \mathcal{T})$ such that $v \sqsubseteq \bigsqcup M$. Let x_i be an arbitrary element of $\{x_1, \ldots, x_n\}$. Then we have that $v(x_i) \leq \bigsqcup M(x_i) = \bigsqcup(M(x_i))$, that $v(x_i)$ is a compact element, and that $\{u_k(x_i); k \in K\}$ is directed. Therefore, there is $u_{k_i} \in M$ such that $v(x_i) \leq u_{k_i}(x_i)$, and we obtain such u_{k_i} for $i = 1, \ldots, n$. Since M is directed, there is $u \in M$ such that $u_{k_i} \sqsubseteq u$ for $i = 1, \ldots, n$, and it now clearly follows that $v \sqsubseteq u$. Hence, v is compact.

---

[20]For further details here and in the next three subsections, see [Seda, 2002].

In the converse direction, suppose that u is any valuation on X. Let M denote the set of all finite valuations v such that $v \sqsubseteq u$. Let $v_1, v_2 \in M$ and suppose that $x \in X$ is such that not both $v_1(x)$ and $v_2(x)$ are equal to the bottom element (there are only finitely many such x, of course). Noting that approx$(u(x))$ in $\mathcal{T}$ is directed, that $v_1(x), v_2(x) \in$ approx$(u(x))$ and by considering one-point valuations (namely, those valuations w such that $w(x)$ is not equal to the bottom element at at most one value of x), we see that there is $v_3(x) \in$ approx$(u(x))$ such that both $v_1(x) \leq v_3(x)$ and $v_2(x) \leq v_3(x)$. It follows that there is an element v_3 of M such that $v_1 \sqsubseteq v_3$ and $v_2 \sqsubseteq v_3$ and, hence, that M is directed. Moreover, given $x \in X$ and any $a \in$ approx$(u(x))$, let v_a^x denote the one-point valuation which satisfies $v_a^x(x) = a$ and $v_a^x(y) = \bot$ for all $y \neq x$. Then $v_a^x \in M$, and $\bigsqcup \{v_a^x(x) \mid a \in$ approx$(u(x))\} = u(x)$. Thus, $\bigsqcup M = u$.

It now follows from the observations just made that if u is compact, then there is $v \in M$ such that $u \sqsubseteq v$, and hence the set $\{x \in X \mid u(x) \neq \bot\}$ is finite. We claim that $u(x)$ is a compact element in $(\mathcal{T}, \leq)$ for each $x \in X$. Suppose otherwise, that is, that there is $x_0 \in X$ with $u(x_0)$ non-compact in $(\mathcal{T}, \leq)$. Then there is a directed set N in $\mathcal{T}$ with $u(x_0) \leq \bigsqcup N$ for which there is no $n \in N$ with $u(x_0) \leq n$. Define the family N_n consisting of the elements u_n of $I(X, \mathcal{T}), n \in N$, by setting $u_n(x) = u(x)$ for all $x \neq x_0$ and setting $u_n(x_0) = n$. Then N_n is directed and $u \sqsubseteq \bigsqcup \{u_n \mid n \in N\}$, yet we do not have $u \sqsubseteq u_n$ for any $n \in N$. This contradicts the fact that u is a compact element, and hence, for each $x \in X$, $u(x)$ is a compact element. Thus, the compact elements are indeed the finite valuations, and, moreover, we now see that approx(u) is directed and that $\bigsqcup$approx$(u) = u$ for each valuation $u \in I(X, \mathcal{T})$.

Finally, if u_1 and u_2 are two consistent finite elements in $I(X, \mathcal{T})$, then the valuation v defined by $v(x) = \bigsqcup\{u_1(x), u_2(x)\}$, for each $x \in X$, is the supremum of u_1 and u_2 (and is, in fact, a finite element). This completes the proof. ∎

1.3.2 Valuations in Two-Valued and Other Logics

The most prominent declarative semantics for logic programs employ classical two-valued logic, three-valued logic, or, to a lesser extent, four-valued logic. The corresponding truth sets $\mathcal{T}$ for these logics are $\mathcal{TWO}$, $\mathcal{THREE}$, and $\mathcal{FOUR}$, as already discussed. We examine these cases next in some detail in light of Theorem 1.3.2 and also introduce some convenient notation for these special cases. We begin by considering the orderings involved on the three sets of truth values that we are currently discussing.

In the case of classical two-valued logic, the ordering usually taken is the *truth ordering*. This is the partial ordering $\leq_t$ satisfying $\mathbf{f} <_t \mathbf{t}$ and is often denoted just by $\leq$; it turns $\mathcal{TWO}$ into a complete lattice with $\mathbf{f}$ as the bottom element.

For three-valued logic, there are two natural orderings usually considered:

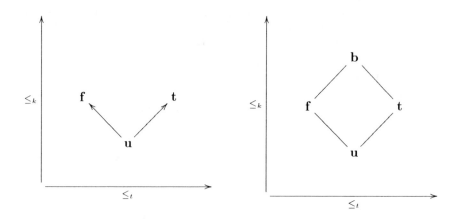

FIGURE 1.1: Hasse diagrams for $\mathcal{THREE}$ (left) and $\mathcal{FOUR}$ (right).

the *knowledge ordering* $\leq_k$ and the *truth ordering* $\leq_t$. The first of these, $\leq_k$, is the partial order indicated by the Hasse diagram to the left in Figure 1.1 in which **u** is the bottom element. This ordering turns $\mathcal{THREE}$ into a complete upper semi-lattice, but not a complete lattice. The second ordering, $\leq_t$, is the partial ordering satisfying **f** $<_t$ **u** and **u** $<_t$ **t**; it turns $\mathcal{THREE}$ into a complete lattice with **f** as the bottom element.

Finally, on $\mathcal{FOUR}$, there are again the two orderings: $\leq_k$, the knowledge ordering, and $\leq_t$, the truth ordering. They are indicated by the Hasse diagram on the right-hand side of Figure 1.1. In each of them, $\mathcal{FOUR}$ is a complete lattice and indeed is a complete bilattice, with bottom elements as indicated by the Hasse diagram.

At this point, having defined the orderings we want on $\mathcal{FOUR}$, it will be convenient to record the definition we use of implication before resuming the study of orderings on valuations. Note that the definition reduces to material implication in two-valued logic and gives the definition we want later for Kleene's strong three-valued logic.

1.3.3 Definition For all truth values t_1 and t_2 in $\mathcal{FOUR}$, we define *implication* by taking the truth value of $t_1 \leftarrow t_2$ to be **f** if and only if $t_1 <_t t_2$ in the truth ordering $\leq_t$, and **t** otherwise.

In each of the three cases we are considering, the truth set $\mathcal{T}$ is easily seen to be a Scott domain in the truth ordering and also in the knowledge ordering in the latter two cases. Furthermore, each element is compact. Therefore, on applying Theorem 1.3.2 with the induced pointwise orderings involved, we obtain the following result, which summarizes the previous discussion.

1.3.4 Theorem Let X be an arbitrary set. Then the following statements hold.

(a) In case $\mathcal{T}$ is the truth set $\mathcal{TWO}$, the set $I(X, \mathcal{T})$ is a complete lattice in the ordering $\sqsubseteq_t$.

(b) In case $\mathcal{T}$ is the truth set $\mathcal{THREE}$, the set $I(X, \mathcal{T})$ is a complete upper semi-lattice in the ordering $\sqsubseteq_k$, but not a complete lattice, and is a complete lattice in the ordering $\sqsubseteq_t$.

(c) In case $\mathcal{T}$ is the truth set $\mathcal{FOUR}$, the set $I(X, \mathcal{T})$ is a complete lattice in each of the orderings $\sqsubseteq_k$ and $\sqsubseteq_t$.

Furthermore, in each case and in each ordering, the set $I(X, \mathcal{T})$ is a Scott domain whose compact elements are precisely those valuations v for which the set $\{x \in X \mid v(x) \neq \bot\}$ is finite, where $\bot$ denotes the appropriate bottom element. ∎

Notice that the order structure here is independent of the actual logic involved, as distinct from the underlying truth set. Thus, for example, Kleene's strong and weak three-valued logics give rise to precisely the same order structure on $I(X, \mathcal{THREE})$; the difference between them is in the definitions of the connectives, rather than in their order structure.

We next take up the point made in Remark 1.3.1, concerning the representation of a valuation in terms of the sets on which it takes various truth values in $\mathcal{TWO}$, $\mathcal{THREE}$, or $\mathcal{FOUR}$.

Let v be a valuation, and let $v_u = v^{-1}(\mathbf{u})$, let $v_f = v^{-1}(\mathbf{f})$, let $v_t = v^{-1}(\mathbf{t})$, and let $v_b = v^{-1}(\mathbf{b})$; these sets are pairwise disjoint subsets of X, and some may be empty. A valuation v taking values in $\mathcal{TWO}$ is clearly completely determined by the subset $I = v_t$ of X and therefore can be identified with I. A valuation taking values in $\mathcal{THREE}$ can be identified either with the pair $I = (v_t, v_f)$ of subsets of X or with the pair $I = (v_t, v_u)$. The former choice will be made when we are concerned with the ordering $\sqsubseteq_k$, so that the bottom element is $\mathbf{u}$ and this is also the "default" value in the sense that $v_u = X \setminus (v_t \cup v_f)$. The latter choice will be made when we are concerned with the ordering $\sqsubseteq_t$, so that the bottom element is $\mathbf{f}$ and this is also the default value in that $v_f = X \setminus (v_t \cup v_u)$. Finally, a valuation v with values in $\mathcal{FOUR}$ can be identified either with the triple $I = (v_t, v_f, v_b)$ of subsets of X when $\mathbf{u}$ is the bottom and default value or with the triple $I = (v_t, v_u, v_b)$ when $\mathbf{f}$ is the bottom and default value.

Conversely, a subset I of X determines a valuation $v : X \to \mathcal{TWO}$ with the property that $v(x) = \mathbf{t}$ if and only if $x \in I$. Given the ordering $\sqsubseteq_k$, a pair $I = (I_t, I_f)$ of disjoint subsets of X determines a valuation $v : X \to \mathcal{THREE}$ which takes value $\mathbf{t}$ on I_t, takes value $\mathbf{f}$ on I_f, and, by default, takes value $\mathbf{u}$ on $X \setminus (I_t \cup I_f)$. Similarly, given the ordering $\sqsubseteq_t$, a pair $I = (I_t, I_u)$ of disjoint subsets of X determines a valuation $v : X \to \mathcal{THREE}$ which takes value $\mathbf{t}$ on

I_t, takes value $\mathbf{u}$ on $I_\mathbf{u}$, and, by default, takes value $\mathbf{f}$ on $X \setminus (I_t \cup I_\mathbf{u})$. Precisely the same remarks apply to triples $I = (I_t, I_f, I_\mathbf{b})$ and to triples $I = (I_t, I_\mathbf{u}, I_\mathbf{b})$ in relation to valuations $v : X \to \mathcal{FOUR}$.

This passage between mappings and tuples of subsets will often be made without explicit mention. However, as noted in Remark 1.3.1, we will, in the main, use the term *valuation* to refer to mappings and the term *interpretation* to refer to tuples of sets, and it will be convenient to employ the following terminology.

1.3.5 Definition A valuation or interpretation taking values in $\mathcal{TWO}$, $\mathcal{THREE}$, or $\mathcal{FOUR}$ will be called *two-valued*, *three-valued*, or *four-valued*, respectively.

The identification above, of valuations with tuples of sets, carries the point-wise ordering of valuations over to the "pointwise" ordering of interpretations, and we employ exactly the same notation for the orderings in the corresponding cases. We obtain the following result, whose proof is straightforward and will be omitted. (There is the possibility of confusion here unless one remembers that coordinate positions in the tuples are labelled with truth values and that the truth value not present is the default value. Thus, for example, in the case of three-valued valuations, the two coordinate positions are either ordered with $\mathbf{t}$ and $\mathbf{f}$ in that order or ordered with $\mathbf{t}$ and $\mathbf{u}$ in that order, and similarly for four-valued valuations. The only way to avoid this minor irritation is to use pairs of sets to represent two-valued valuations, triples of sets to represent three-valued valuations, and quadruples of sets to represent four-valued valuations. However, this is not customarily done.)

1.3.6 Theorem The following statements hold in relation to interpretations on X.

(a) If I and K are two-valued interpretations, then $I \sqsubseteq_t K$ if and only if $I \subseteq K$ as subsets of X. The bottom element for the set of two-valued interpretations is given by the empty set, $\emptyset$.

(b) If I and K are three-valued interpretations, then $I \sqsubseteq_k K$ if and only if $I_t \subseteq K_t$ and $I_f \subseteq K_f$. Also, $I \sqsubseteq_t K$ if and only if $I_t \subseteq K_t$ and $K_f \subseteq I_f$. In both orderings, the bottom element for the set of three-valued interpretations is given by the appropriate pair $(\emptyset, \emptyset)$.

(c) If I and K are four-valued interpretations, then $I \sqsubseteq_k K$ if and only if $I_t \subseteq K_t \cup K_\mathbf{b}$, $I_f \subseteq K_f \cup K_\mathbf{b}$, and $I_\mathbf{b} \subseteq K_\mathbf{b}$. Also, $I \sqsubseteq_t K$ if and only if $I_t \subseteq K_t$, $I_\mathbf{u} \subseteq K_\mathbf{u} \cup K_t$, and $I_\mathbf{b} \subseteq K_\mathbf{b} \cup K_t$. In both orderings, the bottom element for the set of four-valued interpretations is given by the appropriate triple $(\emptyset, \emptyset, \emptyset)$. ∎

Notice that the difference in the form of the statements in (b) and (c) in Theorem 1.3.6 concerning the truth ordering $\sqsubseteq_t$ results from the fact that $\sqsubseteq_t$ is a total order in (b), but it is not a total order in (c).

In all cases we are currently considering, except one, we are working in a complete lattice. Hence, the valuation mapping each element of X to the appropriate top element is itself a top element. The one exception is the case of three-valued interpretations in the order $\sqsubseteq_k$. In this case, it is clear that those interpretations $I = (I_t, I_f)$ for which $I_t \cup I_f = X$ are maximal elements for the ordering $\sqsubseteq_k$. Moreover, each maximal element $I = (I_t, I_f)$ gives rise to the two-valued interpretation I_t, and, conversely, each two-valued interpretation I gives rise to a maximal three-valued interpretation $(I, X \setminus I)$. Moreover, this correspondence is evidently one-to-one. Thus, the two-valued interpretations can be thought of as maximal three-valued interpretations. Indeed, the maximal elements are called *total interpretations*, while the remaining elements are called *partial interpretations*.

1.3.3 Signed Sets and Three-Valued Interpretations

As mentioned in Remark 1.3.1, there is an alternative and useful way of thinking of three-valued interpretations relative to the ordering $\sqsubseteq_k$ (so that $\mathbf{u}$ is the current default value in the representation of interpretations as pairs of sets), and we consider it next.

Let X denote an arbitrary set, and form the set $\neg X$ of symbols $\neg x$ for $x \in X$. If X happens to be a set of atoms or of literals, then $\neg x$ is meaningful; otherwise, we are working formally. In any case, we assume that x and $\neg x$ are never equal. Given a subset I of X, we let $\neg I$ denote the subset of $\neg X$ consisting of those $\neg x$ for $x \in I$. A subset of $X \cup \neg X$ is called a *signed subset* of X and is called *consistent* if it does not contain both x and $\neg x$ for any x. Clearly, any signed subset of X has the form $I^+ \cup \neg I^-$, where I^+ and I^- are subsets of X, and is consistent if and only if I^+ and I^- are disjoint.

Every consistent signed subset $I = I^+ \cup \neg I^-$ of X gives rise to the three-valued interpretation (I^+, I^-). Then, thinking of I as this three-valued interpretation, we have $I_t = I^+ = \{x \in X \mid x \in I\}$ and $I_f = I^- = \{x \in X \mid \neg x \in I\}$. Conversely, every three-valued interpretation $I = (I_t, I_f) = (I^+, I^-)$ gives rise to the consistent signed subset $I^+ \cup \neg I^-$ of X. Moreover, this correspondence is evidently one-to-one, and so $I(X, THREE)$ can be identified with the set of all consistent signed subsets of X, and we will quite frequently use this fact later on without further notice. Indeed, in this representation, we have $I \sqsubseteq_k K$ if and only if $I^+ \cup \neg I^- \subseteq K^+ \cup \neg K^-$, and so $\sqsubseteq_k$ corresponds to subset inclusion of signed subsets, and, furthermore, the bottom element is the empty set thought of as a consistent signed subset of X.

Now let X denote a set of atoms in a first-order language $\mathcal{L}$, and let I be a three-valued interpretation viewed as a consistent signed subset of X. For a literal $L = A$, where A is an atom, we write $L \in I$ if $A \in I$, and we write $\neg L \in I$ if $\neg A \in I$. Similarly, if $L = \neg A$, we write $L \in I$ if $\neg A \in I$, and we write $\neg L \in I$ if $A \in I$. Using these observations, we now say that a literal L is *true* in I if $L \in I$, that L is *false* in I if $\neg L \in I$, and that L is *undefined* in I otherwise. Notice that these facts depend on, and indeed are equivalent to, defining the negation operator $\neg$ from $\mathcal{THREE}$ into itself by means of Table 1.1, so that $\neg(\mathbf{t}) = \mathbf{f}$, $\neg(\mathbf{f}) = \mathbf{t}$, and $\neg(\mathbf{u}) = \mathbf{u}$.

Finally, we note that four-valued interpretations can be treated in the same sort of way as we have just handled three-valued interpretations by including inconsistent signed sets in the discussion, but we omit the details of this as we have no need of them.

1.3.4   Operators on Spaces of Valuations

As we have seen, an ordering on a space $\mathcal{T}$ of truth values induces an ordering on the corresponding spaces $I(X, \mathcal{T})$. Similarly, various connectives defined on $\mathcal{T}$ induce operators defined on $I(X, \mathcal{T})$, and we close this chapter by briefly discussing these next. They will be considered further in Chapter 3.

In fact, we concentrate on Belnap's four-valued logic, in which the truth set is $\mathcal{FOUR}$ and the connectives are determined by the truth table, Table 1.1. Since classical two-valued logic and Kleene's strong three-valued logic are sublogics of $\mathcal{FOUR}$, they are subsumed in our discussion of $\mathcal{FOUR}$ and therefore need not be considered separately.

The first of these operators arises through negation, and is the operator mapping $I(X, \mathcal{T})$ into itself, and still denoted by $\neg$, in which $(\neg v)(x) = \neg(v(x))$ for each $x \in X$, where v is an arbitrary element of $I(X, \mathcal{T})$.

Likewise, the connectives $\vee$ and $\wedge$ determine (binary) operators mapping $I(X, \mathcal{T}) \times I(X, \mathcal{T})$ into $I(X, \mathcal{T})$ defined by $(u \vee v)(x) = u(x) \vee v(x)$ and $(u \wedge v)(x) = u(x) \wedge v(x)$, for each $x \in X$, where u and v are arbitrary elements of $I(X, \mathcal{T})$. We note that the overloading of the symbols $\vee$ and $\wedge$ should not cause any difficulties. Of course, one can similarly deal with other connectives such as $\rightarrow$ and $\leftrightarrow$.

If $v_1, v_2 \in I(X, \mathcal{T})$ satisfy the conditions $v_1 \sqsubseteq_t v_2$, $v_1(x) = \mathbf{f}$ and $v_2(x) = \mathbf{t}$ for some x, then it is clear that $\neg v_1 \not\sqsubseteq_t \neg v_2$. Hence, $\neg$ is not monotonic in this case. Thus, $\neg$ is not order continuous in the truth orderings $\sqsubseteq_t$. It is, however, order continuous in the orderings $\sqsubseteq_k$, as we shall see in Chapter 3, where we also consider the continuity of the other operators $\vee$ and $\wedge$.

The following observation is just one of the many interesting properties possessed by $I(X, \mathcal{T})$ when we take $\mathcal{T}$ to be the logic $\mathcal{FOUR}$, as we are currently doing.

1.3.7 Proposition The operators $\vee$ and $\wedge$ are monotonic in each argument.

Proof: Given $v \in I(X, \mathcal{T})$, it must be shown that the mappings $u \mapsto u \vee v$ and $u \mapsto v \vee u$ are both monotonic, and, since $\vee$ is commutative, it suffices to show that either is monotonic. It is straightforward to check this from the truth table, Table 1.1, and the Hasse diagram for $\mathcal{FOUR}$, Figure 1.1, and we omit details. Precisely the same comments apply also to the operator $\wedge$.   ■

Another interesting fact about $\mathcal{FOUR}$, which emerges from its truth table and its Hasse diagram, is the following result.

1.3.8 Proposition Relative to the truth ordering $\leq_t$ on $\mathcal{FOUR}$, we have $t_1 \vee t_2 = \bigsqcup\{t_1, t_2\}$ and $t_1 \wedge t_2 = \bigsqcap\{t_1, t_2\}$ for all truth values t_1 and t_2. In particular, in classical two-valued logic and Kleene's strong three-valued logic relative to $\leq_t$, we have $t_1 \vee t_2 = \max\{t_1, t_2\}$ and $t_1 \wedge t_2 = \min\{t_1, t_2\}$ for all truth values t_1 and t_2.

Chapter 2

The Semantics of Logic Programs

The objective of this chapter is to introduce the central topic of study in this work, namely, *logic programs*, together with several of the main issues and questions which will be addressed in later chapters. In order to ensure that our treatment is as self-contained as possible, we will take care to formally define all concepts which we consider in detail here and later on. In addition, to assist the reader, we give ample references to those topics which we encounter, but do not treat in detail.

For the course of this and subsequent chapters, our main focus will be on declarative semantics, and, as already noted in the Introduction, issues concerning procedural aspects will play only a minor role. In particular, in this chapter and later in Chapter 5, we will introduce some of the best known declarative semantics for logic programs, and we will develop a uniform treatment of them applicable not only to resolution-based logic programming, but also to non-monotonic reasoning as well.

Frequently, a declarative semantics is given by assigning *intended models* to logic programs. This is done by selecting from the set of all models for a logic program, a subset which contains those models with some properties deemed to be desirable depending on one's objectives and intended applications. All the semantics which we will discuss can be described in terms of fixed points of operators associated with logic programs, and they are all well-established. Our new and novel contribution in this chapter is the development of a uniform and operator-free characterization of them.

Our first task, however, is to introduce formally some of the basic concepts and notation which will be needed throughout the sequel.[1]

2.1 Logic Programs and Their Models

2.1.1 Definition Given a first-order language $\mathcal{L}$, a *clause*, *program clause*, or *rule* in $\mathcal{L}$ is a formula of the form

$$(\forall x_1)\ldots(\forall x_l)(A \leftarrow L_1 \wedge \ldots \wedge L_n),$$

---

[1] We follow the presentation of semantics from [Hitzler and Wendt, 2002, Hitzler, 2003b, Hitzler and Wendt, 2005, Hitzler, 2005, Knorr and Hitzler, 2007].

where $l, n \in \mathbb{N}$; A is an atom in $\mathcal{L}$; $L_1, \ldots, L_n$ are literals in $\mathcal{L}$; and $x_1, \ldots, x_l$ are all the variable symbols occurring in the formula. We will follow common practice and abbreviate such a clause by writing simply

$$A \leftarrow L_1, \ldots, L_n,$$

so that the universal quantifiers are understood, and the conjunction symbol $\wedge$ is replaced by a comma. The atom A is called the *head* of the clause, and the conjunction $L_1, \ldots, L_n$ is called the *body* of the clause; the literals L_i, $i = 1, \ldots, n$, in the body $L_1, \ldots, L_n$ are called *body literals*. If a body literal L is an atom B, say, then we say that B *occurs positively* in the body of the clause. If L is a negated atom $\neg B$, then we say that B *occurs negatively* in the body of the clause. By an abuse of notation, we allow $n = 0$, by which we mean that the body can be empty, and in this case the clause $A \leftarrow$, or simply A, is also called a *unit clause* or a *fact*. It will sometimes be convenient to further abbreviate a clause by writing

$$A \leftarrow \mathsf{body},$$

wherein body denotes the body of the clause. Furthermore, we will use body not only to denote a conjunction of literals, but also to denote the corresponding set containing these literals. This further abuse of notation will substantially ease matters in some places and will not cause confusion. Note that in doing this, we are ignoring the ordering of the literals in clause bodies. This will not matter most of the time, since we are not much concerned with procedural matters, as already noted, and for this reason we often denote a typical clause by $A \leftarrow A_1, \ldots, A_n, \neg B_1, \ldots, \neg B_k$, say, where all the A_i, $i = 1, \ldots, n$, and all the B_j, $j = 1, \ldots, k$, are atoms in $\mathcal{L}$. Notice that we allow ourselves a bit of latitude in the subscripts we employ in writing down clauses, and, for example, the roles of n in the clause just considered and in the clause $A \leftarrow L_1, \ldots, L_n$ above are not identical in general, unless there are no negated atoms present, of course.

A *normal logic program* is a finite set of clauses. A *definite logic program* is a normal logic program in which no negation symbols occur. The term *program* will subsequently always mean a normal program. Definite programs are sometimes called *positive programs*, and obviously every definite program is a normal program. A *propositional logic program* is a program in which all predicate symbols are of arity zero.   ∎

In most cases, the underlying first-order language, or simply the underlying language, $\mathcal{L}_P$ of a program P will not be given explicitly, but will be understood to be the (first-order) language generated by the constant, variable, function, and predicate symbols occurring in P. However, when P does not contain any constant symbols, we add one to $\mathcal{L}_P$, so that the underlying language always contains at least one constant symbol. Propositional programs will be treated slightly differently, and we will return to this point later, see the examples following Definition 2.1.6.

We illustrate Definition 2.1.1 with a number of example programs, to which we will return frequently later. At all times, unless stated to the contrary, we will adhere to the following notational conventions concerning programs: constant, function, and predicate symbols start with a lowercase letter and are set in `typewriter` font unless they consist of a single letter only; variable symbols start with an uppercase letter.

2.1.2 Program (Tweety1) Let Tweety1[2] be the program consisting of the following clauses.

$$\text{penguin}(\text{tweety}) \leftarrow$$
$$\text{bird}(\text{bob}) \leftarrow$$
$$\text{bird}(X) \leftarrow \text{penguin}(X)$$
$$\text{flies}(X) \leftarrow \text{bird}(X), \neg\text{penguin}(X)$$

Tweety1 is intended to represent the following knowledge: `tweety` is a penguin, `bob` is a bird, all penguins are birds, and every bird which is not a penguin can fly.

2.1.3 Program (Even) Let Even be the program consisting of the following clauses.

$$\text{even}(a) \leftarrow$$
$$\text{even}(s(X)) \leftarrow \neg\text{even}(X)$$

The intended meaning of this program is as follows: a is the natural number 0, and s is the successor function on natural numbers. Thus, the program represents the knowledge that 0 is even, and if some number is not even, then its successor is even.

Many of our later examples will be variations of the Even program theme and will employ the successor notation for natural numbers. Consider, for example, the following program.

2.1.4 Program (Length) Let Length be the program consisting of the following clauses.

$$\text{length}([\,], a) \leftarrow$$
$$\text{length}([H\,|\,T], s(X)) \leftarrow \text{length}(T, X)$$

Following Prolog conventions, [] denotes the empty list, and [· | ·] denotes

---

[2]We borrow *Tweety* programs, in which a penguin usually called Tweety appears, from the literature discussing the semantics of non-monotonic reasoning.

a binary function whose intended meaning is the list constructor whose first argument is the head of the list and whose second argument is its tail. Thus, the program Length is intended to be a recursive definition of the "length of lists" using the successor notation for natural numbers as in Program 2.1.3. Length is an example of a definite program.

Thus far, we have specified the syntax of logic programs. We now turn our attention to dealing with their semantics, and this is based on Definitions 1.2.7 and 1.2.8 of Chapter 1 with some notation peculiar to logic programming.

2.1.5 Definition Let P be a program with underlying language $\mathcal{L}_P$, and let D be a non-empty set. A *preinterpretation* J for P with *domain D* is a preinterpretation J for $\mathcal{L}_P$ with domain D.

Let J be a preinterpretation for the program P, with domain D, and let θ be a J-variable assignment. For a typical clause C in P of the form $A \leftarrow A_1, \ldots, A_n, \neg B_1, \ldots, \neg B_k$, we let $(C\theta)^J$ denote

$$(A\theta)^J \leftarrow (A_1\theta)^J, \ldots, (A_n\theta)^J, \neg(B_1\theta)^J, \ldots, \neg(B_k\theta)^J.$$

We call $(C\theta)^J$ a *J-ground instance*[3] of C. By $\mathrm{ground}_J(P)$, we denote the set of all J-ground instances of clauses in P. We denote by $B_{P,J}$ the set $B_{\mathcal{L}_P,J}$ of all J-ground instances of atoms in $\mathcal{L}_P$, that is, the collection of all elements of the form $p(d_1, \ldots, d_n)$, where p is an n-ary predicate symbol in $\mathcal{L}_P$ and $d_1, \ldots, d_n \in D$. Usually, we will be working over a fixed, but arbitrary, preinterpretation J. In order to ease notation, we will often omit mention of J if it causes no confusion, and instead of writing $B_{P,J}$, $\mathrm{ground}_J(P)$, J-ground instance, etc., we will simply write B_P, $\mathrm{ground}(P)$, ground instance, etc. We will frequently abuse notation even further by referring to elements of $\mathrm{ground}_J(P)$ as *(ground) clauses* and by applying to ground clauses terminology, such as "definite", already defined for program clauses.

Of particular interest is the so-called *Herbrand preinterpretation* of a program. Its importance rests on the fact that, for many purposes, restricting to Herbrand preinterpretations causes no loss of generality.[4] For example, in classical first-order logic, a set of clauses has a model if and only if it has a Herbrand model. Indeed, in many cases in the literature on the subject, discussions of logic programming semantics refer only to Herbrand (pre)interpretations and Herbrand models.

2.1.6 Definition Given a program P with underlying language $\mathcal{L}_P$, the *Herbrand universe* $\mathcal{U}_P$ of P is the set of all ground terms in $\mathcal{L}_P$. The *Herbrand*

---

[3]This extends the notion of a J-ground instance of an atom to a J-ground instance of a clause, see [Lloyd, 1987, Page 12].

[4]Nevertheless, we prefer to formulate the basic definitions in complete generality. For one thing this is at no extra cost, and for another we require quite general preinterpretations in our treatment of acceptable programs in Chapter 5.

preinterpretation J, say, for P, has domain $\mathcal{U}_P$ and assigns constant and function symbols as follows, where we use the notation of Definition 1.2.7.

(1) For each constant symbol $c \in \mathcal{L}_P$, c^J is equal to c.

(2) For each n-ary function symbol $f \in \mathcal{L}_P$, $f^J : \mathcal{U}_P^n \to \mathcal{U}_P$ is the mapping defined by $f^J(t_1, \ldots, t_n) = f(t_1, \ldots, t_n)$.

We illustrate these definitions by discussing some of the previous examples in relation to them. For this purpose, and indeed for all example programs unless otherwise noted, we consider the Herbrand preinterpretation.

For the program Tweety1 (Program 2.1.2), we obtain

$$
\begin{aligned}
\mathcal{U}_{\text{Tweety1}} = {} & \{\text{bob}, \text{tweety}\}, \\
B_{\text{Tweety1}} = {} & \{\text{penguin(bob)}, \text{penguin(tweety)}, \\
& \text{bird(bob)}, \text{bird(tweety)}, \\
& \text{flies(bob)}, \text{flies(tweety)}\},
\end{aligned}
$$

and ground(Tweety1) consists of the following clauses.

$$
\begin{aligned}
\text{penguin(tweety)} &\leftarrow \\
\text{bird(bob)} &\leftarrow \\
\text{bird(tweety)} &\leftarrow \text{penguin(tweety)} \\
\text{bird(bob)} &\leftarrow \text{penguin(bob)} \\
\text{flies(tweety)} &\leftarrow \text{bird(tweety)}, \neg\text{penguin(tweety)} \\
\text{flies(bob)} &\leftarrow \text{bird(bob)}, \neg\text{penguin(bob)}
\end{aligned}
$$

For the successor notation used in the program Even (Program 2.1.3), the following convention will be convenient: for $n \in \mathbb{N}$, we denote the term $s(s(\ldots s(x) \ldots))$, with n occurrences of s, by $s^n(x)$. We then obtain for the Even program

$$
\begin{aligned}
\mathcal{U}_{\text{Even}} &= \{s^n(a) \mid n \in \mathbb{N}\}, \\
B_{\text{Even}} &= \{\text{even}\,(s^n(a)) \mid n \in \mathbb{N}\},
\end{aligned}
$$

and ground(Even) consists of the following clauses.

$$
\begin{aligned}
\text{even}(a) &\leftarrow \\
\text{even}\,(s^{n+1}(a)) &\leftarrow \neg\text{even}\,(s^n(a)) \qquad \text{for all } n \in \mathbb{N}
\end{aligned}
$$

We note that the set ground(Even) is infinite. In fact, ground(Even) can be thought of as an infinite propositional program consisting of clauses $p_0 \leftarrow$ and $p_{n+1} \leftarrow \neg p_n$, where, for each $n \in \mathbb{N}$, p_n is a propositional variable replacing $\text{even}\,(s^n(a))$. Often, it is conceptually easier to think of ground(P) as a (countably) infinite propositional program and to study it rather than P.

Indeed, many authors even define a logic program to be a set of propositional clauses, with the advantage that notation can be considerably eased in some places. For many of the example programs which we will discuss later, we will also take advantage of this simpler notation, as in the following.

2.1.7 Program Let P be the following program.

$$p \leftarrow \neg q$$
$$q \leftarrow \neg p$$

Then $B_P = \{p, q\}$ and $\text{ground}(P) = P$. Preinterpretations play no role in this case.

We now come to the fundamental notions of *interpretation* and *model* for programs. Interpretations and models as defined next are the particular forms of Definitions 1.2.7 and 1.2.8 that we will use henceforth in studying the semantics of programs.

2.1.8 Definition Let P be a program, let J be a preinterpretation for P with domain D, and let $\mathcal{T}$ be a logic. An *interpretation* or *valuation for* P *(based on J) with values in $\mathcal{T}$* is an interpretation or valuation defined on $B_{P,J}$ with values in $\mathcal{T}$. An interpretation I for P is a *model* for P if $I(C) = \mathbf{t}$ for each clause $C \in \text{ground}_J(P)$. As in Definition 1.2.8, we sometimes refer to valuations, interpretations, and models for P based on J as J-valuations, J-interpretations, and J-models, respectively.

We will in future use the notation $I_{P,J,2}$ for the set of all two-valued interpretations for P based on J. As usual, reference to the preinterpretation J will often be omitted if it is fixed and understood. Similarly, the number 2 will be omitted if it is understood, and hence the set of all two-valued interpretations for P based on a given, fixed preinterpretation J will often be denoted by $I_{P,2}$ or just by I_P. Similar comments apply to the set $I_{P,J,3}$ of all three-valued interpretations for P based on J and to the set $I_{P,J,4}$ of all four-valued interpretations for P based on J.

The three sets just defined have the order-theoretic structure described in Theorem 1.3.4 relative to the orders we discussed in Chapter 1. In particular, $I_{P,2}$ can be identified with the power set of B_P.

With these structures in place, we are now ready to begin the main subject of our study in this chapter, namely, the semantics of logic programs.

2.2　Supported Models

As already noted, a declarative semantics for logic programs is usually given by selecting models for the programs which satisfy certain desirable conditions. This selection is often most conveniently described by an operator, mapping interpretations to interpretations, whose fixed points are exactly the models being sought. In this section, we will introduce the first of a number of operators we study in the context of declarative semantics, namely, the single-step or immediate consequence operator due to Kowalski and van Emden, see [van Emden and Kowalski, 1976]. The single-step operator was historically the first to be studied in relation to logic programming semantics and in many ways is the most natural. Indeed, it turns out that for definite programs the single-step operator is order continuous and that its least fixed point, as given by Kleene's theorem, Theorem 1.1.9, accords well with a programmer's expectations of what a declarative semantics should be and how it should relate to the procedural semantics.[5]

For the remainder of this section and for the next, we will work in classical two-valued logic. Hence, I_P or $I_{P,J}$ means $I_{P,J,2}$ here and in the subsequent section, where J is a given preinterpretation, and we will on occasions remind the reader of this notational convenience.

The following is an important definition.

2.2.1 Definition Let P be a normal logic program, and let J be a preinterpretation for $\mathcal{L}_P$. The *single-step operator* or *immediate consequence operator* $T_{P,J} : I_{P,J} \to I_{P,J}$ is defined, for $I \in I_{P,J}$, by setting $T_{P,J}(I)$ to be the set of all $A \in B_{P,J}$ for which there is a clause $A \leftarrow L_1, \ldots, L_n$ in $\mathrm{ground}_J(P)$ satisfying $I \models L_1 \wedge \ldots \wedge L_n$, that is, satisfying $I(L_1 \wedge \ldots \wedge L_n) = \mathbf{t}$.

Consistent with our earlier remarks concerning notation, we will usually denote $T_{P,J}$ simply by T_P when J is understood. Furthermore, we will sometimes find it convenient to refer to T_P as the T_P-*operator*.

The importance of the immediate consequence operator is clear from the following proposition.

2.2.2 Proposition The models for P are exactly the pre-fixed points of T_P.

Proof: Let $I \in I_P$ be a model for P, and let $A \in T_P(I)$. Then there is a clause $A \leftarrow L_1, \ldots, L_n$ in $\mathrm{ground}(P)$ with $I(L_1 \wedge \ldots \wedge L_n) = \mathbf{t}$; let us denote this clause by C. Since I is a model for P, we have $I(C) = \mathbf{t}$. Hence, $I(A) = \mathbf{t}$, and so $A \in I$, giving $T_P(I) \subseteq I$, as required.

Conversely, suppose $T_P(I) \subseteq I$, and let $A \leftarrow L_1, \ldots, L_n$ be a clause C in $\mathrm{ground}(P)$ with $I(L_1 \wedge \ldots \wedge L_n) = \mathbf{t}$. Then $A \in T_P(I) \subseteq I$. Hence, $I(A) = \mathbf{t}$, and in consequence $I(C) = \mathbf{t}$, as required. ∎

The notion of model is far too general to capture the declarative semantics of logic programs without some restrictions being imposed upon it. Indeed, B_P itself is always a model for P, but in general B_P fails by far to give a reasonable "intended meaning" for a program. Standard approaches to declarative

---

[5]As already noted, we will not consider procedural aspects in depth and instead refer the reader to [Apt, 1997, Lloyd, 1987] for details of procedural semantics.

semantics therefore involve the imposition of certain additional conditions which models must satisfy in order to qualify as *intended models*. However, just what conditions it is reasonable to choose in this context depends on one's particular understanding of what "intended" could mean, and the remainder of this chapter will be devoted, in the main, to the presentation and study of different conditions which have been proposed in the literature to solve this problem.

The observation that B_P is too large, as a two-valued model, suggests the selection of *minimal models*. Of particular interest are the cases when there exists a *least model*.

2.2.3 Theorem Let P be a definite program, and let J denote a fixed preinterpretation for $\mathcal{L}_P$. Then the following statements hold.

(a) T_P is order continuous on I_P.

(b) P has a least (J-)model, which coincides with the least fixed point of T_P and is equal to $T_P \uparrow \omega$.

(c) The intersection of any non-empty collection of (J-)models for P is itself a model for P. Therefore, a definite program cannot have two distinct minimal models. Furthermore, the intersection of the collection of all models for P coincides with the least model for P.

Proof: (a) We first show that T_P is monotonic. Let $I, K \in I_P$ with $I \subseteq K$, and suppose $A \in T_P(I)$. Then there is a clause $A \leftarrow$ body in ground(P) with body $\subseteq I$. Hence, body $\subseteq K$, and so $A \in T_P(K)$, as required.

Now let $\mathcal{I} = \{I_\lambda \mid \lambda \in \Lambda\}$ be a directed family of two-valued interpretations, and let $I = \bigsqcup \mathcal{I} = \bigcup \mathcal{I}$. Since the order under consideration is set-inclusion and T_P is monotonic, we immediately have that $T_P(\mathcal{I})$ is directed. By the remarks following Definition 1.1.7, it remains to show that $T_P(I) \subseteq \bigcup T_P(\mathcal{I})$. So suppose that A belongs to $T_P(I)$. Then there is a (definite) clause C of the form $A \leftarrow A_1, \ldots, A_n$ in ground(P) satisfying $A_1, \ldots, A_n \in I$. Therefore, there exist $I_{\lambda_1}, \ldots, I_{\lambda_n}$ in $\mathcal{I}$ with $A_i \in I_{\lambda_i}$ for $i = 1, \ldots, n$. Since $\mathcal{I}$ is directed, there is $I_\lambda \in \mathcal{I}$ with $I_{\lambda_i} \subseteq I_\lambda$ for $i = 1, \ldots, n$. Hence, the body of C is true in I_λ, and we obtain that $A \in T_P(I_\lambda)$ and, consequently, that $A \in \bigcup T_P(\mathcal{I})$, as required.

(b) By (a), we can apply Kleene's theorem, Theorem 1.1.9, to see that T_P has a least pre-fixed point, that this least pre-fixed point is in fact the least fixed point of T_P, and that it coincides with $T_P \uparrow \omega$. Hence, by Proposition 2.2.2, $T_P \uparrow \omega$ is the least model for P.

(c) The details of the proof of this claim are straightforward and therefore are omitted.   ∎

It can be shown, furthermore, that the least model for definite programs corresponds rather well with the procedural behaviour of logic programming systems based on resolution.[6] Thus, in summary, the *least model semantics* is very satisfactory for definite logic programs from all points of view.

Attempts to generalize Theorem 2.2.3 to normal programs, however, fail in several ways, as we show next.

2.2.4 Program Let P be the normal logic program consisting of the following clauses.

$$p \leftarrow \neg q$$
$$q \leftarrow \neg p$$
$$r \leftarrow \neg r$$

Then $\{p, r\}$ and $\{q, r\}$ are minimal, but incomparable, models so that P has no least model, T_P has no fixed points at all (and hence P has no supported models, see Proposition 2.2.6), and, since $T_P(\emptyset) = \{p, q, r\}$ and $T_P(\{p, q, r\}) = \emptyset$, we see that T_P is not monotonic.

It is not entirely clear how to cope with the negative results presented by Program 2.2.4. Various different methods have been discussed in the literature, leading to different declarative semantics with varying degrees of success. We will discuss the more prominent of these approaches in the remainder of this chapter.

A rather straightforward attack is to study *minimal models* instead of least models. However, consider the program Even (Program 2.1.3) with models

$$K_1 = \{ \text{even} \left(s^{2n}(a) \right) \mid n \in \mathbb{N} \} \qquad \text{and}$$
$$K_2 = \{ \text{even} \left(s^{2n+1}(a) \right) \mid n \in \mathbb{N} \} .$$

Both models are minimal, but it seems to be rather obvious that K_1 captures the intended meaning of Even, while K_2 does not. Essentially, this arises from the fact that $\text{even}(s(a))$ is true with respect to K_2, although the program itself gives no justification for this. Thus, it would seem intuitively reasonable that whenever an atom is true in an intended model for a program P, then it should be true for a reason provided by the program itself. This idea is captured by the following definition, see [Apt et al., 1988].

2.2.5 Definition An interpretation I for a program P is called *supported* if for each $A \in I$ there is a clause $A \leftarrow$ body in ground(P) with $I(\text{body}) = \mathbf{t}$.

Continuing the Even program discussion above, note that K_1 is supported, whereas K_2 is not. Indeed, K_1 is the only supported model for Even, as we will see later. So, for some programs, supportedness is an appropriate requirement of models. Supportedness is also captured by the immediate consequence operator, as follows.

---

[6]A detailed account of resolution-based logic programming can be found in [Apt, 1997, Lloyd, 1987].

2.2.6 Proposition The supported interpretations for a program P are exactly the post-fixed points of T_P. The supported models for P are exactly the fixed points of T_P.

Proof: Let I be a supported interpretation for P, and suppose that $A \subset I$. Then there is a clause $A \leftarrow \text{body}$ in ground(P) with $I(\text{body}) = \mathbf{t}$. But then $A \in T_P(I)$, showing that $I \subseteq T_P(I)$, as required to see that I is a post-fixed point of T_P.

Conversely, assume that $I \subseteq T_P(I)$ is a post-fixed point of T_P, and let $A \in I$. Then $A \in T_P(I)$. Therefore, there exists a clause $A \leftarrow \text{body}$ in ground(P) with $I(\text{body}) = \mathbf{t}$, showing that I is a supported model for P.

Finally, using Proposition 2.2.2, we obtain that an interpretation for P is a supported model for P if and only if it is both a pre-fixed point and a post-fixed point of T_P, that is, if and only if it is a fixed point of T_P.   ∎

2.2.7 Example Tweety1 from Program 2.1.2 has supported model M, where $M = \{\text{penguin}(\text{tweety}), \text{bird}(\text{bob}), \text{bird}(\text{tweety}), \text{flies}(\text{bob})\}$, as is easily verified. Careful inspection will also convince the reader that M is the unique supported model for Tweety1, and we give a formal proof of this in Example 5.1.7.

From a procedural point of view in the context of resolution-based logic programming, supported models are better than minimal ones. They capture the probable intention of a programmer who may think of a clause as a form of equivalence[7] rather than as an implication.

Since the least model for a definite program is a fixed point, by Theorem 2.2.3, we obtain as a corollary that the least model is always supported. In proving Theorem 2.2.3, we applied Kleene's theorem. For normal programs, this theorem is not applicable, nor is the Knaster-Tarski theorem, due to the non-monotonicity of the immediate consequence operator in general. In order to study the supported model semantics, that is, in order to obtain fixed points of non-monotonic immediate consequence operators, it seems natural to employ fixed-point theorems for mappings which are not necessarily monotonic. This is the main theme of Chapter 4.

2.3   Stable Models

One of the drawbacks of the supported model semantics is that definite programs may have more than one supported model.

---

[7]One formal approach to understanding clauses as equivalences is via the notion of the Clark completion of a program and is related to SLDNF-resolution, see [Clark, 1978].

2.3.1 Program Let P be the program consisting of the single clause $p \leftarrow p$. Then both $\emptyset$ and $\{p\}$ are supported models for P.

This unsatisfactory situation is resolved by the introduction of *stable models*. Before we give the definition, let us make the following observation.

2.3.2 Proposition The least model $T_P \uparrow \omega$ for a definite program P is the unique model M for P satisfying the following condition: there exists a mapping $l : B_P \rightarrow \alpha$, for some ordinal α, such that for each $A \in M$ there is a clause $A \leftarrow$ body in ground(P) with $M(\text{body}) = \mathbf{t}$ and $l(B) < l(A)$ for each $B \in$ body.

Proof: To start with, take M to be the least model $T_P \uparrow \omega$, choose $\alpha = \omega$, and define $l : B_P \rightarrow \alpha$ by setting $l(A) = \min\{n \mid A \in T_P \uparrow (n+1)\}$, if $A \in M$, and by setting $l(A) = 0$, if $A \notin M$. Since $\emptyset \subseteq T_P \uparrow 1 \subseteq \ldots \subseteq T_P \uparrow n \subseteq \ldots \subseteq T_P \uparrow \omega = \bigcup_{m<\omega} T_P \uparrow m$, for each n, we see that l is well-defined and that the least model $T_P \uparrow \omega$ for P has the desired properties.

Conversely, if M is a model for P which satisfies the given condition for some mapping $l : B_P \rightarrow \alpha$, then it is easy to show, by induction on $l(A)$, that $A \in M$ implies $A \in T_P \uparrow (l(A) + 1)$. This yields that $M \subseteq T_P \uparrow \omega$ and hence that $M = T_P \uparrow \omega$ by minimality of the model $T_P \uparrow \omega$. ∎

Mappings l from B_P into an ordinal are commonly called *level mappings*. They will play an important role in several places in the book. On occasions, we will need to extend such mapping to literals, and unless stated to the contrary, we will always assume that the extension satisfies $l(\neg A) = l(A)$ for all atoms A.

The following definition of stable model merges the property of M_P just established with that of supportedness.[8]

2.3.3 Definition An interpretation I for a program P is called a *well-supported interpretation* if there exists a level mapping $l : B_P \rightarrow \alpha$, for some ordinal α, with the property that, for each $A \in I$, there is a clause C in ground(P) of the form $A \leftarrow A_1, \ldots, A_n, \neg B_1, \ldots, \neg B_k$ such that the body of C is true in I and $l(A_i) < l(A)$ for $i = 1, \ldots, n$. A *well-supported model* for P is called a *stable model* for P.

2.3.4 Theorem The following statements hold.

(a) Every stable model is supported, but not vice-versa.

(b) Every stable model is a minimal model, but not vice-versa.

(c) Every definite program has a unique stable model, which is its least model.

---

[8]It is shown in [Fages, 1994] that stable models can be introduced as in Definition 2.3.3. The original formulation used the Gelfond–Lifschitz operator from Definition 2.3.6.

Proof: (a) Supportedness of stable models follows immediately from the definition. The supported model $\{p\}$ for Program 2.3.1 is not stable.

(b) Let P be a program, let M be a stable model for P, and let l be a level mapping with respect to which M is well-supported. Assume that K is a model for P with $K \subset M$. Then there exists $A \in M \setminus K$, and we can assume without loss of generality that A is also such that $l(A)$ is minimal. By the well-supportedness of M, there is a clause C of the form $A \leftarrow A_1, \ldots, A_n, \neg B_1, \ldots, \neg B_k$ in ground(P) such that for $i = 1, \ldots, n$ and $j = 1, \ldots, k$ we have $A_i \in M$, $l(A) > l(A_i)$ and $B_j \notin M$. Since $K \subset M$, we obtain, for $j = 1, \ldots k$, that $B_j \notin K$, and by minimality of $l(A)$ we obtain $A_i \in K$ for $i = 1, \ldots, n$. Since K is a model for P and the body of C is true with respect to K, we conclude that $A \in K$, which contradicts the assumption that $A \in M \setminus K$. Hence, M must be a minimal model.

In the opposite direction, Program 2.3.5 below has $\{p\}$ as its only model, and hence, this is a minimal model. It is clearly not a stable model, however.

(c) By Proposition 2.3.2, we see that the least model is indeed stable. Uniqueness follows from (b) and Theorem 2.2.3 (c). ∎

There are programs with unique supported models which are not stable.

2.3.5 Program The program P consisting of the two clauses

$$p \leftarrow p$$

$$p \leftarrow \neg p$$

has unique supported model $\{p\}$, and this model is not stable.

A unique stable model is always a least model by Theorem 2.3.4 (b). If a program has a least model, however, this model is not guaranteed to be stable, as Program 2.3.5 shows in having $\{p\}$ as its only model.

A characterization of stable models as fixed points of an operator can be given, and we proceed with this next.

2.3.6 Definition Let P be a normal logic program, and let $I \in I_P$. The *Gelfond–Lifschitz transform* P/I of P is the set of all clauses $A \leftarrow A_1, \ldots, A_n$ for which there exists a clause $A \leftarrow A_1, \ldots, A_n, \neg B_1, \ldots, \neg B_k$ in ground(P) with $B_1, \ldots, B_k \notin I$.

We note that the Gelfond–Lifschitz transform P/I of a program P is always definite (as a set of ground clauses) and therefore has a least model $T_{P/I} \uparrow \omega$ by Theorem 2.2.3. The operator $\mathrm{GL}_P : I \mapsto T_{P/I} \uparrow \omega$ is called the *Gelfond–Lifschitz operator*[9] associated with P.

2.3.7 Theorem The following hold.

---

[9]The Gelfond–Lifschitz operator is named after the authors of the well-known paper [Gelfond and Lifschitz, 1988] and was introduced by them in defining the stable model semantics.

(a) The Gelfond–Lifschitz operator is antitonic and, in general, is not monotonic.

(b) An interpretation I is a stable model for a program P if and only if it is a fixed point of GL_P, that is, if and only if it satisfies $GL_P(I) = I$.

Proof: (a) Let P be a program, and let I, K be interpretations for P with $I \subseteq K$. Then $P/K \subseteq P/I$, and it is a straightforward proof by induction to show that $T_{P/K} \uparrow n \subseteq T_{P/I} \uparrow n$ for all $n \in \mathbb{N}$. Hence, $GL_P(K) = T_{P/K} \uparrow \omega \subseteq T_{P/I} \uparrow \omega = GL_P(I)$, which shows that GL_P is antitonic. To see that it is not generally monotonic, take P to be Program 2.3.5. On setting $I = \emptyset$, we obtain that P/I is the definite program consisting of the clauses $p \leftarrow p$ and $p \leftarrow$, and $GL_P(I) = \{p\}$; on setting $I = \{p\}$, we obtain that P/I consists of the single clause $p \leftarrow p$, and $GL_P(I) = \emptyset$. This establishes (a).

For (b), we start by supposing that $GL_P(I) = T_{P/I} \uparrow \omega = I$. Then I is the least model for P/I, and hence, is also a model for P, and, by Proposition 2.3.2, is well-supported with respect to any level mapping l satisfying $l(A) = \min\{n \mid A \in T_{P/I} \uparrow (n+1)\}$ for each $A \in I$. Conversely, let I be a stable model for P. Then I is well-supported relative to some level mapping l, say. Thus, for every $A \in I$, there is a clause C in ground(P) of the form $A \leftarrow A_1, \ldots, A_n, \neg B_1, \ldots, \neg B_k$ such that the body of C is true in I and $l(A_i) < l(A)$ for $i = 1, \ldots, n$. But then, for every $A \in I$, there is a clause $A \leftarrow A_1, \ldots, A_n$ in P/I whose body is true in I and such that $l(A_i) < l(A)$ for $i = 1, \ldots, n$. By Proposition 2.3.2, this means that I is the least model for P/I, that is, $I = T_{P/I} \uparrow \omega = GL_P(I)$. ∎

The Gelfond–Lifschitz transform can be considered as a two-step process: first, delete each ground clause which has a negative literal $\neg B$ in its body with $B \in I$; second, delete all negative literals in the bodies of the remaining clauses. Indeed, the intuition behind it is as follows. We can think of P as a set of premises and of I as a set of beliefs that a rational agent might hold and wants to test, given the premises P. Any ground clause that contains $\neg B$ in its body, where $B \in I$, is useless to the agent and can be discarded. Among the remaining ground clauses, an occurrence of $\neg B$ with $B \notin I$ is trivial. Thus, we can simplify the premises to P/I. If I happens to be the set of atoms that logically follow from P/I, then the agent is rational.

We will now give some examples.

2.3.8 Example Consider again Tweety1 from Program 2.1.2 and its supported model M as given in Example 2.2.7. We show that M is stable. The program Tweety1/M is as follows.

$$\text{penguin(tweety)} \leftarrow$$
$$\text{bird(bob)} \leftarrow$$
$$\text{bird(tweety)} \leftarrow \text{penguin(tweety)}$$
$$\text{bird(bob)} \leftarrow \text{penguin(bob)}$$
$$\text{flies(bob)} \leftarrow \text{bird(bob)}$$

The least model for this program turns out to be M, which shows that M is stable.

A strange feature of the supported model semantics is that the addition of clauses of the form $p \leftarrow p$ may change the semantics.

2.3.9 Program (Tweety2) Consider the following program Tweety2.

$$\text{penguin(tweety)} \leftarrow$$
$$\text{bird(bob)} \leftarrow$$
$$\text{bird}(X) \leftarrow \text{penguin}(X)$$
$$\text{flies}(X) \leftarrow \text{bird}(X), \neg\text{penguin}(X)$$
$$\text{penguin(bob)} \leftarrow \text{penguin(bob)}$$

Tweety2 results from Tweety1 by adding the clause penguin(bob) $\leftarrow$ penguin(bob). Intuitively, this addition should not change the semantics of the program. However, in addition to the supported model M from Example 2.2.7, Tweety2 also has

$$M' = \{\text{penguin(tweety)}, \text{penguin(bob)}, \text{bird(tweety)}, \text{bird(bob)}\}$$

as a supported model. While M is also a stable model for Tweety2, M' is not. This can be seen by inspecting the program Tweety2/M', as follows, which has $\{\text{penguin(tweety)}, \text{bird(bob)}, \text{bird(tweety)}\} \neq M'$ as its least model.

$$\text{penguin(tweety)} \leftarrow$$
$$\text{bird(bob)} \leftarrow$$
$$\text{bird(tweety)} \leftarrow \text{penguin(tweety)}$$
$$\text{bird(bob)} \leftarrow \text{penguin(bob)}$$
$$\text{penguin(bob)} \leftarrow \text{penguin(bob)}$$

We can also use the stable model semantics for modelling *choice*.

2.3.10 Program (Tweety3) Consider the program Tweety3, as follows.

$$\text{eagle(tweety)} \leftarrow \neg\text{penguin(tweety)}$$
$$\text{penguin(tweety)} \leftarrow \neg\text{eagle(tweety)}$$
$$\text{bird}(X) \leftarrow \text{eagle}(X)$$
$$\text{bird}(X) \leftarrow \text{penguin}(X)$$
$$\text{flies}(X) \leftarrow \text{bird}(X), \neg\text{penguin}(X)$$

This program has the two stable models

$$\{\text{eagle(tweety)}, \text{bird(tweety)}, \text{flies(tweety)}\}$$

and

$$\{\text{penguin(tweety)}, \text{bird(tweety)}\}.$$

2.4 Fitting Models

The stable model semantics is more satisfactory than the supported model semantics in that each definite program has a unique stable model which coincides with its least model. However, for normal logic programs in general, uniqueness cannot be guaranteed, as can be seen from Program 2.1.7, which has two stable models $\{p\}$ and $\{q\}$. It is desirable to be able to associate with each program a unique model in some natural way. One way of doing this is by means of three-valued logic, and we discuss this next.[10]

In fact, we will work with Kleene's strong three-valued logic as discussed in Chapter 1 and, in particular, with the knowledge ordering, $\leq_k$, on the truth values. We find it convenient here to represent three-valued interpretations as signed sets, see Section 1.3.3, so that the corresponding ordering $\sqsubseteq_k$ is subset inclusion of signed sets.

Given a normal logic program P, we define the following operators T_P' and F_P on $I_P = I_{P,3} = I_{P,J,3}$. First, $T_P'(I)$ is the set of all $A \in B_P$ for which there is a clause $A \leftarrow$ body in $\text{ground}(P)$ with body true in I with respect to Kleene's strong three-valued logic. Second, $F_P(I)$ is the set of all $A \in B_P$ such that for all clauses $A \leftarrow$ body in $\text{ground}(P)$ we have that body is false in I with respect to Kleene's strong three-valued logic. Finally, we define

$$\Phi_P(I) = T_P'(I) \cup \neg F_P(I)$$

for all $I \in I_P$. We will call the operator Φ_P the *Fitting operator* for P or the Φ_P-*operator*.

---

[10]The resulting Kripke-Kleene semantics, herein called the Fitting semantics, is due to Fitting [Fitting, 1985].

Notice that, for any three-valued interpretation I, we have $A \in \Phi_P(I)$ whenever A is the head of a ground clause and $\neg A \in \Phi_P(I)$ whenever there is no ground clause whose head is A.

2.4.1 Example We illustrate the calculation of $\Phi_P(I)$, taking P to be the program Tweety1 and starting with the three-valued interpretation $I = \emptyset$ thought of as a signed subset; of course, $\emptyset$ gives truth value **u** to all ground atoms in our present context.

We have

$$T_P'(\emptyset) = \{\texttt{penguin(tweety)}, \texttt{bird(bob)}\}$$

and

$$\neg F_P(\emptyset) = \neg\{\texttt{penguin(bob)}\}.$$

Therefore,

$$\Phi_P(\emptyset) = \{\texttt{penguin(tweety)}, \texttt{bird(bob)}, \neg\texttt{penguin(bob)}\}.$$

Continuing, we have

$$T_P'(\Phi_P(\emptyset)) = \{\texttt{penguin(tweety)}, \texttt{bird(bob)}, \texttt{bird(tweety)}, \texttt{flies(bob)}\},$$

and

$$\neg F_P(\Phi_P(\emptyset)) = \neg\{\texttt{penguin(bob)}, \texttt{flies(tweety)}\}.$$

Thus, $\Phi_P(\Phi_P(\emptyset)) = T_P'(\Phi_P(\emptyset)) \cup \neg F_P(\Phi_P(\emptyset))$ is a total three-valued interpretation. It follows from this fact and Proposition 2.4.4 below that $\Phi_P(\Phi_P(\emptyset))$ is, in fact, the least fixed point of Φ_P, as can readily be checked in any case by iterating Φ_P once more.

The development of the operator Φ_P somewhat parallels that of T_P except that there are two orderings involved, and the following result is analogous to Proposition 2.2.2.

2.4.2 Proposition Let P be a normal logic program. Then the three-valued models for P are exactly the pre-fixed points of Φ_P in the truth ordering $\sqsubseteq_t$.

Proof: Suppose that M is a three-valued interpretation for P satisfying $\Phi_P(M) \sqsubseteq_t M$, and let $A \in B_P$ be arbitrary. Suppose that $\Phi_P(M)(A) = \mathbf{u}$. Then we must have $M(A)$ equal to **u** or to **t**. Since no clause $A \leftarrow \texttt{body}$ in ground(P) can have $M(\texttt{body}) = \mathbf{t}$, otherwise $\Phi_P(M)(A)$ would be equal to **t**, we must have $M(\texttt{body})$ equal to **u** or to **f** for each clause $A \leftarrow \texttt{body}$ in ground(P). But then, on recalling the truth value given to $\leftarrow$ in Definition 1.3.3, we see that $A \leftarrow \texttt{body}$ is true in M. The other possible values for $\Phi_P(M)(A)$ are handled similarly, and so M is a model for P.

The converse is also handled similarly, and we omit the details. ∎

2.4.3 Program Consider the following program P.

$$p \leftarrow \neg q$$
$$p \leftarrow \neg r$$
$$q \leftarrow q$$
$$r \leftarrow r$$

Define M as follows: $M(p) = \mathbf{f}$, $M(q) = \mathbf{u}$, and $M(r) = \mathbf{t}$. Then M is a three-valued interpretation for P satisfying $\Phi_P(M) \sqsubseteq_k M$, and yet M is not a model for P.

On the other hand, take P to be Program 2.2.4. Define M as follows: $M(p) = \mathbf{t}$, $M(q) = \mathbf{u}$, and $M(r) = \mathbf{t}$. Then M is a three-valued model for P, but it does not satisfy the inequality $\Phi_P(M) \sqsubseteq_k M$.

Therefore, neither implication of Proposition 2.4.2 holds in the case of the knowledge ordering.

The following fact about Φ_P is fundamental.

2.4.4 Proposition Let P be a program. Then Φ_P is monotonic on $I_{P,3}$ in the knowledge ordering $\sqsubseteq_k$.

Proof: Let $I, K \in I_{P,3}$ with $I \subseteq K$. We show $\Phi_P(I) \subseteq \Phi_P(K)$. Let $A \in \Phi_P(I)$ be an atom. Then $A \in T'_P(I)$. Therefore, there is a ground clause $A \leftarrow \mathsf{body}$ such that body is true in I. From Table 1.1, each literal in body must be true and therefore, noting the results of Section 1.3.3, must belong to I. Hence, each literal in body belongs to K since $I \subseteq K$ and is therefore true in K. Hence, body is also true in K, and we obtain that $A \in T'_P(K) \subseteq \Phi_P(K)$. Now let $\neg A \in \Phi_P(I)$ be a negated atom. Then $A \in F_P(I)$, and so, for all ground clauses $A \leftarrow \mathsf{body}$, we have that body is false in I. So, given such a clause, from Table 1.1 we see that at least one literal L_j, say, in body, is false. Hence, by the results of Section 1.3.3 again, we have $\neg L_j \in I$. But $I \subseteq K$ and hence $\neg L_j \in K$. Therefore, L_j is also false in K, and consequently body is false in K. Thus, we obtain $A \in F_P(K)$, and hence $\neg A \in \Phi_P(K)$, as required. ■

2.4.5 Example Take P to be Program 2.2.4 again. Define three-valued interpretations I and K for P as follows: $I(p) = I(q) = I(r) = \mathbf{f}$, and $K(p) = K(q) = K(r) = \mathbf{t}$. Then $I \sqsubset_t K$. Yet $\Phi_P(K)$ is constant with value $\mathbf{f}$, and $\Phi_P(I)$ is constant with value $\mathbf{t}$. Hence, $\Phi(K) \sqsubset_t \Phi(I)$, and so Φ_P is not monotonic relative to the truth ordering.

Since the operator Φ_P is monotonic relative to the ordering $\sqsubseteq_k$, it has a least fixed point by the Knaster-Tarski theorem, Theorem 1.1.10, and this least fixed point is an ordinal power $\Phi_P \uparrow \alpha$, as defined in Section 1.1, for some ordinal α. The least fixed point of Φ_P is called the *Kripke-Kleene model* or *Fitting model* for P. It turns out, as we show later, that Φ_P is not order continuous, indeed not even ω-continuous, relative to $\sqsubseteq_k$, and so Kleene's theorem, Theorem 1.1.9, is not generally applicable to Φ_P.

2.4.6 Proposition Let P be a program. Then every fixed point M of Φ_P is a model for P with the following properties. (a) If $A \in B_P$ is such that $M(A) = \mathbf{t}$, then there exists a clause $A \leftarrow$ body in ground(P) with $M(\text{body}) = \mathbf{t}$. (b) If $A \in B_P$ is such that for all clauses $A \leftarrow$ body in ground(P) we have $M(\text{body}) = \mathbf{f}$, then $M(A) = \mathbf{f}$.

Proof: Let $A \leftarrow$ body be a clause in ground(P). If $M(\text{body}) = \mathbf{t}$, then $M(A) = \Phi_P(M)(A) = M(\text{body}) = \mathbf{t}$. If $M(A) = \mathbf{f}$, then $\Phi_P(M)(A) = M(A) = \mathbf{f}$, and hence $M(\text{body}) = \mathbf{f}$. Finally, if $M(A) = \mathbf{u}$, then $\Phi_P(M)(A) = M(A) = \mathbf{u}$, and therefore $M(\text{body}) = \mathbf{f}$ or $M(\text{body}) = \mathbf{u}$. By definition of the truth value given to $\leftarrow$, we see that this suffices to show that M is a model for P.

In order to show (a), let $A \in B_P$, and suppose that $M(A) = \mathbf{t}$. Then $\Phi_P(M)(A) = M(A) = \mathbf{t}$, and there is a clause $A \leftarrow$ body in ground(P) with $M(\text{body}) = \mathbf{t}$ by definition of Φ_P.

To show (b), let $A \in B_P$, and assume that for all clauses $A \leftarrow$ body in ground(P) we have $M(\text{body}) = \mathbf{f}$. Then $M(A) = \Phi_P(M)(A) = \mathbf{f}$, again by definition of Φ_P. ∎

Proposition 2.4.6 shows that fixed points of Φ_P are *three-valued supported models* for P, meaning that they satisfy (a) and (b) of Proposition 2.4.6. Note that a total three-valued supported model is a supported model in the sense of Definition 2.2.5.

2.4.7 Proposition Let P be a program. Then the fixed points of Φ_P are exactly the three-valued supported models for P.

Proof: Certainly, every fixed point of Φ_P is a three-valued supported model for P by Proposition 2.4.6. Conversely, let M be a three-valued supported model for P, and let $A \in B_P$. If $M(A) = \mathbf{t}$, then, by definition of a three-valued supported model, there exists a clause $A \leftarrow$ body in ground(P) such that $M(\text{body}) = \mathbf{t}$, and hence $\Phi_P(M)(A) = M(\text{body}) = \mathbf{t} = M(A)$. If $M(A) = \mathbf{f}$, then for all clauses $A \leftarrow$ body in ground(P) we have that $M(\text{body}) = \mathbf{f}$, since M is a model for P. Hence, $\Phi_P(M)(A) = M(\text{body}) = \mathbf{f} = M(A)$. It follows that M is a fixed point of Φ_P, as required. ∎

Before discussing further properties of the Fitting model, we give an alternative characterization of it.

For a program P and a three-valued interpretation $I \in I_{P,3}$, an *I-partial level mapping* for P is a partial mapping $l : B_P \to \alpha$ with domain dom$(l) = \{A \mid A \in I \text{ or } \neg A \in I\}$, where α is some ordinal. Again, we extend every such mapping to literals by setting $l(\neg A) = l(A)$ for all $A \in$ dom(l).

2.4.8 Definition Let P be a normal logic program, let I be a three-valued model for P, and let l be an I-partial level mapping for P. We say that P *satisfies* (F) *with respect to I and l* if each $A \in \mathrm{dom}(l)$ satisfies one of the following conditions.

(Fi) $A \in I$, and there is a clause $A \leftarrow L_1, \ldots, L_n$ in $\mathrm{ground}(P)$ such that $L_i \in I$ and $l(A) > l(L_i)$ for $i = 1, \ldots, n$.

(Fii) $\neg A \in I$, and for each clause $A \leftarrow L_1, \ldots, L_n$ in $\mathrm{ground}(P)$ there exists $i \in \{1, \ldots, n\}$ with $\neg L_i \in I$ and $l(A) > l(L_i)$.

If $A \in \mathrm{dom}(l)$ satisfies (Fi), then we say that A *satisfies* (Fi) *with respect to I and l*, with similar terminology if $A \in \mathrm{dom}(l)$ satisfies (Fii).

2.4.9 Theorem Let P be a normal logic program with Fitting model M_P. Then, in the knowledge ordering $\sqsubseteq_k$, M_P is the greatest model among all three-valued models I for which there exists an I-partial level mapping l for P such that P satisfies (F) with respect to I and l.

Proof: We have $M_P = \Phi_P \uparrow \alpha$ for some ordinal α, and indeed α may be taken to be the closure ordinal for M_P. Define the M_P-partial level mapping $l_P : B_P \to \alpha$ as follows: $l_P(A) = \beta$, where β is the least ordinal such that A is not undefined in $\Phi_P \uparrow (\beta + 1)$. The proof will be established by showing the following facts. (1) P satisfies (F) with respect to M_P and l_P. (2) If I is a three-valued model for P and l is an I-partial level mapping such that P satisfies (F) with respect to I and l, then $I \subseteq M_P$.

(1) Let $A \in \mathrm{dom}(l_P)$, and suppose that $l_P(A) = \beta$. We consider the two cases corresponding to (Fi) and (Fii).

Case (Fi). If $A \in M_P$, then $A \in T_P'(\Phi_P \uparrow \beta)$. Hence, there exists a clause $A \leftarrow \mathtt{body}$ in $\mathrm{ground}(P)$ such that $\mathtt{body}$ is true in $\Phi_P \uparrow \beta$. Therefore, for all $L_i \in \mathtt{body}$, we have that $L_i \in \Phi_P \uparrow \beta$, and hence $l_P(L_i) < \beta$, and also that $L_i \in M_P$ for all i. Consequently, A satisfies (Fi) with respect to M_P and l_P.

Case (Fii). If $\neg A \in M_P$, then $A \in F_P(\Phi_P \uparrow \beta)$. Hence, for each clause $A \leftarrow \mathtt{body}$ in $\mathrm{ground}(P)$, there is a literal $L \in \mathtt{body}$ with $\neg L \in \Phi_P \uparrow \beta$. But then $l_P(L) < \beta$ and $\neg L \in M_P$. Consequently, A satisfies (Fii) with respect to M_P and l_P, and we have established that fact (1) holds.

(2) We show via transfinite induction on $\beta = l(A)$ that, whenever $A \in I$, or $\neg A \in I$, we have $A \in \Phi_P \uparrow (\beta + 1)$, or $\neg A \in \Phi_P \uparrow (\beta + 1)$), respectively. For the base case, note that if $l(A) = 0$, then $A \in I$ implies that A occurs as the head of a fact in $\mathrm{ground}(P)$, hence $A \in \Phi_P \uparrow 1$, and $\neg A \in I$ implies that there is no clause with head A in $\mathrm{ground}(P)$, hence $\neg A \in \Phi_P \uparrow 1$. So assume now that the induction hypothesis holds for all $B \in B_P$ with $l(B) < \beta$ and that $l(A) = \beta$. We consider two cases.

Case i. If $A \in I$, then it satisfies (Fi) with respect to I and l. Hence, there is a clause $A \leftarrow \mathtt{body}$ in $\mathrm{ground}(P)$ such that $\mathtt{body} \subseteq I$ and $l(K) < \beta$ for all $K \in \mathtt{body}$. Hence, $\mathtt{body} \subseteq M_P$ by the induction hypothesis, and since M_P is a model for P, we obtain $A \in M_P$.

Case ii. If $\neg A \in I$, then A satisfies (Fii) with respect to I and l. Hence, for each clause $A \leftarrow$ body in ground(P), there is $K \in$ body with $\neg K \in I$ and $l(K) < \beta$. But then, by the induction hypothesis, we have $\neg K \in M_P$, and consequently for each clause $A \leftarrow$ body in ground(P) we obtain that body is false in M_P. Since $M_P = \Phi_P(M_P)$ is a fixed point of the Φ_P-operator, we obtain $\neg A \in M_P$. This establishes Fact (2) and concludes the proof. ∎

The following corollary follows immediately as a special case of the previous result.

2.4.10 Corollary A normal logic program P has a total Fitting model if and only if there is a total model I for P and a (total) level mapping l for P such that P satisfies (F) with respect to I and l.

2.4.11 Example Example 2.4.1 shows that Tweety1 (Program 2.1.2) has total Fitting model $M \cup \neg(B_{\text{Tweety1}} \setminus M)$, where M is as in Example 2.2.7.
    Tweety2 (Program 2.3.9) has Fitting model

$$\{\texttt{penguin(tweety)}, \texttt{bird(bob)}, \texttt{bird(tweety)}, \neg\texttt{flies(tweety)}\}.$$

Thus, we cannot decide whether or not bob is a penguin. Hence, the Fitting semantics suffers from the same deficiency as the supported model semantics, see our discussion of Program 2.3.9.
    Tweety3 (Program 2.3.10) has $\emptyset$ as its Fitting model.

The Fitting operator is not ω-continuous in general, not even for definite programs, as shown by the next example.

2.4.12 Program Consider the program P consisting of the following clauses.

$$p(s(X)) \leftarrow p(X)$$
$$q \leftarrow p(X)$$

Then $\Phi_P \uparrow n = \{\neg p\left(s^k(0)\right) \mid k < n\}$ for all $n \in \mathbb{N}$ and $\Phi_P \uparrow \omega = \{\neg p(s^n(0)) \mid n \in \mathbb{N}\}$. However, $\Phi_P \uparrow (\omega + 1) = \{\neg q, \neg p(s^n(0)) \mid n \in \mathbb{N}\}$ is the least fixed point of the operator.

The Fitting operator can be thought of as an approximation to the immediate consequence operator, in the sense of the following proposition.

2.4.13 Proposition Let P be a program. Then for all $I \in I_{P,3}$, we have that $\Phi_P(I)^+ \subseteq T_P(I^+) \subseteq B_P \setminus \Phi_P(I)^-$. Furthermore, the Fitting operator maps total interpretations to total interpretations and coincides with the immediate consequence operator on these.

Proof: Let $I = I^+ \cup \neg I^-$ be a three-valued interpretation, and let $A \in \Phi_P(I)^+$. Then there is a clause $A \leftarrow \text{body}$ in $\text{ground}(P)$, where body equals $A_1, \ldots, A_n, \neg B_1, \ldots, \neg B_k$, say, and is true in the three-valued interpretation I. Therefore, for all i and j, we have $A_i \in I^+$ and $B_j \in I^-$ so that $A_i \in I^+$ and $B_j \notin I^+$. Therefore, body is true in the two-valued interpretation I^+, and so $A \in T_P(I^+)$. Conversely, if I is total, then $B_j \notin I^+$ means that $B_j \in I^-$, and hence whenever $A \in T_P(I^+)$ we have $A \in \Phi_P(I)^+$. This deals with the first inclusion.

For the second inclusion, $A \in \Phi_P(I)^-$ if and only if for all clauses $A \leftarrow \text{body}$ in $\text{ground}(P)$ we have body false in the three-valued interpretation I. But then one of the literals in body is false, and so, using the notation already established for body, either some $A_i \in I^-$ or some $B_j \in I^+$, that is, either some $A_i \notin I^+$ or some $B_j \in I^+$. Therefore, body is also false in the two-valued interpretation I^+ leading to $A \notin T_P(I^+)$. We thus obtain $\Phi_P(I)^- \subseteq B_P \setminus T_P(I^+)$ so that $T_P(I^+) \subseteq B_P \setminus \Phi_P(I)^-$. If I is total, then $B_P \setminus \Phi_P(I)^- = \Phi_P(I)^+ = T'_P(I) = T_P(I^+)$. ∎

From Proposition 2.4.13, we immediately obtain that total Fitting models are always supported. They are, in fact, also stable in general, as we will see later in Section 2.6. However, if a program has a unique stable model, it does not necessarily have a total Fitting model.

2.4.14 Program The program consisting of the three clauses

$$p \leftarrow \neg q$$
$$q \leftarrow \neg p$$
$$p \leftarrow \neg p$$

has unique (two-valued) supported model $\{p\}$, which is also stable. However, its (three-valued) Fitting model is everywhere equal to $\mathbf{u}$.

2.5 Perfect Models

The approach using three-valued models, which was presented in Section 2.4, has the advantage that a unique model, namely, the least fixed point of the Fitting operator, or the Fitting model, can be associated with each given program. This avoids the ambiguity present in semantics based on classical logic, such as the stable model semantics, where a program may have many associated models.

An alternative way of avoiding this problem is to restrict syntax of programs in such a way that only programs are allowed whose semantics is unambiguous. The restriction is usually put in place by conditions which prevent recursion in certain situations, and the most convenient way of expressing these conditions is again by the use of level mappings. For example, the alternative characterization of the Fitting model in Definition 2.4.8 and Theorem 2.4.9 can be viewed from this standpoint, and we will return to this point later on in this section and in Section 2.6.

The approach which we present in this section is based on the following idea: the introduction of negation, and in particular the possibility of allowing recursive dependencies between negated atoms, causes ambiguity from a declarative point of view. However, if recursion is only allowed through positive atoms, a standard model, namely, the least model, can be obtained. So it seems natural to disallow recursion through negative dependencies, while at the same time allowing recursion through positive ones. This idea is captured in the following definition.

2.5.1 Definition A program P is called *locally stratified*[11] if there exists a level mapping $l : B_P \rightarrow \alpha$ such that for each clause

$$A \leftarrow A_1, \ldots, A_n, \neg B_1, \ldots, \neg B_m$$

in ground(P) the following hold.

(S1) $l(A) \geq l(A_i)$ for $i = 1, \ldots, n$.

(S2) $l(A) > l(B_j)$ for $j = 1, \ldots, m$.

Furthermore, P is called *stratified* if it is locally stratified, and for all atoms $A, B \in B_P$ with the same predicate symbol, we have $l(A) = l(B)$.

Note that for stratified programs the image of the level mapping involved is finite, in contrast to locally stratified programs. Stratified programs are particularly interesting from the procedural point of view. Nevertheless, we will concentrate here on the more general locally stratified programs.

Along with the introduction of locally stratified programs, a semantics was developed called the *perfect model semantics*. We will discuss this semantics only in passing in this chapter. Indeed, we will focus here on the more general *weakly perfect semantics*, which is introduced later in this section and is also defined for locally stratified programs. However, we will consider the perfect model semantics in some detail in Section 6.3.

2.5.2 Definition Let P be a locally stratified program, and let l denote the associated level mapping. Given two distinct models M and N for P, we say that N is *preferable* to M if, for every ground atom A in $N \setminus M$, there is a ground atom B in $M \setminus N$ such that $l(A) > l(B)$. A model M for P is called *perfect* if there are no models for P preferable to M.

---

[11]The notion of local stratification and the perfect model semantics were introduced in the paper [Przymusinski, 1988]. Stratified programs and certain procedural apects of them were studied in [Apt et al., 1988].

2.5.3 Example Tweety2 (Program 2.3.9) is locally stratified, indeed stratified, since `flies` depends both on `penguin` and on `bird`, where "depends on" is defined below, `bird` depends only on `penguin`, and `penguin` does not depend on any predicate symbol other than itself. We will see in Example 6.3.12 that it has M from Example 2.2.7 as its perfect model.

Tweety3 (Program 2.3.10) is obviously not locally stratified.

We will see later in Section 6.3 that every locally stratified program has a unique perfect model and that this model is independent of the choice of the level mapping with respect to which the program is locally stratified. In fact, we are more interested here in a generalization of the perfect model semantics to three-valued logic, and of course the objective underlying this generalization is the usual one, namely, to provide a single *intended model* for each given program.

We will proceed next with presenting the rather involved definition of the weakly perfect model due to Przymusinska and Przymusinski.[12] For ease of notation, it will be convenient to consider (countably infinite) propositional programs instead of programs over a first-order language, and we recall that we have already observed in Section 2.1 that this results in no loss of generality for our purposes.

Let P be a (countably infinite propositional) normal logic program. We say that an atom $A \in B_P$ *refers to* an atom $B \in B_P$ if either B or $\neg B$ occurs as a body literal in a clause $A \leftarrow$ body in P with head A. We say that A *refers negatively to* B if $\neg B$ occurs as a body literal in such a clause. We say that A *depends on* B, written $B \leq A$, if the pair (A, B) is in the transitive closure of the relation *refers to*. We say that A *depends negatively on* B, written $B < A$, if there are $C, D \in B_P$ such that C refers negatively to D and the following conditions hold: (1) $C \leq A$ or $C = A$ (the latter meaning identity), and (2) $B \leq D$ or $B = D$. For $A, B \in B_P$, we write $A \sim B$ if either $A = B$ or A and B depend negatively on each other, so that $A < B$ and $B < A$ both hold in this latter case.[13] The relation $\sim$ is an equivalence relation, and its equivalence classes are called *components* of P. A component is *trivial* if it consists of a single element A with $A \not< A$.

Notice that the definitions above can be viewed in a rather intuitive way by means of the *dependency graph* G_P of a program P, defined as follows. The vertices of G_P are the ground atoms appearing in P; for each clause $A \leftarrow$ body in ground(P) there is a positive directed edge in G_P from B to A if B occurs in body, and there is a negative directed edge from B to A in G_P if $\neg B$ occurs in body. Then, in these terms, we have $B \leq A$ if and only if there is a directed path in G_P from B to A, and we have $B < A$ if and only if there is a directed path in G_P from B to A passing through a negative edge.

---

[12] The notions of weak stratification and the weakly perfect model were introduced in the paper [Przymusinska and Przymusinski, 1990].

[13] It is noted in [Przymusinska and Przymusinski, 1990] that such mutual recursion is the primary cause of difficulties in defining declarative semantics for logic programs.

Let C_1 and C_2 be two components of a program P. We write $C_1 \prec C_2$ if and only if $C_1 \neq C_2$ and for each $A_1 \in C_1$ there is $A_2 \in C_2$ with $A_1 < A_2$. A component C_1 is called *minimal* if there is no component C_2 with $C_2 \prec C_1$.

Given a normal logic program P, the *bottom stratum* $S(P)$ of P is the union of all minimal components of P. The *bottom layer* of P is the subprogram $L(P)$ of P which consists of all clauses from P with heads belonging to $S(P)$.

Given a three-valued interpretation I for P, thought of as a signed subset, we define the *reduct of P with respect to I* to be the program P/I obtained from P by performing the following reductions. (1) Remove from P all clauses which contain a body literal L such that $\neg L \in I$ or whose head belongs to I. (2) Remove from all remaining clauses all body literals L with $L \in I$. (3) Remove from the resulting program all non-unit clauses whose heads appear also as heads of unit clauses in the program.

Note that the definition of P/I used here differs from that given in Definition 2.3.6 in the context of stable models. The new definition just given will only be used in the present section.

2.5.4 Definition The *weakly perfect model* M_P for a program P is defined by transfinite induction as follows. Let $P_0 = P$, and let $M_0 = \emptyset$. For each (countable) ordinal $\alpha > 0$ such that programs P_δ and three-valued interpretations M_δ have already been defined for all $\delta < \alpha$, let

$$N_\alpha = \bigcup_{\delta < \alpha} M_\delta,$$
$$P_\alpha = P/N_\alpha,$$

R_α is the set of all atoms which are undefined in N_α and were eliminated from P by reducing it with respect to N_α,

$$S_\alpha = S(P_\alpha), \text{ and}$$
$$L_\alpha = L(P_\alpha).$$

The construction then proceeds with one of the following three cases. (1) If P_α is empty, then the construction stops, and $M_P = N_\alpha \cup \neg R_\alpha$ is the (*total*) *weakly perfect model* for P. (2) If the bottom stratum S_α is empty or if the bottom layer L_α contains a negative literal, then the construction also stops, and $M_P = N_\alpha \cup \neg R_\alpha$ is the (*partial*) *weakly perfect model* for P. (3) In the remaining case, L_α is a definite program, and we define $M_\alpha = H \cup \neg R_\alpha$, where H is the total three-valued model corresponding to the least two-valued model for L_α, and the construction continues.

For every α, the set $S_\alpha \cup R_\alpha$ is called the *α-th stratum* of P, and the program L_α is called the *α-th layer* of P.

We now present a detailed example of the calculation of the weakly perfect model; see also Program 2.6.12 for further discussion of this example.

2.5.5 Example Consider the program Tweety4, as follows; it is a modification of Tweety2 (Program 2.3.9), where the last clause has been changed.

$$\text{penguin(tweety)} \leftarrow$$
$$\text{bird(bob)} \leftarrow$$
$$\text{bird}(X) \leftarrow \text{penguin}(X)$$
$$\text{flies}(X) \leftarrow \text{bird}(X), \neg\text{penguin}(X)$$
$$\text{penguin(bob)} \leftarrow \text{penguin(bob)}, \neg\text{flies(bob)}$$

This program has the weakly perfect model

$$\{\text{bird(bob)}, \text{bird(tweety)}, \text{penguin(tweety)}, \neg\text{flies(tweety)}\},$$

and we show here how this model is calculated. We begin by setting $P = P_0 = \text{ground}(\text{Tweety4})$, as follows.

$$\text{penguin(tweety)} \leftarrow$$
$$\text{bird(bob)} \leftarrow$$
$$\text{bird(tweety)} \leftarrow \text{penguin(tweety)}$$
$$\text{bird(bob)} \leftarrow \text{penguin(bob)}$$
$$\text{flies(tweety)} \leftarrow \text{bird(tweety)}, \neg\text{penguin(tweety)}$$
$$\text{flies(bob)} \leftarrow \text{bird(bob)}, \neg\text{penguin(bob)}$$
$$\text{penguin(bob)} \leftarrow \text{penguin(bob)}, \neg\text{flies(bob)}$$

Next, we set $M_0 = \emptyset$ and carry out reduction of P_0 with respect to M_0 to obtain $P_1 = P_0/M_0$, which turns out to be equal to P_0 with the fourth clause removed. The dependency graph G_{P_1} of P_1 is shown in Figure 2.1, where we use the obvious abbreviations for the ground atoms in P_1 such as p(t) for penguin(tweety) and so on. Using G_{P_1}, it is simple to check that the components of P_1 are {bird(bob)}, {bird(tweety)}, {penguin(tweety)}, {flies(tweety)}, and {flies(bob), penguin(bob)} and that the minimal components are the first three of these. Therefore, the bottom stratum $S_1 = S(P_1)$ of P_1 is {penguin(tweety), bird(bob), bird(tweety)}. Hence, the bottom layer $L_1 = L(P_1)$ of P_1 is the definite program

$$\text{penguin(tweety)} \leftarrow$$
$$\text{bird(bob)} \leftarrow$$
$$\text{bird(tweety)} \leftarrow \text{penguin(tweety)}$$

whose least two-valued model is clearly equal to S_1. Note that $N_1 = \bigcup_{\delta < 1} M_\delta = M_0 = \emptyset$. Reduction of P_0 with respect to M_0 removed one clause, but did not eliminate any atoms from P; hence, $R_1 = \emptyset$. Since L_1 is definite, we put $M_1 = H \cup \neg R_1$, where H is the total three-valued model corresponding to S_1; thus, $M_1 = S_1$, and the process continues.

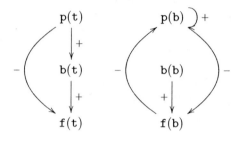

FIGURE 2.1: Dependency graph for P_1.

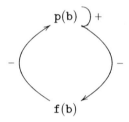

FIGURE 2.2: Dependency graph for P_2.

The program $P_2 = P_1/M_1$ is

$$\text{flies(bob)} \leftarrow \neg\text{penguin(bob)}$$
$$\text{penguin(bob)} \leftarrow \text{penguin(bob)}, \neg\text{flies(bob)}$$

The dependency graph G_{P_2} of P_2, shown in Figure 2.2, has only one component $\{\text{penguin(bob)}, \text{flies(bob)}\}$, which is therefore equal to the bottom stratum $S_2 = S(P_2)$ of P_2. Furthermore, $N_2 = M_0 \cup M_1 = M_1$ and $R_2 = \{\text{flies(tweety)}\}$. Since the bottom layer $L_2 = L(P_2)$ is equal to P_2, it is not definite. Therefore, the construction stops, and the weakly perfect model is $N_2 \cup \neg R_2 = M_1 \cup \neg R_2$, as claimed.

2.5.6 Proposition Let P be a program, and let M be its (partial) weakly perfect model. Then M is a model with respect to Kleene's strong three-valued logic.

Proof: It is straightforward to show that $\Phi_P(M) = M$, and we leave the details to the reader. ∎

A *weakly stratified program* is a program with a total weakly perfect model. The set of all its strata is then called its *weak stratification*.

2.5.7 Remark We remark that our definition of weakly perfect model, as given in Definition 2.5.4, differs slightly from the version introduced in [Przymusinska and Przymusinski, 1990]. In order to obtain the original definition, points (2) and (3) of Definition 2.5.4 have to be replaced with the following: $(2)'$ If the bottom stratum S_α is empty or if the bottom layer L_α *has no least two-valued model*, then the construction stops, and $M_P = N_\alpha \cup \neg R_\alpha$ is the (partial) weakly perfect model for P. $(3)'$ In the remaining case, L_α *has a least two-valued model*, and we define $M_\alpha = H \cup \neg R_\alpha$, where H is the three-valued model for L_α corresponding to its least two-valued model, and the construction continues. The original definition is more general due to the fact that every definite program has a least two-valued model. However, while the least two-valued model for a definite program can be obtained as the least fixed point of the monotonic (and even continuous) operator T_P, we know of no similar result, nor of a general operator, for obtaining the least two-valued model, if it exists, for programs which are not definite. The original definition therefore seems to be rather awkward, and indeed, even in [Przymusinska and Przymusinski, 1990], when defining weakly stratified programs, the more general version was dropped in favour of requiring definite layers. So Definition 2.5.4 is an adaptation taking the original notion of weakly stratified program into account and appears to be more natural. Our use, therefore, of the term *weakly perfect model* will refer to Definition 2.5.4 unless stated to the contrary.

Again, an alternative characterization of the weakly perfect model can be provided using level mappings.

2.5.8 Definition Let P be a normal logic program, let I be a three-valued model for P, and let l be an I-partial level mapping for P. We say that P *satisfies* (WS) *with respect to I and l* if each $A \in \mathrm{dom}(l)$ satisfies one of the following conditions.

(WSi) $A \in I$, and there is a clause $A \leftarrow L_1, \ldots, L_n$ in $\mathrm{ground}(P)$ such that $L_i \in I$ and $l(A) > l(L_i)$ for all i.

(WSii) $\neg A \in I$, and for each clause $A \leftarrow A_1, \ldots, A_n, \neg B_1, \ldots, \neg B_m$ in $\mathrm{ground}(P)$ one (at least) of the following conditions holds.

(WSiia) There exists i with $\neg A_i \in I$ and $l(A) > l(A_i)$.

(WSiib) For all k we have $l(A) \geq l(A_k)$, for all j we have $l(A) > l(B_j)$, and there exists i with $\neg A_i \in I$.

(WSiic) There exists j with $B_j \in I$ and $l(A) > l(B_j)$.

Noting that the condition (Fii) in Definition 2.4.8 implies that either (WSiia) or (WSiic) holds, we see that the condition (WSii) above is more general than (Fii); conditions (WSi) and (Fi) are identical.

2.5.9 Theorem Let P be a normal logic program with weakly perfect model

M_P. Then, in the knowledge ordering $\sqsubseteq_k$, M_P is the greatest model among all models I for which there exists an I-partial level mapping l for P such that P satisfies (WS) with respect to I and l.

We prepare for the proof of Theorem 2.5.9 by introducing some notation which will help make the presentation transparent.

It will be convenient to consider level mappings which map into *pairs* (β, n) of ordinals, where $n \le \omega$. So let α be a (countable) ordinal, and consider the set $\mathcal{A}$ of all pairs (β, n), where $\beta < \alpha$ and $n \le \omega$. Of course, $\mathcal{A}$ endowed with the lexicographic ordering is isomorphic to an ordinal. So any mapping from B_P to $\mathcal{A}$ can be considered to be a level mapping.

Let P be a program with (partial) weakly perfect model M_P. We define the M_P-partial level mapping l_P as follows: $l_P(A) = (\beta, n)$, where $A \in S_\beta \cup R_\beta$ and n is least with $A \in T_{L_\beta} \uparrow (n+1)$, if such an n exists, and $n = \omega$ otherwise. We observe that if $l_P(A) = l_P(B)$, then there exists α with $A, B \in S_\alpha \cup R_\alpha$, and if $A \in S_\alpha \cup R_\alpha$ and $B \in S_\beta \cup R_\beta$ with $\alpha < \beta$, then $l(A) < l(B)$.

The following notion will help to ease later notation.

2.5.10 Definition Let P and Q be two programs, and let I be an interpretation.

(1) Suppose that $C_1 = (A \leftarrow L_1, \ldots, L_n)$ and $C_2 = (B \leftarrow K_1, \ldots, K_m)$ are two clauses. Then we say that C_1 *subsumes* C_2, written $C_1 \preccurlyeq C_2$, if $A = B$ and $\{L_1, \ldots, L_n\} \subseteq \{K_1, \ldots, K_m\}$.

(2) We say that P *subsumes* Q, written $P \preccurlyeq Q$, if for each clause C_1 in P there exists a clause C_2 in Q with $C_1 \preccurlyeq C_2$.

(3) We say that P *subsumes* Q *model-consistently (with respect to I)*, written $P \preccurlyeq_I Q$, if the following conditions hold.

   (i) For each clause $C_1 = (A \leftarrow L_1, \ldots, L_n)$ in P, there exists a clause $C_2 = (B \leftarrow K_1, \ldots, K_m)$ in Q with $C_1 \preccurlyeq C_2$ and $\{K_1, \ldots, K_m\} \setminus \{L_1, \ldots, L_n\} \subseteq I$.

   (ii) For each clause $C_2 = (B \leftarrow K_1, \ldots, K_m)$ in Q which satisfies $\{K_1, \ldots, K_m\} \subseteq I$ and $B \notin I$, there exists a clause C_1 in P such that $C_1 \preccurlyeq C_2$.

Definition 2.5.10 will facilitate the proof of Theorem 2.5.9 by employing the following lemma.

2.5.11 Lemma With the notation established in Definition 2.5.4, we have $P/N_\alpha \preccurlyeq_{N_\alpha} P$ for all α.

Proof: Condition 3(i) of Definition 2.5.10 holds because every clause $C_1 = (A \leftarrow L_1, \ldots, L_n)$ in P/N_α is obtained from a clause $C_2 = (A \leftarrow K_1, \ldots, K_m)$ in P by deleting body literals which are contained in N_α. Clearly, $C_1 \preccurlyeq C_2$, and the set difference $\{K_1, \ldots, K_m\} \setminus \{L_1, \ldots, L_n\}$ contains only elements of N_α. Condition 3(ii) holds because for each clause $C_2 = (A \leftarrow K_1, \ldots, K_m)$ in P with head $A \notin N_\alpha$ whose body is true under N_α, Step 2 in the reduction of P with respect to N_α removes all the body literals K_i. Therefore, we have that $C_1 = (A \leftarrow)$ is a fact in P/N_α, and clearly, $C_1 \preccurlyeq C_2$. ∎

The next lemma establishes the induction step in Part (2) of the proof of Theorem 2.5.9.

2.5.12 Lemma If I is a non-empty three-valued model for a (infinite propositional normal) logic program P' and l is an I-partial level mapping such that P' satisfies (WS) with respect to I and l, then the following hold for $P = P'/\emptyset$.

(a) The bottom stratum $S(P)$ of P is non-empty and consists of trivial components only.

(b) The bottom layer $L(P)$ of P is definite.

(c) The three-valued model N corresponding to the least two-valued model for $L(P)$ is consistent with I in the following sense: we have $I' \subseteq N$, where I' is the restriction of I to all atoms which are not undefined in N.

(d) P/N satisfies (WS) with respect to $I \setminus N$ and $l|_N$, where $l|_N$ is the restriction of l to the atoms in $I \setminus N$.

Proof: (a) Assume that there exists some component $C \subseteq S(P)$ which is not trivial. Then there must exist atoms $A, B \in C$ with $A < B$, $B < A$, and $A \neq B$. Without loss of generality, we can assume that A is chosen such that $l(A)$ is minimal. Now let A' be any atom occurring in the body of a clause with head A. If A' occurs positively, then $A > B > A \geq A'$, and so $A > A'$; if A' occurs negatively, then $A > A'$ also. Therefore, by minimality of the component, we must also have $A' > A$. Thus, we obtain that all atoms occurring positively or negatively in the bodies of clauses with head A must be contained in C. We consider two cases.

Case i. If $A \in I$, then there must be a fact $A \leftarrow$ in P; otherwise, by (WSi) we have a clause $A \leftarrow L_1, \ldots, L_n$ (for some $n \geq 1$) with $L_1, \ldots, L_n \in I$ and $l(A) > l(L_i)$ for all i, contradicting the minimality of $l(A)$. Since $P = P'/\emptyset$, we obtain that $A \leftarrow$ is the only clause in P with head A, contradicting the existence of $B \neq A$ with $B < A$.

Case ii. If $\neg A \in I$, then since A was chosen to be minimal with respect to l, we obtain that condition (WSiib) must hold for each clause $A \leftarrow A_1, \ldots, A_n, \neg B_1, \ldots, \neg B_m$ with respect to I and l and that $m = 0$. Furthermore, all A_i must be contained in C, as already noted above, and $l(A) \geq l(A_i)$ for all i by (WSiib). Also, from Case i, we obtain that no A_i can be contained in I. We have now established that, for all A_i in the body of any clause with head A, we have $l(A) = l(A_i)$ and $\neg A_i \in I$. The same argument holds for all clauses with head A_i, for all i, and the argument repeats itself. Now, from $A > B$, we obtain $D, E \in C$ with $A \geq E$ (or $A = E$), $D \geq B$ (or $D = B$), and E refers negatively to D. As we have just seen, we obtain $\neg E \in I$ and $l(E) = l(A)$. Since E refers negatively to D, there is a clause containing E in its head and $\neg D$ in its body. Since (WSii) holds for this clause, there must be a literal L in its body with level less than $l(E)$, so that $l(L) < l(A)$ and $L \in C$, which is a contradiction. We thus have established that all components are trivial.

We show next that the bottom stratum is non-empty. Indeed, let A be an atom such that $l(A)$ is minimal. We will show that $\{A\}$ is a component. Assume that this is not the case, that is, assume that there is B with $B < A$. Then there exist $D_1, \ldots, D_k$, for some $k \in \mathbb{N}$, such that $D_1 = A$, D_j refers to D_{j+1} for all $j = 1, \ldots, k-1$, and D_k refers negatively to some B' with $B' \geq B$ (or $B' = B$).

We show by induction that, for all $j = 1, \ldots, k$, the following statements hold: $\neg D_j \in I$, $B < D_j$, and $l(D_j) = l(A)$. Indeed, note that for $j = 1$, that is, when $D_j = A$, we have that $B < D_j = A$ and $l(D_j) = l(A)$. Assuming $A \in I$, we obtain, by minimality of $l(A)$, that $A \leftarrow$ is the only clause in $P = P'/\emptyset$ with head A, contradicting the existence of $B < A$. So, $\neg A \in I$, and the assertion holds for $j = 1$. Now assume that the assertion holds for some $j < k$. Then obviously $D_{j+1} > B$ since $A \geq D_2 \geq \ldots \geq D_{k-1} \geq D_k > B' \geq B$. Since $\neg D_j \in I$ and $l(D_j) = l(A)$, we obtain that (WSii) must hold, and, by the minimality of $l(A)$, we infer that (WSiib) must hold and that no clause with head D_j contains negated atoms. So, $l(D_{j+1}) = l(D_j) = l(A)$ holds by (WSiib) and the minimality of $l(A)$. Furthermore, the assumption $D_{j+1} \in I$ can be rejected by the same argument as for A above; otherwise, $D_{j+1} \leftarrow$ would be the only clause with head D_{j+1} by minimality of $l(D_{j+1}) = l(A)$, contradicting $B < D_{j+1}$. This concludes the inductive proof.

Summarizing, we obtain that D_k refers negatively to B' and that $\neg D_k \in I$. But then there is a clause satisfying (WSii) with head D_k and $\neg B'$ in its body, and this contradicts the minimality of $l(D_k) = l(A)$. This concludes the proof of statement (a).

(b) Assume that $L(P)$ is not definite. Then there exists a clause $A \leftarrow \mathsf{body}$ in $L(P)$ with a negated literal $\neg B$ occurring in body. But then $B < A$, and since the bottom stratum consists of minimal components only, we also have $A < B$, that is, A and B are in the same component, contradicting (a).

(c) First, note that in forming the reduct P of P' with respect to $\emptyset$, the third step is the only one in the process which has any effect in that it removes all non-unit clauses whose heads appear also as heads of unit clauses. Now let $A \in I'$ be an atom with $A \notin N$, and assume without loss of generality that A is chosen such that $l(A)$ is minimal with these properties. By the first observation and the hypothesis that P' satisfies (WS) with respect to I and l, there must be a clause $A \leftarrow L_1, \ldots, L_n$ in P such that, for all i, L_i is true with respect to I, and hence true with respect to I', and $l(A) > l(L_i)$. Hence, all the literals L_i are true with respect to N by minimality of $l(A)$. Thus,

$L_1, \ldots, L_n$ is true in N, and, since N is a model for $L(P)$, we obtain $A \in N$, which contradicts our assumption.

Now let $A \in N$ be an atom with $A \notin I'$, and assume without loss of generality that A is chosen such that n is minimal with $A \in T_{L(P)} \uparrow (n + 1)$. Then there is a definite clause $A \leftarrow$ body in $L(P)$ such that all atoms in body are true with respect to $T_{L(P)} \uparrow n$. Hence, these atoms are also true with respect to I', and, since I' is a model for $L(P)$, we obtain $A \in I'$, which contradicts our assumption.

Finally, let $\neg A \in I'$. Then we cannot have $A \in N$; otherwise, $A \in I'$. So, $\neg A \in N$ since N is a total model for $L(P)$.

(d) From Lemma 2.5.11, we know that $P/N \preccurlyeq_N P$. We distinguish two cases.

Case i. If $A \in I \setminus N$, then there must be a clause $A \leftarrow L_1, \ldots, L_k$ in P such that $L_i \in I$ and $l(A) > l(L_i)$ for all i. Since it is not possible for A to belong to N, there must also be a clause in P/N which subsumes $A \leftarrow L_1, \ldots, L_k$ and which therefore satisfies (WSi). So, A satisfies (WSi).

Case ii. If $\neg A \in I \setminus N$, then, for each clause $A \leftarrow$ body1 in P/N, there must be a clause $A \leftarrow$ body in P which is subsumed by $A \leftarrow$ body1, and, since $\neg A \in I$, we obtain that condition (WSii) must be satisfied by A and also by the clause $A \leftarrow$ body. Since reduction with respect to N removes only body literals which are true in N, condition (WSii) is still fulfilled. ∎

We can now proceed with the proof of Theorem 2.5.9.

Proof of Theorem 2.5.9: The proof will proceed by establishing the following facts: (1) P satisfies (WS) with respect to M_P and l_P. (2) If I is a model for P and l is an I-partial level mapping such that P satisfies (WS) with respect to I and l, then $I \subseteq M_P$.

(1) Let $A \in \mathrm{dom}(l_P)$, and suppose that $l_P(A) = (\alpha, n)$. We consider two cases.

Case i. $A \in M_P$. Then $A \in T_{L_\alpha} \uparrow (n + 1)$. Hence, there is a definite clause $A \leftarrow A_1, \ldots, A_k$ in L_α with $A_1, \ldots, A_k \in T_{L_\alpha} \uparrow n$. Thus, $A_1, \ldots, A_k \in M_P$ and $l_P(A) > l_P(A_i)$ for all i. By Lemma 2.5.11, $P/N_\alpha \preccurlyeq_{N_\alpha} P$. So there must be a clause $A \leftarrow A_1, \ldots, A_k, L_1, \ldots, L_m$ in P with literals $L_1, \ldots, L_m \in N_\alpha \subseteq M_P$, and we obtain $l_P(L_j) < l_P(A)$ for all $j = 1, \ldots, m$. So, (WSi) holds in this case.

Case ii. $\neg A \in M_P$. Let $A \leftarrow A_1, \ldots, A_k, \neg B_1, \ldots, \neg B_m$ be a clause in P, noting that (WSii) is trivially satisfied in case no such clause exists. We consider the following two subcases.

Subcase ii.a. Assume A is undefined in N_α and was eliminated from P by reducing it with respect to N_α, that is, $A \in R_\alpha$. Then, in particular, there must be some $\neg A_i \in N_\alpha$, or some $B_j \in N_\alpha$, which yields $l_P(A_i) < l_P(A)$, or $l_P(B_j) < l_P(A)$, respectively, and hence one of (WSiia), (WSiic) holds.

Subcase ii.b. Assume $\neg A \in H$, where H is the three-valued model corresponding to the least two-valued model for L_α. Since P/N_α subsumes P

model consistently with respect to N_α, we obtain that there must be some A_i with $\neg A_i \in H$, and, by definition of l_P, we obtain $l_P(A) = l_P(A_i) = (\alpha, \omega)$ and, hence, also $l_P(A_{i'}) \leq l_P(A_i)$ for all $i' \neq i$. Furthermore, since P/N_α is definite, we obtain that $\neg B_j \in N_\alpha$ for all j, and hence $l_P(B_j) < l_P(A)$ for all j. So, condition (WSiib) is satisfied.

(2) Suppose that I is a non-empty three-valued model for P and that l is an I-partial level mapping such that P satisfies (WS) with respect to I and l. First, note that for all models M, N of P with $M \subseteq N$, we have $(P/M)/N = P/(M \cup N) = P/N$ and $(P/N)/\emptyset = P/N$.

Let I_α denote I restricted to the atoms which are not undefined in $N_\alpha \cup R_\alpha$. It suffices to show the following: for all $\alpha > 0$, we have $I_\alpha \subseteq N_\alpha \cup R_\alpha$, and $I \setminus M_P = \emptyset$.

We show next by induction that if $\alpha > 0$ is an ordinal, then the following statements hold. (a) The bottom stratum of P/N_α is non-empty and consists of trivial components only. (b) The bottom layer of P/N_α is definite. (c) $I_\alpha \subseteq N_\alpha \cup R_\alpha$. (d) $P/N_{\alpha+1}$ satisfies (WS) with respect to $I \setminus N_{\alpha+1}$ and $l|_{N_{\alpha+1}}$.

Note that P satisfies the hypothesis of Lemma 2.5.12 and, hence, also its conclusions. So, on taking $\alpha = 1$, we have that $P/N_1 = P/\emptyset$ satisfies (WS) with respect to $I \setminus N_1$ and $l|_{N_1}$, and by application of Lemma 2.5.12, we obtain that statements (a) and (b) hold. For (c), note that no atom in R_1 can be true in I, because no atom in R_1 can appear as head of a clause in P, and now apply Lemma 2.5.12 (c). For (d), apply Lemma 2.5.12, noting that $P/N_2 \preceq_{N_2} P$.

For α a limit ordinal, we can show, exactly as in the proof of Lemma 2.5.12 (d), that P satisfies (WS) with respect to $I \setminus N_\alpha$ and $l|_{N_\alpha}$. So, Lemma 2.5.12 is applicable, and statements (a) and (b) follow. For (c), let $A \in R_\alpha$. Then every clause in P with head A contains a body literal which is false in N_α. By the induction hypothesis, this implies that no clause with head A in P can have a body which is true in I. So, $A \notin I$. Together with Lemma 2.5.12 (c), this proves statement (c). For (d), apply again Lemma 2.5.12 (d), noting that $P/N_{\alpha+1} \preceq_{N_{\alpha+1}} P$.

For $\alpha = \beta + 1$ a successor ordinal, we obtain by the induction hypothesis that P/N_β satisfies the hypothesis of Lemma 2.5.12. So, again statements (a) and (b) follow immediately from this lemma, and (c) and (d) follow as in the case when α is a limit ordinal.

It remains to show that $I \setminus M_P = \emptyset$. Indeed, by the transfinite induction argument just given, we obtain that P/M_P satisfies (WS) with respect to $I \setminus M_P$ and $l|_{M_P}$. If $I \setminus M_P$ is non-empty, then by Lemma 2.5.12 the bottom stratum $S(P/M_P)$ is non-empty, and the bottom layer $L(P/M_P)$ is definite and has model M corresponding to the least two-valued model for $L(P/M_P)$. Hence, by definition of the weakly perfect model M_P for P, we must have that $M \subseteq M_P$, which contradicts the fact that M is the least model for $L(P/M_P)$. Hence, $I \setminus M_P$ must be empty, and this concludes the proof. ∎

The following corollary follows immediately as a special case.

2.5.13 Corollary A normal logic program P is weakly stratified, that is, has a total weakly perfect model if and only if there is a total model I for P and a (total) level mapping l for P such that P satisfies (WS) with respect to I and l.

The weakly perfect model is in general different from the Fitting model.

2.5.14 Proposition Let P be a program, let M_1 be its Fitting model, and let M_2 be its (partial) weakly perfect model. Then $M_1 \subseteq M_2$.

Proof: Let l_1 be an M_1-partial level mapping such that P satisfies (F) with respect to M_1 and l_1. Then, trivially, P satisfies (WS) with respect to M_1 and l_1. Since M_2 is the largest model among all models I for which there exists an I-partial level mapping l for P such that P satisfies (WS) with respect to I and l, by Theorem 2.5.9, we have that $M_1 \subseteq M_2$. ∎

The Fitting model does not in general coincide with the (partial) weakly perfect model, nor does it coincide in general with the perfect model for locally stratified programs.

2.5.15 Program Let P be the program consisting of the single clause $p \leftarrow p$. Then the Fitting model for P is $\emptyset$, but the (partial) weakly perfect model for P is $\{\neg p\}$. Note that P is locally stratified with perfect (two-valued) model in which p is false.

We will see later in Section 6.3 that if P is a locally stratified program, then P is weakly stratified, and its (total) weakly perfect model is also its perfect model. So, the weakly perfect model semantics unifies two separate approaches. On the one hand, it is a generalization of the Fitting semantics and allows one to assign a single intended model to each program; on the other hand, it generalizes the perfect model semantics for locally stratified programs.

2.5.16 Theorem Definite programs are locally stratified and have a total weakly perfect model.

Proof: The first statement is trivial. For the second statement, let P be a definite program with least model I. Assign levels $l(A)$ to all $A \in I$ according to Proposition 2.3.2, and set $l(B) = 0$ for all $B \notin I$. Considering the characterization of the weakly perfect model from Theorem 2.5.9, we observe that all $A \in I$ satisfy (WSi), while all other atoms satisfy (WSiib), and this suffices to establish the result. ∎

2.6 Well-Founded Models

If we compare Definitions 2.4.8 and 2.5.8 and keep in mind that the main idea underlying stratification is to restrict recursion through negation, one may be led to ask whether Definition 2.5.8 is the most natural way to achieve this in a three-valued setting. Indeed, one may be led to propose the following definition.

2.6.1 Definition Let P be a normal logic program, let I be a model for P, and let l be an I-partial level mapping for P. We say that P *satisfies* (WF) *with respect to I and l* if each $A \in \mathrm{dom}(l)$ satisfies one of the following conditions.

(WFi) $A \in I$, and there is a clause $A \leftarrow L_1, \ldots, L_n$ in ground(P) such that $L_i \in I$ and $l(A) > l(L_i)$ for all i.

(WFii) $\neg A \in I$, and for each clause $A \leftarrow A_1, \ldots, A_n, \neg B_1, \ldots, \neg B_m$ in ground(P) one (at least) of the following conditions holds.

 (WFiia) There exists i with $\neg A_i \in I$ and $l(A) \geq l(A_i)$.

 (WFiib) There exists j with $B_j \in I$ and $l(A) > l(B_j)$.

If $A \in \mathrm{dom}(l)$ satisfies (WFi), then we say that A *satisfies* (WFi) *with respect to I and l*, and similarly if $A \in \mathrm{dom}(l)$ satisfies (WFii).

We note that conditions (Fi), (WSi), and (WFi) are identical, and, furthermore, if P satisfies (WS) with respect to I and l, then it satisfies (WF) with respect to I and l. However, replacing (WFi) by a "stratified version" such as the following is not satisfactory.

(SFi) $A \in I$, and there is a clause $A \leftarrow A_1, \ldots, A_n, \neg B_1, \ldots, \neg B_m$ in ground(P) such that $A_i, \neg B_j \in I$, $l(A) \geq l(A_i)$, and $l(A) > l(B_j)$ for all i and j.

Indeed, if we do replace condition (WFi) by condition (SFi), then it is not guaranteed that, for a given program, there is a greatest model satisfying the desired properties. Consider the program consisting of the two clauses $p \leftarrow p$ and $q \leftarrow \neg p$, the two (total) models $\{p, \neg q\}$ and $\{\neg p, q\}$, and the level mapping l with $l(p) = 0$ and $l(q) = 1$. These models are incomparable, yet in both cases the conditions obtained by replacing (WFi) by (SFi) in (WF) are satisfied.

So, in the light of Theorem 2.4.9, Definition 2.6.1 should provide a natural stratified version of the Fitting semantics, and indeed it does, see Program 2.6.12 for an instructive example. Furthermore, the resulting semantics coincides with another well-known semantics, called the *well-founded semantics*, which is a very satisfactory result. To establish this claim, we need to introduce well-founded models, and this we do next.

Given a normal logic program P and $I \in I_{P,4}$, we say that $U \subseteq B_P$ is an *unfounded set* (*of* P) *with respect to* I if each atom $A \in U$ satisfies the following condition. For each clause $A \leftarrow$ body in ground(P) at least one of the following holds.

(US1) Some (positive or negative) literal in body is false in I.

(US2) Some (non-negated) atom in body occurs in U.

2.6.2 Proposition Let P be a program, and let $I \in I_{P,4}$. Then there exists a greatest unfounded set of P with respect to I.

Proof: If $(U_i)_{i \in \mathcal{I}}$ is a family of sets, each of which is an unfounded set of P with respect to I, then it is easy to see that $\bigcup_{i \in \mathcal{I}} U_i$ is also an unfounded set of P with respect to I. ∎

Let P be a program, and recall the definition of the operator T'_P from Section 2.4. It is straightforward to lift T'_P to an operator on $I_{P,4}$, namely, by defining $T'_P(I)$, for $I \in I_{P,4}$, to be the set of all $A \in B_P$ for which there is a clause $A \leftarrow$ body in ground(P) with body true in I with respect to Kleene's strong three-valued logic. For all $I \in I_{P,4}$, define $U_P(I)$ to be the greatest unfounded set (of P) with respect to I. Finally, define[14]

$$W_P(I) = T'_P(I) \cup \neg U_P(I)$$

for all $I \in I_{P,4}$. We call W_P the W_P-*operator*.

We note that W_P does not restrict to a function on $I_{P,3}$, which necessitates using $I_{P,4}$ instead.

2.6.3 Example Consider Program 2.3.1 and $I = \{p\} \in I_{P,3}$. Then $T'_P(I) = \{p\}$ and $U_P(I) = \{p\}$, so $W_P(I) = \{p, \neg p\} \notin I_{P,3}$.

2.6.4 Proposition Let P be a program. Then W_P is monotonic on $I_{P,4}$.

Proof: Let $I, K \in I_{P,4}$ with $I \subseteq K$. Then we obtain $T'_P(I) \subseteq T'_P(K)$ as in the proof of Proposition 2.4.4. So it suffices to show that every unfounded set of P with respect to I is also an unfounded set of P with respect to K, and this fact follows immediately from the definition. ∎

Since W_P is monotonic, it has a least fixed point by the Knaster-Tarski theorem, Theorem 1.1.10. The least fixed point of W_P is called the *well-founded model* for P, giving the *well-founded semantics* of P. We will show shortly that the well-founded model is always in $I_{P,3}$, but let us remark first that the operator W_P is not order continuous in general nor even ω-continuous, as the following example shows.

---

[14]The operator W_P and the well-founded semantics are due to Van Gelder, Ross, and Schlipf, see [Van Gelder et al., 1991]. However, in the original definition, the operator W_P was not introduced using $\mathcal{FOUR}$.

2.6.5 Program Let P be the following program.

$$p(0) \leftarrow$$
$$p(s(X)) \leftarrow p(X)$$
$$q(s(X)) \leftarrow \neg p(X)$$
$$r \leftarrow \neg q(s(X))$$

Then $W_P \uparrow n = \{p(s^k(0)) \mid k < n\} \cup \{\neg q(s^k(0)) \mid 0 < k < n\}$, and

$$\begin{aligned}
W_P \uparrow \omega &= \{p(s^n(0)) \mid n \in \mathbb{N}\} \cup \{\neg q(s^n(0)) \mid n \in \mathbb{N}, n > 0\} \\
&\neq \{p(s^n(0)) \mid n \in \mathbb{N}\} \cup \{\neg q(s^n(0)) \mid n \in \mathbb{N}, n > 0\} \cup \{\neg r\} \\
&= W_P \uparrow (\omega + 1).
\end{aligned}$$

2.6.6 Theorem Let P be a program. Then $W_P \uparrow \alpha \in I_{P,3}$ for all ordinals α. In particular, the well-founded model for P is in $I_{P,3}$.

Proof: We first need some notation. Let M denote the least fixed point of W_P, and for each atom $A \in M^+$ let $l(A)$ be the least ordinal β such that $A \in W_P \uparrow (\beta + 1)$.

Now assume that there is an ordinal γ which is least under the condition that $W_P \uparrow \gamma \notin I_{P,3}$. Then γ must be a successor ordinal, since $I_{P,3}$ is a complete partial order; so let $I = W_P \uparrow (\gamma - 1) \in I_{P,3}$. Now consider the set $U = T'_P(I) \cap U_P(I)$. Then for each $A \in U$ and each clause $A \leftarrow$ body in ground(P) such that body is true in I, we have that some (non-negated) atom B in body occurs in $U_P(I)$. We obtain $B \in U_P(I) \cap I$, and since $I \subseteq T'_P(I)$ we get $B \in U$. Now let $A \in U$ be chosen such that it is minimal with respect to $l(A) = \beta$, and notice that necessarily $\beta < \gamma$. Then there exists a clause $A \leftarrow$ body in ground(P) with body true in $W_P \uparrow \beta \subseteq I$, and in particular $B \in I$ and $l(B) < l(A)$ for all (non-negated) atoms B which occur in body. But now we have just shown that $B \in U$, contradicting minimality of $l(A)$. ∎

2.6.7 Proposition Let P be a program, and let $I \in I_{P,3}$. Then $\Phi_P(I) \subseteq W_P(I)$. Furthermore, the three-valued fixed points of W_P are three-valued supported models for P with respect to Kleene's strong three-valued logic.

Proof: Let $A \in F_P(I)$. Then for each clause $A \leftarrow$ body in ground(P), we have that $I(\text{body}) = \mathbf{f}$, and so there is a literal $L \in \text{body}$ with $I(L) = \mathbf{f}$. But then A is in the greatest unfounded set of P with respect to I, and so $A \in U_P(I)$. This shows that $\Phi_P(I) \subseteq W_P(I)$.

Now let $M = W_P(M) = T'_P(M) \cup \neg U_P(M)$. We show that $M = \Phi_P(M) = T'_P(M) \cup \neg F_P(M)$. For this it suffices to show that $U_P(M) \subseteq F_P(M)$. Let $A \in U_P(M)$, and let $A \leftarrow$ body be an arbitrary clause in ground(P) with head A. Noting that $U_P(M)$ is an unfounded set of P with respect to M, if condition (US1) in the definition of an unfounded set holds, then body is false in M in Kleene's strong three-valued logic. If (US2) holds, then some atom in body occurs in $U_P(M)$ and, therefore, is false in M. Consequently, body is again false in M in Kleene's strong three-valued logic. Hence, $A \in F_P(M)$, as required. ∎

We will now show formally that the well-founded model can be characterized using Definition 2.6.1.[15]

2.6.8 Theorem Let P be a normal logic program with well-founded model M. Then, in the knowledge ordering, M is the greatest model among all models I for which there exists an I-partial level mapping l for P such that P satisfies (WF) with respect to I and l.

Proof: Let M_P be the well-founded model for P, and define the M_P-partial level mapping l_P as follows: $l_P(A) = \alpha$, where α is the least ordinal such that A is not undefined in $W_P \uparrow (\alpha + 1)$. The proof will proceed by establishing the following facts. (1) P satisfies (WF) with respect to M_P and l_P. (2) If I is a model for P and l is an I-partial level mapping such that P satisfies (WF) with respect to I and l, then $I \subseteq M_P$.

(1) Let $A \in \text{dom}(l_P)$, and suppose that $l_P(A) = \alpha$. We consider the two cases corresponding to (WFi) and (WFii).

Case i. $A \in M_P$. Then $A \in T'_P(W_P \uparrow \alpha)$. Hence, there exists a clause $A \leftarrow \text{body}$ in ground(P) such that body is true in $W_P \uparrow \alpha$. Thus, for all $L_i \in \text{body}$, we have that $L_i \in W_P \uparrow \alpha$. Hence, $l_P(L_i) < \alpha = l_P(A)$ and $L_i \in M_P$ for all i. Consequently, A satisfies (WFi) with respect to M_P and l_P.

Case ii. $\neg A \in M_P$. Then $A \in U_P(W_P \uparrow \alpha)$, and so A is contained in the greatest unfounded set of P with respect to $W_P \uparrow \alpha$. Hence, for each clause $A \leftarrow \text{body}$ in ground(P), either (US1) or (US2) holds for this clause with respect to $W_P \uparrow \alpha$ and the unfounded set $U_P(W_P \uparrow \alpha)$. If (US1) holds, then there exists some literal $L \in \text{body}$ with $\neg L \in W_P \uparrow \alpha$. Hence, $l_P(L) < \alpha$ and condition (WFiia) holds relative to M_P and l_P if L is an atom, or condition (WFiib) holds relative to M_P and l_P if L is a negated atom. On the other hand, if (US2) holds, then some (non-negated) atom B in body occurs in $U_P(W_P \uparrow \alpha)$. Hence, $l_P(B) \le l_P(A)$, and A satisfies (WFiia) with respect to M_P and l_P. Thus, we have established that the statement (1) holds.

(2) We show via transfinite induction on $\alpha = l(A)$ that if $A \in I$, or $\neg A \in I$, then $A \in W_P \uparrow (\alpha + 1)$, or $\neg A \in W_P \uparrow (\alpha + 1)$), respectively. For the base case, note that if $l(A) = 0$, then $A \in I$ implies that A occurs as the head of a fact in ground(P). Hence, $A \in W_P \uparrow 1$. If $\neg A \in I$, then consider the set U of all atoms B with $l(B) = 0$ and $\neg B \in I$. We show that U is an unfounded set of P with respect to $W_P \uparrow 0$, and this suffices since it implies $\neg A \in W_P \uparrow 1$ by the fact that $A \in U$. So let $C \in U$, and let $C \leftarrow \text{body}$ be a clause in ground(P).

---

[15] A different characterization using level mappings, which is nevertheless in the same spirit, can be found in [Lifschitz et al., 1995].

Since $\neg C \in I$, and $l(C) = 0$, we have that C satisfies (WFiia) with respect to I and l, and so condition (US2) is satisfied showing that U is an unfounded set of P with respect to I. Assume now that the induction hypothesis holds for all $B \in B_P$ with $l(B) < \alpha$. We consider two cases.

Case i. $A \in I$. Then A satisfies (WFi) with respect to I and l. Hence, there is a clause $A \leftarrow$ body in ground(P) such that body $\subseteq I$ and $l(K) < \alpha$ for all $K \in$ body. Hence, body $\subseteq W_P \uparrow \alpha$, and we obtain $A \in T'_P(W_P \uparrow \alpha)$, as required.

Case ii. $\neg A \in I$. Consider the set U of all atoms B with $l(B) = \alpha$ and $\neg B \in I$. We show that U is an unfounded set of P with respect to $W_P \uparrow \alpha$, and this suffices since it implies $\neg A \in W_P \uparrow (\alpha + 1)$ by the fact that $A \in U$. So let $C \in U$, and let $C \leftarrow$ body be a clause in ground(P). Since $\neg C \in I$, we have that C satisfies (WFii) with respect to I and l. If there is a literal $L \in$ body with $\neg L \in I$ and $l(L) < l(C)$, then by the induction hypothesis we obtain $\neg L \in W_P \uparrow \alpha$, and therefore condition (US1) is satisfied for the clause $C \leftarrow$ body with respect to $W_P \uparrow \alpha$ and U. In the remaining case, we have that C satisfies condition (WFiia), and there exists an atom $B \in$ body with $\neg B \in I$ and $l(B) = l(C)$. Hence, $B \in U$ showing that condition (US2) is satisfied for the clause $C \leftarrow$ body with respect to $W_P \uparrow \alpha$ and U. Hence, U is an unfounded set of P with respect to $W_P \uparrow \alpha$. ∎

As a special case, we immediately obtain the following corollary.

2.6.9 Corollary A normal logic program P has a total well-founded model if and only if there is a total model I for P and a (total) level mapping l such that P satisfies (WF) with respect to I and l.

The well-founded model is in general different from the weakly perfect model, but always contains it.

2.6.10 Proposition Let P be a program, let M_1 be its (partial) weakly perfect model, and let M_2 be its well-founded model. Then $M_1 \subseteq M_2$.

Proof: Let l_1 be an M_1-partial level mapping such that P satisfies (WS) with respect to M_1 and l_1. Then P satisfies (WF) with respect to M_1 and l_1, as noted earlier. By Theorem 2.6.8, M_2 is largest among all models I for which there exists an I-partial level mapping l for P such that P satisfies (WF) with respect to I and l, and hence $M_1 \subseteq M_2$. ∎

2.6.11 Program Let P be the program consisting of the two clauses

$$p \leftarrow q, \neg p$$
$$q \leftarrow p$$

Then the reduct P_1 of P with respect to the empty set is P itself, that is,

$P_1 = P/\emptyset = P$. The only minimal component of P_1 is the set $\{p, q\}$, and hence the bottom layer of P_1 is P; it follows that the (partial) weakly perfect model for P is $\emptyset$. However, by applying Theorem 2.6.8, it is easy to see that $\{\neg p, \neg q\}$ is the well-founded model for P. Indeed, more directly, we have $T_P'(\emptyset) = \emptyset$, and $U_P(\emptyset) = \{p, q\}$. Therefore, $W_P \uparrow 2 = W_P(W_P \uparrow 1) = W_P(\emptyset \cup \{\neg p, \neg q\}) = \{\neg p, \neg q\} = W_P \uparrow 1$, and it follows that the well-founded model for P is indeed $\{\neg p, \neg q\}$.

An irregular property of the weakly perfect model semantics is that certain changes in the program affect the semantics, although inutitively they should not.

2.6.12 Program (Tweety4) Consider again the program Tweety4 of Example 2.5.5. As noted earlier, this program is a variation of Tweety2 (Program 2.3.9), with the last clause changed; it is intuitively clear that this change should not alter the semantics of the program.

While the program Tweety2, which is locally stratified, has the expected weakly perfect model as discussed in Example 2.5.3, the program Tweety4 has weakly perfect model

$$\{\texttt{penguin(tweety)}, \texttt{bird(bob)}, \texttt{bird(tweety)}, \neg\texttt{flies(tweety)}\},$$

as shown in Example 2.5.5. So again we are unable to determine whether or not bob is a penguin.

The well-founded semantics, however, does not suffer from the same deficiency. Indeed, it turns out to be $M \cup \neg(B_P \setminus M)$, where M is as in Example 2.2.7. So in this semantics bob is not a penguin and flies.

An alternative way of characterizing the well-founded semantics is via the Gelfond–Lifschitz operator from Section 2.3. Recall from Theorem 2.3.7 that the Gelfond–Lifschitz operator is antitonic. In particular, this means that for any program P, the operator GL_P^2, obtained by applying GL_P twice, is monotonic. Therefore, by the Knaster-Tarski theorem, GL_P^2 has a least fixed point, L_P. Note further that $I_{P,2}$ is a complete lattice in the dual of the truth ordering on $I_{P,2}$. So, on applying the Knaster-Tarski theorem again, we also obtain that GL_P^2 has a greatest fixed point, G_P. Since $L_P \subseteq G_P$, we obtain that $L_P \cup \neg(B_P \setminus G_P)$ is a three-valued interpretation for P and is, in fact, a model for P, as we show next, called the *alternating fixed point model* for P.

We are going to show that the alternating fixed point model coincides with the well-founded model. Let us first introduce some temporary notation, where P is an arbitrary program.

$$
\begin{aligned}
L_0 &= \emptyset & G_0 &= B_P & \\
L_{\alpha+1} &= \mathrm{GL}_P(G_\alpha) & G_{\alpha+1} &= \mathrm{GL}_P(L_\alpha) & \text{for any ordinal } \alpha \\
L_\alpha &= \bigcup_{\beta < \alpha} L_\beta & G_\alpha &= \bigcap_{\beta < \alpha} G_\beta & \text{for a limit ordinal } \alpha.
\end{aligned}
$$

Since $\emptyset \subseteq B_P$, we obtain $L_0 \subseteq L_1 \subseteq G_1 \subseteq G_0$, and, by transfinite induction, it can easily be shown that $L_\alpha \subseteq L_\beta \subseteq G_\beta \subseteq G_\alpha$ whenever $\alpha \leq \beta$.

2.6.13 Theorem Let P be a program. Then the following hold.

(a) $L_P = \mathrm{GL}_P(G_P)$ and $G_P = \mathrm{GL}_P(L_P)$.

(b) For every stable model S for P, we have $L_P \subseteq S \subseteq G_P$.

(c) $M = L_P \cup \neg(B_P \setminus G_P)$ is the well-founded model for P.

Proof: (a) We obtain $\mathrm{GL}_P^2(\mathrm{GL}_P(L_P)) = \mathrm{GL}_P(\mathrm{GL}_P^2(L_P)) = \mathrm{GL}_P(L_P)$, so $\mathrm{GL}_P(L_P)$ is a fixed point of GL_P^2, and hence $L_P \subseteq \mathrm{GL}_P(L_P) \subseteq G_P$. Similarly, $L_P \subseteq \mathrm{GL}_P(G_P) \subseteq G_P$. Since $L_P \subseteq G_P$, we get from the antitonicity of GL_P that $L_P \subseteq \mathrm{GL}_P(G_P) \subseteq \mathrm{GL}_P(L_P) \subseteq G_P$. Similarly, since $\mathrm{GL}_P(L_P) \subseteq G_P$, we obtain $\mathrm{GL}_P(G_P) \subseteq \mathrm{GL}_P^2(L_P) = L_P \subseteq \mathrm{GL}_P(G_P)$, so $\mathrm{GL}_P(G_P) = L_P$, and hence $G_P = \mathrm{GL}_P^2(G_P) = \mathrm{GL}_P(L_P)$.

(b) It suffices to note that S is a fixed point of GL_P, by Theorem 2.3.7, and, hence, is a fixed point of GL_P^2.

(c) We prove this statement by applying Theorem 2.6.8. First, we define an M-partial level mapping l. For convenience, we will take as image set of l, pairs (α, n) of ordinals, where $n \leq \omega$, with the lexicographic ordering. This can be done without loss of generality because any set of pairs of ordinals, lexicographically ordered, is certainly well-ordered and therefore order-isomorphic to an ordinal, as noted earlier. For $A \in L_P$, let $l(A)$ be the pair (α, n), where α is the least ordinal such that $A \in L_{\alpha+1}$, and n is the least ordinal such that $A \in T_{P/G_\alpha} \uparrow (n+1)$. For $B \notin G_P$, let $l(B)$ be the pair (β, ω), where β is the least ordinal such that $B \notin G_{\beta+1}$. We show next by transfinite induction that P satisfies (WF) with respect to M and l.

Let $A \in L_1 = T_{P/B_P} \uparrow \omega$. Since P/B_P consists of exactly all clauses from ground(P) which contain no negation, we have that A is contained in the least two-valued model for a definite subprogram of P, namely, P/B_P, and (WFi) is satisfied, by Proposition 2.3.2. Now let $\neg B \in \neg(B_P \setminus G_P)$ be such that $B \in (B_P \setminus G_1) = B_P \setminus T_{P/\emptyset} \uparrow \omega$. Since $P/\emptyset$ contains all clauses from ground(P) with all negative literals removed, we obtain that each clause in ground(P) with head B must contain a positive body literal $C \notin G_1$, which, by definition of l, must have the same level as B; hence, (WFiia) is satisfied.

Assume now that, for some ordinal α, we have shown that A satisfies (WF) with respect to M and l for all $n \leq \omega$ and all $A \in B_P$ with $l(A) \leq (\alpha, n)$.

Let $A \in L_{\alpha+1} \setminus L_\alpha = T_{P/G_\alpha} \uparrow \omega \setminus L_\alpha$. Then $A \in T_{P/G_\alpha} \uparrow n \setminus L_\alpha$ for some $n \in \mathbb{N}$; note that all (negative) literals which were removed by the Gelfond–Lifschitz transformation from clauses with head A have level less than $(\alpha, 0)$. Then the assertion that A satisfies (WF) with respect to M and l follows again by Proposition 2.3.2.

Let $A \in (B_P \setminus G_{\alpha+1}) \cap G_\alpha$. Then we have $A \notin T_{P/L_\alpha} \uparrow \omega$. Let $A \leftarrow A_1, \ldots, A_k, \neg B_1, \ldots, \neg B_m$ be a clause in ground(P). If $B_j \in L_\alpha$ for some j, then $l(A) > l(B_j)$. Otherwise, since $A \notin T_{P/L_\alpha} \uparrow \omega$, we have that there exists A_i with $A_i \notin T_{P/L_\alpha} \uparrow \omega$, and hence $l(A) \geq l(A_i)$, and this suffices.

This finishes the proof that P satisfies (WF) with respect to M and l. It therefore only remains to show that M is greatest with this property.

So assume that $M_1 \neq M$ is the greatest model such that P satisfies (WF) with respect to M_1 and some M_1-partial level mapping l_1.

Assume $L \in M_1 \setminus M$, and, without loss of generality, let the literal L be chosen such that $l_1(L)$ is minimal. We consider the following two cases.

Case i. If $L = A$ is an atom, then there exists a clause $A \leftarrow$ body in $\mathrm{ground}(P)$ such that body is true in M_1 and $l_1(L) < l_1(A)$ for all literals L in body. Hence, body is true in M, and $A \leftarrow$ body transforms to a clause $A \leftarrow A_1, \ldots, A_n$ in P/G_P with $A_1, \ldots, A_n \in L_P = T_{P/G_P} \uparrow \omega$. But this implies $A \in M$, contradicting $A \in M_1 \setminus M$.

Case ii. If $L = \neg A \in M_1 \setminus M$ is a negated atom, then $\neg A \in M_1$ and $A \in G_P = T_{P/L_P} \uparrow \omega$, so $A \in T_{P/L_P} \uparrow n$ for some $n \in \mathbb{N}$. We show by induction on n that this leads to a contradiction to finish the proof.

If $A \in T_{P/L_P} \uparrow 1$, then there is a unit clause $A \leftarrow$ in P/L_P, and any corresponding clause $A \leftarrow \neg B_1, \ldots, \neg B_k$ in $\mathrm{ground}(P)$ satisfies $B_1, \ldots, B_k \notin L_P$. Since $\neg A \in M_1$, we also obtain by Theorem 2.6.8 that there is $i \in \{1, \ldots, k\}$ such that $B_i \in M_1$ and $l_1(B_i) < l_1(A)$. By minimality of $l_1(A)$, we obtain $B_i \in M$, and hence $B_i \in L_P$, which contradicts $B_i \notin L_P$.

Now assume that there is no $\neg B \in M_1 \setminus M$ with $B \in T_{P/L_P} \uparrow k$ for any $k < n+1$, and let $\neg A \in M_1 \setminus M$ with $A \in T_{P/L_P} \uparrow (n+1)$. Then there is a clause $A \leftarrow A_1, \ldots, A_m$ in P/L_P with $A_1, \ldots, A_m \in T_{P/L_P} \uparrow n \subseteq G_P$, and we note that we cannot have $\neg A_i \in M_1 \setminus M$ for any $i \in \{1, \ldots, m\}$ by our current induction hypothesis. Furthermore, it is also impossible for $\neg A_i$ to belong to M for any i; otherwise, we would have $A_i \in B_P \setminus G_P$. Thus, we conclude that we cannot have $\neg A_i \in M_1$ for any i. Moreover, there is a corresponding clause $A \leftarrow A_1, \ldots, A_m, \neg B_1, \ldots, \neg B_{m_1}$ in $\mathrm{ground}(P)$ with $B_1, \ldots, B_{m_1} \notin L_P$. Hence, by Theorem 2.6.8, we know that there is $i \in \{1, \ldots, m_1\}$ such that $B_i \in M_1$ and $l_1(B_i) < l_1(A)$. By minimality of $l_1(A)$, we conclude that $B_i \in M$, so that $B_i \in L_P$, and this contradicts $B_i \notin L_P$. ∎

It follows from Theorem 2.6.13 (b) that total well-founded models are unique stable models. The converse, however, does not hold. Indeed, Program 2.4.14 has well-founded model $\emptyset$, as can easily be seen by noting that $\mathrm{GL}_P(\emptyset) = B_P$ and $\mathrm{GL}_P(B_P) = \emptyset$.

2.6.14 Theorem Let P be a program with a total Fitting model. Then P has a total well-founded model and a total weakly perfect model. Moreover, P also has a unique stable and a unique supported model. Furthermore, all these models coincide.

Proof: By Propositions 2.5.14 and 2.6.10, P has a total well-founded and a total weakly perfect model, both of which coincide with the Fitting model. By Theorem 2.6.13 (b), P has a unique stable model, and this coincides with the well-founded model by Theorem 2.6.13 (c). Finally, by Proposition 2.4.13, P has a unique supported model, and this model coincides with its Fitting model.   ∎

Chapter 3

Topology and Logic Programming

In this chapter, we consider the role of topology in logic programming semantics. There is a considerable history of topology being used in computer science in general, much of it stemming from the role of the Scott topology in domain theory and in conventional programming language semantics. However, topological methods have been employed in a number of other areas of importance in computing, including digital topology in image processing, software engineering, and the use of metric spaces in concurrency, for example. In addition, topological methods and ideas have been used in foundational investigations via the topology of observable properties of M.B. Smyth, see [Smyth, 1992]. Again, Blair et al. have made considerable use of convergence spaces in unifying discrete and continuous models of computation and, hence, in providing models for hybrid systems. Indeed, these authors, see [Blair et al., 1999] and [Blair and Remmel, 2001], for example, view any model of computation in which there is a notion of evolving state as a dynamical system. Such models of computation include, of course, Turing machines, finite state machines, logic programs, neural networks, etc. On the other hand, convergence spaces, as already noted earlier, provide a very general framework in which to study convergence and continuity, either by means of nets or by filters, and include topologies as a special case. It is shown in [Blair et al., 1999] and [Blair and Remmel, 2001] that the execution traces of a dynamical system can be realized as those solutions of a certain type of constraint on a convergence space that yield continuous instances of the constraint. This work provides a foundation for hybrid systems. Furthermore, the papers [Blair et al., 1997a, Blair et al., 1997b, Blair, 2007, Blair et al., 2007] give many other interesting applications of ideas of a dynamical systems and analytical nature to the theory of computation, including logic programming in particular.

Here, we want to explore the role of topology in finding models for logic programs and its role as a foundational framework for logic programming semantics.[1] Thus, our focus is the study of topologies and their properties on spaces $I(X, \mathcal{T})$ of interpretations, and we work with general truth sets $\mathcal{T}$ wherever possible, only imposing conditions as appropriate and necessary. There are two main topologies which we discuss in this chapter and which have

---

[1]The thesis [Ferry, 1994] and the paper [Heinze, 2003] contain results concerning the characterization in topological terms of the various standard models for logic programs discussed in Chapter 2.

important properties in relation to logic programming semantics, namely, the well-known Scott topology and a topology, called the Cantor topology by us,[2] which has connections with the Scott topology. Our goal is to establish the basic facts about these two topologies and to consider continuity of semantic operators in them. In fact, we deal with continuity in the Scott topology in this chapter, but postpone our discussion of continuity in the Cantor topology until Chapter 5. Later on, we will see how the results we establish can be employed in studying acceptable programs and termination issues, and we will also see that the topologies we discuss underlie the fixed-point structures we introduce in later chapters.

In fact, in many ways it is the convergence properties of these topologies which are most important, as already noted in the Introduction, and therefore we take convergence as a fundamental notion and base our discussion upon it. Nevertheless, we quite easily obtain descriptions of the topologies we study in terms of more familiar notions such as basic open sets. Actually, convergence per se is formalized completely generally via the concept of convergence spaces, and therefore we take convergence spaces as our starting point. In fact, we focus mainly on the so-called convergence classes, which form a subclass of the convergence spaces, because convergence classes correspond to conventional topologies, whereas convergence spaces give more general theories of convergence than are needed here.

As can be seen from the results of Chapter 2, the notion of order is not entirely satisfactory as a foundation for logic programming semantics due to the failure in general of the immediate consequence operator to be monotonic in the natural order present. However, order can be expressed through convergence, as we show here. Indeed, convergence spaces and convergence classes are to a considerable extent appropriate structures with which to investigate semantical questions in computer science in general and in logic programming in particular.

3.1   Convergence Spaces and Convergence Classes

The theory of convergence can be based either on nets or on filters,[3] and these two approaches are equivalent in that any result which can be established by the one can equally well be established by the other. We will work exclusively with nets since they give rather intuitive descriptions of the sort of conditions we want to consider in logic programming. The facts we need

---

[2]The Cantor topology was introduced in [Batarekh and Subrahmanian, 1989a] and in [Batarekh and Subrahmanian, 1989b], see also [Batarekh, 1989], under a restriction called the matching condition and was treated in complete generality in [Seda, 1995].

[3]Our basic references to the theory of nets and filters are the books [Kelley, 1975] and [Willard, 1970].

concerning nets, and our notation in this respect, can be found in the Appendix.[4] Indeed, all the basic facts we need concerning general topology have been collected together in the Appendix.

We begin with some basic definitions.

3.1.1 Definition Let X be a non-empty set. We call the pair $(X, \mathcal{S}) = (X, (\mathcal{S}_s)_{s \in X})$ a *convergence space* if, for each $s \in X$, $\mathcal{S}_s$ is a non-empty collection of nets in X with the following properties.

(1) If (s_i) is a constant net, that is, $s_i = s \in X$ for all i, then $(s_i) \in \mathcal{S}_s$.

(2) If $(s_i)_{i \in \mathcal{I}} \in \mathcal{S}_s$ and $(t_j)_{j \in \mathcal{J}}$ is a subnet of (s_i), then $(t_j)_{j \in \mathcal{J}} \in \mathcal{S}_s$.

If $(s_i) \in \mathcal{S}_s$, we say s_i *converges to* s and sometimes write $s_i \to s$ to indicate this.

3.1.2 Definition Let X be a non-empty set, and suppose that $\mathcal{C}$ is a class of pairs $((s_i), s)$, where $(s_i)_{i \in \mathcal{I}}$ is a net in X and s is an element of X. We call $\mathcal{C}$ a *convergence class* if it satisfies the conditions below, in which we will write that s_i *converges* $(\mathcal{C})$ *to* s or that $\lim_i s_i \equiv s$ $(\mathcal{C})$ if and only if $((s_i), s) \in \mathcal{C}$.

(1) (Constant nets) If (s_i) is a net such that $s_i = s$ for all i, then $((s_i), s) \in \mathcal{C}$.

(2) (Convergence of subnets) If (s_i) converges $(\mathcal{C})$ to s, then so does every subnet of (s_i).

(3) (Non-convergence)[5] If (s_i) does not converge $(\mathcal{C})$ to s, then there is a subnet of (s_i), of which no subnet converges $(\mathcal{C})$ to s.

(4) (Iterated limits) Suppose that I is a directed set and that J_m is a directed set for each $m \in I$. Form the fibred product $F' = I \times_I \bigcup_{m \in I} J_m = \{(m, n) \mid m \in I, n \in J_m\}$, and suppose that $x : F' \to X$. Let F denote the product directed set[6] $I \times \prod_{m \in I} J_m$, and let $r : F \to F'$ be defined by $r(m, f) = (m, f(m))$. If $\lim_m \lim_n x(m, n) \equiv s$ $(\mathcal{C})$, then the net $x \circ r$ converges $(\mathcal{C})$ to s.

The principal result concerning convergence classes, see [Kelley, 1975, Chapter 2] or [Seda et al., 2003], is that each convergence class $\mathcal{C}$ on X induces a closure operator on X which in turn induces a topology on X, in accordance with Theorem A.2.9, in which the convergent nets and their limits are precisely those given in $\mathcal{C}$. More precisely, we have the following result which shows that the notion of convergence may be taken as fundamental.

---

[4]We refer the reader again to [Kelley, 1975] for more details.

[5]This formulation is as given in [Kelley, 1975]. An equivalent form, given in positive terms, is as follows: if every subnet of a net (s_i) has a subnet converging to s, then (s_i) converges to s.

[6]By a product directed set $\prod_{m \in I} I_m$, we understand, of course, the pointwise ordering on the product $\prod_{m \in I} I_m$ of the directed sets I_m; thus, for elements f and g of $\prod_{m \in I} I_m$, we have $f \leq g$ if and only if $f(m) \leq g(m)$ for each $m \in I$.

3.1.3 Theorem Let $\mathcal{C}$ be a convergence class in a non-empty set X. For each $A \subseteq X$, let $A^c = \{s \in X \mid \text{there is a net } (s_i) \text{ in } A \text{ with } ((s_i), s) \in \mathcal{C}\}$. Then $\cdot^c$ is a closure operator on X and, hence, defines a topology τ on X, called the topology *associated with* $\mathcal{C}$. Moreover, we have $((s_i), s) \in \mathcal{C}$ if and only if $s_i \to s$ with respect to τ.

Conversely, suppose that τ is a topology on a non-empty set X. Let $\mathcal{C}$ denote the set of all pairs $((s_i), s)$, where $s \in X$ and $(s_i)_{i \in \mathcal{I}}$ is a net in X which converges to s in the topology τ. Then $\mathcal{C}$ is a convergence class in X whose associated topology coincides with τ.

Proof: The proof of the first part of the theorem is well-known and will be omitted, and we refer the reader to [Kelley, 1975] or [Seda et al., 2003] for details.

For the converse, we note that properties (1), (2), and (3) in the definition of a convergence class are immediate for the class $\mathcal{C}$ by elementary properties of nets converging in a topology (see Definition A.3.3). Property (4) of the definition follows from the Theorem on Iterated Limits, see [Kelley, 1975, Page 69], and, hence, the class $\mathcal{C}$ is a convergence class. Finally, let $A \subseteq X$ be an arbitrary subset of X. By the definition of the closure operator determined by $\mathcal{C}$ as given in the first statement in the theorem, we have $s \in A^c$ if and only if there is a net (s_i) in A converging to s. But this is equivalent to $s \in \overline{A}$ by statement (a) of Theorem A.3.5, and it follows that the associated topology of $\mathcal{C}$ coincides with τ. ∎

Another basic definition is that of continuous function, as follows.

3.1.4 Definition Let $(X, \mathcal{S})$ and $(Y, \mathcal{T})$ be convergence spaces. Then a function $f : X \to Y$ is said to be *continuous at* $s \in X$ if $(f(s_i)) \in \mathcal{T}_{f(s)}$ whenever $(s_i) \in \mathcal{S}_s$, that is, if $f(s_i)$ converges to $f(s)$ whenever s_i converges to s.

There are a few points to be made about these definitions. First, suppose that $\mathcal{C}$ is a convergence class on X. For each $s \in X$, let $\mathcal{S}_s$ denote the collection of nets (s_i) such that $((s_i), s) \in \mathcal{C}$. Then conditions (1) and (2) in the definition of $\mathcal{C}$ show that $(X, (\mathcal{S}_s)_{s \in X})$ is, in fact, a convergence space. Second, since a function $f : X \to Y$ between topological spaces is continuous at $s \in X$ if and only if $f(s_i)$ converges to $f(s)$ whenever the net s_i converges to s, see (d) of Theorem A.3.5, we note that the notion of continuity just defined coincides with topological continuity when the convergence spaces in question are actually convergence classes. Finally, definitions equivalent to these can be given entirely in terms of filters, but we omit the details.[7]

It is known that the full generality of convergence spaces is needed in modelling hybrid systems, as observed earlier. Here, in fact, all the convergence conditions we consider give rise to convergence classes and, hence, to topologies, rather than to strict convergence spaces, and therefore our focus is on convergence classes as already noted.

---

[7] We refer the reader to [Seda et al., 2003] for a treatment in terms of filters.

3.2 The Scott Topology on Spaces of Valuations

The Scott topology is normally encountered in domain theory in the context of solving recursive domain equations and in understanding self reference. However, it also has a role in logic programming, which we discuss in this section, and indeed, in a certain sense, it naturally underpins definite programs.

We begin with the following basic definition and refer the reader to the Appendix, both for proofs of the results we simply state here and also for a development of the elements of the Scott topology.

3.2.1 Definition Let $(D, \sqsubseteq)$ be a complete partial order. A set $O \subseteq D$ is called *Scott open*[8] if it satisfies the following two conditions: (1) O is *upwards closed* in the sense that whenever $x \in O$ and $x \sqsubseteq y$, we have $y \in O$, and (2) whenever $A \subseteq D$ is directed and $\bigsqcup A \in O$, then $A \cap O \neq \emptyset$.

In the case of a domain D, this topology has a rather simple description in that the collection $\{\uparrow a \mid a \in D_c\}$ is a base for the Scott topology on D, where $\uparrow x = \{y \in D \mid x \sqsubseteq y\}$ for any $x \in D$, as we see in the next proposition.

3.2.2 Proposition Let $(D, \sqsubseteq)$ be a domain. Then the following statements hold.

(a) The Scott-open sets form a topology on D called the *Scott topology*.

(b) For each compact element $a \in D_c$, the set $\uparrow a$ is a Scott-open set.

(c) The collection $\{\uparrow a \mid a \in D_c\}$ is a base for the Scott topology on D.

Proof: (a) That $\emptyset$ and D are Scott open is easy to see. If O_1 and O_2 are Scott open, if $x \in O_1 \cap O_2$, and if $x \sqsubseteq y$, then it is clear that $y \in O_1 \cap O_2$. Suppose that A is directed and $\bigsqcup A \in O_1 \cap O_2$. Then there are $a_1, a_2 \in A$ such that $a_1 \in O_1$ and $a_2 \in O_2$. Therefore, by directedness of A, there is $a_3 \in A$ such that $a_1 \sqsubseteq a_3$ and $a_2 \sqsubseteq a_3$. But then $a_3 \in O_1 \cap O_2$, and hence $a_3 \in A \cap (O_1 \cap O_2)$, as required to see that $O_1 \cap O_2$ is Scott open. Finally, it is easy to check that a union $\bigcup_{i \in \mathcal{I}} O_i$ of Scott-open sets $O_i, i \in \mathcal{I}$, is itself Scott open.

(b) If $x \in \uparrow a$ and $x \sqsubseteq y$, then it is immediate that $y \in \uparrow a$. Now suppose that A is directed and $\bigsqcup A \in \uparrow a$. Then a is compact and $a \sqsubseteq \bigsqcup A$. Therefore, there is $a' \in A$ such that $a \sqsubseteq a'$. Hence, $a' \in \uparrow a$ by definition of $\uparrow a$, that is, $a' \in A \cap \uparrow a$ showing that $A \cap \uparrow a \neq \emptyset$, as required.

(c) First we show that this collection is a base for some topology on D. Let $x \in D$ be arbitrary. Then approx(x) is directed and is non-empty; let $a \in$ approx(x). Then, $a \in D_c$ and $a \sqsubseteq x$, so that $x \in \uparrow a$, and hence $\bigcup_{a \in D} \uparrow a = D$.

---

[8]See [Abramsky and Jung, 1994, Gierz et al., 2003, Stoltenberg-Hansen et al., 1994].

Now suppose that a_1 and a_2 are compact elements and that $z \in \uparrow a_1 \cap \uparrow a_2$. Then $a_1, a_2 \in \mathrm{approx}(z)$, and by directedness there is $a_3 \in \mathrm{approx}(z)$ such that $a_1 \sqsubseteq a_3$ and $a_2 \sqsubseteq a_3$. Hence, we have $a_3 \in \uparrow a_1 \cap \uparrow a_2$. But $\uparrow a_1 \cap \uparrow a_2$ is clearly upwards closed, and so we obtain $z \in \uparrow a_3 \subseteq \uparrow a_1 \cap \uparrow a_2$ and $a_3 \in D_c$, as required.

Finally, we show that the collection $\{\uparrow a \mid a \in D_c\}$ is a base for the Scott topology on D. Let O be any Scott-open set, and let $x \in O$. Then $\mathrm{approx}(x)$ is directed, and we have that $\bigsqcup \mathrm{approx}(x) = x \in O$. Therefore, there is some $a \in \mathrm{approx}(x)$ such that $a \in O$. But then $a \in D_c$ and $a \sqsubseteq x$. Therefore, $x \in \uparrow a \subseteq O$, where a is a compact element, as required. ∎

We refer to the elements of the Scott topology as Scott-open sets. Likewise, we refer to neighbourhoods in the Scott topology as Scott neighbourhoods, and so on.

We next give a simple example of the Scott topology in the context of $I_{P,2}$.

3.2.3 Example Consider the definite program P as follows.

$$p(a) \leftarrow$$
$$p(s(X)) \leftarrow p(X)$$

This program is intended to compute the natural numbers, where a is the natural number 0, and s is the successor function on the natural numbers.

In accordance with Theorem 1.3.4, the set $I_P = I_{P,2}$ of all two-valued interpretations for P is a domain, and, furthermore, its compact elements are the finite subsets I of B_P, where as usual we are identifying a two-valued interpretation with the set of ground atoms which are true in I. Therefore, a typical basic open set in the Scott topology on I_P is the set $\uparrow I = \{I' \subseteq B_P \mid I \subseteq I'\}$ of all supersets of the finite set I.

One of our main aims here is to present the Scott topology in terms of convergence, and we proceed to do this next.[9]

3.2.4 Theorem Let $(D, \sqsubseteq)$ denote a domain, let (s_i) be a net in D, and let s denote an element of D. Define $\lim_i s_i \equiv s$ $(\mathcal{C})$ to mean that

for each $a \in \mathrm{approx}(s)$, there is an index i_0 such that $a \sqsubseteq s_i$ whenever $i_0 \leq i$.

Then the condition just given determines a convergence class $\mathcal{C}$ whose associated topology is the Scott topology on D. Therefore, a net s_i converges to s in the Scott topology on D if and only if it satisfies the condition just stated.

Proof: We first verify that the conditions (1), (2), (3), and (4) in the definition of a convergence class, see Definition 3.1.2, hold with the given meaning of $\lim_i s_i \equiv s$ $(\mathcal{C})$.

---

[9]For further details of this result and of several more in this chapter, see [Seda, 2002].

(1) Suppose that $s_i = s$ for all $i \in \mathcal{I}$ is a constant net, and let $a \in$ approx(s). Thus, a is a compact element satisfying $a \sqsubseteq s$. Therefore, we have $a \sqsubseteq s_i$ for all i. So, $((s_i), s) \in \mathcal{C}$.

(2) Suppose that $((s_i), s) \in \mathcal{C}$ and that $(t_j)_{j \in \mathcal{J}}$ is a subnet of $(s_i)_{i \in \mathcal{I}}$. Thus, there is a function $\phi : \mathcal{J} \to \mathcal{I}$ such that (i) $t_j = s_{\phi(j)}$ for all $j \in \mathcal{J}$, and (ii) for each $i_0 \in \mathcal{I}$, there is $j_0 \in \mathcal{J}$ such that $i_0 \leq \phi(j)$ whenever $j_0 \leq j$. Let $a \in$ approx(s) be arbitrary. Then because $((s_i), s) \in \mathcal{C}$, there is an $i_0 \in \mathcal{I}$ such that $a \sqsubseteq s_i$ whenever $i_0 \leq i$. Since t_j is a subnet of s_i, there is $j_0 \in \mathcal{J}$ such that $i_0 \leq \phi(j)$ whenever $j_0 \leq j$. But then we have $a \sqsubseteq s_{\phi(j)}$ whenever $j_0 \leq j$, that is, $a \sqsubseteq t_j$ whenever $j_0 \leq j$. Therefore, $((t_j), s) \in \mathcal{C}$.

(3) Suppose that $((s_i), s) \notin \mathcal{C}$. Then there exists $a \in$ approx(s) such that for each index i_0 there is an index $j_0 \geq i_0$ with $a \not\sqsubseteq s_{j_0}$. Let $\mathcal{J}$ denote the collection of all these j_0. Then clearly $\mathcal{J}$ is cofinal in $\mathcal{I}$, and hence $(t_j)_{j \in \mathcal{J}}$ is a subnet of (s_i), where $t_j = s_j$ for each $j \in \mathcal{J}$. It is clear that if (r_k) is any subnet of (t_j), then we have $((r_k), s) \notin \mathcal{C}$.

(4) Suppose that the conditions stated in (4) of Definition 3.1.2 all hold and that $\lim_m \lim_n x(m, n) \equiv s$ $(\mathcal{C})$, where $x : F' \to D$. Let $a \in$ approx(s) be arbitrary. Because $\lim_m \lim_n x(m, n) \equiv s$ $(\mathcal{C})$, there is an index $m_0 \in I$ such that $a \sqsubseteq \lim_n x(m, n)$ whenever $m \geq m_0$. But now we see that $a \in$ approx$(\lim_n x(m, n))$. Therefore, for each fixed $m \geq m_0$, there is an index $n_m \in J_m$ such that $a \sqsubseteq x(m, n)$ whenever $n \geq n_m$. Define $f \in \prod_{m \in I} J_m$ by setting $f(m) = n_m \in J_m$ whenever $m \geq m_0$, and otherwise letting $f(m) \in J_m$ be arbitrary. Suppose that $(m', g) \geq (m_0, f)$. Then $m' \geq m_0$ and $g \geq f$, so that $g(m') \geq f(m') = n_{m'}$, that is, $g(m') \geq n_{m'}$. Thus, $a \sqsubseteq x(m', g(m'))$ whenever $(m', g) \geq (m_0, f)$. Hence, $a \sqsubseteq x \circ r(m', g)$ whenever $(m', g) \geq (m_0, f)$, and it follows that $(x \circ r, s) \in \mathcal{C}$, as required.

Next, we verify that the topology induced on D by the convergence condition coincides with the Scott topology on D. Let O be open in the topology associated with the convergence class $\mathcal{C}$, let $x \in O$, and suppose that $x \sqsubseteq y$; suppose further that $y \notin O$, that is, suppose that y is in the closed set $D \setminus O$. Then there is a net $s_i \to y$ with $s_i \in D \setminus O$ for all i. Let $a \in$ approx(x) be arbitrary. Then $a \in$ approx(y) and, hence, $a \sqsubseteq s_i$ eventually. It follows from this that $s_i \to x$. Therefore, by (b) of Theorem A.3.5, we see that s_i is eventually in O. This contradiction shows that y is, in fact, in O. Next, suppose that A is a directed set with $x = \bigsqcup A \in O$. Then by Proposition A.6.1 we have that, as a net, $A \to x$. Therefore, A is eventually in O, and so $A \cap O \neq \emptyset$. Hence, O is a Scott-open set.

Conversely, suppose that O is a Scott-open set, and let $x \in O$. We show that O is open in the topology associated with the convergence class $\mathcal{C}$ by establishing that, whenever $s_i \to x$, we have s_i eventually in O, and then the result follows from (b) of Theorem A.3.5 again. Now, approx(x) is a directed set, and $x = \bigsqcup$ approx$(x) \in O$. Therefore, there is an element $a \in$ approx(x) such that $a \in O$. Since $s_i \to x$, it now follows that there is i_0 such that for $i_0 \leq i$ we have $a \sqsubseteq s_i$. But then, since $a \in O$ and O is Scott open, we have $s_i \in O$ whenever $i_0 \leq i$, as required to finish the proof. ∎

Of course, a function $f : D \to E$ from a domain D to a domain E is called *Scott continuous* if it is continuous in the Scott topologies on D and E. However, it is well-known that a function f between domains is Scott continuous if and only if it is continuous in the sense of Definition 1.1.7, see Proposition A.6.4. Moreover, by virtue of Theorem 1.3.2 and Proposition A.6.5, we have the following result.

3.2.5 Proposition Suppose that the truth set $\mathcal{T}$ is a domain. Then in the Scott topology $I(X, \mathcal{T})$ is a compact T_0 topological space, but is not T_1 in general.

Nets (and convergence classes), like sequences, are normally simple to handle, and their use makes checking continuity relatively straightforward, as we will see later on in several places. However, we move next to consider the significance of Theorem 3.2.4 in the case of spaces $I(X, \mathcal{T})$ of valuations, where the set $(\mathcal{T}, \leq)$ of truth values is a domain. Indeed, suppose that $(\mathcal{T}, \leq)$ is a domain and that the net (v_i) converges to v in the Scott topology on the domain $I(X, \mathcal{T})$. According to Theorem 3.2.4, this holds if and only if for each finite valuation u with $u \sqsubseteq v$, there is an index i_0 such that $u \sqsubseteq v_i$ whenever $i_0 \leq i$. In fact, when applied to the particular truth sets discussed in Section 1.3.2, Theorem 3.2.4 gives the following result.

3.2.6 Theorem Suppose that (I_i) is a net of interpretations and that I is an interpretation.

(a) Let $\mathcal{T}$ denote the truth set $\mathcal{TWO}$. Then, in the ordering $\sqsubseteq_t$ on $I(X, \mathcal{T})$, we have that (I_i) converges to I in the Scott topology if and only if whenever $x \in I$, eventually $x \in I_i$.

(b) Let $\mathcal{T}$ denote the truth set $\mathcal{THREE}$. Then the following statements hold.

    (i) In the ordering $\sqsubseteq_k$ on $I(X, \mathcal{T})$, we have that (I_i) converges to I in the Scott topology if and only if whenever $x \in I_t$, eventually $x \in I_{i_t}$, and whenever $x \in I_f$, eventually $x \in I_{i_f}$.

    (ii) In the ordering $\sqsubseteq_t$ on $I(X, \mathcal{T})$, we have that (I_i) converges to I in the Scott topology if and only if whenever $x \in I_t$, eventually $x \in I_{i_t}$, and whenever $x \in I_u$, eventually $x \in I_{i_u} \cup I_{i_t}$.

(c) Let $\mathcal{T}$ denote the truth set $\mathcal{FOUR}$. Then the following statements hold.

    (i) In the ordering $\sqsubseteq_k$ on $I(X, \mathcal{T})$, we have that (I_i) converges to I in the Scott topology if and only if whenever $x \in I_t$, eventually $x \in I_{i_t} \cup I_{i_b}$, whenever $x \in I_f$, eventually $x \in I_{i_f} \cup I_{i_b}$, and whenever $x \in I_b$, eventually $x \in I_{i_b}$.

    (ii) In the ordering $\sqsubseteq_t$ on $I(X, \mathcal{T})$, we have that (I_i) converges to I in the Scott topology if and only if whenever $x \in I_u$, eventually $x \in I_{i_u} \cup I_{i_t}$, whenever $x \in I_b$, eventually $x \in I_{i_b} \cup I_{i_t}$, and whenever $x \in I_t$, eventually $x \in I_{i_t}$.

Proof: We prove the first of the claims in (c), with the others being proved similarly. Let v denote the valuation corresponding to the interpretation I, and, for each index i, let v_i denote the valuation corresponding to the interpretation I_i. Suppose first that (v_i) converges to v in the Scott topology on $I(X, \mathcal{T})$, and let $x \in X$. Suppose further that $x \in v_{\mathbf{t}}$, so that $v(x) = \mathbf{t}$. Define $u \in I(X, \mathcal{T})$ by $u(x) = \mathbf{t}$, and, for $y \neq x$, set $u(y) = \mathbf{u}$. Then u is a finite element satisfying $u \sqsubseteq_k v$. Therefore, by Theorem 3.2.4, there exists i_0 such that $u \sqsubseteq_k v_i$ whenever $i \geq i_0$, and hence eventually either $v_i(x) = \mathbf{t}$ or $v_i(x) = \mathbf{b}$. Thus, eventually $x \in v_{i_{\mathbf{t}}} \cup v_{i_{\mathbf{b}}}$. A similar argument holds in case $x \in v_{\mathbf{f}}$ or $x \in v_{\mathbf{b}}$, and hence we obtain the stated condition.

Conversely, suppose that the given condition holds. Let u be a finite valuation such that $u \sqsubseteq_k v$, and suppose further that u takes value $\mathbf{u}$ at all points of X except possibly at one point x, say. Let us first suppose that $u(x) = \mathbf{t}$. Then either $x \in v_{\mathbf{t}}$ or $x \in v_{\mathbf{b}}$. But then, by the given condition, either eventually $x \in v_{i_{\mathbf{t}}} \cup v_{i_{\mathbf{b}}}$, or eventually $x \in v_{i_{\mathbf{b}}}$, and in either case, eventually $u \sqsubseteq_k v_i$. A similar argument holds in case $u(x) = \mathbf{f}$ or $u(x) = \mathbf{b}$. By a standard argument using the directedness of the index set of the net v_i, it follows that, for any finite valuation $u \sqsubseteq_k v$, we have eventually $u \sqsubseteq_k v_i$. Hence, (v_i) converges to v in the Scott topology on $I(X, \mathcal{T})$, as required. ∎

Thus, we obtain a uniform description of net convergence in the Scott topology on $(I(X, \mathcal{T}), \sqsubseteq)$, where $(\mathcal{T}, \leq)$ is any one of the main sets of truth values which are important in logic programming. Indeed, the convergence conditions involved are simple, natural, and intuitive, and this is one of the advantages of approaching this topic via convergence.

In fact, it is Part (a) of Theorem 3.2.6 which we will use most often, and we illustrate its use next with an example.

3.2.7 Example The following statements concerning convergence in the Scott topology hold in two-valued logic.[10]

(1) Any net (I_λ) of interpretations converges to the empty interpretation $\emptyset$.

(2) If (I_λ) is a net of interpretations which is monotonic in the sense that $I_\lambda \subseteq I_\gamma$ whenever $\lambda \leq \gamma$, then (I_λ) converges to $\bigcup_\lambda I_\lambda$.

(3) If a net (I_λ) of interpretations converges to an interpretation I, and $J \subseteq I$, then (I_λ) converges to J. Thus, in general, a net (I_λ) of interpretations has many limits. A specific example of this can be given as follows. Suppose that $\mathcal{L}$ is a first-order language containing a unary predicate symbol p, a unary function symbol s, and a constant symbol a, such as the language underlying Example 3.2.3, say. Consider the sequence (I_n) of interpretations defined as follows: I_n is the set $\{p(a), p(s(a))\}$ if n is even and is the set $\{p(a), p(s(a)), p(s^2(a))\}$ if n is odd. Then (I_n) converges to

---

[10]For further results in this direction, see [Seda, 1995].

each of the interpretations $\emptyset$, $\{p(a)\}$, $\{p(s(a))\}$, $\{p(a), p(s(a))\}$, but not to $\{p(a), p(s(a)), p(s^2(a))\}$.

Again, if I_n is the interpretation defined by taking it to be the set $\{p(a), p(s(a)), \ldots, p(s^n(a))\}$ if n is even and taking it to be the set $\{p(a), p(s(a)), \ldots, p(s^{2n}(a))\}$ if n is odd, then the sequence (I_n) converges to the interpretation $\{p(a), p(s(a)), p(s^2(a)), \ldots\}$; note that (I_n) is not monotonic in the sense of Part (2).

Although we have taken convergence as the basic concept, it is easy to exhibit properties of the Scott topology in other familiar terms, as the following example shows.

3.2.8 Example In the context of spaces of interpretations, Proposition 3.2.2 gives a simple description of the basic open sets in the Scott topology, and we briefly consider this point here. In the case of $\mathcal{TWO}$, for example, let $A_1, \ldots, A_n \in X$ and let $\mathcal{G}(A_1, \ldots, A_n) = \{I \in I(X, \mathcal{TWO}) \mid A_1, \ldots, A_n \in I\}$. By means of (f) of Theorem 1.3.2 and (c) of Proposition 3.2.2, it is clear that the sets $\mathcal{G}(A_1, \ldots, A_n)$ form a base for the Scott topology on $I(X, \mathcal{TWO})$. Indeed, the sets $\mathcal{G}(A) = \{I \in I(X, \mathcal{TWO}) \mid A \in I\}$ form a subbase for the Scott topology, since $\mathcal{G}(A_1, \ldots, A_n) = \bigcap_{i \in \{1, \ldots, n\}} \mathcal{G}(A_i)$. As another example, consider this time the knowledge ordering $\sqsubseteq_k$ in the case of $\mathcal{THREE}$. Take elements $A_1, \ldots, A_n, B_1, \ldots, B_m \in X$, where $n, m \geq 0$, and let $\mathcal{G}(A_1, \ldots, A_n; B_1, \ldots, B_m)$ be the set $\{I \in I(X, \mathcal{THREE}) \mid A_1, \ldots, A_n \in I_t \text{ and } B_1, \ldots, B_m \in I_f\}$. Then these sets form a base for the Scott topology on $I(X, \mathcal{THREE})$. Indeed, the sets $\mathcal{G}(A; B)$ clearly form a subbase for this topology, where $\mathcal{G}(A; B) = \{I \in I(X, \mathcal{THREE}) \mid A \in I_t \text{ and } B \in I_f\}$.

The other cases dealt with in Section 1.3.2 can be treated similarly.

We turn next to consider the continuity of the immediate consequence operator in the Scott topology. By virtue of (a) of Theorem 2.2.3 and Proposition A.6.4, we have immediately that T_P is Scott continuous whenever P is a definite program. However, we will take the trouble to include a self-contained proof of this fact next.

3.2.9 Theorem Let P be a definite program. Then T_P is continuous in the Scott topology on $I_{P,2}$.

Proof: Let $I \in I_{P,2}$, and let $I_i \to I$ be a net converging to I in the Scott topology; we show that $T_P(I_i) \to T_P(I)$ in the Scott topology. If $T_P(I) = \emptyset$, then the required conclusion is immediate since, by Theorem 3.2.4, every net in a domain converges in the Scott topology to the bottom element. So suppose that $T_P(I) \neq \emptyset$, and let A belong to $T_P(I)$. Then there is a ground instance $A \leftarrow A_1, \ldots, A_n$ of a clause in P such that $I(A_1 \wedge \ldots \wedge A_n) = \mathbf{t}$, where $n \geq 0$. Since $I_i \to I$, we have, by (a) of Theorem 3.2.6, that eventually $I_i(A_1 \wedge \ldots \wedge A_n) = \mathbf{t}$. Therefore, $A \in T_P(I_i)$ eventually. It now follows from Theorem 3.2.6 that $T_P(I_i) \to T_P(I)$ in the Scott topology, as required. ∎

It is not difficult to see that the converse of the previous result fails. For example, the program P_1 with clauses $p(a) \leftarrow p(a)$, $p(a) \leftarrow \neg p(a)$, and $p(b) \leftarrow p(a)$ and the program P_2 with clauses $p(a) \leftarrow$ and $p(b) \leftarrow p(a)$ have the same (Scott continuous) immediate consequence operator.

By contrast, recall that Program 2.4.12 showed that the Fitting operator is not order continuous, and hence not Scott continuous, for definite programs. Nevertheless, Theorem 3.2.9 justifies our earlier statement that the Scott topology naturally underpins definite programs.

A theme which is important in this chapter and in later ones concerns the convergence to some interpretation I of sequences $T_P^n(M)$ of iterates of T_P on an interpretation M, and under what conditions I is a model for P. We discuss this briefly now for definite programs and take it up in more detail in the next section for normal programs.

In general, if (v_i) is a net converging to v in the Scott topology on $I(X, \mathcal{T})$, then it is clear from Theorem 3.2.4, see also Example 3.2.7, that (v_i) converges to u whenever $u \sqsubseteq v$ and, hence, that the set of limits of (v_i) is downwards closed.[11] Indeed, since (v_i) always converges to $\bot$, this latter set is always non-empty also. Furthermore, when $\mathcal{T}$ denotes the complete lattice TWO, we have by Theorem 1.3.4 that $I(X, \mathcal{T})$ is itself a complete lattice. Thus, in this case, the supremum of the set of all limits, in the Scott topology, of a net (v_i) exists and is easily seen to be a limit of (v_i) also, by Theorem 3.2.6. We refer to this limit as the *greatest limit* of (v_i) and denote it by $gl(v_i)$. In fact, it is readily checked that $gl(v_i)$ takes value **t** precisely on the set of all $x \in X$ at which eventually v_i takes value **t**, and this property completely determines $gl(v_i)$, see [Seda, 1995] for more details.

Of course, a sequence $T_P^n(M)$ always converges to the empty interpretation $\emptyset$, as already noted, but the interpretation $\emptyset$ need not be a model for P. However, we do have the following result.

3.2.10 Proposition Let P be a definite logic program, and let M be an interpretation for P. Then the greatest limit $gl(T_P^n(M))$ of the sequence $(T_P^n(M))$ is a model for P.

Proof: Let I denote $gl(T_P^n(M))$. Then the sequence $(T_P^n(M))$ converges to I in the Scott topology. Hence, by the Scott continuity of T_P, the sequence $(T_P(T_P^n(M)))$ converges to $T_P(I)$. Thus, $(T_P^n(M))$ converges to $T_P(I)$, and we obtain, by definition of the greatest limit, that $T_P(I) \subseteq I$, as required. ∎

Finally, we note that if we take M to be the bottom element in $I(X, \mathcal{T})$, then $gl(T_P^n(M))$ coincides with the least fixed point of T_P and, hence, is the least model for the definite logic program P, see [Seda, 1995]. Thus, the usual two-valued semantics for definite programs can be expressed entirely in terms of convergence in the Scott topology.

---

[11] A subset O of a partially ordered set $(D, \sqsubseteq)$ is called *downwards closed* if, whenever $x \in O$ and $y \sqsubseteq x$, we have $y \in O$.

We close this section with an example which, despite its simplicity, illustrates the main points discussed previously.

3.2.11 Example Consider again the program P of Example 3.2.3.

$$p(a) \leftarrow$$
$$p(s(X)) \leftarrow p(X)$$

Let $M = \emptyset$, thought of as a two-valued interpretation, and let I_n denote the n-th iterate of T_P on M. Then $I_n = \{p(a), p(s(a)), \ldots, p(s^{n-1}(a))\}$ for any $n \geq 1$. By Part (2) of Example 3.2.7, the sequence (I_n) converges in the Scott topology to the set $I = \{p(a), p(s(a)), \ldots, p(s^n(a)), \ldots\}$ of all natural numbers. Moreover, I is clearly the greatest limit of the sequence (I_n) and, hence, by Theorem 3.2.10, is a model for P. Indeed, by the comments immediately prior to this example, I is the least model for P by the results of [Seda, 1995].

3.3   The Cantor Topology on Spaces of Valuations

As just noted in the previous section, one of the sources of motivation for studying topology in relation to logic programming is the role of convergence of sequences of iterates of the immediate consequence operator in relation to semantics and also, in fact, in relation to termination. We take this discussion further now, but this time in the context of normal programs and the construction of certain standard models for them, and in more detail in Chapter 5. We also refer the reader to Chapter 5 for details of how convergence enters into questions concerned with the so-called acceptable programs and problems concerned with termination, see Corollary 5.2.5, Proposition 5.2.7, Theorem 5.2.8 and Theorem 5.4.14, for example.

We begin with a result concerning product topologies.

Let X and Y be arbitrary sets, and let $[X \rightarrow Y]$ denote the set of all total functions mapping X into Y. When Y is ordered, perhaps as a set of truth values $\mathcal{T}$, then so is $[X \rightarrow Y]$, and, as we have just seen, important topologies can be defined on $[X \rightarrow Y]$ by quite natural convergence conditions which make use of the order. However, important topologies can also be defined on $[X \rightarrow Y]$ using natural convergence conditions which do not depend on any order, as we show next.[12]

3.3.1 Theorem Let (s_i) be a net in $[X \rightarrow Y]$, and let $s \in [X \rightarrow Y]$. Then the condition

---

[12] Again, see [Seda, 2002].

$\lim_i s_i \equiv s\ (\mathcal{C})$ *if and only if for each $x \in X$ eventually $s_i(x) = s(x)$*

determines a convergence class on $[X \to Y]$ whose associated topology Q is the product of X copies of the discrete topology on Y.

Proof: We must verify that the conditions (1), (2), (3), and (4) in the definition of a convergence class, see Definition 3.1.2, hold with the given meaning of $\lim_i s_i \equiv s\ (\mathcal{C})$.

(1) Suppose that $s_i = s$ for all $i \in \mathcal{I}$ is a constant net. Then $s_i(x) = s(x)$ for all x and all i. Hence, for all x, eventually $s_i(x) = s(x)$, and so $((s_i), s) \in \mathcal{C}$.

(2) Suppose that $((s_i), s) \in \mathcal{C}$ and that $(t_j)_{j \in \mathcal{J}}$ is a subnet of $(s_i)_{i \in \mathcal{I}}$. Let $x \in X$ be arbitrary, and let i_0 be such that $s_i(x) = s(x)$ for all $i \geq i_0$. Since (t_j) is a subnet of (s_i), there is $\phi : \mathcal{J} \to \mathcal{I}$ and $j_0 \in \mathcal{J}$ such that $i_0 \leq \phi(j)$ whenever $j_0 \leq j$. But then, if $j_0 \leq j$, we have $t_j(x) = s_{\phi(j)}(x) = s(x)$, and hence $((t_j), s) \in \mathcal{C}$.

(3) Suppose that $(s_i)_{i \in \mathcal{I}}$ does not converge $(\mathcal{C})$ to s. Then there is $x \in X$ and a cofinal subset $\mathcal{J}$ of $\mathcal{I}$ such that, whenever $j \in \mathcal{J}$, we have $s_j(x) \neq s(x)$. Let $t_j = s_j$ for each $j \in \mathcal{J}$. Then (t_j) is a subnet of (s_i), and clearly no subnet of (t_j) converges $(\mathcal{C})$ to s.

(4) Suppose that the conditions stated in (4) of Definition 3.1.2 all hold and that $\lim_m \lim_n x(m, n) \equiv s\ (\mathcal{C})$, where $x : F' \to [X \to Y]$. Consider the net $x \circ r : F \to [X \to Y]$. Let $y \in X$ be arbitrary. Since $\lim_m \lim_n x(m, n) \equiv s\ (\mathcal{C})$, there is $m_0 \in I$ such that, for all $m \geq m_0$, $\lim_n x(m, n) \equiv s_m\ (\mathcal{C})$ for some $s_m \in [X \to Y]$, and $\lim_m s_m \equiv s\ (\mathcal{C})$. Therefore, for $m \geq m_0$, there is $n_m \in J_m$ such that $x(m, n)(y) = s_m(y)$ for all $n \geq n_m$. But for $m \geq m_0$, $s_m(y) = s(y)$. Define $f \in \prod_{m \in I} J_m$ by setting $f(m) = n_m \in J_m$ whenever $m \geq m_0$ and otherwise letting $f(m) \in J_m$ be arbitrary. Suppose $(m, g) \geq (m_0, f)$. Then $m \geq m_0$ and $g \geq f$ so that $g(m) \geq f(m) = n_m$. But then we have $x(m, g(m))(y) = s_m(y) = s(y)$. In other words, $(x \circ r)(m, g)(y) = x(m, g(m))(y) = s(y)$ whenever $(m, g) \geq (m_0, f)$. Thus, $(x \circ r)(y)$ is eventually equal to $s(y)$, and hence $x \circ r$ converges $(\mathcal{C})$ to s.

Finally, viewing $[X \to Y]$ as the product $\prod_{x \in X} Y_x$, where $Y_x = Y$ for each $x \in X$, then, as is well-known, a net (s_i) converges in such a product to s if and only if $s_i(x) \to s(x)$ in Y for each x, see Theorem A.5.2 (e). But, given that Y is endowed with the discrete topology, this latter condition $s_i(x) \to s(x)$ holds if and only if $s_i(x)$ is eventually equal to $s(x)$, as required. ∎

Theorem 3.3.1 holds with X taken as B_P ($= B_{P,J}$), where P is a normal logic program, and Y taken as any set $\mathcal{T}$ of truth values, and in particular it holds with $\mathcal{T}$ taken as $\mathcal{TWO}$. With these choices, we obtain the following result, which is analogous to Proposition 3.2.10, but applies to normal programs in general.

3.3.2 Proposition Let P be a normal logic program. Suppose that $\mathcal{C}$ is any convergence class on $I_{P,2}$ whose elements satisfy the condition stated in Theorem 3.3.1:

if $((I_i), I) \in \mathcal{C}$, then, for each $A \in B_P$, eventually $I_i(A) = I(A)$.

Then, whenever M is an interpretation for P such that $((T_P^n(M)), I) \in \mathcal{C}$, we have that I is a model for P.

Proof: By Proposition 2.2.2, it suffices to show that $T_P(I) \sqsubseteq I$. So, suppose therefore that $T_P(I)(A) = \mathbf{t}$. Then there is a ground instance $A \leftarrow A_1, \ldots, A_n, \neg B_1, \ldots, \neg B_m$ of a clause in P such that $I(A_1 \wedge \ldots \wedge A_n \wedge \neg B_1 \wedge \ldots \wedge \neg B_m) = \mathbf{t}$. Taking the sequence $T_P^n(M)$, we have, by the property stated in the hypothesis (applied to each literal in the conjunction under consideration), that eventually $T_P^n(M)(A_1 \wedge \ldots \wedge A_n \wedge \neg B_1 \wedge \ldots \wedge \neg B_m) = I(A_1 \wedge \ldots \wedge A_n \wedge \neg B_1 \wedge \ldots \wedge \neg B_m) = \mathbf{t}$. Therefore, eventually $T_P^n(M)(A) = \mathbf{t}$, and, by the property stated in the hypothesis again, we obtain $I(A) = \mathbf{t}$. Hence, whenever $T_P(I)(A) = \mathbf{t}$, we have $I(A) = \mathbf{t}$. Thus, $T_P(I) \sqsubseteq I$, as required. ∎

3.3.3 Remark (1) Theorem 3.3.1 shows that the largest convergence class $\mathcal{C}$ to which Proposition 3.3.2 applies is the convergence class $\mathcal{C}(Q)$ determined by the topology Q. Therefore, Q is the coarsest topology among the topologies determined by those convergence classes to which Proposition 3.3.2 can be applied.

(2) In topological terms, Proposition 3.3.2 says that if M is an interpretation for a normal logic program P such that the sequence $(T_P^n(M))$ of iterates converges in the topology Q to some interpretation I for P, then I is a model for P.

In fact, we note that the construction of the perfect model semantics for locally stratified programs P, which we give in Chapter 6, rests on the second of the facts stated in the previous remark.

Notice that Proposition 3.3.2 holds in any convergence class contained in $\mathcal{C}(Q)$. In other words, it holds for any convergence class determined by a topology finer than Q. Furthermore, Q is not the only naturally definable topology determined by a convergence class for which Proposition 3.3.2 holds. For example, if we define $\lim_i v_i \equiv v$ $(\mathcal{C})$ to mean that eventually $v_i = v$, we obtain another natural convergence class which trivially satisfies Proposition 3.3.2, and this convergence class generates the discrete topology on $I(X, \mathcal{T})$.

Next, we want to investigate the properties of $I(X, \mathcal{T})$ when endowed with the topology Q, and indeed the representation of Q given in Theorem 3.3.1 as a product space makes this relatively easy.

3.3.4 Theorem Let P be a normal logic program, let J be a preinterpretation for P with domain D, let $X = B_{P,J}$, and let $\mathcal{T}$ be a truth set endowed with the discrete topology. Then in the topology Q on $I(X, \mathcal{T})$ we have the following results.

(a) A net (I_i) of interpretations converges to an interpretation I if and only if, for each ground atom A, we have that $I_i(A)$ is eventually equal to $I(A)$.

(b) $I(X, \mathcal{T})$ is a totally disconnected Hausdorff space.

(c) $I(X, \mathcal{T})$ is compact if and only if $\mathcal{T}$ is a finite set.

(d) $I(X, \mathcal{T})$ is metrizable[13] if and only if D is countable.

(e) $I(X, \mathcal{T})$ is second countable if and only if D and $\mathcal{T}$ are both countable.

(f) Suppose that D is denumerable and that $\mathcal{T}$ is finite. Then $I(X, \mathcal{T})$ is homeomorphic to the Cantor set in the closed unit interval within the real line.

Proof: Statement (a) follows immediately from Theorem 3.3.1, and all the remaining statements follow from general and well-known results concerning product spaces, see the Appendix. Specifically, they can be found in [Willard, 1970], where unfamiliar terms are also defined, as follows: for (b), see Page 72, Theorem 13.8, and Page 210, Theorem 29.3; (c) follows from Tychonoff's theorem (Page 120, Theorem 17.8) and the fact that a discrete space is compact if and only if it is finite; for (d), see Page 161, Theorem 22.3; for (e), see Page 108, Theorem 16.2; and finally, for (f), see Page 217, Corollary 30.6. ∎

Because of Part (f) of Theorem 3.3.4, we refer to the topology Q as the *Cantor topology*.

Notice that $I(X, \mathcal{T})$ is a Hausdorff space in the topology Q, and hence the limit of any net convergent in Q is unique, see Theorem A.4.2, unlike the situation in the Scott topology where a convergent net has many limits in general, as shown by Example 3.2.7.

In the case of two-valued interpretations, we have the following result. It follows immediately from Part (a) of Theorem 3.3.4 and will be used quite often later on.

3.3.5 Proposition A net (I_i) of interpretations in $I_{P,2}$ converges to I in the topology Q if and only if whenever $A \in I$, eventually $A \in I_i$, and whenever $A \notin I$, eventually $A \notin I_i$. Moreover, the unique limit I coincides with the set $\{A \in B_P \mid A \text{ eventually belongs to } I_i\}$.

The following example illustrates Proposition 3.3.5.

---

[13]Metrics are defined in Section 4.2 and studied extensively in Chapter 4. A topological space is said to be *metrizable* if its open sets can be defined in terms of some metric as discussed in Section 4.1. The representation of Q as a product topology makes it easy to determine metrics for Q, see [Seda, 1995].

3.3.6 Example Consider again the program Even, see Program 2.1.3. To ease notation here, it will be convenient to denote this program by P and also to replace the predicate symbol even by p. Thus P denotes the program

$$p(a) \leftarrow$$
$$p(s(X)) \leftarrow \neg p(X)$$

We consider the iterates of T_P on the interpretation $\emptyset$, as follows.

$$T_P^0(\emptyset) = \emptyset$$
$$T_P^1(\emptyset) = \{p(a), p(s(a)), p(s^2(a)), p(s^3(a)), p(s^4(a)), \ldots\}$$
$$T_P^2(\emptyset) = \{p(a)\}$$
$$T_P^3(\emptyset) = \{p(a), p(s^2(a)), p(s^3(a)), p(s^4(a)), p(s^5(a)), \ldots\}$$
$$T_P^4(\emptyset) = \{p(a), p(s^2(a))\}$$
$$T_P^5(\emptyset) = \{p(a), p(s^2(a)), p(s^4(a)), p(s^5(a)), p(s^6(a)), \ldots\}$$
$$T_P^6(\emptyset) = \{p(a), p(s^2(a)), p(s^4(a))\}$$
$$T_P^7(\emptyset) = \{p(a), p(s^2(a)), p(s^4(a)), p(s^6(a)), p(s^7(a)), \ldots\}$$
$$T_P^8(\emptyset) = \{p(a), p(s^2(a)), p(s^4(a)), p(s^6(a))\}$$

and so on. On letting I_n denote $T_P^n(\emptyset)$ and also letting I denote the set $\{p(a), p(s^2(a)), p(s^4(a)), \ldots\}$ of "even" natural numbers, we note that the sequence (I_n) oscillates quite wildly about I. Nevertheless, it is easy to see by means of Proposition 3.3.5 that (I_n) converges in Q to I. Therefore, by Remark 3.3.3, I is a model for P. Indeed, I is a fixed point of T_P and is the unique supported model for P.

In fact, the oscillatory behaviour exhibited in this example in relation to the single-step operator is typical of programs containing negation. Indeed, for this example, T_P is not Scott continuous, and therefore Theorem 1.1.9 is not applicable to T_P. Hence, the theory developed for the semantics of definite programs in Chapter 2 is not applicable here either.

3.3.7 Example It is immediate from (a) of Theorem 3.2.6 and Proposition 3.3.5 that whenever a net (I_i) converges to I in Q, then it converges to I in the Scott topology, and this is borne out by Example 3.2.8 and Corollary 3.3.10, just below, which show that the topology Q is finer than the Scott topology in the case of two-valued interpretations.

On the other hand, the sequence (I_n) defined in the first paragraph of (3) of Example 3.2.7 converges in the Scott topology (to several interpretations), but does not converge (to anything) in Q.

The point of view that the topology Q is appropriate for studying the semantics of logic programs with negation is given strong support by examples such as Example 3.3.6. It is given further support in the most usual case, where the domain of interpretation is countable, as shown in the following example. In fact, in this next example, we show that a sequence (I_n) of two-valued interpretations converges in Q to a two-valued interpretation I if and only if the symmetric difference[14] $I_n \triangle I$ of the sets representing I_n and I can be made arbitrarily small (in the sense described in Example 3.3.8), and this fact appears to be in accord with one's intuition regarding negation. Indeed, the symmetric difference provides a simple metric for the topology Q, as we see next.

3.3.8 Example Let P denote a normal logic program, and, to make the discussion non-trivial, suppose that the underlying first-order language $\mathcal{L}$ of P contains at least one function symbol. Thus, B_P is denumerable, and we can suppose that the elements of B_P are given some fixed listing, so that $B_P = (A_1, A_2, A_3, \ldots)$, say. (In fact, the exact nature of B_P plays no role here, and we could work equally well over any preinterpretation J for $\mathcal{L}$ whose domain is denumerable and can therefore be listed.) Now let d_i be a real number satisfying $0 < d_i < 1$, for each i, and such that $\sum_{i=1}^{\infty} d_i = 1$; each d_i is a *weight* to be attached to the element A_i of B_P. Now define the metric d on I_P by

$$d(I, I') = \sum_{A_i \in I \triangle I'} d_i,$$

for $I, I' \in I_P$. Note that it is routine to check that d does indeed define a metric on I_P, and we show that d generates the topology Q on I_P. To do this, it suffices to show that an arbitrary sequence (I_n) converges to I, say, in Q if and only if it converges to I in the metric d.

Suppose that (I_n) is a sequence of interpretations in I_P, and $I_n \to I$ in the metric d. Thus, $d(I_n, I) \to 0$ as $n \to \infty$. So, given $\epsilon > 0$, there is a natural number n_0 such that whenever $n \geq n_0$ we have $d(I_n, I) = \sum_{A_i \in I_n \triangle I} d_i < \epsilon$. Suppose that $A_j \in I$. Choose ϵ so small that $\epsilon < d_j$, and obtain the corresponding n_0 such that $\sum_{A_i \in I_n \triangle I} d_i < \epsilon$ whenever $n \geq n_0$. Then obviously d_j does not occur in this sum for any $n \geq n_0$. In other words, $A_j \in I_n \cap I$ for all $n \geq n_0$, and so A_j is eventually in I_n. On the other hand, suppose that $A_j \notin I$. If A_j belongs to infinitely many I_n, then $\sum_{A_i \in I_n \triangle I} d_i \geq d_j$ infinitely often, contradicting $d(I_n, I) \to 0$. Thus, A_j belongs to only finitely many I_n, and so A_j is eventually not in I_n. Therefore, by Proposition 3.3.5, convergence in d implies convergence in Q.

Conversely, suppose $I_n \to I$ in Q. Given $\epsilon > 0$, choose integers n_0 so large that $\sum_{i \geq n_0} d_i < \epsilon$ and $n'_0 \geq n_0$ so large that whenever $n \geq n'_0$, $I_n \triangle I$ only contains elements A_j with $j \geq n_0$ or is empty (this situation can be achieved by finitely many applications of Proposition 3.3.5 since the set $\{A_j; j < n_0\}$ is finite and, in fact, contains $n_0 - 1$ elements). Then, whenever $n \geq n'_0$, we have

$$d(I_n, I) = \sum_{A_j \in I_n \triangle I} d_j \leq \sum_{i \geq n_0} d_i < \epsilon$$

---

[14]We remind the reader that the symmetric difference of sets A and B is defined by $A \triangle B = (A \setminus B) \cup (B \setminus A)$.

and so $I_n \to I$ in the metric d. Thus, d generates Q, as claimed.

Furthermore, we note that, in particular, the weights d_i can be taken to be $\frac{1}{2^i}$ for each i, in which case the metric d takes the natural form

$$d(I, I') = \sum_{A_i \in I \triangle I'} \frac{1}{2^i},$$

for $I, I' \in I_P$. In any case, if $I_n \to I$ in Q, then $I_n \to I$ in d, and hence, given any $\epsilon > 0$, there is n_0 such that $d(I_n, I) = \sum_{A_i \in I_n \triangle I} d_i < \epsilon$ whenever $n \geq n_0$, and conversely. It is in this sense that the symmetric difference $I_n \triangle I$ can be made arbitrarily small if $I_n \to I$ in Q.   ∎

Because Q is a product topology, it is easy to describe the basic open sets of $I(X, \mathcal{T})$ in Q as follows (the nature of X is actually irrelevant, although it is being taken here to be $B_{P,J}$). First, given any truth value $t \in \mathcal{T}$, the singleton set $\{t\}$ is open in $\mathcal{T}$, since $\mathcal{T}$ is endowed with the discrete topology. Therefore, see Section A.5, the basic open sets here are of the form $\pi_{i_1}^{-1}(t_{i_1}) \cap \ldots \cap \pi_{i_n}^{-1}(t_{i_n})$. They therefore can be written in the form $\mathcal{G}(A_{i_1}, \ldots, A_{i_n}; t_{i_1}, \ldots, t_{i_n}) = \{I \in I(X, \mathcal{T}) \mid I(A_{i_j}) = t_{i_j} \text{ for } j = 1, \ldots, n\}$, where $A_{i_1}, \ldots, A_{i_n}$ are arbitrary, but fixed, elements of X.

Thus, we have the following result, which describes Q in the familiar terms of basic open sets.

3.3.9 Proposition With the notation above, the basic open sets in the topology Q on the set $I(X, \mathcal{T})$ take the form $\mathcal{G}(A_{i_1}, \ldots, A_{i_n}; t_{i_1}, \ldots, t_{i_n}) = \{I \in I(X, \mathcal{T}) \mid I(A_{i_j}) = t_{i_j} \text{ for } j = 1, \ldots, n\}$, where $A_{i_1}, \ldots, A_{i_n}$ are arbitrary, but fixed, elements of X and $t_{i_1}, \ldots, t_{i_n}$ are arbitrary, but fixed, elements of $\mathcal{T}$ for $j = 1, \ldots, n$. Furthermore, the subbasic open sets in Q are those basic open sets $\mathcal{G}(A; t)$ determined by taking $n = 1$ in the set $\mathcal{G}(A_{i_1}, \ldots, A_{i_n}; t_{i_1}, \ldots, t_{i_n})$.

We denote by $\mathcal{G}$ the subbase for Q consisting of the sets $\mathcal{G}(A; t)$, where $A \in X$ and $t \in \mathcal{T}$.

In particular, the previous proposition has the following corollary when $\mathcal{T}$ is the truth set $\mathcal{TWO}$.

3.3.10 Corollary When $\mathcal{T}$ is the truth set $\mathcal{TWO}$, the basic open sets in Q take the form $\mathcal{G}(A_1, \ldots, A_n; B_1, \ldots, B_m) = \{I \in I(X, \mathcal{T}) \mid A_i \in I, \text{ for } i = 1, \ldots, n, \text{ and, for } j = 1, \ldots, m, B_j \notin I\}$, where the A_i and the B_j are fixed, but arbitrary, elements of X, and $n, m \geq 0$. Furthermore, the subbasic open sets can be described similarly on taking n and m to be at most 1 in the set $\mathcal{G}(A_1, \ldots, A_n; B_1, \ldots, B_m)$.

Finally, we close this section by noting that a natural question to consider is that of the continuity of the T_P operator relative to the topology Q. However, as already noted, we defer a discussion of this matter until Chapter 5, see Theorem 5.4.11, since we treat this question in more generality there in a context within which it naturally arises; in particular, we provide necessary and sufficient conditions for the continuity of T_P in Q to hold. Some results are also known which ensure discontinuity of T_P, see [Seda, 1995], for example, and we pause briefly to consider an interesting example of this.

3.3.11 Example Consider the program P consisting of the single clause $p \leftarrow \neg q(X)$, whose underlying first-order language $\mathcal{L}$ is assumed to contain a constant symbol o, a function symbol s, and predicate symbols r and t in addition to the symbols present in P. For each binary sequence $a = (a_n)_{n \in \mathbb{N}}$ (of 0s and 1s), we form the set $A_a = \{A_1, A_2, A_3, ...\}$, where $A_i = r(s^i(o))$ if $a_i = 0$ and $A_i = t(s^i(o))$ if $a_i = 1$. Finally, let $K_n = \{q(0), q(s(0)), ..., q(s^n(0))\}$ for each $n \in \mathbb{N}$.

Then for each binary sequence a, the sequence of interpretations $I_n = A_a \cup K_n$ converges in Q to the interpretation $I_a = A_a \cup \{q(s^n(o)) \mid n \in \mathbb{N}\}$ by Theorem 3.3.4. On the other hand, $T_P(I_n) = \{p\}$, whereas $T_P(I_a) = \emptyset$. Hence, $T_P(I_n)$ does not converge to $T_P(I_a)$ in Q, and so T_P is discontinuous at I_a.

Since we have uncountably many binary sequences a, T_P has uncountably many points of discontinuity in Q.

3.4 Operators on Spaces of Valuations Revisited

Finally, we want to briefly return to the operators defined on $I(X, \mathcal{T})$, which were discussed in Section 1.3.4, namely, the operators $\neg$, $\vee$, and $\wedge$. We have already noted in Section 1.3.4 that $\neg$ is not order continuous and, hence, not Scott continuous relative to the orderings $\leq_t$, in which $\mathbf{f} \leq_t \mathbf{t}$. It is, however, Scott continuous in the orderings $\leq_k$, as we now see. Of course, one can similarly deal with other connectives such as $\rightarrow$ and $\leftrightarrow$ in the same way. However, as we have seen earlier, these are usually made to depend on the three connectives we have already considered and therefore need not be pursued further.

Our objective here is to examine the continuity of the operators $\neg$, $\vee$, and $\wedge$ relative to the Scott and Cantor topologies, and we first deal with the Scott topology. Again, we concentrate on the truth set $\mathcal{FOUR}$ for precisely the same reasons as stated in Section 1.3.4.

3.4.1 Theorem Let $\mathcal{T}$ denote Belnap's logic $\mathcal{FOUR}$. Then the following statements hold.

(a) The negation operator $\neg : I(X, \mathcal{T}) \rightarrow I(X, \mathcal{T})$ is continuous in the Scott topology relative to the knowledge ordering $\sqsubseteq_k$, but not relative to the truth ordering $\sqsubseteq_t$. The same statement is true in the case of Kleene's strong three-valued logic.

(b) Take $\leq$ to be either $\leq_k$ or $\leq_t$ on the logic $\mathcal{FOUR}$. Form the domain $I(X, \mathcal{T})$ with the corresponding pointwise order $\sqsubseteq$ and the corresponding product domain $I(X, \mathcal{T}) \times I(X, \mathcal{T})$. Then both $\vee$ and $\wedge$ are Scott continuous as mappings from $I(X, \mathcal{T}) \times I(X, \mathcal{T})$ to $I(X, \mathcal{T})$. The same statements are true in the case of classical two-valued logic (where the ordering has to be $\leq_t$) and Kleene's strong three-valued logic.

Proof: For (a), the statements concerning the truth ordering $\sqsubseteq_t$ have already been established. To deal with $\sqsubseteq_k$, we use the criteria for convergence presented in Theorem 3.2.6. Let (v_i) be a net converging in the Scott topology to v in $I(X, \mathcal{T})$. Suppose that $x \in (\neg v)_\mathbf{t}$. Then $(\neg v)(x) = \mathbf{t}$, and hence $x \in v_\mathbf{f}$. Since $v_i \to v$, we have that eventually $x \in v_{i_\mathbf{f}} \cup v_{i_\mathbf{b}}$, that is, eventually $v_i(x) = \mathbf{f}$ or $v_i(x) = \mathbf{b}$. But then eventually $\neg v_i(x) = \mathbf{t}$ or $\neg v_i(x) = \mathbf{b}$, and so eventually $x \in (\neg v_i)_\mathbf{t} \cup (\neg v_i)_\mathbf{b}$. The other cases are handled similarly. Thus, the net $(\neg v_i)$ converges to $\neg v$ in the Scott topology, as required.

For (b), we establish the result stated concerning $\vee$, noting that the proof for $\wedge$ is entirely similar. Now, as is well-known, it suffices to show continuity in each argument[15] of $\vee$, and, by commutativity, it in fact suffices to show continuity in one argument, the first, say. So, fix $v \in I(X, \mathcal{T})$, and suppose that $u_i \to u$ in the Scott topology on $I(X, \mathcal{T})$. Let $x \in X$ be arbitrary. Then $(u \vee v)(x) = u(x) \vee v(x)$. Since $u_i \to u$, we have eventually that $u(x) \leq u_i(x)$ by Theorem 3.2.6. Therefore, by Proposition 1.3.7, we have eventually that $u(x) \vee v(x) \leq u_i(x) \vee v(x)$, and this suffices, by Theorem 3.2.6, to show that $u_i \vee v \to u \vee v$, as required. ∎

We now turn our attention to these same operators in relation to the topology Q. Indeed, we close this chapter with the following result.

3.4.2 Theorem Let $\mathcal{T}$ denote Belnap's logic $\mathcal{FOUR}$. Then the following statements hold.

(a) The negation operator $\neg : I(X, \mathcal{T}) \to I(X, \mathcal{T})$ is continuous in the topology Q. Hence, it is continuous in Q when $\mathcal{T}$ denotes either classical two-valued logic or Kleene's strong three-valued logic.

(b) Both $\vee$ and $\wedge$ are continuous as mappings from $I(X, \mathcal{T}) \times I(X, \mathcal{T})$ to $I(X, \mathcal{T})$, where $I(X, \mathcal{T}) \times I(X, \mathcal{T})$ is endowed with the product topology of Q with itself. Hence, the same result holds relative to either classical two-valued logic or Kleene's strong three-valued logic.

Proof: For (a), let (v_i) be a net converging to v in $I(X, \mathcal{T})$ relative to the topology Q, and let $x \in X$ be arbitrary. Then eventually $v_i(x) = v(x)$. Therefore, eventually $(\neg v_i)(x) = (\neg v)(x)$. Therefore, $\neg v_i \to \neg v$ in Q, and the result follows.

For (b), let $(u_i, v_i) \to (u, v)$ in the product topology. Then $u_i \to u$ in Q

---

[15] See Proposition 2.4 of [Stoltenberg-Hansen et al., 1994].

and $v_i \to v$ in Q. Let $x \in X$ be arbitrary. Then there exist i_1 and i_2 such that $u_i(x) = u(x)$ whenever $i \geq i_1$ and $v_i(x) = v(x)$ whenever $i \geq i_2$. By directedness, there is i_3 such that, for $i \geq i_3$, we have both $u_i(x) = u(x)$ and $v_i(x) = v(x)$. Therefore, whenever $i \geq i_3$, we have $u_i(x) \vee v_i(x) = u(x) \vee v(x)$ and $u_i(x) \wedge v_i(x) = u(x) \wedge v(x)$. Therefore, $u_i \vee v_i \to u \vee v$ and $u_i \wedge v_i \to u \wedge v$, as required. ∎

There are several interesting topics relating to topology and logic programming semantics which are examined in the literature on the subject, but are not pursued here. These include, among other things, the consistency of program completions and of the union of program completions, see [Batarekh and Subrahmanian, 1989b]; compactness of spaces of models for a program; and continuity in Q of T_P for a normal program P at the point $T_P \downarrow \omega$ and the coincidence of $T_P \downarrow \omega$ with the greatest fixed point of T_P. For further discussion of all these points and others, see [Seda, 1995].

In conclusion, we note that order is a very satisfactory foundation for the semantics of procedural and imperative programming languages as exemplified through the denotational semantics approach to programming language theory. On the other hand, order is not an entirely satisfactory foundation for the semantics of logic programming languages in the presence of negation, and yet negation is a natural part of most logics. However, our treatment here and in later chapters shows that one can consider convergence instead as a foundation for a unified approach by which one can recover conventional order-theoretic semantics and at the same time display some important standard models in logic programming languages as limits of a sequence of iterates. In addition, convergence conditions involving nets arise very naturally in a number of areas within theoretical computer science and are simple to state and to comprehend. Moreover, nets usually give short and technically simple proofs, as demonstrated in several places in this chapter.

Chapter 4

Fixed-Point Theory for Generalized Metric Spaces

In Chapters 1 and 2, we gave ample evidence of the fundamental role played by the Kleene and Knaster-Tarski fixed-point theorems, Theorems 1.1.9 and 1.1.10, in logic programming semantics. Moreover, we have also seen that the operator T_P need not be monotonic for normal programs and, hence, that the theorems just cited are not generally applicable to T_P in this case. It is, therefore, of interest to consider possible alternatives to Theorems 1.1.9 and 1.1.10, and in this chapter we discuss a number of such fixed-point theorems and some related results which will be put to use later on.

Almost always, alternatives to the theorems of Kleene and Knaster-Tarski employ distance functions in their formulations and in their applications.[1] Logic programming is no exception to this rule, and we will consider a number of ways in which distance functions can be naturally introduced into this subject along with appropriate fixed-point theorems. Part of this process consists of working with quite general distance functions, relaxing in one way or another the standard axioms for a metric, and establishing corresponding fixed-point theorems analogous to the Banach contraction mapping theorem. Nevertheless, the applications we make later and the examples we discuss show that these general distance functions do quite easily and naturally arise in logic programming, although applications will be deferred until Chapter 5. Indeed, Sections 4.1 to 4.7 in this chapter deal with the different generalized metrics and corresponding fixed-point theorems we develop for single-valued mappings, while in Section 4.8 we examine the interconnections between the spaces underlying the various distance functions we study and also discuss a number of relevant examples. In Sections 4.9 to 4.14, we consider the corresponding results for multivalued mappings. Hence, in summary, this chapter is a self-contained account of the pure metric fixed-point theory appropriate to logic programming and also provides the tools needed for the application of distance functions in developing a unified approach to the fixed-point theory of very general and significant classes of logic programs in Chapters 5 and 6. In addition, the methods and results discussed in this chapter have potential applications to a wider spectrum of topics in computer science than just simply logic programming, but none of these will be pursued here.

---

[1] We refer again to [Kirk and Sims, 2001] as an excellent source of information on fixed-point theory in general.

Remark We refer the reader to the paper [Seda and Hitzler, 2010] for a discussion of many recent and fairly recent applications of distance functions to various parts of computer science. The areas in question range from conventional semantics ([Arnold and Nivat, 1980b, Arnold and Nivat, 1980a, Bukatin and Scott, 1997, O'Neill, 1996, Smyth, 1992]) and the study of concurrency ([de Bakker and de Vink, 1996, Reed et al., 1991]) to domain theory ([Künzi et al., 2006, Krötzsch, 2006, Martin, 2000, Waszkiewicz, 2003]) to information theory, cognitive processes and unique fingerprinting of time series ([Albeverio et al., 1999, Khrennikov, 1998, Khrennikov, 2004, Murtagh, 2004, Murtagh, 2005]) to abstract interpretation ([Crazzolara, 1997]) to complexity and and its connections with semantics ([Castro-Company et al., 2007, Romaguera and Schellekens, 2003, Rodríguez-López et al., 2008]), to neural-symbolic integration ([Bader et al., 2006, Hitzler et al., 2004, Seda, 2006]), to measuring the distance between programs in software engineering ([Bukatin, 2002, Seda and Lane, 2003]), through to bioinformatics and the properties of p-adic numbers of DNA sequences and degeneracy of genetic codes ([Dragovich and Dragovich, 2006, Khrennikov and Kozyrev, 2007]), and beyond.

4.1   Distance Functions in General

At a completely general level, a *distance function* d defined on a set X is simply a mapping $d : X \times X \to A$, where A is some suitable set of values (a *distance set or value set*), and the distance between x and y is taken to be the element $d(x, y)$ of A. Second, and again at a completely general level, the related notion of closeness can be defined by assigning to each element x of a set X a family $\mathcal{U}_x$ of subsets U of X; then y can be thought of as *close to* x if y belongs to some element U of $\mathcal{U}_x$. These notions are somewhat dual to each other, even synonymous, as we shall see shortly. However, the present level of generality is too high to be useful, and therefore we will impose a variety of restrictions as we proceed.[2] In fact, it is our intention to begin by briefly considering a uniform, conceptual framework, namely, *continuity spaces*,[3] within which all the particular distance functions we encounter can be described. Indeed, this framework is such that the notions of distance function and closeness are actually dual to each other when the set $\mathcal{U}_x$ is taken, for each $x \in X$, to be the neighbourhood base of x, as defined in the Appendix,

---

[2][Waszkiewicz, 2002] contains a very general study of spaces based on the notion of distance function.

[3]Our treatment of continuity spaces follows [Kopperman, 1988] closely. We refer also to [Flagg and Kopperman, 1997] and related papers, where the notion of continuity space has been developed further in a number of directions, and to [Künzi, 2001] for further background.

see Theorem A.2.5 in particular. This last observation connects topology and distance in full generality, and this setting, while not the most general to have been found to be of interest in computer science, as already noted in Chapter 3, is sufficient for our purposes here. In fact, we shall make no actual use of continuity spaces and present them purely as a framework within which to work. However, continuity spaces do provide a smooth transition from the topology presented in Chapter 3 to the work of this chapter, and indeed they bridge the two chapters.

Before turning to the details of continuity spaces in general, it will be worth considering first the familiar case of distance functions d which are metrics, see Definition 4.2.1 and Remark 4.2.2. In this case, the usual value set A of d is the interval $[0, \infty)$. Given some real number $\varepsilon > 0$, one defines the *(open) ball* $N_\varepsilon(x)$ *of radius* ε *about a point* $x \in X$ by setting $N_\varepsilon(x) = \{y \in X \mid d(x, y) < \varepsilon\}$. A subset O of X is then declared to be *open* if, for each $x \in X$, there is some $\varepsilon > 0$ such that $N_\varepsilon(x) \subseteq O$. It is easy to see that the collection of such open sets O forms a topology on X. Notice that in defining "open" sets O here, one can equivalently require $B_{\varepsilon'}(x) \subseteq O$ for suitable $\varepsilon' > 0$, where $B_\varepsilon(x) = \{y \in X \mid d(x, y) \leq \varepsilon\}$ denotes the *(closed) ball of radius* ε *about a point* $x \in X$.

However, it is not true that every topology on X arises thus via a metric d, and, for example, this statement applies to the Scott topology since this topology in not even T_1 in general, see Proposition A.6.5, whereas every metrizable topology is Hausdorff. Nevertheless, every topology can be generated by means of a suitable distance function, as already noted, and we next consider briefly the details of one way of establishing this claim, beginning with several definitions.

4.1.1 Definition A *semigroup* is a set A together with an (additive) associative binary operation $+ : A \times A \to A$. If $+$ is also commutative, then the semigroup is called *commutative* or *Abelian*. A semigroup A is called a *semigroup with identity* if there exists an element $0 \in A$, called the *identity*, such that $0 + a = a + 0 = a$ for all $a \in A$. We note that an (additive) Abelian semigroup with identity is also called a *commutative monoid* or *Abelian monoid*.

By an *ordered semigroup with identity* we mean a semigroup A with 0, say, on which there is defined an ordering $\leq$ satisfying: $0 \leq a$ for all $a \in A$, and if $a_1 \leq a_2$ and $a_1' \leq a_2'$, then $a_1 + a_1' \leq a_2 + a_2'$ for all $a_1, a_1', a_2, a_2' \in A$.

4.1.2 Definition A *value semigroup* A is an additive Abelian semigroup with identity 0 and *absorbing element* ∞,[4] where $\infty \neq 0$, satisfying the following axioms.

(1) For all $a, b \in A$, if $a + x = b$ and $b + y = a$ for some $x, y \in A$, then $a = b$. (Note that, using this property, we can define a partial order $\leq$ on A by setting $a \leq b$ if and only if $b = a + x$ for some $x \in A$; we call $\leq$ the *partial*

---

[4] An element satisfying $a + \infty = \infty + a = \infty$ for all $a \in A$.

order induced on A by the operation $+$. It is immediate that A equipped with this partial order is an ordered semigroup, as just defined.)

(2) For each $a \in A$, there is a unique $b \, (= \frac{a}{2}) \in A$ such that $b + b = a$.

(3) For all $a, b \in A$, the infimum $a \wedge b$ of a and b exists in A relative to the partial order $\leq$ defined in (1).

(4) For all $a, b, c \in A$, $(a \wedge b) + c = (a + c) \wedge (b + c)$.

Note that if $\{(A_i, +_i, 0_i, \infty_i) \mid i \in \mathcal{I}\}$ is a family of value semigroups, then so is their product $(A, +, 0, \infty)$, where $+, 0$, and ∞ are defined coordinatewise.

4.1.3 Definition A set P of *positives* in a value semigroup A is a subset P of A satisfying the following axioms.

(1) If $r, s \in P$, then $r \wedge s \in P$.

(2) If $r \in P$ and $r \leq a$, then $a \in P$.

(3) If $r \in P$, then $\frac{r}{2} \in P$.

(4) If $a \leq b + r$ for all $r \in P$, then $a \leq b$.

4.1.4 Example The set $\mathcal{R}$ of extended real numbers $[0, \infty]$ together with addition forms a value semigroup, the set $(0, \infty]$ is a set of positives for this example, and the induced partial order $\leq$ is the usual one on $\mathcal{R}$.

4.1.5 Definition A *continuity space* is a quadruple $\mathcal{X} = (X, d, A, P)$, where X is a non-empty set, A is a value semigroup, P is a set of positives in A, and $d : X \times X \to A$ is a function, called a *continuity function*, satisfying the following axioms.

(1) For all $x \in X$, $d(x, x) = 0$.

(2) For all $x, y, z \in X$, $d(x, z) \leq d(x, y) + d(y, z)$.

Finally, we define the topology generated by a continuity space.

4.1.6 Definition Suppose that $\mathcal{X} = (X, d, A, P)$ is a continuity space. Let $x \in X$, and let $b \in P$. Then $B_b(x) = \{y \in X \mid d(x, y) \leq b\}$ is called the *ball* of radius b about x. The *topology* $\mathcal{T}(\mathcal{X})$ *generated by* $\mathcal{X}$ consists of all those subsets O of X satisfying the property: if $x \in O$, then $B_b(x) \subseteq O$ for some $b \in P$.

The main result concerning continuity spaces is the following theorem due to R. Kopperman [Kopperman, 1988].

4.1.7 Theorem Given a continuity space $\mathcal{X} = (X, d, A, P)$, the collection $\mathcal{T}(\mathcal{X})$ of subsets of X is a topology on X. Conversely, given a topology $\mathcal{T}$ on a set X, there is a continuity space $\mathcal{X} = (X, d, A, P)$ with the property that $\mathcal{T} = \mathcal{T}(\mathcal{X})$.

Given a topology $\mathcal{T}$ on X, it is worth noting that the continuity space $\mathcal{X} = (X, d, A, P)$ with the property that $\mathcal{T} = \mathcal{T}(\mathcal{X})$ used in the proof of Theorem 4.1.7 is obtained, see [Kopperman, 1988], by taking A to be the product of $\mathcal{T}$ copies of $\mathcal{R}$ and P to be the product of $\mathcal{T}$ copies of $(0, \infty]$. The continuity function d is defined coordinatewise by $d(x, y)(S) = d_S(x, y)$ for each $S \in \mathcal{T}$, where $d_S(x, y) = 0$ if ($x \in S$ implies $y \in S$), and $d_S(x, y) = q$ otherwise, where q is an element of $(0, \infty]$ fixed once and for all.

4.2 Metrics and Their Generalizations

As already noted, it is our intention, with applications in mind, to choose suitable value sets for distance functions and to impose various useful conditions on the distance functions themselves. We begin by considering the most familiar of these, where the value set is taken to be the set of non-negative real numbers.

4.2.1 Definition Let X be a set, and let $\varrho : X \times X \to \mathbb{R}_0^+$ be a distance function, where $\mathbb{R}_0^+$ denotes the set of non-negative real numbers. We consider the following conditions on ϱ.

(M1) For all $x \in X$, $\varrho(x, x) = 0$.

(M2) For all $x, y \in X$, if $\varrho(x, y) = \varrho(y, x) = 0$, then $x = y$.

(M3) For all $x, y \in X$, $\varrho(x, y) = \varrho(y, x)$.

(M4) For all $x, y, z \in X$, $\varrho(x, y) \leq \varrho(x, z) + \varrho(z, y)$.

(M5) For all $x, y, z \in X$, $\varrho(x, y) \leq \max\{\varrho(x, z), \varrho(z, y)\}$.

If ϱ satisfies conditions (M1) to (M4), it is called a *metric* and is called an *ultrametric* if it also satisfies (M5).[5] If it satisfies conditions (M1), (M3), and (M4), it is called a *pseudometric*. If it satisfies (M2), (M3), and (M4), we will call it a *dislocated metric* (or simply a *d-metric*). Finally, if it satisfies conditions (M1), (M2), and (M4), it is called a *quasimetric*. Condition (M4) is usually

---

[5]For elementary properties and notions relating to conventional metrics, such as *Cauchy sequences* and *completeness*, we refer to [Willard, 1970]; these notions will, in any case, be defined later in this chapter in greater generality.

TABLE 4.1: Generalized metrics: Definition 4.2.1.

notion satisfies	(M1)	(M2)	(M3)	(M4)	(M5)
metric	×	×	×	×	
ultrametric	×	×	×	(×)	×
pseudometric	×		×	×	
pseudo-ultrametric	×		×	(×)	×
quasimetric	×	×		×	
quasi-ultrametric	×	×		(×)	×
dislocated metric		×	×	×	
dislocated ultrametric		×	×	(×)	×
dislocated quasimetric		×		×	
dislocated quasi-ultrametric		×		(×)	×
quasi-pseudometric	×			×	
quasi-pseudo-ultrametric	×			(×)	×

called the *triangle inequality*. Furthermore, if a (pseudo, quasi, d-)metric satisfies the *strong triangle inequality* (M5), then it is called a (pseudo-, quasi-, d-)*ultrametric*. These notions are displayed in Table 4.1, where the symbol × indicates that the respective condition is satisfied and the symbol (×) indicates that the respective condition is automatically satisfied; for example, since the condition (M5) implies (M4), any distance function satisfying (M5) automatically satisfies (M4).

Note that one can take the codomain of ϱ to be $[0, \infty]$ in Definition 4.2.1 rather than $\mathbb{R}_0^+$. We note then that all the distance functions just considered in Definition 4.2.1, apart from dislocated metrics, are continuity functions, as is easily checked. However, even dislocated metrics give rise to topologies, and essentially the same correspondence between them and topologies holds between continuity spaces and topologies, as we see later.[6] Indeed, each d-metric gives rise to its associated metric, see Definition 4.8.9, and each d-generalized ultrametric gives rise to its associated generalized ultrametric, see Definition 4.8.19.

4.2.2 Remark As far as notation for distance functions is concerned, we will, generally, although not rigidly, use d and occasionally λ to denote metrics, ultrametrics, pseudometrics, and quasimetrics, all as just defined; we will use ϱ and occasionally ρ to denote d-metrics, to denote generalized ultrametrics as introduced in Section 4.3, and to denote the extensions of these notions studied in Section 4.4 and beyond. This convention will be employed both in the context of single-valued mappings and in the context of multivalued

---

[6]See [Hitzler and Seda, 2000] for full details of the topology determined by a d-metric.

mappings and is intended to help the reader to remember the nature of the distance function under consideration at any given time. The one exception to this occurs in Section 4.8.4, where we encounter two generalized ultrametrics the second of which is derived from the first. In this instance, we retain the notation ϱ for the first of these generalized ultrametrics and d for the second; essentially, the same comment applies to Section 5.1, where the results of Section 4.8.4 are applied.

The most widely used of the distance functions just defined is that of metric, and to that extent we regard metric distance functions as basic and think of departures from them as variants.

The following well-known theorem, usually referred to as the Banach contraction mapping theorem, is fundamental in many areas of mathematics. It is prototypical of a large number of extensions and refinements, including all those we discuss in this chapter. We give the well-known proof in detail for later reference.

4.2.3 Theorem (Banach) Let (X, d) be a complete metric space, let $0 \leq \lambda < 1$, and let $f : X \to X$ be a *contraction* with *contractivity factor* λ, that is, f is a (single-valued) function satisfying $d(f(x), f(y)) \leq \lambda d(x, y)$ for all $x, y \in X$ with $x \neq y$. Then f has a unique fixed point, which can be obtained as the limit of the sequence $(f^n(y))$ for any $y \in X$.

Proof: The proof consists of the following three steps. It is shown that (1) $(f^n(y))_{n \geq 0}$ is a Cauchy sequence for all $y \in X$, (2) the limit of this Cauchy sequence is a fixed point of f, and (3) this fixed point is unique.

(1) Let $m, n \in \mathbb{N}$, suppose that $m > n$, and put $k = m - n$. Then we obtain

$$d\left(f^n(y), f^m(y)\right) = d\left(f^n(y), f^n\left(f^k(y)\right)\right) \leq \lambda^n d\left(y, f^k(y)\right)$$

$$\leq \lambda^n \sum_{i=0}^{k-1} d\left(f^i(y), f^{i+1}(y)\right) \leq \lambda^n \sum_{i=0}^{k-1} \lambda^i d(y, f(y))$$

$$= \lambda^n d(y, f(y)) \sum_{i=0}^{k-1} \lambda^i \leq \lambda^n d(y, f(y)) \sum_{i=0}^{\infty} \lambda^i$$

$$= \frac{\lambda^n}{1 - \lambda} d(y, f(y)).$$

The latter term converges to 0 as $n \to \infty$, and this establishes (1).

(2) Now X is complete, and so $(f^n(y))_{n \geq 0}$ has a limit x. Thus, we obtain

$$f(x) = f(\lim f^n(y)) = \lim f^{n+1}(y) = x$$

by continuity of f. Therefore, x is a fixed point of f.

(3) Assume now that z is also a fixed point of f. Then $d(x, z) = d(f(x), f(z)) \leq \lambda d(x, z)$. Since $\lambda < 1$, we obtain $d(x, z) = 0$, and hence, by (M2), we have $x = z$, as required. ∎

Notice that the condition $x \neq y$ is not actually needed in the statement of the previous result, but is included for the sake of consistency with what we want to say next, namely, that it is well-known[7] that the requirement $\lambda < 1$ cannot be relaxed in general. This can be seen by considering the function $f : \mathbb{R} \to \mathbb{R}$ defined by

$$f(x) = \begin{cases} x + \frac{1}{x} & \text{for } x \geq 1, \\ 2 & \text{otherwise.} \end{cases}$$

This function satisfies the condition $d(f(x), f(y)) < d(x, y)$ for all $x, y \in \mathbb{R}$ with $x \neq y$, where d is the usual metric on $\mathbb{R}$, but has no fixed point since $f(x) > x$ for all $x \in \mathbb{R}$. If X is compact, however, the requirement on λ can be relaxed.

4.2.4 Theorem Let (X, d) be a compact metric space, and let $f : X \to X$ be a function which is *strictly contracting*, that is, f satisfies $d(f(x), f(y)) < d(x, y)$ for all $x, y \in X$ with $x \neq y$. Then f has a unique fixed point.

Proof: The function $\overline{d}(x) = d(x, f(x))$ is continuous since f is continuous. It therefore achieves a minimum m on X. Assume $\overline{d}(x_0) = m > 0$. Then $\overline{d}(f(x_0)) = d(f(x_0), f(f(x_0))) < d(x_0, f(x_0)) = \overline{d}(x_0) = m$, which is a contradiction. Hence, $m = 0$, and so f has a fixed point.

   Assume x and y are fixed points of f and $x \neq y$. Then $d(x, y) = d(f(x), f(y)) < d(x, y)$, which is a contradiction. Therefore, the fixed point of f is unique. ∎

There is quite a lot of interest in establishing results which can be viewed in one way or another as converses of the Banach theorem.[8] The following is such a result. It was originally inspired by certain applications to logic programming, to be given in Chapters 5 and 6, of the results presented in this chapter.

4.2.5 Theorem Let (X, τ) be a T_1 topological space, and let $f : X \to X$ be a function which has a unique fixed point a and is such that, for each $x \in X$, the sequence $(f^n(x))$ converges to a in τ. Then there exists a function $d : X \times X \to \mathbb{R}$ such that (X, d) is a complete ultrametric space and such that for all $x, y \in X$ we have $d(f(x), f(y)) \leq \frac{1}{2}d(x, y)$.

Proof: The proof is divided into several steps, numbered consecutively.

   (1) Given $x \in X$, we define the set $T(x) \subseteq X$ to be the smallest subset of X which is closed under the following rules.

   (1.1) $x \in T(x)$.

---

[7]The results of Section 4.2 can be found in many places including [Kirk and Sims, 2001, Dugundji and Granas, 1982], for example.

   [8]A discussion of this question can be found in [Kirk and Sims, 2001] and its references and in [Istrăţescu, 1981].

(1.2) If $y \in T(x)$ and $f(y) \neq a$, then $f(y) \in T(x)$.

(1.3) If $y \in T(x)$ and $y \neq a$, then $f^{-1}(y) \subseteq T(x)$.

It is clear that the intersection of the family of all sets closed under these rules is itself closed under these rules, and hence $T(x)$ exists. Moreover, it is also clear that each of the sets $T(x)$ is non-empty. Now let $\mathcal{T} = \{T(x) \mid x \in X\}$, and observe the following facts.

(i) $T(a) = \{a\}$. To see this, we note that (1.1), (1.2), and (1.3) are all true relative to the set $\{a\}$. Therefore, by minimality, we have $T(a) = \{a\}$.

(ii) If $x \neq a$, then $a \notin T(x)$, and so $T(a) \cap T(x) = \emptyset$. Hence, either $T(a)$ and $T(x)$ are equal or they are disjoint. To see this, suppose $x \neq a$, and consider rule (1.3). Clearly, we cannot have $a \in f^{-1}(x)$; otherwise, $f(a) = x$, and hence $a = x$, which is a contradiction. Thus, rules (1.2) and (1.3) applied repeatedly and starting with x never place a in $T(x)$, and, by minimality, the process just described generates $T(x)$.

(iii) If $T(x) \neq T(a)$ and $T(y) \neq T(a)$, then either $T(x)$ and $T(y)$ are equal or they are disjoint. To see this, suppose $z \in T(x) \cap T(y)$. Then the rules (1.1), (1.2), and (1.3) under repeated application starting with z force $T(x) = T(y)$. Thus, the collection $\mathcal{T}$ is a partition of X.

(2) We next inductively define a mapping $l : \mathcal{T} \to \mathbb{Z} \cup \{\infty\}$ on each $T \in \mathcal{T}$.

(2.1) We set $l(a) = \infty$, and this defines l on $T = T(a)$. If $T \neq T(a)$, we choose an arbitrary $x \in T$ and set $l(x) = 0$ (of course, $x \neq a$) and proceed as follows.

(2.2) For each $y \in T$ with $f(y) \neq a$ and $l(y) = k$, let $l(f(y)) = k + 1$.

(2.3) For each $y \in T$ with $l(y) = k$, let $l(z) = k - 1$ for all $z \in f^{-1}(y)$.

We will henceforth assume that all this is done for every $T \in \mathcal{T}$ so that l is a function defined on all of X. It is clear that the mapping l is well-defined since (X, τ) is a T_1 space.[9] For, if there is a cycle in the sequence $f^n(x)$ of iterates for some $x \in X$, then we can arrange for some element y in this sequence to be frequently not in some neighbourhood of a, using the fact that X is T_1, which contradicts the convergence of the sequence $f^n(x)$ to a.

(3) Define a mapping $\iota : \mathbb{Z} \cup \{\infty\} \to \mathbb{R}$ by

$$\iota(k) = \begin{cases} 0 & \text{if } k = \infty, \\ 2^{-k} & \text{otherwise.} \end{cases}$$

Furthermore, define a mapping $\delta : X \times X \to \mathbb{R}$ by

$$\delta(x, y) = \max\{\iota(l(x)), \iota(l(y))\}$$

and a mapping $d : X \times X \to \mathbb{R}$ by

$$d(x, y) = \begin{cases} \delta(x, y) & \text{if } x \neq y, \\ 0 & \text{if } x = y. \end{cases}$$

---

[9]We can weaken the requirement of τ being T_1 by replacing it with the following condition: for every $y \in X$ there exists an open neighbourhood U of a with $y \notin U$.

(4) We show that (X, d) is an ultrametric space. (M1) Let $d(x, y) = 0$, and assume that $x \neq y$. Then we have $\delta(x, y) = d(x, y) = 0$. Therefore, we obtain $\max\{\iota(l(x)), \iota(l(y))\} = 0$, so $\iota(l(x)) = \iota(l(y)) = 0$. Hence, $l(x) = l(y) = \infty$ and $x = y = a$ by construction of l, which is a contradiction.

(M2) This is true by definition of d.

(M3) This is true by symmetry of δ and, hence, of d.

(M5) Let $x, y, z \in X$. Assume without loss of generality that $\iota(l(x)) < \iota(l(z))$ so that $d(x, z) = \iota(l(z))$. If $\iota(l(y)) \leq \iota(l(z))$, then $d(y, z) = \iota(l(z))$. If $\iota(l(y)) > \iota(l(z))$, then $d(y, z) = \iota(l(y)) > \iota(l(z))$. In both cases we get $d(y, z) \geq d(x, z)$, as required.

(5) (X, d) is complete as a metric space. In order to show this, let (x_n) be a Cauchy sequence in X. If (x_n) is eventually constant, then it converges trivially. So now assume that (x_n) is not eventually constant. We proceed to show that x_n converges to a in d, for which it suffices to show that $(\iota(l(x_n)))_{n \in \mathbb{N}}$ converges to 0. Let $\varepsilon > 0$. Then there exists $n_0 \in \mathbb{N}$ such that for all $m, n \geq n_0$ we have $d(x_m, x_n) < \varepsilon$. In particular, we have $d(x_m, x_{n_0}) < \varepsilon$ for all $m \geq n_0$, and, since (x_n) is not eventually constant, we thus obtain $\iota(l(x_{n_0})) < \varepsilon$ and also $\iota(l(x_m)) < \varepsilon$ for all $m \geq n_0$. Since ε was chosen arbitrarily, we see that $(\iota(l(x_n)))_{n \in \mathbb{N}}$ converges to 0.

(6) We note that for $f(x) \neq a$, we have $l(f(x)) = l(x) + 1$ by definition of l, and hence $\iota(l(f(x))) = \frac{1}{2}\iota(l(x))$.

(7) For all $x, y \in X$, we have that $d(f(x), f(y)) \leq \frac{1}{2}d(x, y)$. In order to establish this claim, let $x, y \in X$, and assume without loss of generality that $x \neq y$. Now let $d(x, y) = 2^{-k}$, say, so that $\max\{\iota(l(x)), \iota(l(y))\} = 2^{-k}$. Then $d(f(x), f(y)) = \max\{\iota(l(f(x))), \iota(l(f(y)))\} = \frac{1}{2}\max\{\iota(l(x)), \iota(l(y))\} = \frac{1}{2}d(x, y)$, as required. ∎

It should be noted that Theorem 4.2.5 is not a true converse of the Banach theorem in that we do not start out with a metrizable space and attempt to obtain a metric for it relative to which f is a contraction. Thus, Theorem 4.2.5 is quite different from those discussed, for example, in Section 3.6 of the text [Istrăţescu, 1981], in which a number of converses of the Banach theorem are considered. Even the result of Bessaga discussed there, which applies to an abstract set, is very different from ours in that we do not require all iterations of f to have a unique fixed point, but we do require topological convergence of the iterates of any point. Indeed, we can only make the following observations on the relationship between the original topology and the one created by the metric constructed in the proof of Theorem 4.2.5.

4.2.6 Proposition With the notation of the proof of Theorem 4.2.5, the following hold.

(a) Any $x \neq a$ is an isolated point with respect to d, that is, $\{x\}$ is open and closed in the topology generated by d.

(b) If (x_n) is a sequence in X which converges in d to some $x \neq a$, then the sequence (x_n) is eventually constant.

(c) The metric d does not in general generate τ, but the iterates $(f^n(x))$ of f converge to a both with respect to τ and with respect to d.

Proof: (a) Let $x \neq a$, and let $\iota(l(x)) = 2^{-k}$, say. Then, for any $y \in X$, we have $\delta(x, y) \geq 2^{-k}$, and hence, for each $y \neq x$, we have $d(x, y) \geq 2^{-k}$. Therefore, $\{y \in X \mid d(x, y) < 2^{-k}\} = \{x\}$, which is consequently open in d. Closedness is trivial.

(b) In order to see this, it suffices to show that $\{x\}$ is open with respect to d for any $x \neq a$, which is true by (i) in Step (1) of the proof of Theorem 4.2.5.

(c) Indeed, the topology τ is not in general metrizable. By the proof of the Banach contraction mapping theorem, $(f^n(x))$ converges to a with respect to d. Convergence with respect to τ follows from the hypothesis of Theorem 4.2.5. ∎

4.3 Generalized Ultrametrics

The first generalization of the standard notion of metric which we consider is actually obtained from Definition 4.2.1 by replacing the codomain of ϱ (the value set of ϱ), namely, the set $\mathbb{R}_0^+$ of non-negative real numbers, by an arbitrary partially ordered set rather than by relaxing any axioms. This leads to the notion of "generalized ultrametric" found in parts of algebra such as valuation theory and first applied to logic programming semantics by Prieß-Crampe and Ribenboim. Indeed, the main theorem of this section, Theorem 4.3.6, is due to Prieß-Crampe and Ribenboim.[10]

4.3.1 Definition Let X be a set, and let Γ be a partially ordered set with least element 0. We call (X, ϱ, Γ), or simply (X, ϱ), a *generalized ultrametric space (gum)* if $\varrho : X \times X \to \Gamma$ is a function such that the following statements hold for all $x, y, z \in X$ and all $\gamma \in \Gamma$.

(U1) $\varrho(x, x) = 0$.

(U2) If $\varrho(x, y) = 0$, then $x = y$.

(U3) $\varrho(x, y) = \varrho(y, x)$.

(U4) If $\varrho(x, z) \leq \gamma$ and $\varrho(z, y) \leq \gamma$, then $\varrho(x, y) \leq \gamma$.

If ϱ satisfies conditions (U2), (U3), and (U4), but not necessarily (U1), we call (X, ϱ) a *dislocated generalized ultrametric space* or simply a *d-gum space*,

---

[10]The material contained in Section 4.3 up to Theorem 4.3.6 can be found in the following three papers: [Prieß-Crampe and Ribenboim, 1993, Prieß-Crampe and Ribenboim, 2000a, Prieß-Crampe and Ribenboim, 2000c].

TABLE 4.2: (Dislocated) generalized ultrametrics: Definition 4.3.1.

notion satisfies	(U1)	(U2)	(U3)	(U4)
generalized ultrametric (gum)	×	×	×	×
dislocated generalized ultrametric (d-gum)		×	×	×

see Table 4.2. Condition (U4) will be called the *strong triangle inequality for gums*. We note that any gum is a d-gum.

4.3.2 Remark It is clear that every ultrametric space is also a generalized ultrametric space. However, at the level of generality of the previous definition, the function ϱ this time is not a continuity function, that is, Γ need not be a value semigroup. However, in the applications we will actually consider, Γ will be a value semigroup, and ϱ will indeed be a continuity function, and we consider this point next.

Let $\gamma > 0$ denote an arbitrary ordinal, and denote by Γ_γ the set $\{2^{-\alpha} \mid \alpha < \gamma\}$ of symbols $2^{-\alpha}$. Then Γ_γ is totally ordered by $2^{-\alpha} < 2^{-\beta}$ if and only if $\beta < \alpha$. Notice that Γ_γ is really nothing other than γ endowed with the dual of the usual ordering on ordinals, but it is convenient to use the symbols $2^{-\alpha}$ rather than the symbols α to denote typical elements, as will be seen later in Section 4.8.2 and beyond. Notice also, as is commonly done, that we view an ordinal γ as the set of all ordinals n such that $n \in \gamma$, that is, as the set of ordinals n such that $n < \gamma$. Finally, we define the binary operation $+$ on Γ_γ by

$$2^{-\alpha} + 2^{-\beta} = \max\{2^{-\alpha}, 2^{-\beta}\}$$

noting that 2^{-0} is an absorbing element for this operation. In particular, applying this construction to the ordinal $\gamma + 1$, we note that $2^{-\gamma}$ is both the bottom element of $\Gamma_{\gamma+1}$ and the identity element for the operation $+$ defined on $\Gamma_{\gamma+1}$. Furthermore, $2^{-\gamma} \neq 2^{-0}$ since $\gamma > 0$, where 0 denotes the finite limit ordinal zero, and we note that we will sometimes also use 0 to denote $2^{-\gamma}$ where this does not cause confusion. Then $\Gamma_{\gamma+1}$ is a value semigroup in which $\frac{a}{2} = a$, where $a = 2^{-\alpha}$ denotes a typical element of $\Gamma_{\gamma+1}$, and moreover, the partial order induced on $\Gamma_{\gamma+1}$ by $+$ coincides with that already defined. Furthermore, the set $\{2^{-\alpha} \mid \alpha < \gamma\}$ is a set of positives in $\Gamma_{\gamma+1}$. It is the case $\Gamma = \Gamma_{\gamma+1}$ which is of most interest to us. Therefore, in these cases of most interest, (X, ϱ, Γ) is a continuity space. In fact, we shall take these points further later on in this chapter by turning a domain $(D, \sqsubseteq)$ into a generalized ultrametric space, see Sections 4.8.2 and 4.8.3 (and also Section 5.1.1).

The following definitions prepare the way for the main result of this section, namely, Theorem 4.3.6, which provides the main fixed-point theorem applicable to gums. We note that the requisite form of completeness here is that of spherical completeness, defined next, and that the next two definitions and the following lemma apply to gums as a special case of d-gums.

4.3.3 Definition Let (X, ϱ, Γ) be a d-gum space. For $0 \neq \gamma \in \Gamma$ and $x \in X$, the set $B_\gamma(x) = \{y \in X \mid \varrho(x, y) \leq \gamma\}$ is called a $(\gamma\text{-})ball$ in X with *centre* or *midpoint* x. A d-gum space is called *spherically complete* if, for any chain $\mathcal{C}$, with respect to set-inclusion, of non-empty balls in X we have $\bigcap \mathcal{C} \neq \emptyset$.

The stipulation in the definition of spherical completeness that all balls be non-empty can be dropped when working in a gum rather than in a d-gum, since in the former case all balls are clearly non-empty.

4.3.4 Definition Let (X, ϱ, Γ) be a d-gum space, and let $f : X \to X$ be a function.

(1) f is called *non-expanding* if $\varrho(f(x), f(y)) \leq \varrho(x, y)$ for all $x, y \in X$.

(2) f is called *strictly contracting on orbits*[11] if $\varrho(f^2(x), f(x)) < \varrho(f(x), x)$ for every $x \in X$ with $x \neq f(x)$.

(3) f is called *strictly contracting* (on X) if $\varrho(f(x), f(y)) < \varrho(x, y)$ for all $x, y \in X$ with $x \neq y$.

We will need the following observations, which are well-known for ordinary ultrametric spaces.

4.3.5 Lemma Let (X, ϱ, Γ) be a d-gum space. For $\alpha, \beta \in \Gamma$ and $x, y \in X$, the following statements hold.

(a) If $\alpha \leq \beta$ and $B_\alpha(x) \cap B_\beta(y) \neq \emptyset$, then $B_\alpha(x) \subseteq B_\beta(y)$.

(b) If $B_\alpha(x) \cap B_\alpha(y) \neq \emptyset$, then $B_\alpha(x) = B_\alpha(y)$. In particular, each element of a ball is also its centre.

(c) $B_{\varrho(x,y)}(x) = B_{\varrho(x,y)}(y)$.

Proof: Let $a \in B_\alpha(x)$, and let $b \in B_\alpha(x) \cap B_\beta(y)$. Then $\varrho(a, x) \leq \alpha$ and $\varrho(b, x) \leq \alpha$; hence, $\varrho(a, b) \leq \alpha \leq \beta$. Since $\varrho(b, y) \leq \beta$, we have $\varrho(a, y) \leq \beta$ and, hence, $a \in B_\beta(y)$, and this proves the first statement. The second follows by symmetry and the third by replacing $\varrho(x, y)$ by α and applying (b). ∎

The following theorem is the analogue of the Banach contraction mapping theorem applicable to generalized ultrametrics.[12] It will be proved later by virtue of proving the more general Theorem 4.5.1.

---

[11] An *orbit* of f is a subset of X of the form $\{f^n(x) \mid n \in \mathbb{N}\}$ for some $x \in X$.

[12] Theorem 4.3.6 can be found in [Prieß-Crampe and Ribenboim, 2000c]. An earlier and less general version appeared in [Prieß-Crampe, 1990].

4.3.6 Theorem (Prieß-Crampe and Ribenboim) Let (X, ϱ, Γ) be a spherically complete generalized ultrametric space, and let $f : X \to X$ be non-expanding and strictly contracting on orbits. Then f has a fixed point. Moreover, if f is strictly contracting on X, then f has a unique fixed point.

Note that every compact ultrametric space is spherically complete by the finite intersection property. The converse is not true: let X be an infinite set, and let d be the ultrametric defined by setting $d(x, y) = 1$ if $x \neq y$ and taking $d(x, x) = 0$ for all $x \in X$. Then (X, d) is not compact but is spherically complete.

The relationship between spherical completeness and completeness is given by the next proposition.[13]

4.3.7 Proposition Let (X, d) be an ultrametric space. If X is spherically complete, then it is complete. The converse does not hold in general.

Proof: Assume that (X, d) is spherically complete and that (x_n) is a Cauchy sequence in (X, d). Then, for every $k \in \mathbb{N}$, there exists a least $n_k \in \mathbb{N}$ such that for all $n, m \geq n_k$ we have $d(x_n, x_m) \leq \frac{1}{k}$. We note that n_k increases with k. Now consider the set of balls $\mathcal{B} = \left\{ B_{\frac{1}{k}}(x_{n_k}) \mid k \in \mathbb{N} \right\}$. By (U4), $\mathcal{B}$ is a decreasing chain of balls and has non-empty intersection B by spherical completeness of (X, d). Let $a \in B$. Then it is easy to see that (x_n) converges to a. Hence, $B = \{a\}$ is a one-point set since limits in (X, d) are unique. Therefore, (X, d) is complete.

In order to show that the converse does not hold in general, define an ultrametric d on $\mathbb{N}$ as follows. For $n, m \in \mathbb{N}$, let $d(n, m) = 1 + 2^{-\min\{m,n\}}$ if $n \neq m$, and set $d(n, n) = 0$ for all $n \in \mathbb{N}$. The topology induced by d is the discrete topology on $\mathbb{N}$, and the Cauchy sequences with respect to d are exactly the sequences which are eventually constant; hence, $(\mathbb{N}, d)$ is complete. Now consider the chain of balls B_n of the form $\{m \in \mathbb{N} \mid d(m, n) \leq 1 + 2^{-n}\}$. Then we obtain $B_n = \{m \mid m \geq n\}$ for all $n \in \mathbb{N}$. Hence, $\bigcap B_n = \emptyset$. ∎

Note also that, with the notation from the second part of the proof, the successor function $n \mapsto n + 1$ is strictly contracting, but does not have a fixed point. By Proposition 4.3.7 and the remarks preceding it, we see that the notion of spherical completeness is strictly less general than completeness and is strictly more general than compactness.

Spherical completeness can also be characterized by means of transfinite sequences, and we consider this next.[14]

---

[13] Similar studies of this issue have been undertaken in [Prieß-Crampe, 1990] in the case of totally ordered distance sets. The topology of generalized ultrametric spaces is investigated in [Heckmanns, 1996].

[14] Here, we follow a line of thought developed in [Prieß-Crampe, 1990], only slightly changed (the original version was established under the assumption that the distance sets in question were linearly ordered) and with the proofs adapted to the more general setting.

4.3.8 Definition Let $(x_\delta)_{\delta<\eta}$ be a (possibly transfinite) sequence of elements of a gum (X, ϱ, Γ). Then (x_δ) is said to be *pseudo-convergent* if, for all $\alpha < \beta < \gamma < \eta$, we have $\varrho(x_\beta, x_\gamma) < \varrho(x_\alpha, x_\beta)$. The transfinite sequence $(\pi_\delta)_{\delta+1<\eta}$ with $\pi_\delta = \varrho(x_\delta, x_{\delta+1})$ is then strictly monotonic decreasing. If η is a limit ordinal, then any $x \in X$ with $\varrho(x, x_\delta) \leq \pi_\delta$ for all $\delta < \eta$ is called a *pseudo-limit* of the transfinite sequence $(x_\delta)_{\delta<\eta}$.

The space (X, ϱ, Γ) is called *trans-complete* if every pseudo-convergent transfinite sequence $(x_\delta)_{\delta<\eta}$, where η is a limit ordinal, has a pseudo-limit in X.

4.3.9 Proposition Suppose that x is a pseudo-limit of $(x_\delta)_{\delta<\eta}$, where η is a limit ordinal. Then the set of all pseudo-limits of (x_δ) is given by $\mathrm{Lim}(x_\delta) = \{z \in X \mid \varrho(x, z) < \pi_\delta \text{ for all } \delta < \eta\}$.

Proof: Let $z \in \mathrm{Lim}(x_\delta)$. Since $\varrho(z, x) < \pi_\delta$ and $\varrho(x, x_\delta) \leq \pi_\delta$, we obtain $\varrho(z, x_\delta) \leq \pi_\delta$ for all δ, and hence z is a pseudo-limit. Conversely, let z be a pseudo-limit of (x_δ). Since $\varrho(x, x_{\delta+1}), \varrho(z, x_{\delta+1}) \leq \pi_{\delta+1}$ for all $\delta < \eta$, we obtain $\varrho(x, z) \leq \pi_{\delta+1} < \pi_\delta$ for all $\delta < \eta$, as required. ■

4.3.10 Proposition A generalized ultrametric space is spherically complete if and only if it is trans-complete.

Proof: Let X be trans-complete, and let $\mathcal{B}$ be a decreasing chain of balls in X. Without loss of generality, assume that $\mathcal{B}$ does not have a minimal element and is, in fact, strictly decreasing. Then we can select a coinitial subchain $(B_\delta)_{\delta<\eta}$ of $\mathcal{B}$, where η is a limit ordinal, so that $(B_\delta)_{\delta<\eta}$ is a transfinite sequence of balls. Since this transfinite sequence is strictly decreasing, we know that for every δ there exists $x_\delta \in B_\delta \setminus B_{\delta+1}$, and the transfinite sequence $(x_\delta)_{\delta<\eta}$ is pseudo-convergent; hence, it has a pseudo-limit x. Since $\varrho(x, x_\delta) \leq \varrho(x_\delta, x_{\delta+1})$ and $x_\delta, x_{\delta+1} \in B_\delta$, we obtain $x \in B_\delta$ for all δ, and therefore, $x \in \bigcap \mathcal{B}$.

Conversely, let X be spherically complete, and let (x_δ) be pseudo-convergent. Let $\pi_\delta = \varrho(x_\delta, x_{\delta+1})$, and let $B_\delta = B_{\pi_\delta}(x_\delta)$. For $\alpha < \beta$, we have that $x_\beta \in B_\alpha \cap B_\beta$, and therefore (B_δ) is a decreasing chain of balls by Lemma 4.3.5. By spherical completeness, there is some $x \in \bigcap B_\delta$, and it is immediate that x is a pseudo-limit of (x_δ). ■

We close this section by considering briefly how pseudo-convergent sequences may be generated when the set Γ is linearly ordered. Thus, in what follows, let (X, ϱ, Γ) be a generalized ultrametric space in which Γ is a linearly ordered set.

4.3.11 Lemma Let $x, y, z \in X$ with $\varrho(x, y) < \varrho(y, z)$. Then $\varrho(x, z) = \varrho(y, z)$.

Proof: We have $\varrho(x, z) \leq \max\{\varrho(x, y), \varrho(y, z)\} \leq \varrho(y, z)$ on using the strong triangle inequality. Now assume $\varrho(y, z) \not\leq \varrho(x, z)$. Then, because Γ is linearly ordered, we have $\varrho(x, z) < \varrho(y, z)$, and by the strong triangle inequality again we obtain $\varrho(y, z) \leq \max\{\varrho(x, y), \varrho(x, z)\} < \varrho(y, z)$, which is impossible. ∎

4.3.12 Lemma Let $n \geq 2$, and suppose that $(x_1, x_2, \ldots, x_n)$ is an n-tuple of elements of X satisfying $\varrho(x_{i+1}, x_{i+2}) < \varrho(x_i, x_{i+1})$ for $i = 1, \ldots, n - 2$. Then $\varrho(x_1, x_n) = \varrho(x_1, x_2)$.

Proof: We show by induction on n that the identity $\varrho(x_1, x_2) = \varrho(x_1, x_n)$ holds. This is trivial for $n = 2$. So assume $n > 2$ and that the assertion holds for $n - 1$. Then $\varrho(x_1, x_2) = \varrho(x_1, x_{n-1})$, and consequently $\varrho(x_{n-1}, x_n) < \varrho(x_1, x_2) = \varrho(x_1, x_{n-1})$. So Lemma 4.3.11 applies to the points x_1, x_{n-1} and x_n and gives $\varrho(x_1, x_n) = \varrho(x_1, x_{n-1}) = \varrho(x_1, x_2)$, as required. ∎

We can now establish the following result.

4.3.13 Proposition Let (X, ϱ, Γ) be a generalized ultrametric space in which Γ is a linearly ordered set. Furthermore, let $f : X \to X$ be strictly contracting, let $x_0 \in X$, and let $x_i = f^i(x_0)$ for all $i < \omega$. Then the sequence $(x_i)_{i<\omega}$ is pseudo-convergent.

Proof: Let $\alpha < \beta < \gamma < \omega$, and note then that $(x_\alpha, x_{\alpha+1}, \ldots, x_\beta, \ldots, x_\gamma)$ satisfies the hypothesis of Lemma 4.3.12 because f is strictly contracting. So we obtain $\varrho(x_\alpha, x_\beta) = \varrho(x_\alpha, x_{\alpha+1})$ and $\varrho(x_\beta, x_\gamma) = \varrho(x_\beta, x_{\beta+1})$. Thus, $\varrho(x_\beta, x_\gamma) = \varrho(x_\beta, x_{\beta+1}) < \varrho(x_\alpha, x_{\alpha+1}) = \varrho(x_\alpha, x_\beta)$, as desired. ∎

4.4   Dislocated Metrics

Dislocated metrics were first studied by S.G. Matthews under the name of *metric domains* in the context of Kahn's dataflow model.[15] We proceed now with the definitions needed for stating the main theorem of Matthews, which, in fact, is the form of the Banach contraction mapping theorem applicable to these spaces. Thus, we will define the notions of convergence, Cauchy sequence, and completeness for dislocated metrics. As it turns out, these notions can be carried over directly from the corresponding conventional ones.

---

[15]The contents of Section 4.4, including Theorem 4.4.6, can be found in [Matthews, 1986]. Matthews and other authors have argued that the slightly less general notion of (*weak*) *partial metric* is more appropriate than that of dislocated metric from a domain-theoretic point of view. We refer the reader to [Matthews, 1994, Heckmann, 1999, Waszkiewicz, 2002] for an account of this, since we have no direct need of it, and indeed dislocated metrics are well-suited to our purposes.

4.4.1 Definition A sequence (x_n) in a d-metric space (X, ϱ) *converges with respect to ϱ or in ϱ* if there exists $x \in X$ such that $\varrho(x_n, x)$ converges to 0 as $n \to \infty$. In this case, x is called a *limit* of (x_n) *in* ϱ.

4.4.2 Proposition Limits in d-metric spaces are unique.

Proof: Let x and y be limits of the sequence (x_n) in a d-metric space (X, ϱ). By properties (M3) and (M4) of Definition 4.2.1, it follows that $\varrho(x, y) \leq \varrho(x_n, x) + \varrho(x_n, y) \to 0$ as $n \to \infty$. Hence, $\varrho(x, y) = 0$, and by property (M2) of Definition 4.2.1, we obtain $x = y$. ∎

4.4.3 Definition A sequence (x_n) in a d-metric space (X, ϱ) is called a *Cauchy sequence* if, for each $\varepsilon > 0$, there exists $n_0 \in \mathbb{N}$ such that for all $m, n \geq n_0$ we have $\varrho(x_m, x_n) < \varepsilon$.

4.4.4 Proposition Every convergent sequence in a d-metric space is a Cauchy sequence.

Proof: Let (x_n) be a sequence which converges to some x in a d-metric space (X, ϱ), and let $\varepsilon > 0$ be chosen arbitrarily. Then there exists $n_0 \in \mathbb{N}$ with $\varrho(x_n, x) < \frac{\varepsilon}{2}$ for all $n \geq n_0$. For $m, n \geq n_0$, we then obtain $\varrho(x_m, x_n) \leq \varrho(x_m, x) + \varrho(x, x_n) < 2 \cdot \frac{\varepsilon}{2} = \varepsilon$. Hence, (x_n) is a Cauchy sequence. ∎

4.4.5 Definition A d-metric space (X, ϱ) is called *complete* if every Cauchy sequence in X converges with respect to ϱ. Furthermore, a function $f : X \to X$ is called a *contraction* if there exists $0 \leq \lambda < 1$ such that $\varrho(f(x), f(y)) \leq \lambda \varrho(x, y)$ for all $x, y \in X$.

4.4.6 Theorem (Matthews' theorem) Let (X, ϱ) be a complete d-metric space, and let $f : X \to X$ be a contraction. Then f has a unique fixed point.

Proof: The proof follows the pattern of the proof of Theorem 4.2.3. Indeed, Parts (1) and (3) of that proof do not make use of condition (M1) and therefore can be carried over literally. Part (2), however, needs to be modified since we do not have a suitable notion of topological convergence available for dislocated metric spaces.[16] With the notation from the proof of Theorem 4.2.3, so that x denotes the limit of the Cauchy sequence $(f^n(y))$, we make the

---

[16]It is possible to carry over the complete proof of Theorem 4.2.3, but the constructions needed are rather involved. Details can be found in [Hitzler and Seda, 2000, Hitzler, 2001]; see also [Hitzler and Seda, 2003].

following calculations for all $n \in \mathbb{N}$:

$$\varrho(f(x), x) \leq \varrho(f(x), f^n(x)) + \varrho(f^n(x), x)$$
$$< \varrho(x, f^{n-1}(x)) + \varrho(f^n(x), x)$$
$$\leq \varrho(x, f^{n-1}(y)) + \varrho(f^{n-1}(y), f^{n-1}(x)) + \varrho(f^n(x), f^n(y))$$
$$+ \varrho(f^n(y), x)$$
$$\leq \varrho(x, f^{n-1}(y)) + \lambda^{n-1}\varrho(y, x) + \lambda^n\varrho(x, y) + \varrho(f^n(y), x).$$

Since all four terms in the last line converge to 0 as $n \to \infty$, we obtain $\varrho(f(x), x) = 0$, and therefore $f(x) = x$ by (M3) and (M2). ∎

4.5   Dislocated Generalized Ultrametrics

The following theorem gives a partial unification of Matthews' theorem, Theorem 4.4.6, and the Prieß-Crampe and Ribenboim theorem, Theorem 4.3.6.[17]

4.5.1 Theorem Let (X, ϱ, Γ) be a spherically complete d-gum, and let $f : X \to X$ be non-expanding and strictly contracting on orbits. Then f has a fixed point. If f is strictly contracting on X, then the fixed point is unique.

Proof: Assume that f has no fixed point. Then for all $x \in X$, we have $\varrho(x, f(x)) \neq 0$. We now define the set $\mathcal{B}$ by $\mathcal{B} = \{B_{\varrho(x,f(x))}(x) \mid x \in X\}$, and note that each ball in this set is non-empty. We also note that $B_{\varrho(x,f(x))}(x) = B_{\varrho(x,f(x))}(f(x))$ by Lemma 4.3.5. Now let $\mathcal{C}$ be a maximal chain in $\mathcal{B}$. Since X is spherically complete, there exists $z \in \bigcap \mathcal{C}$. We show that $B_{\varrho(z,f(z))}(z) \subseteq B_{\varrho(x,f(x))}$ for all $x \in X$ and, hence, by maximality, that $B_{\varrho(z,f(z))}(z)$ is the smallest ball in the chain. Let $B_{\varrho(x,f(x))}(x) \in \mathcal{C}$. Since $z \in B_{\varrho(x,f(x))}(x)$, and noting our earlier observation that $B_{\varrho(x,f(x))}(x) = B_{\varrho(x,f(x))}(f(x))$ for all x, we get $\varrho(z, x) \leq \varrho(x, f(x))$ and $\varrho(z, f(x)) \leq \varrho(x, f(x))$. By non-expansiveness of f, we get $\varrho(f(z), f(x)) \leq \varrho(z, x) \leq \varrho(x, f(x))$. It follows by (U4) that $\varrho(z, f(z)) \leq \varrho(x, f(x))$ and therefore by Lemma 4.3.5 that $B_{\varrho(z,f(z))}(z) \subseteq B_{\varrho(x,f(x))}(x)$ for all $x \in X$, since x was chosen arbitrarily. Now, since f is strictly contracting on orbits, $\varrho(f(z), f^2(z)) < \varrho(z, f(z))$, and therefore $z \notin B_{\varrho(f(z),f^2(z))}(f(z)) \subset B_{\varrho(z,f(z))}(f(z))$. By Lemma 4.3.5, this is equivalent to $B_{\varrho(f(z),f^2(z))}(f(z)) \subset B_{\varrho(z,f(z))}(z)$, which is a contradiction to the maximality of $\mathcal{C}$. So f has a fixed point.

---

[17]The proof of Theorem 4.4.6 given here is, in fact, identical to that of Theorem 4.3.6 from [Prieß-Crampe and Ribenboim, 1993].

Now let f be strictly contracting on X, and assume that x and y are two distinct fixed points of f. Then we get $\varrho(x,y) = \varrho(f(x), f(y)) < \varrho(x,y)$, which is impossible. So the fixed point of f is unique in this case. ∎

We next give an iterative proof of a special case of Theorem 4.5.1.

4.5.2 Theorem Let (X, ϱ, Γ) be a spherically complete, dislocated generalized ultrametric space with $\Gamma = \{2^{-\alpha} \mid \alpha \leq \gamma\}$ for some ordinal γ. We order Γ by $2^{-\alpha} < 2^{-\beta}$ if and only if $\beta < \alpha$, and denote $2^{-\gamma}$ by 0. Thus, Γ is the set $\Gamma_{\gamma+1}$ of Remark 4.3.2. If $f : X \to X$ is any strictly contracting function on X, then f has a unique fixed point.

Proof: Let $x \in X$. Then we have $f(x) \in f(X)$ and $\varrho(f(x), x) \leq 2^{-0}$, since 2^{-0} is the maximum possible distance between any two points in X. Now, $\varrho(f(f(x)), f(x)) \leq 2^{-1} \leq 2^{-0}$ since f is strictly contracting, and by (U4), it follows that $\varrho(f^2(x), x) \leq 2^{-0}$. By the same argument, we obtain $\varrho(f^3(x), f^2(x)) \leq 2^{-2} \leq 2^{-1}$, and therefore $\varrho(f^3(x), f(x)) \leq 2^{-1}$. In fact, an easy induction argument along these lines shows that $\varrho(f^{n+1}(x), f^m(x)) \leq 2^{-m}$ for $m \leq n$. Again by (U4), we obtain that the sequence of balls of the form $B_{2^{-n}}(f^n(x))$ is a descending chain (with respect to set-inclusion) if n is increasing and, therefore, has non-zero intersection B_ω since X is assumed to be spherically complete. We therefore conclude that there is $x_\omega \in B_\omega$ with $\varrho(x_\omega, f^n(x)) \leq 2^{-n}$ for each $n \in \mathbb{N}$.

Next, for each $n \in \mathbb{N}$, we now argue as follows. Since $\varrho(f(x_\omega), f^{n+1}(x)) < \varrho(x_\omega, f^n(x)) \leq 2^{-n}$ and also $\varrho(x_\omega, f^{n+1}(x)) \leq 2^{-(n+1)} \leq 2^{-n}$, we therefore obtain $\varrho(f(x_\omega), x_\omega) \leq 2^{-n}$. Since this is the case for all $n \in \mathbb{N}$, it follows that $\varrho(f(x_\omega), x_\omega) \leq 2^{-\omega}$.

It is straightforward to cast the above observations into a transfinite induction argument, and we obtain the following construction. Choose $x \in X$ arbitrarily. For each ordinal $\alpha \leq \gamma$, we define $f^\alpha(x)$ as follows. If α is a successor ordinal, then $f^\alpha(x) = f(f^{\alpha-1}(x))$, as usual. If α is a limit ordinal, then we choose $f^\alpha(x)$ as some x_α which has the property that $\varrho(x_\alpha, f^\beta(x)) \leq 2^{-\beta}$, noting that the existence of such an x_α is guaranteed by spherical completeness of X.

The resulting transfinite sequence $f^\alpha(x)$ has the property that, for all $\alpha \leq \gamma$, $\varrho(f^{\alpha+1}(x), f^\alpha(x)) \leq 2^{-\alpha}$. Consequently, $\varrho(f^{\gamma+1}(x), f^\gamma(x)) = 2^{-\gamma} = 0$, and therefore $f^\gamma(x)$ must be a fixed point of f.

Finally, $x_\gamma = f^\gamma(x)$ can be the only fixed point of f. To see this, suppose $y \neq x_\gamma$ is another fixed point of f. Then we obtain $\varrho(y, x_\gamma) = \varrho(f(y), f(x_\gamma)) < \varrho(y, x_\gamma)$, from the fact that f is strictly contracting, and this is impossible. ∎

4.6   Quasimetrics

Quasimetrics are a convenient way of reconciling metric and order structures, see Example 4.6.4. We give the relevant definitions in order to state and prove the Rutten-Smyth theorem,[18] which is the appropriate analogue of the Banach theorem for quasimetric spaces.

4.6.1 Definition A sequence (x_n) in a quasimetric space (X, d) is a (*forward*) *Cauchy sequence* if, for all $\varepsilon > 0$, there exists $n_0 \in \mathbb{N}$ such that for all $n \geq m \geq n_0$ we have $d(x_m, x_n) < \varepsilon$. A Cauchy sequence (x_n) *converges* to $x \in X$ if, for all $y \in X$, $d(x, y) = \lim_{n \to \infty} d(x_n, y)$. Finally, X is called *CS-complete* if every Cauchy sequence in X converges.

Note that limits of Cauchy sequences in quasimetric spaces are unique. Given a quasimetric space (X, d), d induces a partial order $\leq_d$ on X, called the *partial order induced by* d, by setting $x \leq_d y$ if and only if $d(x, y) = 0$. Furthermore, if (X, d) is a quasimetric space, then (X, d^*) is a metric space, where $d^*(x, y) = \max\{d(x, y), d(y, x)\}$, and d^* is called the *metric induced by* d. We call a quasimetric space (X, d) *totally bounded* if for every $\varepsilon > 0$ there exists a finite set $E \subseteq X$ such that for every $y \in X$ there is an $e \in E$ with $d^*(e, y) < \varepsilon$.

4.6.2 Definition Let X be a quasimetric space, and let $f : X \to X$ be a function.

(1) f is called *CS-continuous* if, for all Cauchy sequences (x_n) in X which converge to x, $(f(x_n))$ is a Cauchy sequence which converges to $f(x)$.

(2) f is called *non-expanding* if $d(f(x), f(y)) \leq d(x, y)$ for all $x, y \in X$.

(3) f is called *contractive* if there exists some c with $0 \leq c < 1$ such that $d(f(x), f(y)) \leq c \cdot d(x, y)$ for all $x, y \in X$.

Contractive mappings are not necessarily CS-continuous: consider the set $\mathbb{N} \cup \{\infty\}$ with the natural order and the distance function

$$
d(x, y) = \begin{cases} 0 & \text{if } x \leq y, \\ \frac{1}{2} & \text{if } x = 1 \text{ and } y = 0, \\ 1 & \text{otherwise.} \end{cases}
$$

Then the function f which maps any $n \in \mathbb{N}$ to 0 and ∞ to 1 is contractive, but not continuous since $\lim_{n \in \mathbb{N}} n = \infty$, whereas $\lim f(n) = 0 \neq 1 = f(\infty)$.

---

[18] We give Theorem 4.6.3 in the form in which it appears in [Rutten, 1996]; see also the paper [Rutten, 1995]. A more general version of this result was given in [Smyth, 1987] in the context of quasi-uniformities.

4.6.3 Theorem (Rutten-Smyth) Let (X, d) be a CS-complete quasimetric space, and let $f : X \to X$ be non-expanding.

(a) If f is CS-continuous and there exists $x \in X$ with $x \leq_d f(x)$, then f has a fixed point, and this fixed point is least above x with respect to $\leq_d$.

(b) If f is CS-continuous and contractive, then f has a unique fixed point.

Moreover, in both cases the fixed point can be obtained as the limit of the Cauchy sequence $(f^n(x))$, where in (a) x is the given point, and in (b) x can be chosen arbitrarily.

Proof: (a) For all $n, k \in \mathbb{N}$ and $k \geq 1$, we have $d(f^n(x), f^{n+1}(x)) \leq d(x, f(x)) = 0$ and $d(f^n(x), f^{n+k}(x)) \leq \sum_{i=0}^{k-1} d(f^{n+i}(x), f^{n+i+1}(x)) = 0$. Hence, $(f^n(x))$ is a Cauchy sequence and has a unique limit y, say. Since $f(y) = f(\lim f^n(x)) = \lim f(f^n(x)) = \lim f^n(x) = y$, y is a fixed point of f. Now let z be a fixed point of f with $x \leq_d z$. Then $d(y, z) = \lim d(f^n(x), z) = 0$, since $d(f^n(x), f^n(z)) \leq d(x, z) = 0$. Hence, $y \leq_d z$.

(b) The proof given for Theorem 4.2.3 does not depend on condition (M3) other than implicitly for deriving continuity of f from the fact that it is a contraction. Since CS-continuity is a hypothesis in statement (b), the proof of Theorem 4.2.3 can be carried over by simply replacing "Cauchy sequence" by "forward Cauchy sequence" and "continuous" by "CS-continuous", etc. ∎

4.6.4 Example Let $(X, \leq)$ be a partially ordered set. Define a function $d_\leq$ on $X \times X$ by

$$d_\leq(x, y) = \begin{cases} 0 & \text{if } x \leq y, \\ 1 & \text{otherwise.} \end{cases}$$

Then it is easily checked that $(X, d_\leq)$ is a quasi-ultrametric space; we call $d_\leq$ the *discrete quasimetric* on X. Note that $\leq_{d_\leq}$ and $\leq$ coincide for a given partial order $\leq$, and moreover (X, d) is totally bounded if and only if X is finite. By virtue of this definition and the definition of $\leq_d$ for a given quasimetric d, Part (a) of Theorem 4.6.3 generalizes Kleene's theorem, Theorem 1.1.9, and Part (b) of Theorem 4.6.3 generalizes the Banach contraction mapping theorem, Theorem 4.2.3.[19]

4.6.5 Example Note that it is easy to see that a sequence (I_n) in $I_{P,2}$ is forward Cauchy relative to the discrete quasimetric d if and only if it is eventually increasing in the sense that there is a natural number k with the property that $I_n \subseteq I_{n+1}$ whenever $k \leq n$, see [Seda, 1997, Proposition 1].

Consider the sequence (I_n) in the power set $\mathcal{P}(\mathbb{N})$ of the natural numbers determined by setting $I_n = \mathbb{N}$ if n is even and setting $I_n = \{0\}$ otherwise. Then $\{0\}$ is the greatest limit, $gl(I_n)$, of (I_n), yet (I_n) is not forward Cauchy

---

[19] For further observations on this point, see [Smyth, 1987, Rutten, 1996].

in the discrete quasimetric simply because it is not eventually increasing. Thus, it appears not to be possible to directly characterize the property of being forward Cauchy relative to the discrete quasimetric in terms of convergence in the Scott topology. This contrasts with the situation where the (forward) Cauchy sequences relative to the quasimetric determined by a level mapping, see Definition 4.6.9, can be described in terms of convergence in Q, see Proposition 4.6.8 and Corollary 4.6.12. ∎

Using the observations made thus far, it is straightforward to recover the usual fixed-point semantics of definite logic programs, namely, to recover Theorem 2.2.3 Part (b) in terms of quasimetrics, by employing Theorem 4.6.3 Part (a) and the discrete quasimetric on $(I_P, \subseteq)$. We briefly sketch this next and refer the reader to [Seda, 1997] for full details.

4.6.6 Example Let P denote an arbitrary definite logic program, and let d denote the discrete quasimetric defined on the partially ordered set $(I_{P,2}, \subseteq)$. Then it is shown in [Seda, 1997] that $(I_{P,2}, d)$ is a CS-complete quasimetric space and that T_P is CS-continuous. We show here that, in fact, T_P is non-expansive and hence that Theorem 4.6.3 is applicable.

Suppose first that $d(I_1, I_2) = 0$. Then $I_1 \subseteq I_2$ so that $T_P(I_1) \subseteq T_P(I_2)$, and hence $d(T_P(I_1), T_P(I_2)) = 0$, as required. Next suppose that $d(I_1, I_2)$ takes value 1. Then immediately $d(I_1, I_2) \geq d(T_P(I_1), T_P(I_2))$, as required. Thus, T_P is indeed non-expansive relative to d. We note that, in contrast, T_P is not usually a contraction relative to any metric or quasimetric, since fixed points of T_P are not usually unique. In any event, we are now in a position to apply Theorem 4.6.3 since we have the following facts.

(1) (I_P, d) is a CS-complete quasimetric space.

(2) $T_P : I_{P,2} \to I_{P,2}$ is non-expansive and CS-continuous.

(3) The empty set $\emptyset$ is a point in $I_{P,2}$ such that $d(\emptyset, T_P(\emptyset)) = 0$.

Thus, on applying Theorem 4.6.3 and examining its proof, we conclude that T_P has a fixed point equal to the greatest limit $gl(T_P^n(\emptyset))$, and this, in turn, is equal to $\bigcup T_P^n(\emptyset) = T_P \uparrow \omega$, as shown in Chapter 3. Thus, we recover the classical least fixed point of T_P, as required.

We will now use quasimetrics to characterize continuity in the Cantor topology of the immediate consequence operator for normal logic programs.[20]

4.6.7 Definition Let $(D, \sqsubseteq)$ be a domain, and let $r : D_c \to \mathbb{N}$ be a function,

---

[20]For more details of the results presented in this section, see [Seda, 1997].

called a *rank function*,[21] such that $r^{-1}(n)$ is a finite set for each $n \in \mathbb{N}$. Define $d_r : D \times D \to \mathbb{R}$ by[22]

$$d_r(x, y) := \inf\{2^{-n} \mid (c \sqsubseteq x \Longrightarrow c \sqsubseteq y) \text{ for all } c \in D_c \text{ with } r(c) < n\}.$$

Then d_r is called the quasi-ultrametric *induced by* r.

It is straightforward to see that (D, d_r) is a quasi-ultrametric space. Furthermore, d_r induces the Scott topology on D, and (D, d_r) is totally bounded, see Proposition 4.6.10.

In order to discuss the relationships between quasimetrics and the Cantor topology on spaces of interpretations, we need the following proposition.

4.6.8 Proposition Let (X, d) be a totally bounded quasimetric space, and let (x_n) be a Cauchy sequence in X. Then, for all $\varepsilon > 0$, there exists $k \in \mathbb{N}$ such that for all $l, m \geq k$, $d^*(x_l, x_m) < \varepsilon$. (A sequence with this property is usually called a *bi-Cauchy sequence*.)

Proof: Choose $\varepsilon > 0$ and a finite subset $E \subseteq X$ together with a map $h : \mathbb{N} \to E$ such that $d^*(x_n, h(n)) < \frac{\varepsilon}{3}$, using total boundedness. Since (x_n) is a Cauchy sequence, there exists $k_0 \in \mathbb{N}$ such that for all $m \geq l \geq k_0$, $d(x_l, x_m) < \frac{\varepsilon}{3}$. Now choose $k_1 \geq k_0$ such that for every $e \in E$, the set $h^{-1}(e) \cap \{n \mid n \geq k_1\}$ is either infinite or empty. Choose now $l, m \geq k_1$, and let $p \geq l$ be minimal such that $h(p) = h(m)$. Then

$$d(x_l, x_m) \leq d(x_l, x_p) + d(x_p, h(p)) + d(h(p), x_m) < 3 \cdot \frac{\varepsilon}{3} = \varepsilon,$$

and by symmetry $d^*(x_l, x_m) < \varepsilon$. ∎

We next define totally bounded quasi-ultrametrics on I_P, for a given program P, by using level mappings and show that these are closely related to the Cantor topology Q.

4.6.9 Definition Let P be a normal logic program, and let $l : B_P \to \mathbb{N}$ be a level mapping for P such that $l^{-1}(n)$ is finite for every $n \in \mathbb{N}$. The mapping l induces a rank function $r : I_c \to \mathbb{N}$ defined by

$$r(I) = \max_{A \in I}\{l(A)\},$$

where we take $I_c = (I_P)_c$ to be the set of all finite subsets of B_P. By Definition 4.6.7, r induces a quasi-ultrametric d_r on I_P.

For a given normal logic program P, we will denote $I_{P,2}$ by I_P for the rest of this section.

---

[21]The notion of rank function will be given in more generality in Definition 4.8.12.

[22]The definition of d_r is similar to one made by M.B. Smyth in Example 5 of the paper [Smyth, 1991].

4.6.10 Proposition With the notation established above, (I_P, d_r) is a totally bounded quasi-ultrametric space.

Proof: Choose $\varepsilon = 2^{-n}$, where $n \in \mathbb{N}$, and let E be the set of all subsets of B_P, the atoms of which are all of level less than or equal to n. Then E is finite by our assumption on l. For every $I \in I_P$, let e be the restriction of I to atoms of level less than or equal to n. Then $d_r^*(e, I) < \varepsilon$, as is easily verified. ∎

We have the following characterization of Cauchy sequences in I_P.

4.6.11 Proposition A sequence (I_n) in (I_P, d_r) is a Cauchy sequence if and only if for every $n \in \mathbb{N}$ there exists $k_n \in \mathbb{N}$ such that for all $l, m \geq k_n$ we have that I_l and I_m agree on all atoms of level less than n.

Proof: Let (I_n) be a Cauchy sequence in I_P. Choose $n \in \mathbb{N}$, and let $\varepsilon = 2^{-n}$. Since I_P is totally bounded, there exists $k_n \in \mathbb{N}$ such that for all $l, m \geq k_n$, $d_r^*(I_l, I_m) \leq 2^{-n}$. By definition of d_r, we obtain that I_l and I_m agree on all atoms of level less than n. The converse follows since the argument above clearly reverses. ∎

4.6.12 Corollary Let (I_n) be a sequence in (I_P, d_r). Then (I_n) is a Cauchy sequence if and only if (I_n) converges in Q to some I. Moreover, $\lim I_n = I$, so (I_P, d_r) is complete.

Proof: By Proposition 3.3.5 and the previous proposition, (I_n) is a Cauchy sequence if and only if (I_n) converges in Q to some I. It is easily verified that $\lim I_n = I$ by noting that $I = \{A \in B_P \mid A \in I_n \text{ eventually}\}$. It follows that (I_P, d_r) is complete. ∎

The previous result allows us to characterize CS-continuity in terms of Q.

4.6.13 Proposition Suppose that $l : B_P \to \mathbb{N}$ is a level mapping such that $l^{-1}(n)$ is finite for all n. Then the immediate consequence operator T_P is CS-continuous if and only if it is continuous in Q.

Proof: Suppose that T_P is CS-continuous and that (I_n) is an arbitrary sequence in I_P which converges in Q to some $I \in I_P$. Then (I_n) is a Cauchy sequence, and by Corollary 4.6.12, $\lim I_n = I$. By CS-continuity of T_P, we have $\lim T_P(I_n) = T_P(I)$, and again by Corollary 4.6.12, we have $T_P(I_n) \to T_P(I)$ in Q, as required.

Conversely, suppose T_P is continuous in Q and that (I_n) is a Cauchy sequence with $\lim I_n = I$, say. By Corollary 4.6.12, $I_n \to I$ in Q, and, by continuity of T_P in Q, we get $T_P(I_n) \to T_P(I)$, which yields $\lim T_P(I_n) = T_P(I)$, again by Corollary 4.6.12. ∎

Our next observation shows that non-expansiveness implies CS-continuity.

4.6.14 Proposition Let $l : B_P \to \mathbb{N}$ be an arbitrary level mapping satisfying the condition that $l^{-1}(n)$ is finite for each $n \in \mathbb{N}$. If T_P is non-expanding, then T_P is continuous in Q and hence is CS-continuous.

Proof: Let T_P be non-expanding, and let (I_n) be a Cauchy sequence with $\lim I_n = I$. Since T_P is non-expansive, we obtain

$$0 \le d_r(T_P(I_n), T_P(I)) \le d_r(I_n, I) \to 0$$

and

$$0 \le d_r(T_P(I), T_P(I_n)) \le d_r(I, I_n) \to 0$$

by total boundedness of I_P. By definition of d_r and Proposition 4.6.11, it follows that $T_P(I_n)$ is a Cauchy sequence and, by Proposition 3.3.5 and the previous inequalities, $T_P(I_n)$ converges in Q to $T_P(I)$. Hence, $\lim T_P(I_n) = T_P(I)$, again by Corollary 4.6.12. ∎

We close with a brief discussion of several simple examples illustrating the methods and results of this section as applied to normal logic programs P relative to T_P defined on I_P. For full details the reader is again referred to [Seda, 1997]. Thus, suppose that P is a normal logic program, that d_r is the quasimetric determined by a level mapping l defined on B_P and satisfying the property that $l^{-1}(n)$ is finite for all n, and that T_P is CS-continuous relative to d_r or equivalently that T_P is continuous in the topology Q.

4.6.15 Example Consider again the program P of Example 3.2.3

$$p(a) \leftarrow$$
$$p(s(X)) \leftarrow p(X)$$

and define l on B_P by $l(p(s^n(a))) = n$. Then we see that $d_r(T_P(I_1), T_P(I_2)) \le \frac{1}{2} d_r(I_1, I_2)$ for all $I_1, I_2 \in I_P$. Therefore, T_P is a contraction and is continuous in Q and, hence, is CS-continuous. Thus, Theorem 4.6.3 applies and produces a unique fixed point of T_P. Of course, this fixed point coincides with the usual one produced by considering powers $T_P^n(\emptyset)$ of $\emptyset$.

4.6.16 Example Consider the program P

$$p(s(X), a) \leftarrow p(s(X), a)$$

with the level mapping l defined on B_P by $l(p(s^n(a), s^m(a))) = n + m$. Then it is readily checked that T_P is non-expansive (and therefore continuous in Q), but not contractive, relative to the quasimetric d_r determined by l, since it is easy to find distinct I_1 and I_2 such that $d_r(T_P(I_1), T_P(I_2)) = d_r(I_1, I_2)$. Thus, Theorem 4.6.3 is applicable and, needless to say, produces numerous fixed points of T_P. For this reason, it follows that T_P cannot be a contraction relative to any metric. Thus, the approach to finding fixed points based on metrics and the Banach contraction mapping theorem fails even for the rather simple program P.

4.6.17 Example Consider again the program P of Example 3.3.6

$$p(a) \leftarrow$$
$$p(s(X)) \leftarrow \neg p(X)$$

and note that P is not stratified nor even locally stratified. Define the level mapping l on B_P by $l(p(s^n(a))) = n$ for each n. We note that in this case T_P is not non-expansive, for if we take $I_1 = \{p(a), p(s(a))\}$ and $I_2 = \{p(a), p(s(a)), p(s^2(a))\}$, then $T_P(I_1) = \{p(a), p(s^3(a)), p(s^4(a)), p(s^5(a)), \ldots\}$ and $T_P(I_2) = \{p(a), p(s^4(a)), p(s^5(a)), \ldots\}$. Thus, we have $d_r(I_1, I_2) = 0$ yet $d_r(T_P(I_1), T_P(I_2)) = 2^{-2}$, and therefore T_P is not non-expansive. Next, consider powers $I_n = T_P^n(\emptyset)$, the first few of which, as we have already seen, are as follows: $I_1 = B_P$, $I_2 = \{p(a)\}$, $I_3 = B_P \setminus \{p(s(a))\}$, $I_4 = \{p(a), p(s^2(a))\}$, $I_5 = B_P \setminus \{p(s(a)), p(s^3(a))\}$, etc. Then we obtain that $d_r(I_n, I_{n+1})$ takes value 0 if n is even and takes value 2^{-n+1} if n is odd. Therefore, the sequence (I_n) is Cauchy and converges to I, say, in Q. By Proposition 3.3.5, we have that (I_n) converges in Q to the set $\{p(a), p(s^2(a)), p(s^4(a)), \ldots\}$, which therefore coincides with I. It follows that I is a fixed point of T_P, since T_P is continuous in Q, and indeed I is the only fixed point of T_P, as already noted in Example 3.3.6.

4.6.18 Example Let P be the program

$$p(X) \leftarrow \neg q(X)$$
$$r(s(X)) \leftarrow r(X)$$
$$q(X) \leftarrow q(a), \neg r(X)$$

which is a slight modification of an example in [Apt et al., 1988, Page 97] and is stratified. Again, T_P is continuous relative to Q, but in this case T_P is not non-expansive for any choice of level mapping l and corresponding quasimetric d_r. To see this, put $I_1 = \{q(a)\}$ and $I_2 = T_P(I_1) = \{p(s(a)), p(s^2(a)), \ldots\} \cup \{q(a), q(s(a)), \ldots\}$. Then $d_r(I_1, I_2) = 0$ for any d_r simply because $I_1 \subseteq I_2$. Since $T_P(I_2) = \{q(a), q(s(a)), \ldots\}$, we must have $d_r(T_P(I_1), T_P(I_2)) > 0$ for any d_r or in other words for any choice of l and corresponding d_r, so that T_P is never non-expansive. Taking $I = \{r(a)\}$ and setting $I_n = T_P^n(I)$, we have $I_n = \{r(s^n(a))\} \cup \{p(a), p(s(a)), p(s^2(a)), \ldots\}$. Clearly, (I_n) is Cauchy (for any choice of level mapping and corresponding d_r), and I_n converges in Q to the fixed point $\{p(a), p(s(a)), p(s^2(a)), \ldots\}$.

4.7 A Hierarchy of Fixed-Point Theorems

For the reader's convenience, we have collected together in Table 4.3 the main fixed-point theorems presented in this chapter, at least for single-valued

TABLE 4.3: Summary of single-valued fixed-point theorems.

space	name of theorem	reference number	symbol
ω-cpo	Kleene	1.1.9	K
cpo	Knaster-Tarski	1.1.10	KT
complete metric	Banach	4.2.3	B
compact metric	—	4.2.4	cp
gum	Prieß-Crampe and Ribenboim	4.3.6	PCR
d-metric	Matthews	4.4.6	M
d-gum	—	4.5.1	dPCR
quasimetric	Rutten-Smyth	4.6.3	RS

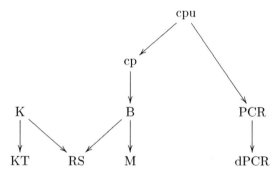

FIGURE 4.1: Dependencies between fixed-point theorems from Chapters 1 and 4. The lower a theorem is placed in the diagram, the more general it is. See Table 4.3 for the abbreviations.

mappings. In fact, we will consider generalizations of several of them to multivalued mappings as well in the later sections of this chapter. Furthermore, the dependencies between these theorems are depicted in Figure 4.1, where the letters abbreviate the theorems as listed in Table 4.3. (The abbreviation "cpu" represents the statement that strictly contracting functions on compact ultrametric spaces have unique fixed points, which follows immediately from Theorem 4.2.4.)

4.8 Relationships Between the Various Spaces

We move on next to study the relationships which exist between the various different spaces we have introduced in this chapter. In particular, we focus on the representation of certain relationships in terms of others. This will in some cases lead to alternative proofs of fixed-point theorems we have already considered. The one exception to this comment is the interplay between quasimetrics and partial orders. It is clear from the results of Section 4.6 that this interplay is strong. But we will not consider it again other than in the context of multivalued mappings, see Sections 4.10 and 4.13; see also [Smyth, 1987, Smyth, 1991, Bonsangue et al., 1996, Rutten, 1996] for further details.

4.8.1 Metrics and Dislocated Metrics

Our intention here is to establish relationships between metrics and dislocated metrics. Furthermore, we will examine several methods of obtaining dislocated metrics from metrics, some of which will be applied later, and we will show how Matthews' theorem can be derived from the Banach contraction mapping theorem.

We begin by noting that if f is a contraction with contractivity factor λ on a d-metric space (X, ϱ), then we have $\varrho(f(x), f(x)) \leq \lambda \varrho(x, x)$ for all $x \in X$. Furthermore, the property $\varrho(x, x) = 0$ for all $x \in X$, if ϱ happens to satisfy this, simply means that the d-metric ϱ is actually a metric. It follows, therefore, that we are interested in studying the function $u_\varrho : X \to \mathbb{R}$ associated with any d-metric ϱ.

4.8.1 Definition Let (X, ϱ) be a d-metric space. We define the function $u_\varrho : X \to \mathbb{R}$ by $u_\varrho(x) = \varrho(x, x)$, for all $x \in X$, and call it the *dislocation function* of ϱ.

Depending on the context, dislocation functions are sometimes also called *weight functions*, see, for example, [Matthews, 1994, Waszkiewicz, 2002].

The following result gives a rather general method by which d-metrics can be obtained from metrics.

4.8.2 Proposition Let (X, d) be a metric space, let $u : X \to \mathbb{R}_0^+$ be a function, and let $T : \mathbb{R}_0^+ \times \mathbb{R}_0^+ \to \mathbb{R}_0^+$ be a symmetric function which satisfies the triangle inequality. Then (X, ϱ), where

$$\varrho(x, y) = d(x, y) + T(u(x), u(y))$$

for all $x, y \in X$ is a d-metric space, and $u_\varrho(x) = T(u(x), u(x))$ for all $x \in X$. In particular, if $T(x, x) = x$ for all $x \in \mathbb{R}_0^+$, then $u_\varrho = u$.

Proof: We check the axioms for a d-metric. (M2) If $\varrho(x, y) = 0$, then $d(x, y) + T(u(x), u(y)) = 0$. Hence, $d(x, y) = 0$, and so $x = y$. (M3) Obvious by symmetry of d and T. (M4) Obvious since d and T satisfy the triangle inequality. ∎

Completeness also carries over if some continuity conditions are imposed.

4.8.3 Proposition Using the notation of Proposition 4.8.2, let u be continuous as a function from (X, d) to $\mathbb{R}_0^+$ (where X is endowed with the topology determined by d, and $\mathbb{R}_0^+$ is endowed with its usual topology), and let T be continuous as a function from the topological product space $(\mathbb{R}_0^+)^2$ to $\mathbb{R}_0^+$, satisfying the additional property $T(x, x) = x$ for all x. If (X, d) is a complete metric space, then (X, ϱ) is a complete d-metric space.

Proof: Let (x_n) be a Cauchy sequence in (X, ϱ). Thus, for each $\varepsilon > 0$, there exists $n_0 \in \mathbb{N}$ such that for all $m, n \geq n_0$ we have $d(x_m, x_n) \leq d(x_m, x_n) + T(u(x_m), u(x_n)) = \varrho(x_m, x_n) < \varepsilon$. So (x_n) is also a Cauchy sequence in (X, d) and therefore has a unique limit x in (X, d). In particular, we have $x_n \to x$ in (X, d), and also $u(x_n) \to u(x)$ and $T(u(x_n), u(x)) \to T(u(x), u(x)) = u(x)$. We have to show that $\varrho(x_n, x)$ converges to 0 as $n \to \infty$. For all $n \in \mathbb{N}$, we obtain $\varrho(x_n, x) = d(x_n, x) + T(u(x_n), u(x)) \to u(x) = u_\varrho(x)$, and it remains to show that $\varrho(x, x) = 0$. But this follows from the fact that (x_n) is a Cauchy sequence, since it implies that $u(x_n) = u_\varrho(x_n) = \varrho(x_n, x_n) \to 0$ as $n \to \infty$, and hence by continuity of u we obtain $u(x) = 0$. ∎

An example of a natural function T which satisfies the requirements of Propositions 4.8.2 and 4.8.3 is

$$T : \mathbb{R}_0^+ \times \mathbb{R}_0^+ \to \mathbb{R}_0^+ : (x, y) \mapsto \frac{1}{2}(x + y).$$

We discuss a few more examples of d-metrics; they are partly taken from [Matthews, 1992].

4.8.4 Example Let d be the metric $d(x, y) = \frac{1}{2}|x-y|$ on $\mathbb{R}_0^+$, let $u : \mathbb{R}_0^+ \to \mathbb{R}_0^+$ be the identity function, and define $T(x, y) = \frac{1}{2}(x + y)$. Then ϱ as defined in Proposition 4.8.2 is a d-metric, and $\varrho(x, y) = \frac{1}{2}|x - y| + \frac{1}{2}(x + y) = \max\{x, y\}$ for all $x, y \in \mathbb{R}_0^+$.

4.8.5 Example Let $\mathcal{I}$ be the set of all closed intervals in $\mathbb{R}$. Then $d : \mathcal{I} \times \mathcal{I} \to \mathbb{R}_0^+$ defined by

$$d([a, b], [c, d]) = \frac{1}{2}(|a - c| + |b - d|)$$

is a metric on $\mathcal{I}$. Let $u : \mathcal{I} \to \mathbb{R}_0^+$ be defined by

$$u([a, b]) = b - a$$

and let T be defined as in Example 4.8.4. Then the construction in Proposition 4.8.2 yields a d-metric ϱ such that

$$\varrho([a,b],[c,d]) = \max\{b,d\} - \min\{a,c\}$$

for all $[a,b],[c,d] \in \mathcal{I}$.

Indeed, we obtain

$$\varrho([a,b],[c,d]) = d([a,b],[c,d]) + \frac{1}{2}b - \frac{1}{2}a + \frac{1}{2}d - \frac{1}{2}c$$

$$= \frac{1}{2}\left(|b-d| + b + d + |a-c| - a - c\right)$$

$$= \frac{1}{2}\left(|b-d| + (b+d)\right) + \frac{1}{2}\left(|a-c| - (a+c)\right)$$

$$= \max\{b,d\} - \min\{a,c\}.$$

4.8.6 Example $(\mathbb{R}_0^+, \varrho)$ is a dislocated metric space, where ϱ is defined by $\varrho(x,y) = x + y$.

The following proposition gives an alternative way of obtaining d-ultrametrics from ultrametrics. We will apply this later in Section 5.1.2.

4.8.7 Proposition Let (X,d) be an ultrametric space, and let $u : X \to \mathbb{R}_0^+$ be a function. Then (X, ϱ), where

$$\varrho(x,y) = \max\{d(x,y), u(x), u(y)\}$$

for all $x,y \in X$, is a d-ultrametric, and $\varrho(x,x) = u(x)$ for all $x \in X$. If u is continuous as a function on (X,d), then completeness of (X,d) implies completeness of (X,ϱ).

Proof: (M2) and (M3) are obvious.

(M5) We obtain for all $x,y,z \in X$

$$\varrho(x,y) = \max\{d(x,y), u(x), u(y)\}$$

$$\leq \max\{d(x,z), d(z,y), u(x), u(y)\}$$

$$\leq \max\{d(x,z), u(x), u(z), d(z,y), u(y)\}$$

$$= \max\{\varrho(x,z), \varrho(z,y)\}.$$

For completeness, let (x_n) be a Cauchy sequence in (X,ϱ). Then (x_n) is a Cauchy sequence in (X,d) and converges to some $x \in X$. We then obtain $\varrho(x_n,x) = \max\{d(x_n,x), u(x_n), u(x)\} \to u(x)$ as $n \to \infty$. As in the proof of Proposition 4.8.3, we obtain $u(x) = 0$, and this completes the proof. ∎

We want to investigate next the relationship between Matthews' theorem, Theorem 4.4.6, and the Banach contraction mapping theorem, Theorem 4.2.3.

4.8.8 Proposition Let (X, ϱ) be a d-metric space, and define $d : X \times X \to \mathbb{R}$ by setting $d(x, y) = \varrho(x, y)$ for $x \neq y$ and by setting $d(x, x) = 0$ for all $x \in X$. Then d is a metric on X.

Proof: We obviously have $d(x, x) = 0$ for all $x \in X$. If $d(x, y) = 0$, then either $x = y$ or $\varrho(x, y) = 0$, and from the latter we also obtain $x = y$. Symmetry is clear. We want to show that $d(x, y) \leq d(x, z) + d(z, y)$ for all $x, y, z \in X$. If $d(x, z) = \varrho(x, z)$ and $d(z, y) = \varrho(z, y)$, then the inequality is clear. If $d(x, z) = 0$, then $x = z$, and the inequality reduces to $d(x, y) \leq d(x, y)$, which holds. If $d(z, y) = 0$, then $z = y$, and the inequality reduces to $d(x, y) \leq d(x, y)$, which also holds. ∎

4.8.9 Definition The metric d just defined from the d-metric ϱ is called the metric *associated* with ϱ.

Considering Step (3) of the proof of Theorem 4.2.5, we easily verify that δ is a dislocated ultrametric and note also that d is the metric associated with δ.

The following proposition allows one to derive from completeness of d, in general, that ϱ itself is complete.

4.8.10 Proposition Let (X, ϱ) be a d-metric space, and let d denote the metric associated with ϱ. If the metric d is complete, then so is ϱ. If f is a contraction relative to ϱ, then f is a contraction relative to d with the same contractivity factor.

Proof: Suppose that (x_n) is a Cauchy sequence in ϱ. Then for all $\varepsilon > 0$, there exists n_0 such that $\varrho(x_k, x_m) < \varepsilon$ for all $k, m \geq n_0$. Consequently, we also obtain $d(x_k, x_m) < \varepsilon$ for all $k, m \geq n_0$. Since d is complete, the sequence (x_n) converges in d to some x, and $d(x_n, x) \to 0$ as $n \to \infty$. We show that $\varrho(x_n, x) \to 0$ as $n \to \infty$, and to do this we consider two cases.

Case i. Assume that the sequence (x_n) is such that there exists n_0 satisfying the property that for all $m \geq n_0$, we have $x_m \neq x$. Then $\varrho(x_m, x) = d(x_m, x)$ for all $m \geq n_0$ so that $\varrho(x_m, x) \to 0$, and hence $\varrho(x_n, x) \to 0$.

Case ii. Assume that there exist infinitely many $n_k \in \mathbb{N}$ such that $x_{n_k} = x$. Since (x_n) is a Cauchy sequence with respect to ϱ, we obtain $\varrho(x_{n_k}, x) < \varepsilon$ for all $\varepsilon > 0$, and so $\varrho(x, x) = 0$. Hence, $\varrho(x_n, x) = d(x_n, x)$ for all $n \in \mathbb{N}$, and we obtain that $\varrho(x_n, x) \to 0$ as $n \to \infty$, as required.

Let $\lambda \in [0, 1)$ be such that $\varrho(f(x), f(y)) \leq \lambda \varrho(x, y)$ for all $x, y \in X$, and let $x, y \in X$. If $f(x) = f(y)$, then we have $d(f(x), f(y)) = 0$, hence $d(f(x), f(y)) \leq \lambda d(x, y)$. If $f(x) \neq f(y)$, then $x \neq y$, and so $d(f(x), f(y)) = \varrho(f(x), f(y)) \leq \lambda \varrho(x, y) = \lambda d(x, y)$, as required. ∎

4.8.11 Proposition Let (X, ϱ) be a complete d-metric space, and let d denote the metric associated with ϱ. Then the metric d is complete. However, if f is a contraction relative to d, it does not follow that f is necessarily a contraction relative to ϱ.

Proof: Let (x_n) be a Cauchy sequence in d. If (x_n) eventually becomes constant, then it obviously converges in d. So, assume that this is not the case. Then the sequence (x_n) must contain infinitely many distinct points; otherwise, it would not be a Cauchy sequence. We define a subsequence (y_n) of (x_n) which is obtained by removing multiple occurrences of points in (x_n). For each $n \in \mathbb{N}$, let $y_n = x_k$, where k is minimal with the property that, for all $m < n$, we have $y_m \neq x_k$. Since (y_n) is a subsequence of the Cauchy sequence (x_n), we see that (y_n) is also a Cauchy sequence relative to d. But, for any two elements y, z in the sequence (y_n), we have that $d(y, z) = \varrho(y, z)$ by definition of d. Therefore, (y_n) is a Cauchy sequence in ϱ and, hence, converges in ϱ to some $y_\omega \in X$. So, (y_n) also converges in d to y_ω. We show that (x_n) converges to y_ω in d. Let $\varepsilon > 0$ be chosen arbitrarily. Since (x_n) is a Cauchy sequence with respect to d, there exists an index n_1 such that $d(x_k, x_m) < \frac{\varepsilon}{2}$ for all $k, m \geq n_1$. Since (y_n) converges to y_ω in ϱ, we also know that there is an index n_2 with $y_{n_2} = x_{n_3}$ for some index n_3 such that $n_3 \geq n_1$ and $d(y_{n_2}, y_\omega) < \frac{\varepsilon}{2}$. For all x_n with $n \geq n_3$, we then obtain $d(x_n, y_\omega) \leq d(x_n, x_{n_3}) + d(x_{n_3}, y_\omega) < \varepsilon$, as required.

Let $X = \{0, 1\}$, and define the mapping $f : X \to X$ by setting $f(x) = 0$ for all $x \in X$. Let ϱ be constant and equal to 1. Then ϱ is a complete d-metric, and f is a contraction relative to d. However, $\varrho(f(0), f(1)) = \varrho(0, 0) = \varrho(0, 1)$, and so f is not a contraction relative to ϱ. ∎

The results we have just established put us in a position to prove Matthews' theorem, Theorem 4.4.6, by using the Banach contraction mapping theorem, Theorem 4.2.3, and this we do next.

Proof of Theorem 4.4.6 Let (X, ϱ) be a complete d-metric space, and let f be a contraction relative to ϱ. Let d be the metric associated with ϱ. Then d is a complete metric, and f is a contraction relative to d. Hence, f has a unique fixed point by the Banach contraction mapping theorem, Theorem 4.2.3. ∎

4.8.2   Domains as GUMS

It is our intention here to cast Scott domains into ultrametric spaces, a construction we will use later in Chapter 5. Usually, domains are endowed with the Scott topology, see Section A.6. However, as we will see next, domains can be endowed with the structure of a spherically complete ultrametric space. This is not something normally considered in domain theory. However, as already noted at the beginning of the chapter, one of the objectives of the chapter is to discuss a variety of distance functions, including (generalized) ultrametrics, which have applications both in logic programming and more generally in theoretical computer science.[23]

As in Remark 4.3.2, let γ denote an arbitrary ordinal, and let Γ_γ denote the set $\{2^{-\alpha} \mid \alpha < \gamma\}$ of symbols $2^{-\alpha}$ ordered by $2^{-\alpha} < 2^{-\beta}$ if and only if $\beta < \alpha$. As already noted, this ordering is, in effect, the dual of the usual ordering on γ. However, we find it convenient to work with the set Γ_γ and the ordering just defined, rather than with the dual ordering on γ, especially in the context of contraction mappings whose contractivity factor is $\frac{1}{2}$, see, for example, Proposition 4.8.17 and particularly Theorem 5.1.6.

We recall that the set of compact elements in a domain D is denoted by D_c, see Definition 1.1.4.

4.8.12 Definition Let $r : D_c \to \gamma$ be a function, called a *rank function*, form $\Gamma_{\gamma+1}$, and denote $2^{-\gamma}$ by 0. Define $\varrho_r : D \times D \to \Gamma_{\gamma+1}$ by $\varrho_r(x, y) = \inf\{2^{-\alpha} \mid c \sqsubseteq x$ if and only if $c \sqsubseteq y$ for every $c \in D_c$ with $r(c) < \alpha\}$.

It is readily checked that (D, ϱ_r) is a generalized ultrametric space. We call ϱ_r the generalized ultrametric *induced* by the rank function r. Indeed, the intuition behind ϱ_r is that two elements x and y of the domain D are close if they dominate the same compact elements up to a certain rank (and hence *agree* in this sense up to this rank); the higher the rank giving agreement, the closer are x and y. Furthermore, (D, ϱ_r) is spherically complete. The proof of this claim does not make use of the existence of a bottom element of D, so this requirement can be omitted. The main idea of the proof is captured in the next lemma, which shows that chains of balls give rise to chains of elements in the domain. It depends on the following two elementary facts, which result immediately from Lemma 4.3.5: (1) if $\gamma \leq \delta$ and $x \in B_\delta(y)$, then $B_\gamma(x) \subseteq B_\delta(y)$, and (2) if $B_\gamma(x) \subset B_\delta(y)$, then $\delta \not\leq \gamma$ (thus, $\gamma < \delta$, if Γ is totally ordered).

In order to simplify notation in the following proofs, we will denote the ball $B_{2^{-\alpha}}(x)$ by $B^\alpha(x)$.

4.8.13 Lemma Let $B^\beta(y)$ and $B^\alpha(x)$ be arbitrary balls in (D, ϱ_r). Then the following statements hold.

(a) For any $z \in B^\beta(y)$, we have $\{c \in \text{approx}(z) \mid r(c) < \beta\} = \{c \in \text{approx}(y) \mid r(c) < \beta\}$.

(b) $B_\beta = \bigsqcup\{c \in \text{approx}(y) \mid r(c) < \beta\}$ and $B_\alpha = \bigsqcup\{c \in \text{approx}(x) \mid r(c) < \alpha\}$ both exist.

---

[23]This point of view is further developed in a number of papers including the following: [Kuhlmann, 1999], [Ribenboim, 1996], [Bouamama et al., 2000], [Prieß-Crampe, 1990]; also the papers [Prieß-Crampe and Ribenboim, 1993], [Prieß-Crampe and Ribenboim, 2000c], [Prieß-Crampe and Ribenboim, 2000b], [Prieß-Crampe and Ribenboim, 2000a] should be consulted.

(c) $B_\beta \in B^\beta(y)$ and $B_\alpha \in B^\alpha(x)$.

(d) Whenever $B^\alpha(x) \subseteq B^\beta(y)$, we have $B_\beta \sqsubseteq B_\alpha$.

Proof: (a) Since $\varrho_r(z, y) \le 2^{-\beta}$, the first statement follows immediately from the definition of ϱ_r.

(b) Since the set $\{c \in \mathrm{approx}(z) \mid r(c) < \beta\}$ is bounded by z, for any z and β, the second statement follows immediately from the consistent completeness of D.

(c) By definition, we obtain $B_\beta \sqsubseteq y$. Since B_β and y agree on all $c \in D_c$ with $r(c) < \beta$, the first statement in (c) holds, and the second similarly.

(d) First note that $x \in B^\beta(y)$, so that $B^\beta(y) = B^\beta(x)$, and the hypothesis can be written as $B^\alpha(x) \subseteq B^\beta(x)$. We consider two cases.

Case i. If $\beta \le \alpha$, then using (a) and noting again that $x \in B^\beta(y)$, we get $B_\beta = \bigsqcup\{c \in \mathrm{approx}(y) \mid r(c) < \beta\} = \bigsqcup\{c \in \mathrm{approx}(x) \mid r(c) < \beta\} \sqsubseteq \bigsqcup\{c \in \mathrm{approx}(x) \mid r(c) < \alpha\} = B_\alpha$, as required.

Case ii. If $\alpha < \beta$, then we cannot have $B^\alpha(x) \subset B^\beta(x)$, and we therefore obtain $B^\alpha(x) = B^\beta(x)$ and consequently $B^\alpha(B_\beta) = B^\beta(B_\beta) = B^\beta(B_\alpha)$ using (c). With the argument of Case i and noting that $y \in B^\alpha(x)$, it follows that $B_\alpha \sqsubseteq B_\beta$. We want to show that $B_\alpha = B_\beta$. Assume, in fact, that $B_\alpha \sqsubset B_\beta$. Since any point of a ball is its centre, we can take $z = B_\beta$ in (b), twice, to obtain $B_\beta = \bigsqcup\{c \in \mathrm{approx}(B_\beta) \mid r(c) < \beta\}$ and $B_\alpha = \bigsqcup\{c \in \mathrm{approx}(B_\beta) \mid r(c) < \alpha\}$. Thus, the supposition $B_\alpha \sqsubset B_\beta$ means that $\bigsqcup\{c \in \mathrm{approx}(B_\beta) \mid r(c) < \alpha\} \sqsubset \bigsqcup\{c \in \mathrm{approx}(B_\beta) \mid r(c) < \beta\}$. Since $\{c \in \mathrm{approx}(B_\beta) \mid r(c) < \alpha\} \subseteq \{c \in \mathrm{approx}(B_\beta) \mid r(c) < \beta\}$, there must be some $d \in \{c \in \mathrm{approx}(B_\beta) \mid r(c) < \beta\}$ with $d \not\sqsubseteq \bigsqcup\{c \in \mathrm{approx}(B_\beta) \mid r(c) < \alpha\} = B_\alpha$. Thus, there is an element $d \in D_c$ with $r(d) < \beta$ satisfying $d \not\sqsubseteq B_\alpha$ and $d \sqsubseteq B_\beta$. This contradicts the fact that $\varrho_r(B_\alpha, B_\beta) \le 2^{-\beta}$. Hence, $B_\alpha \not\sqsubseteq B_\beta$. Since $B_\alpha \sqsubseteq B_\beta$, it follows that $B_\alpha = B_\beta$ and therefore that $B_\beta \sqsubseteq B_\alpha$, as required. ∎

4.8.14 Theorem The ultrametric space (D, ϱ_r) is spherically complete.

Proof: By the previous lemma, every chain $(B^\alpha(x_\alpha))$ of balls in D gives rise to a chain (B_α) in D in reverse order. Let $B = \bigsqcup B_\alpha$. Now let $B^\alpha(x_\alpha)$ be an arbitrary ball in the chain. It suffices to show that $B \in B^\alpha(x_\alpha)$. Since $B_\alpha \in B^\alpha(x_\alpha)$, we have $\varrho_r(B_\alpha, x_\alpha) \le 2^{-\alpha}$. But ϱ_r is a generalized ultrametric, and so it suffices to show that $\varrho_r(B, B_\alpha) \le 2^{-\alpha}$. For every compact element $c \sqsubseteq B_\alpha$, we have $c \sqsubseteq B$ by construction of B. Now let $c \sqsubseteq B$ with $c \in D_c$ and $r(c) < \alpha$. We have to show that $c \sqsubseteq B_\alpha$. Since c is compact and $c \sqsubseteq B$, there exists B_β in the chain with $c \sqsubseteq B_\beta$. If $B^\alpha(x_\alpha) \subseteq B^\beta(x_\beta)$, then $B_\beta \sqsubseteq B_\alpha$ by Lemma 4.8.13, and therefore $c \sqsubseteq B_\alpha$. If $B^\beta(x_\beta) \subset B^\alpha(x_\alpha)$, then $\alpha < \beta$, and, since $c \sqsubseteq B_\beta$, we see that c is an element of the set $\{c \in \mathrm{approx}(x_\beta) \mid r(c) < \alpha\} = \{c \in \mathrm{approx}(x_\alpha) \mid r(c) < \alpha\}$. Since B_α is the supremum of the latter set, we have $c \sqsubseteq B_\alpha$, as required. ∎

We will apply this result in Section 5.1.1.

4.8.3 GUMS and Chain Complete Posets

In this section, we will invert the point of view of the previous one by associating a chain-complete partial order with any generalized ultrametric space (X, ϱ, Γ) whose distance set Γ is an ordinal endowed with, essentially, the dual ordering as considered in the previous section. Thus, for the duration of this section, Γ is the set $\Gamma_{\gamma+1}$ for some ordinal γ with the ordering described in Remark 4.3.2. For convenience, we will henceforth call such a generalized ultrametric space a *gum with ordinal distances*; recall that we denote $2^{-\gamma}$ by 0.

The motivation for adopting our current point of view is to provide a domain-theoretic proof of the Prieß-Crampe and Ribenboim theorem.[24] In fact, we will prove the Prieß-Crampe and Ribenboim theorem using the Knaster-Tarski theorem in this special case of gums with ordinal distances. As a matter of fact, this special case will suffice for all our purposes since, in applications, all the gums we encounter have ordinal distances, simply because they arise from level mappings.

Our main technical tool is the space of formal balls associated with a given metric space, see [Edalat and Heckmann, 1998]. Our first task is to extend this notion to generalized ultrametrics. [25]

Let (X, ϱ, Γ) be a generalized ultrametric space with ordinal distances, and let $\mathcal{B}'X$ be the set of all pairs (x, α) with $x \in X$ and $\alpha \in \Gamma$. We define an equivalence relation $\sim$ on $\mathcal{B}'X$ by setting $(x_1, \alpha_1) \sim (x_2, \alpha_2)$ if and only if $\alpha_1 = \alpha_2$ and $\varrho(x_1, x_2) \leq \alpha_1$. The quotient space $\mathcal{B}X = \mathcal{B}'X/\sim$ will be called the *space of formal balls* associated with (X, ϱ, Γ), and it carries an ordering $\sqsubseteq$ which is well-defined (on representatives of equivalence classes) by $(x, \alpha) \sqsubseteq (y, \beta)$ if and only if $\varrho(x, y) \leq \alpha$ and $\beta \leq \alpha$. We denote the equivalence class of (x, α) by $[(x, \alpha)]$, and note of course that the use of the same symbol $\sqsubseteq$ between equivalence classes and their representatives should not cause any confusion.

4.8.15 Proposition The set $\mathcal{B}X$ is partially ordered by $\sqsubseteq$. Moreover, X is spherically complete if and only if $\mathcal{B}X$ is chain complete.

Proof: That $\mathcal{B}X$ is partially ordered by $\sqsubseteq$ is clear.

Let X be spherically complete, and let $[(x_\beta, \beta)]$ be an ascending chain in $\mathcal{B}X$. Then $B_\beta(x_\beta)$ is a chain of balls in X with non-empty intersection; let $x \in \bigcap B_\beta(x_\beta)$. Then $\varrho(x_\beta, x) \leq \beta$ for all β. Hence, the chain $[(x_\beta, \beta)]$ in $\mathcal{B}X$ has $[(x, 0)]$ as an upper bound. Now consider the set A of all $\alpha \in \Gamma$ such that $[(x, \alpha)]$ is an upper bound of $[(x_\beta, \beta)]$. Since we are working with ordinal distances only, the set A has a supremum γ, and hence $[(x, \gamma)]$ is the least upper bound of the chain $[(x_\beta, \beta)]$.

Now suppose $\mathcal{B}X$ is chain complete, and let $(B_\beta(x_\beta))_{\beta \in \Lambda}$ be a chain of

---

[24] This approach is inspired by [Edalat and Heckmann, 1998], where the Banach contraction mapping theorem is derived from Kleene's theorem.

[25] For more details, see [Hitzler and Seda, 2003].

balls in X, where $\Lambda \subseteq \Gamma$. Then $[(x_\beta, \beta)]$ is an ascending chain in $\mathcal{B}X$ and has least upper bound (x, γ), and hence $B_\gamma(x) \subseteq \bigcap_{\beta \in \Lambda} B_\beta(x_\beta)$. ∎

4.8.16 Proposition The function $\iota : X \to \mathcal{B}X$, where $\iota(x) = [(x, 0)]$ for each $x \in X$, is injective, and $\iota(X)$ is the set of all maximal elements of $\mathcal{B}X$.

Proof: Injectivity of ι follows from (U2). The observation that the maximal elements of $\mathcal{B}X$ are exactly the elements of the form $[(x, 0)]$ completes the proof. ∎

Now suppose that f is a strictly contracting mapping on a generalized ultrametric space (X, ϱ, Γ) with ordinal distances. We use f to induce a mapping $\mathcal{B}f : \mathcal{B}X \to \mathcal{B}X$ defined by

$$\mathcal{B}f(x, 2^{-\alpha}) = \begin{cases} \left(f(x), 2^{-(\alpha+1)} \right) & \text{if } 2^{-\alpha} \neq 0, \\ (f(x), 0) & \text{if } 2^{-\alpha} = 0. \end{cases}$$

4.8.17 Proposition If f is strictly contracting, then $\mathcal{B}f$ is monotonic.

Proof: Let $(x, 2^{-\alpha}) \sqsubseteq (y, 2^{-\beta})$, so that $\varrho(x, y) \leq 2^{-\alpha}$ and $\alpha \leq \beta$. If $2^{-\alpha} = 0$, there is nothing to show, so assume $2^{-\alpha} \neq 0$. It then remains to show that $\varrho(f(x), f(y)) \leq 2^{-(\alpha+1)}$, and this holds since f is strictly contracting and because the following Statements (i) and (ii) hold, as is easily verified, namely, (i) $\alpha + 1 \leq \beta + 1$ if $2^{-\beta} \neq 0$, and (ii) $\alpha + 1 \leq \beta$ if $2^{-\beta} = 0$ and $\alpha \neq \beta$. ∎

Alternative Proof of Theorem 4.3.6 Let (X, ϱ, Γ) be a spherically complete generalized ultrametric space with ordinal distances, and let $f : X \to X$ be strictly contracting. Then $\mathcal{B}X$ is a chain-complete partially ordered set, and $\mathcal{B}f$ is a monotonic mapping on $\mathcal{B}X$. For $B_0 \in \mathcal{B}X$, we denote by $\uparrow B_0$ the upper cone of B_0, that is, the set of all $B \in \mathcal{B}X$ with $B_0 \sqsubseteq B$, as defined in Section 3.2.

Let $x \in X$ be arbitrarily chosen, assume without loss of generality that $x \neq f(x)$, and also let α be an ordinal such that $\varrho(x, f(x)) = 2^{-\alpha}$. Then $(x, 2^{-\alpha}) \sqsubseteq \left(f(x), 2^{-(\alpha+1)} \right)$, and by monotonicity of $\mathcal{B}f$ we obtain that $\mathcal{B}f$ maps $\uparrow [(x, 2^{-\alpha})]$ into itself. Since $\uparrow [(x, 2^{-\alpha})]$ is a chain-complete partial order with bottom element $[(x, 2^{-\alpha})]$, we obtain by the Knaster-Tarski theorem, Theorem 1.1.10, that $\mathcal{B}f$ has a least fixed point in $\uparrow [(x, 2^{-\alpha})]$, which we will denote by B_0.

It is clear by definition of $\mathcal{B}f$ that B_0 must be maximal in $\mathcal{B}X$ and, hence, is of the form $[(x_0, 0)]$. From $\mathcal{B}f[(x_0, 0)] = [(x_0, 0)]$, we obtain $f(x_0) = x_0$, so that x_0 is a fixed point of f.

Now assume that $y \neq x_0$ is another fixed point of f. Then $\varrho(x_0, y) = \varrho(f(x_0), f(y)) < \varrho(x_0, y)$ since f is strictly contracting. This contradiction establishes that f has no fixed point other than x_0. ∎

We note finally that the constructions used for casting domains into generalized ultrametrics as in Section 4.8.2 and for casting generalized ultrametrics into chain-complete partial orders as in Section 4.8.3 are not inverses of each other, and the exact relationship between these processes remains to be determined.

4.8.4 GUMS and d-GUMS

We move next to study relationships between gums and d-gums and provide results somewhat parallel to those of Section 4.8.1, where we contrasted metrics and d-metrics. Indeed, our main objective here is to investigate the relationship between the Prieß-Crampe and Ribenboim theorem, Theorem 4.3.6, and its dislocated version, Theorem 4.5.2.

4.8.18 Proposition Let (X, ϱ, Γ) be a dislocated generalized ultrametric space, and define $d : X \times X \to \Gamma$ by setting $d(x, y) = \varrho(x, y)$ for $x \neq y$ and setting $d(x, x) = 0$ for all $x \in X$. Then d is a generalized ultrametric.

Proof: The proof is straightforward following Proposition 4.8.8. ∎

4.8.19 Definition The generalized ultrametric d just defined from the d-generalized ultrametric ϱ is called the generalized ultrametric *associated* with ϱ.

4.8.20 Proposition Let (X, ϱ, Γ) be a dislocated generalized ultrametric space, and let d denote the generalized ultrametric associated with ϱ. If d is spherically complete, then ϱ is spherically complete. If f is strictly contracting relative to ϱ, then f is strictly contracting relative to d.

Proof: We first show that non-empty balls in ϱ contain all their midpoints. So let $\{y \mid \varrho(x, y) \leq \alpha\}$ be some non-empty ball in ϱ with midpoint x. Then there is some $z \in \{y \mid \varrho(x, y) \leq \alpha\}$, and we obtain $\varrho(x, x) \leq \varrho(x, z)$ by (U4). Since $\varrho(x, z) \leq \alpha$, we have $x \in \{y \mid \varrho(x, y) \leq \alpha\}$. Hence, every non-empty ball in ϱ is also a ball with respect to d.

Now let $\mathcal{B}$ be a chain of non-empty balls in ϱ. Then $\mathcal{B}$ is also a chain of balls in d and has non-empty intersection by spherical completeness of d, as required.

Let $x, y \in X$ with $x \neq y$, and assume $\varrho(f(x), f(y)) < \varrho(x, y)$. If $f(x) = f(y)$, then $d(f(x), f(y)) = 0$, and hence $d(f(x), f(y)) < d(x, y)$. If $f(x) \neq f(y)$, then $x \neq y$, and so $d(f(x), f(y)) = \varrho(f(x), f(y)) < \varrho(x, y) = d(x, y)$, as required. ∎

4.8.21 Proposition Let (X, ϱ, Γ) be a spherically complete dislocated generalized ultrametric space, and let d denote the generalized ultrametric associated with ϱ. Then d is spherically complete. However, if f is strictly contracting relative to d, it does not follow that f is necessarily strictly contracting relative to ϱ.

Proof: Let $\mathcal{B}$ be a chain of balls in d. If $\mathcal{B}$ contains a ball $B = \{x\}$ for some $x \in X$, then x is in the intersection of the chain. So assume that all balls in $\mathcal{B}$ contain more than one point.

Now let $B_\gamma(x_m) = \{x \mid d(x, x_m) \leq \gamma\}$ be a ball in $\mathcal{B}$, and let $z \in B_\gamma(x_m)$ with $z \neq x_m$. Then $\varrho(x_m, x_m) \leq \varrho(z, x_m) = d(z, x_m) \leq \gamma$; hence $B_\gamma(x_m) = \{x \mid \varrho(x, x_m) \leq \gamma\}$. It follows that $\mathcal{B}$ is also a chain of balls in ϱ and, hence, has non-empty intersection by spherical completeness of ϱ, as required.

Let $X = \{0, 1\}$, and define a mapping $f : X \to X$ by $f(x) = 0$ for all $x \in X$. Let ϱ be constant and equal to 1. Then $(X, \varrho, \{0, 1\})$, where $0 < 1$, is a spherically complete d-gum and f is strictly contracting relative to d. However, $\varrho(f(0), f(1)) = \varrho(0, 0) = \varrho(0, 1)$, and so f is not strictly contracting relative to ϱ. ∎

We can now use Theorem 4.3.6 to give an easy proof of Theorem 4.5.2, as follows. With the notation used in Theorems 4.3.6 and 4.5.2 and using Proposition 4.8.18, we obtain a generalized ultrametric space (X, d, Γ) which is spherically complete by Proposition 4.8.21. By Proposition 4.8.20, the function f is strictly contracting relative to d. Hence, by Theorem 4.3.6, f has a unique fixed point.

We close this section by giving two constructions of d-gums from gums.

4.8.22 Proposition Let (X, d, Γ) be a generalized ultrametric space with ordinal distances, and let $u : X \to \Gamma$ be a function. Then the distance function ϱ defined by

$$\varrho(x, y) = \max\{d(x, y), u(x), u(y)\}$$

is a dislocated generalized ultrametric on X.

Proof: (U2) and (U3) are trivial. For (U4), see the proof of Proposition 4.8.7. ∎

This result will be applied in Section 5.1.3.

4.8.23 Proposition Let (X, d, Γ) be a generalized ultrametric space with ordinal distances, let $z \in X$, and define the distance function ϱ by

$$\varrho(x, y) = \max\{d(x, z), d(y, z)\}.$$

Then (X, ϱ, Γ) is a spherically complete, dislocated generalized ultrametric space.

Proof: Clearly, ϱ is a d-gum. For spherical completeness, note that every non-empty ball in (X, ϱ, Γ) contains z, and this suffices. ∎

This result will be applied in Section 5.1.4.

4.9   Fixed-Point Theory for Multivalued Mappings

We close this chapter with a discussion of multivalued mappings and some of the fixed-point theorems which are applicable to them.

Let X be a set. Then a *multivalued mapping* T defined on X is simply a mapping $T : X \to \mathcal{P}(X)$ from X to the power set $\mathcal{P}(X)$ of X; thus, for each $x \in X$, $T(x)$ is a subset of X. Furthermore, a *fixed point of a multivalued mapping* T is an element x of X such that $x \in T(x)$. Such mappings are important in studying semantics in the presence of non-determinism because at any step in the execution of a non-deterministic program, there will in general be many possible successive states, and therefore the informal meaning of such a program may be taken to be a multivalued mapping defined on the set X of states the program may assume. These comments apply in particular to *disjunctive logic programs* in which the head of a typical program clause contains a disjunction of several atoms, rather than a single atom, and in executing such a program a non-deterministic choice has to be made of an atom in the head of any clause involved in the execution.

Not surprisingly, given their informal meaning, the formal meaning of disjunctive programs involves fixed points of multivalued mappings. Therefore, it is of interest to consider fixed-point theorems in this context and the methods used to establish them. Again, not surprisingly, the methods normally used to establish such theorems depend either on order theory or on generalized metrics of one type or another, and we consider both approaches.

We begin by considering an interesting recent paper by Straccia, Ojeda-Aciego, and Damásio, see [Straccia et al., 2009], and relating their work to ours. In this paper, the authors use methods depending on order theory to establish a number of results guaranteeing the existence of least and greatest fixed points of a multivalued mapping $T : L \to \mathcal{P}(L)$, where L is a complete lattice. In contrast, the methods we will employ mainly depend on the methods of analysis. Furthermore, as noted below, the results of [Straccia et al., 2009] are broadly representative of those obtained by order theory. Therefore, it will help to state a result of [Straccia et al., 2009], which gives a flavour of its contents and is typical of results obtained in the field by order theory. However, to do this requires the statement of some preliminary definitions, but they will be needed in any case as we proceed.

Given the complete lattice $(L, \leq)$ and its power set $\mathcal{P}(L)$, we define three orderings on $\mathcal{P}(L)$ familiar in semantics and domain theory, as follows, see

[Abramsky and Jung, 1994]. First, the *Smyth ordering* $\preceq_S$ defined by $X \preceq_S Y$ if and only if for each $y \in Y$ there exists $x \in X$ such that $x \leq y$. Second, we define the *Hoare ordering* $\preceq_H$ by $X \preceq_H Y$ if and only if for each $x \in X$ there exists $y \in Y$ such that $x \leq y$. Finally, we define the *Egli–Milner ordering* $\preceq_{EM}$ by $X \preceq_{EM} Y$ if and only if $X \preceq_S Y$ and $X \preceq_H Y$. Next, we say that T is *Smyth monotonic* or simply *S-monotonic* if, for all $x, y \in X$ satisfying $x \leq y$, we have $T(x) \preceq_S T(y)$. The notions of *Hoare monotonicity* and *Egli–Milner monotonicity* are defined similarly.

We are now in a position to present the following result of Straccia, Ojeda-Aciego, and Damásio, see [Straccia et al., 2009, Prosposition 3.10].

4.9.1 Proposition Let $T : L \to \mathcal{P}(L)$ be a multivalued mapping, where L is a complete lattice.

(a) If T is S-monotonic and for all $x \in L$, $T(x)$ has a least element, then T has a least fixed point.

(b) If T is H-monotonic and for all $x \in L$, $T(x)$ has a greatest element, then T has a greatest fixed point.

Straccia et al. also introduce a very general class of logic programs $\mathcal{P}$, a class much more general than conventional disjunctive logic programs, and proceed to define a multivalued semantic operator $T_{\mathcal{P}}$ associated with each program $\mathcal{P}$ in the class in question. On applying their fixed-point theorems, they establish a one-to-one correspondence between the models of any program $\mathcal{P}$ and the fixed points of $T_{\mathcal{P}}$. All these results are order-theoretic in nature, although, in summarizing their conclusions, the question of deriving fixed-point theorems for multivalued mappings using methods from analysis is raised by the authors, but not taken up in detail.

Thus, we will focus here mainly on those fixed-point theorems for multivalued mappings which employ analytical methods and results in their formulation or in their proofs, rather than on results which depend primarily on order theory. This is partly for the reason stated at the end of the previous paragraph and partly because the results of [Straccia et al., 2009] largely subsume the order-theoretic results derived by several other contributors to this subject anyway, except that the latter are usually presented in the context of complete partial orders rather than in the less general context of complete lattices employed by Straccia and his co-authors. On the other hand, most other authors require the condition that the multivalued mapping T is *nonempty* in the sense that, for all $x \in X$, we have $T(x) \neq \emptyset$, a condition that Straccia et al. do not impose. However, despite the opening sentence of this paragraph, we do wish to consider a result of our own which gives a form, for multivalued mappings, of the Rutten-Smyth theorem discussed earlier, Theorem 4.6.3, and its role in unifying the order-theoretic and metric approaches to the fixed-point theory of multivalued mappings, and this of course necessitates some discussion of order theory.

In fact, it turns out that the majority of the fixed-point theorems we have already considered earlier in this chapter can be directly carried over to the multivalued setting, and indeed our main task now is to carry out this extension. Thus, we present multivalued versions of the Knaster-Tarski theorem, the Banach contraction mapping theorem, the Rutten-Smyth theorem referred to in the previous paragraph, and Kleene's theorem. We do not, however, include any applications of these results here, although they do indeed have a number of applications to the semantics of (conventional) disjunctive logic programs, see [Khamsi et al., 1993, Khamsi and Misane, 1998, Hitzler and Seda, 1999c, Hitzler and Seda, 2002a].

4.10   Partial Orders and Multivalued Mappings

Throughout, $T : X \to \mathcal{P}(X)$ will denote a multivalued mapping defined on X. Furthermore, unless stated to the contrary, T will be assumed to be non-empty.

We begin by discussing a fixed-point theorem first established by M.A. Khamsi and D. Misane, see [Khamsi and Misane, 1998]. It can be viewed as a multivalued version of the Knaster-Tarski theorem, Theorem 1.1.10; a multivalued version of Kleene's theorem, Theorem 1.1.9 will be presented in Section 4.13.

4.10.1 Definition Let $T : X \to \mathcal{P}(X)$ be a multivalued mapping defined on X. An *orbit* of T is a net $(x_i)_{i \in \mathcal{I}}$ in X, where $\mathcal{I}$ denotes an ordinal, such that $x_{i+1} \in T(x_i)$ for all $i \in \mathcal{I}$. An orbit $(x_i)_{i \in \mathcal{I}}$ of T is called an ω-*orbit* if $\mathcal{I}$ is the first limit ordinal, ω. An orbit $(x_i)_{i \in \mathcal{I}}$ of T will be said to be *eventually constant* if there is a tail $(x_i)_{i_0 \leq i}$ of $(x_i)_{i \in \mathcal{I}}$ which is *constant* in that $x_i = x_j$ for all $i, j \in \mathcal{I}$ satisfying $i_0 \leq i, j$.

If $T : X \to \mathcal{P}(X)$ is a multivalued mapping and x is a fixed point of T, then we obtain an orbit of T which is eventually constant by setting $x = x_0 = x_1 = x_2 \ldots$. Conversely, suppose that $(x_i)_{i \in \mathcal{I}}$ is an orbit of T with the property that $x_{i+1} = x_i$ for all $i \in \mathcal{I}$ satisfying $i_0 \leq i$, for some ordinal $i_0 \in \mathcal{I}$. Then $x_{i_0} = x_{i_0+1} \in T(x_{i_0})$, and we have a fixed point x_{i_0} of T. Thus, having a fixed point and having an orbit which is eventually constant are essentially equivalent conditions on T.

4.10.2 Definition Suppose that T is a multivalued mapping defined on a partially ordered set X. An orbit $(x_i)_{i \in \mathcal{I}}$ of T is said to be *increasing* if we have $x_i \leq x_j$ for all $i, j \in \mathcal{I}$ satisfying $i \leq j$ and is said to be *eventually increasing* if some tail of the orbit is increasing. Finally, an increasing orbit $(x_i)_{i \in \mathcal{I}}$ of T is said to be *tight* if, for all limit ordinals $j \in \mathcal{I}$, we have $x_j = \bigsqcup \{x_i \mid i < j\}$.

Suppose that $(x_i)_{i \in \mathcal{I}}$ is an increasing orbit of T and that $j \in \mathcal{I}$ is a limit ordinal. Then x_{j+1} is an element of $T(x_j)$ such that $x_i \leq x_{j+1}$ for all $i < j$, and of course $\bigsqcup\{x_i \mid i < j\} \leq x_j \leq x_{j+1}$ if the supremum exists. In particular, any increasing orbit $(x_i)_{i \in \mathcal{I}}$ which is tight (if such exists) must satisfy the following condition: for any limit ordinal j, there exists $x = x_{j+1}$ such that

$$x \in T(\bigsqcup\{x_i \mid i < j\}) \quad \text{and} \quad \bigsqcup\{x_i \mid i < j\} \leq x. \tag{4.1}$$

This condition is a slight variant of a condition which was identified by Khamsi and Misane as a sufficient condition for the existence of fixed points of Hoare monotonic multivalued mappings. In fact, the following result was established by them, see [Khamsi and Misane, 1998], except that it was formulated for decreasing orbits and infima, and we have chosen to work with the dual notions instead to be consistent with the form of Kleene's theorem we give later.

4.10.3 Theorem (Knaster-Tarski multivalued) Suppose that X is a complete partial order and that $T : X \to \mathcal{P}(X)$ is a multivalued mapping which is non-empty, Hoare monotonic, and satisfies condition (4.1). Then T has a fixed point.

We omit details of the proof of this result except to observe that, starting with the bottom element $x_0 = \bot$ of X, the condition (4.1) permits the construction, transfinitely, of a tight orbit (x_i) of T. Since this can be carried out for ordinals whose underlying cardinal is greater than that of X, we are forced to conclude that (x_i) is eventually constant and therefore that T has a fixed point.

Noting that $\bigsqcup\{x_i \mid i < j\} = \bigsqcup\{x_{i+1} \mid i < j\}$, one can view condition (4.1) schematically as the statement "$\bigsqcup\{T(x_i) \mid i < j\} \leq T(\bigsqcup\{x_i \mid i < j\})$", and it can therefore be thought of as a rather natural, weak continuity condition on T which is automatically satisfied by any monotonic single-valued mapping T on a complete partial order. The question of when the orbit constructed in the previous paragraph becomes constant in not more than ω steps is a question of continuity, as in the single-valued version, and will be taken up in Section 4.13.

Theorem 4.10.3 was established by Khamsi and Misane in order to show the existence of (consistent) answer sets for a class of disjunctive logic programs called signed programs. We have shown elsewhere, see [Hitzler and Seda, 1999c], that it sometimes is necessary to work transfinitely in practice, a point which justifies the name "Knaster-Tarski theorem" applied to Theorem 4.10.3.

Thus, in summary, Hoare monotonicity of T together with (4.1) gives, for multivalued mappings, an exact analogue of the fixed-point theory for monotonic single-valued mappings due to Knaster-Tarski. Moreover, there are applications of it to the semantics of disjunctive logic programs which parallel those made in the standard, non-disjunctive case.

4.11 Metrics and Multivalued Mappings

We discuss here a result established by M.A. Khamsi, V. Kreinovich, and D. Misane, see [Khamsi et al., 1993], which is a multivalued version of the Banach contraction mapping theorem, Theorem 4.2.3.

4.11.1 Definition Let (X, d) be a metric space. A multivalued mapping $T : X \to \mathcal{P}(X)$ is called a *contraction* if there exists a non-negative real number $\lambda < 1$ such that for every $x \in X$, for every $y \in X$, and for all $a \in T(x)$ there exists $b \in T(y)$ such that $d(a, b) \leq \lambda d(x, y)$.

The result we wish to state is as follows; a proof of it will be given in Section 4.13.

4.11.2 Theorem (Banach multivalued) Let X be a complete metric space, and suppose that T is a multivalued contraction on X such that, for every $x \in X$, the set $T(x)$ is closed and non-empty. Then T has a fixed point.

This theorem was also established with a specific objective in view, namely, to show the existence of answer sets for disjunctive logic programs which are countably stratified, again see [Khamsi et al., 1993].

4.12 Generalized Ultrametrics and Multivalued Mappings

We next turn our attention to multivalued versions of the Prieß-Crampe and Ribenboim theorem, Theorem 4.3.6.

4.12.1 Definition Let (X, ϱ, Γ) be a generalized ultrametric space. A multivalued mapping T defined on X is called *strictly contracting* (on X) (respectively, *non-expanding* (on X)) if, for all $x, y \in X$ with $x \neq y$ and for every $a \in T(x)$, there exists an element $b \in T(y)$ such that $\varrho(a, b) < \varrho(x, y)$ $(\varrho(a, b) \leq \varrho(x, y))$. Furthermore, the mapping T is called *strictly contracting on orbits* if, for every $x \in X$ and for every $a \in T(x)$ with $a \neq x$, there exists an element $b \in T(a)$ such that $\varrho(a, b) < \varrho(a, x)$.

For $T : X \to \mathcal{P}(X)$, let $\Pi_x = \{\varrho(x, y) \mid y \in T(x)\}$, and, for a subset $\Delta \subseteq \Gamma$, denote by $\text{Min } \Delta$ the set of all minimal elements of Δ.

Note that these definitions collapse to those already considered for single-valued mappings if, in fact, T is single valued, meaning that $T(x)$ is a singleton set for each $x \in X$.

The following theorem was proved by Prieß-Crampe and Ribenboim, see [Prieß-Crampe and Ribenboim, 2000c], and is a multivalued version of Theorem 4.3.6.

4.12.2 Theorem (Prieß-Crampe and Ribenboim) Let (X, ϱ, Γ) be a spherically complete, generalized ultrametric space, and let $T : X \to \mathcal{P}(X)$ be non-empty, non-expanding, and strictly contracting on orbits. In addition, assume that for every $x \in X$, $\operatorname{Min} \Pi_x$ is finite and that every element of Π_x has a lower bound in $\operatorname{Min} \Pi_x$. Then T has a fixed point.

This result has several corollaries, due to Prieß-Crampe and Ribenboim, see [Prieß-Crampe and Ribenboim, 2000c], both for multivalued mappings and for single-valued mappings, and we state two of these next for completeness. Theorem 4.12.2 has been applied to establish the stable model semantics for disjunctive logic programs, see [Seda and Hitzler, 2010]. Note that Theorem 4.12.4 is a slight extension of Theorem 4.3.6.

4.12.3 Theorem Let (X, ϱ, Γ) be spherically complete, and let Γ be narrow, that is, such that every trivially ordered subset of Γ is finite. Let $f : X \to \mathcal{P}(X)$ be non-empty, strictly contracting on orbits and such that $f(x)$ is spherically complete for every $x \in X$. Then f has a fixed point.

4.12.4 Theorem Let (X, ϱ, Γ) be a spherically complete, generalized ultrametric space, and let $f : X \to X$ be non-expanding on X. Then either f has a fixed point or there exists a ball $B_\pi(z)$ such that $\varrho(y, f(y)) = \pi$ for all $y \in B_\pi(z)$. If, in addition, f is strictly contracting on orbits, then f has a fixed point. Finally, this fixed point is unique if f is strictly contracting on X.

The following ideas are closely related to the notion of value semigroup given in Definition 4.1.2 and were considered by Khamsi, Kreinovich, and Misane in the context of the stable model semantics for disjunctive logic programs, see [Khamsi et al., 1993]. We show that, in fact, these notions basically coincide with those from generalized ultrametric theory.

4.12.5 Definition Let V be an ordered Abelian semigroup with 0, and let X be an arbitrary set. A *g-metric* on X is a mapping $\rho : X \times X \to V$ which satisfies the following conditions for all $x, y, z \in X$.

(1) $\rho(x, y) = 0$ if and only if $x = y$.

(2) $\rho(x, y) = \rho(y, x)$.

(3) $\rho(x, y) \leq \rho(x, z) + \rho(z, y)$.

A pair (X, ρ) consisting of a set X and a g-metric ρ on X is called a *g-metric space*.

In fact, g-metrics were called generalized metrics by Khamsi, Kreinovich, and Misane, but we have changed the terminology since the term "generalized metric" is, of course, already used differently by us. Actually, we will not work with g-metrics in general since the closely related generalized ultrametrics will suffice for our purposes. Indeed, we consider this relationship next, and we begin by recalling the observations we made in Remark 4.3.2. Thus, let V denote the set of all expressions of the type 0 or $2^{-\alpha}$, where $\alpha > 0$ is an ordinal. An order is defined on V by: $0 \le v$ for every $v \in V$, and $2^{-\alpha} \le 2^{-\beta}$ if and only if $\beta \le \alpha$. As a semigroup operation $u + v$, we will use the maximum $\max(u, v)$. It will be convenient to write $\frac{1}{2}2^{-\alpha} = 2^{-(\alpha+1)}$.

The following definition is due to Khamsi, Kreinovich, and Misane, see [Khamsi et al., 1993].

4.12.6 Definition Assume that α is either a countable ordinal or ω_1, the first uncountable ordinal, and that $\mathbf{v} = (v_\beta)_{\beta<\alpha}$ is a decreasing family of elements of V. Let X be a g-metric space relative to V, and let $(x_\beta)_{\beta<\alpha}$ be a family of elements of X.

(1) (x_β) is said to **v**-*cluster* to $x \in X$ if, for all β, we have $\rho(x_\beta, x) < v_\beta$ whenever $\beta < \alpha$.

(2) (x_β) is said to be **v**-*Cauchy* if, for all β and γ, we have $\rho(x_\beta, x_\gamma) < v_\beta$ whenever $\beta < \gamma < \alpha$.

(3) X is said to be **v**-*complete* or just *complete* if, for every **v**, every **v**-Cauchy family **v**-clusters to some element in X.

(4) A set $Y \subseteq X$ will be called **v**-*complete* or just *complete* if, for every **v**, whenever a **v**-Cauchy family consists of elements of Y, it **v**-clusters to some element of Y.

A close relationship exists between the notion of completeness for g-metrics and the notion of trans-completeness, Definition 4.3.8, for generalized ultra-metrics. Indeed, we show that these notions coincide by showing equivalence between completeness for g-metrics and spherical completeness for generalized ultrametrics, see Proposition 4.3.10.

4.12.7 Definition A multivalued mapping $T : X \to \mathcal{P}(X)$ is called a $\left(\frac{1}{2}\right)$-*contraction* if, for every $x \in X$, for every $y \in X$, and for every $a \in T(x)$, there exists $b \in T(y)$ such that $\rho(a, b) \le \frac{1}{2}\rho(x, y)$.

The following theorem was proved by Khamsi, Kreinovich, and Misane in [Khamsi et al., 1993].

4.12.8 Theorem Let X be a complete g-metric space, let T be a multivalued $\left(\frac{1}{2}\right)$-contraction defined on X such that $T(x)$ is not empty for some $x \in X$ (so that T is not identically empty), and suppose that for every $x \in X$ the set $T(x)$ is complete. Then T has a fixed point.

We next present some results relating those just given to the notion of spherical completeness we discussed earlier. Indeed, we show that if (X, ρ) is a g-metric space with respect to V as given in Definition 4.3.2, then ρ is a generalized ultrametric space, and vice-versa.

4.12.9 Proposition Let (X, ρ) be a complete g-metric space with respect to V. Then X is spherically complete as an ultrametric space.

Proof: Let $\mathcal{B} = \left(B_{v_\beta}(x_\beta)\right)_{\beta < \alpha}$ be a decreasing chain of balls in X, and without loss of generality assume that it is strictly decreasing and that α is a limit ordinal. We have to show that $\bigcap \mathcal{B} \neq \emptyset$. Let $\mathbf{v} = (v_\beta)_\beta$. Since $\mathcal{B}$ is a chain, it is easy to see that $(x_{\beta+1})_\beta$ is $\mathbf{v}$-Cauchy and therefore, by completeness of X, $(x_{\beta+1})$ $\mathbf{v}$-clusters to some $x \in X$. By definition, this means that $\rho(x_{\beta+1}, x) < v_\beta$ and therefore that $x \in B_{v_\beta}(x_{\beta+1}) = B_{v_\beta}(x_\beta)$ for all β. Thus, $x \in \bigcap \mathcal{B}$. ∎

In the opposite direction, we have the following result.

4.12.10 Proposition Let (X, ρ, V) be a spherically complete, generalized ultrametric space. Then X is complete as a g-metric space.

Proof: Let $\mathbf{v} = (v_\beta)$ be a decreasing family of elements of V which is, without loss of generality, strictly decreasing, and let (x_β) be $\mathbf{v}$-Cauchy. For $v \in \mathbf{v}$, for example, $v = 2^{-\alpha}$, let v' denote $2^{-(\alpha+1)}$. Then $\mathcal{B} = \left(B_{v'_\beta}(x_\beta)\right)_\beta$ is a decreasing chain of balls in X. By spherical completeness, it has non-empty intersection. Choose $x \in \bigcap \mathcal{B}$. Then for all β we obtain $\rho(x_\beta, x) \leq v'_\beta < v_\beta$, and so (x_β) $\mathbf{v}$-clusters to x. ∎

This means, by virtue of Theorem 4.12.2, that we can reformulate the assumptions in Theorem 4.12.8 and thereby obtain the following result, which, in fact, is a special case of a theorem of Prieß-Crampe and Ribenboim, see [Prieß-Crampe and Ribenboim, 2000c, (3.4)].

4.12.11 Theorem Let X be a spherically complete, generalized ultrametric space (with respect to V), and let T be a multivalued, non-empty, and strictly contracting mapping defined on X such that $T(x)$ is spherically complete for all $x \in X$. Then T has a fixed point.

4.13   Quasimetrics and Multivalued Mappings

We move next to study a multivalued version of the Rutten-Smyth theorem, Theorem 4.6.3. As a consequence, we obtain a multivalued version of Kleene's theorem, Theorem 1.1.9.[26]

---

[26] For further details, see [Hitzler and Seda, 1999c].

4.13.1 Definition Let (X, d) be a quasimetric space. A multivalued mapping $T : X \to \mathcal{P}(X)$ is called a *contraction* if there is a $\lambda \in [0, 1)$ such that, for all $x, y \in X$ and for all $a \in T(x)$, there exists $b \in T(y)$ satisfying $d(a, b) \leq \lambda d(x, y)$. We say that T is *non-expanding* if, for all $x, y \in X$ and for all $a \in T(x)$, there exists $b \in T(y)$ satisfying $d(a, b) \leq d(x, y)$.

Again, these definitions are clearly extensions of the corresponding definitions made for single-valued mappings and indeed collapse to them in the case where T is single valued. An obvious and natural definition of continuity of T is the following: for every Cauchy sequence (x_n) in X with limit x and for every choice of $y_n \in T(x_n)$, we have that (y_n) is a Cauchy sequence and $\lim y_n \in T(x)$. In fact, the weaker definition following, which is implied by the one just given, suffices for our purposes and will be used throughout.

4.13.2 Definition Let $T : X \to \mathcal{P}(X)$ be a multivalued mapping defined on a quasimetric space (X, d). We say that T is *continuous* if we have $\lim x_n \in T(\lim x_n)$ for every ω-orbit (x_n) of T which is a Cauchy sequence.

Once more, this definition collapses to a natural one if T is single valued. In fact, if T is single valued, it simply states the condition that $\lim T(x_n) = \lim x_{n+1} = \lim x_n = T(\lim x_n)$ for every ω-orbit which is a Cauchy sequence, which is a weaker condition than that of CS-continuity as in Definition 4.6.2(1).

Finally, if (X, d) is a quasimetric space, we define the associated partial order $\leq_d$ on X by $x \leq_d y$ if and only if $d(x, y) = 0$, see Section 4.6.

The main result of this section is the following theorem, generalizing the Rutten-Smyth theorem we gave earlier, Theorem 4.6.3.

4.13.3 Theorem (Rutten-Smyth multivalued) Let (X, d) be a CS-complete quasimetric space, and let $T : X \to \mathcal{P}(X)$ denote a non-empty and continuous multivalued mapping on X. Then T has a fixed point if either of the following two conditions holds.

(a) T is a contraction.

(b) T is non-expanding, and there is $x_0 \in X$ and $x_1 \in T(x_0)$ such that $d(x_0, x_1) = 0$, that is, $x_0 \leq_d x_1$.

Proof: (a) Let $x_0 \in X$. Since $T(x_0) \neq \emptyset$, we can choose $x_1 \in T(x_0)$. Since T is a contraction, there is $x_2 \in T(x_1)$ such that $d(x_1, x_2) \leq \lambda d(x_0, x_1)$. Applying this argument repeatedly, we obtain a sequence (x_n) such that for all $n \geq 0$ we have $x_{n+1} \in T(x_n)$ and $d(x_{n+1}, x_{n+2}) \leq \lambda d(x_n, x_{n+1})$. Thus, (x_n) is an ω-orbit. Using the triangle inequality, we obtain

$$d(x_n, x_{n+m}) \leq \sum_{i=0}^{m-1} d(x_{n+i}, x_{n+i+1}) \leq \sum_{i=0}^{m-1} \lambda^{n+i} d(x_0, x_1).$$

Since the last summation here is dominated by $\frac{\lambda^n}{1-\lambda}d(x_0, x_1)$, we see that (x_n) is a (forward) Cauchy sequence in X and therefore is an ω-orbit of T which is Cauchy. Since X is complete, (x_n) has a limit x_ω. Now, by continuity of T, we obtain $x_\omega \in T(x_\omega)$, and x_ω is a fixed point of T, as required.

(b) Let $x_0 \in X$ and $x_1 \in T(x_0)$ satisfy $d(x_0, x_1) = 0$. Since T is non-expanding, there is $x_2 \in T(x_1)$ with $d(x_1, x_2) \leq d(x_0, x_1) = 0$. Inductively, we obtain a sequence (x_n) such that $x_{n+1} \in T(x_n)$ and $d(x_n, x_{n+k}) \leq \sum_{i=0}^{k-1} d(x_{n+i}, x_{n+i+1}) = 0$. Hence, (x_n) is an orbit of T which is forward Cauchy and therefore has a limit x_ω. By continuity of T again, we see that x_ω is a fixed point of T. ∎

The proof given here of Part (a) of Theorem 4.13.3 is, up to the last step, exactly the same as the first half of the proof of the multivalued Banach contraction mapping theorem, Theorem 4.11.2, established by Khamsi, Kreinovich, and Misane, except that we are working with a quasimetric rather than with a metric and therefore care needs to be taken that no use is made of symmetry. On the other hand, the proof we give next of Theorem 4.11.2, which roughly corresponds to the second half of the proof given by Khamsi, Kreinovich, and Misane, is shorter and technically somewhat simpler than the proof given by them.

Proof of Theorem 4.11.2 We show that the condition that $T(x)$ is closed for every x together with that of T being a contraction implies that T is continuous, and the result then follows from Part (a) of Theorem 4.13.3.

First note that (X, d) being a complete metric space means that (X, d) is complete as a quasimetric space, and obviously T satisfies Part (a) of Theorem 4.13.3. Now suppose that (x_n) is an orbit of T which is a forward Cauchy sequence and, hence, a Cauchy sequence; we want to show that $x_\omega \in T(x_\omega)$, where x_ω is the limit of (x_n).

Since T is a contraction, for every n there exists $y_n \in T(x_\omega)$ such that $d(x_{n+1}, y_n) \leq \lambda d(x_n, x_\omega)$. Therefore, $d(y_n, x_\omega) \leq d(y_n, x_{n+1}) + d(x_{n+1}, x_\omega) \leq \lambda d(x_n, x_\omega) + d(x_{n+1}, x_\omega)$. Hence, we have $y_n \to x_\omega$. But each $y_n \in T(x_\omega)$, and $T(x)$ is closed for every x. Consequently, the limit x_ω of the sequence y_n also belongs to $T(x_\omega)$. So, $x_\omega \in T(x_\omega)$, and it follows that T is continuous, as required. ∎

Thus, Theorem 4.13.3 contains, as a consequence, the multivalued Banach contraction mapping theorem, Theorem 4.11.2, discussed earlier. It also contains a natural extension of Kleene's theorem to multivalued mappings, Theorem 4.13.6 below, as we show next. Thus, Theorem 4.13.3 gives a unification of metric and order-theoretic notions in direct analogy with the corresponding unification given, in the single-valued case, by Theorem 4.6.3.

In order to proceed, we make some preliminary and elementary observations, as follows, concerning partially ordered sets and the quasimetrics they carry, see Section 4.6. The proofs are straightforward and are omitted.

4.13.4 Proposition Let $(X, \leq)$ be a partial order, and let (X, d) denote the associated quasimetric space, so that $d = d_{\leq}$ as in Section 4.6. Then the following hold.

(a) A non-empty multivalued mapping $T : X \to \mathcal{P}(X)$ is Hoare monotonic if and only if it is non-expanding.

(b) A sequence (x_n) in X is eventually increasing in $(X, \leq)$ if and only if it is a Cauchy sequence in (X, d).

(c) The partially ordered set $(X, \leq)$ is ω-complete if and only if (X, d) is complete as a quasimetric space. Furthermore, in the presence of either form of completeness, the limit of any Cauchy sequence is the least upper bound of any increasing tail of the sequence.

Notice that neither Part (c) of this result nor the next definition assumes the presence of a bottom element.

4.13.5 Definition Let the partial order $(X, \leq)$ be ω-complete, and let $T : X \to \mathcal{P}(X)$ be a non-empty multivalued mapping on X. We say that T is ω-*continuous* if T is Hoare monotonic, and for any ω-orbit (x_n) of T which is eventually increasing, we have $\bigsqcup(x_n) \in T(\bigsqcup(x_n))$, where the supremum is taken over any increasing tail of (x_n).

We obtain finally the following form of Kleene's theorem for multivalued mappings as an easy corollary of our Theorem 4.13.3. This theorem has been applied by the present authors to find answer sets for certain classes of disjunctive logic programs, see [Hitzler and Seda, 1999c].

4.13.6 Theorem (Kleene multivalued) Let $(X, \leq)$ be an ω-complete partial order (with bottom element), and let $T : X \to \mathcal{P}(X)$ be a non-empty, ω-continuous multivalued mapping on X. Then T has a fixed point.

Proof: Since $(X, \leq)$ is ω-complete, the associated quasimetric space (X, d) (with $d = d_{\leq}$ as in Section 4.6) is complete by Proposition 4.13.4. Furthermore, T is Hoare monotonic, since it is ω-continuous and is therefore non-expanding by Proposition 4.13.4 again. On taking $x_0 = \bot$ and $x_1 \in T(x_0)$ arbitrarily, we have x_0 and x_1 satisfying $d(x_0, x_1) = 0$. The result will therefore follow from Part (b) of Theorem 4.13.3 as soon as we have established that T is continuous in the sense of Definition 4.13.2.

Let (x_n) be any ω-orbit of T which is a Cauchy sequence. Then (x_n) is eventually increasing, and, by ω-continuity of T, we have $\bigsqcup(x_n) \in T(\bigsqcup(x_n))$, where the supremum is taken over any increasing tail of (x_n). In other words, we have $\lim x_n \in T(\lim x_n)$, and hence we have the continuity of T that we require. ∎

Kleene's theorem for single-valued mappings T asserts that the fixed point produced by the usual proof is the least fixed point of T. This assertion does not immediately carry over to the case of multivalued mappings T without additional assumptions. One such simple, though rather strong, condition is the following: for each $x \in X$, assume that $T(x)$ has a least element M_x and that $M_x \leq M_y$ whenever $x \leq y$. To see that this suffices, suppose that x is any fixed point of T, and construct the orbit (x_n) of T by setting $x_0 = \perp$ and $x_{n+1} = M_{x_n}$ for each n. Then (x_n) converges to a fixed point $\overline{x}$. Noting that $\perp \leq x$ and that $M_x \leq x$, we see that $x_n \leq x$ for all n. Hence, $\overline{x} \leq x$.

4.14   An Alternative to Multivalued Mappings

As already noted earlier, multivalued mappings arise naturally as semantic operators in relation to disjunctive logic programs. However, William Rounds and Guo-Qiang Zhang have shown that the use of multivalued mappings in this context can be avoided by employing single-valued mappings defined on power domains instead (we refer the reader to [Stoltenberg-Hansen et al., 1994] for details of power domains). In fact, this observation is part of a considerable programme of research undertaken by the authors just mentioned in the application of domain theory to logic programming. Since their work complements that presented here, we intend to make a few remarks about a couple of aspects of it, and it is convenient to do this next.

The starting point of this programme of work is the observation that domains and logic are strongly related [Zhang, 1991] and that this relationship may be used as a foundation for a theory of logic programming based on domain theory. In [Zhang and Rounds, 1997a, Zhang and Rounds, 1997b] and [Rounds and Zhang, 2001], Rounds and Zhang use power domains to develop a domain-theoretic view of default logic, which they call *power defaults*. Indeed, in this framework logic programs can be viewed in a rather simple way as *default theories* in the sense of [Reiter, 1980]. Default theories constitute an important formalism in the area of non-monotonic reasoning, and we refer the reader to [Bidoit and Froideveaux, 1991, Gelfond and Lifschitz, 1991, Bochman, 1995, Lifschitz, 2001] and to the references contained in these papers for an interesting discussion of the relationship between default logic and logic programs. Indeed, from this point of view, the standard models of a disjunctive program, such as the stable model, correspond to extensions in default logic: in short, truth in a model corresponds to default theorem. Furthermore, Rounds and Zhang [Rounds and Zhang, 2001, Zhang and Rounds, 1997a, Zhang and Rounds, 1997b, Zhang and Rounds, 2001] study a version of default reasoning from the domain-theoretic point of view. In particular, they focus on the Smyth powerdomain by making the observation that the Smyth powerdomain can be used to model non-monotonicity. This results, for example, in the implementation of a non-monotonic reasoning system, see [Klavins et al., 1998], which bears a significant relationship to other answer set programming systems which have been investigated with implementation in mind, see [Lifschitz, 1999, Marek and Truszczyński, 1999]. In addition, in [Rounds and Zhang, 2001, Zhang and Rounds, 2001], Rounds and Zhang introduced a domain-theoretic framework for the study of the semantics of logic programming, both procedural and non-procedural, including an abstract resolution rule, together with a treatment of negation, which is not negation as (finite) failure, however. [Hitzler, 2003a, Hitzler and Wendt, 2003, Hitzler, 2004, Hitzler and Krötzsch, 2006] further expand on some aspects of the work of Rounds and Zhang and in particular relate it to Formal Concept Analysis [Ganter and Wille, 1999] and to answer set programming.[27]

Of course, the monotonicity notions for multivalued mappings used mainly in this chapter correspond to orderings encountered in power domains. In particular, this applies to Hoare montonicity and to Smyth monotonicity. With this and the comments of the previous paragraph in mind, we note finally that in Chapter 6 of [Zhang and Rounds, 2001], a treatment is given of the semantics of disjunctive logic programs (as considered here) with the same overall objective as our own. The treatment is based on the Smyth powerdomain again. One important feature of this power-domain approach is that by using the right domain, the concept of multivalued function is avoided and continuity can always be taken to be Scott continuity. Thus, in conclusion, we note that overall the developments just described appear to hold out, in particular, the possibility of a domain-theoretic treatment of the declarative semantics of negation in logic programming and therefore to bring logic programming semantics more fully into the realm of domain theory, and vice-versa.

---

[27]See Footnote 3 in the Introduction.

Chapter 5

Supported Model Semantics

Among the various semantics for normal logic programs discussed in Chapter 2, the supported model semantics, whether in two-valued or in three-valued form, is most fundamental: stable and perfect models are two-valued supported models; and well-founded and weakly perfect models are three-valued supported models. Furthermore, as shown in Theorem 2.6.14, if the Fitting model for a program P is total, then P has a unique two-valued supported model which coincides with the unique model assigned to P by the Fitting, the well-founded, the weakly perfect, and the stable semantics: the semantics in this case is unambiguous.

Programs which have unique supported models together with those which have total Fitting models can therefore be considered to be of fundamental importance for understanding logic programming semantics as presented in Chapter 2. The former, namely, programs with unique supported models, are called by us *uniquely determined*, while we call the latter Φ-*accessible* programs. We know from Theorem 2.6.14, as just noted, that every Φ-accessible program has a unique supported model. The converse, however, is not true in general, as the following example shows.

5.0.1 Program The program

$$p \leftarrow p$$
$$p \leftarrow \neg p$$

has a unique supported model $\{p\}$ and Fitting model $\emptyset$.

In this chapter, we study supported models in two-valued and three-valued logic, with particular emphasis on uniquely determined and Φ-accessible programs. In particular, in Section 5.1 we consider two-valued supported models and apply generalized metric fixed-point theorems from Chapter 4 in order to show that certain classes of programs are uniquely determined. As is to be expected, more general fixed-point theorems allow the treatment of more general classes of programs, so that the hierarchy of fixed-point theorems from Section 4.7 gives rise to a hierarchy of program classes, each of which has the property that all programs in the class have unique supported models. Such program classes are consequently called *unique supported model classes*.

The same hierarchy of unique supported model classes will be considered again in Section 5.2, but this time from the point of view of three-valued supported models (more precisely by studying variants of Fitting's Φ-operator). By analogy with Chapter 2, we will establish a correspondence between semantics defined, on the one hand, by means of monotonic operators, and characterizations given by means of level mappings, on the other hand. As a result, we obtain a hierarchy of program classes which extends observations from Chapter 2. All this will be carried out in this chapter in Section 5.3.

Finally, in Section 5.4, we make some brief observations concerning how one may approach the results of this chapter from a much more general point of view.

5.1   Two-Valued Supported Models

We know from Proposition 2.2.6 that the (two-valued) supported models for a given program P are exactly the fixed points of the corresponding single-step operator T_P. From Program 2.2.4, we know that T_P is in general not monotonic. This fact has the particular consequence that the fixed-point theorems from Section 1.1 for monotonic operators are not applicable to T_P in this case. The alternative suggested by our development in Chapter 4 is to apply, to non-monotonic single-step operators, fixed-point theorems utilizing generalized metrics. In particular, it suggests in our current context the application of those theorems which directly generalize the Banach contraction mapping theorem to the extent that they ensure uniqueness of the resulting fixed points, if any. Of course, if we successfully apply any of these particular theorems to a single-step operator, the corresponding program will clearly be uniquely determined. It follows, therefore, that any approach of this type employing fixed-point theorems which guarantee uniqueness of the resulting fixed points cannot, when applied to single-step operators, encompass all (definite) programs. Program 2.3.1, for example, is definite, but has two supported models and, hence, cannot be uniquely determined.

Throughout the present section, it will be convenient to let I_P denote $I_{P,2}$.

5.1.1   Acyclic and Locally Hierarchical Programs

Let us first recall the program Even (Program 2.1.3). Iterates of the corresponding immediate consequence operator T_{Even} are easily computed and are as follows, for all $n \in \mathbb{N}$, see Example 3.3.6.

$$T_{\text{Even}}^{2n} = \left\{ \text{even}\left(s^{2k}(0)\right) \mid 0 \leq k < n \right\},$$
$$T_{\text{Even}}^{2n+1} = B_{\text{Even}} \setminus \left\{ \text{even}\left(s^{2k+1}(0)\right) \mid 0 \leq k < n \right\}$$

We notice that the sequence of iterates is alternating in a certain sense. The iterates with even numbers successively *generate* the atoms in the supported model $M = \{\text{even}\left(s^{2n}(0)\right) \mid n \in \mathbb{N}\}$, while the iterates with odd numbers successively *delete* those atoms which are *not* in M. The order in which the atoms are generated or deleted is such that atoms with more occurrences of the function symbol s are generated or deleted later. This corresponds to the structure of the Even program, whose rules reflect this in the sense that the atom in the head of a ground instance of the second program clause always contains one more function symbol than the corresponding body atom.

The following definition abstracts from this and draws on the observation made in the previous paragraph that iterates of the immediate consequence operator can in some sense be controlled if there is a strong dependency between heads of clauses and their corresponding body atoms. This is a theme which will dominate the discussion of this chapter, and the reader may have already noticed that it is related to the characterizations of semantics using level mappings given in Chapter 2. The precise relationship between these two themes will be made more explicit in Section 5.2.

5.1.1 Definition A normal logic program P is called *locally hierarchical*[1] if there exists a level mapping $l : B_P \to \alpha$, for some ordinal α, such that for each clause $A \leftarrow L_1, \ldots, L_n$ in ground(P) and for all $i = 1, \ldots, n$ we have $l(A) > l(L_i)$. If α can be chosen here to be ω, then P is called *acyclic*.[2]

The Even program is acyclic, as can be seen by defining $l : B_P \to \alpha$ by $l\left(\text{even}\left(s^k(0)\right)\right) = k$ for all $k \in \mathbb{N}$.

5.1.2 Program (ExistsEven) Consider the following program, which extends Even. We call it *ExistsEven* because intuitively, and also when run under Prolog, it is a generate-and-test program which tests whether or not there exists an even number.

$$\text{nat}(0) \leftarrow$$
$$\text{nat}(s(X)) \leftarrow \text{nat}(X)$$
$$\text{even}(0) \leftarrow$$
$$\text{even}(s(X)) \leftarrow \neg\text{even}(X)$$
$$\text{existsEven} \leftarrow \text{nat}(X), \text{even}(X)$$

---

[1] Locally hierarchical programs were studied in [Cavedon, 1989]. It was shown in [Seda and Hitzler, 1999a] that it is possible to compute all partial recursive functions with locally hierarchical programs under SLDNF-resolution if the use of the meta-logical *cut* is allowed.

[2] Acyclic programs were studied in [Cavedon, 1989, Cavedon, 1991] under the name of *ω-locally hierarchical programs*. The notion of *acyclicity* was introduced in [Bezem, 1989], and further studies of it concerning termination properties were undertaken in [Bezem, 1989, Apt and Bezem, 1990].

Certainly, ExistsEven is somewhat pointless as a program. However, it exhibits the basic idea underlying the generate-and-test programming scheme. If Prolog is called with the query

```
?- existsEven.
```

then the interpreter successively *generates* all instantiations of $\mathbf{nat}(X)$ and *tests* for each instance of X whether or not it falls under the predicate $\mathbf{even}$. Obviously, the generator $\mathbf{nat}$ and the test $\mathbf{even}$ could be replaced by something much more sophisticated.

In ExistsEven, the subprogram consisting of the first four clauses is acyclic with respect to the level mapping l with $l\left(\mathbf{even}\left(s^k(0)\right)\right) = l\left(\mathbf{nat}\left(s^k(0)\right)\right) = k$ for all $k \in \mathbb{N}$, and we notice that any level mapping with respect to which this subprogram is acyclic must have an infinite codomain. Consequently, ExistsEven is not acyclic, but it is locally hierarchical, as can be seen by extending the level mapping by setting $l(\mathbf{existsEven}) = \omega$.

We want to apply generalized metric fixed-point theorems from Chapter 4 to acyclic and locally hierarchical programs, that is, we would like to construct a (generalized) metric on the set of all interpretations of a program such that the immediate consequence operator of the program satisfies a corresponding contractivity property. We follow the construction of Section 4.8.2 with a minor modification to suit our present purposes.

5.1.3 Definition Let P be a normal logic program, and let $l : B_P \to \gamma$ be a level mapping for P. We consider symbols $2^{-\alpha}$ for ordinals α, and, essentially as in Section 4.8.2, define $\Gamma_l = \{2^{-\alpha} \mid \alpha \le \gamma\}$. The set Γ_l is again ordered by $2^{-\alpha} < 2^{-\beta}$ if and only if $\beta < \alpha$, and we denote $2^{-\gamma}$ by 0.

In Sections 4.8.2 and 4.8.3, we used this construction for gums with ordinal distances, and with the notation established there we have $\Gamma_l = \Gamma_{\gamma+1}$, where $l : B_P \to \gamma$.

Finally, define a mapping $d_l : I_P \times I_P \to \Gamma_l$ by setting $d_l(I, J) = 0$ if $I = J$, and, when $I \ne J$, by setting $d_l(I, J) = 2^{-\alpha}$, where I and J differ on some ground atom of level α, but agree on all ground atoms β satisfying $\beta < \alpha$.

In case $\gamma = \omega$, we can identify each $2^{-n} \in \Gamma_l$ with the corresponding negative power of two, that is, $2^{-n} = \frac{1}{2^n} \in \mathbb{R}$ and $2^{-\omega} = 0$, and then d_l takes values in the set of real numbers.

5.1.4 Proposition Suppose that P is a normal logic program, and that l is a level mapping. Then the following statements hold.

(a) If P is locally hierarchical with respect to l, then d_l is a spherically complete generalized ultrametric.

(b) If P is acyclic with respect to l, then d_l is a complete ultrametric.

Proof: It suffices to prove (a). We will do this by applying Theorem 4.8.14. For the given level mapping l, define the rank function r_l by setting $r_l(\emptyset) = 0$ and by setting $r_l(I) = \max\{l(A) \mid A \in I\}$ for every non-empty $I \in (I_P)_c$, where we identify each element of $(I_P)_c$ with a finite subset of B_P, as usual. The generalized ultrametric d_{r_l} induced by r_l, as in Definition 4.8.12, is spherically complete by Theorem 4.8.14. The mappings d_l and d_{r_l} coincide since, for each $I \in I_P$, we have $I = \sup\{\{A\} \mid A \in I\}$, with the supremum being taken with respect to subset inclusion. ∎

Under certain conditions similar to those discussed in Section 4.6, we can recover the Cantor topology from d_l.

5.1.5 Proposition Let P be a normal logic program, and let $l : B_P \to \omega$ be a level mapping such that $l^{-1}(n)$ is finite for each $n \in \mathbb{N}$. Then d_l induces the Cantor topology Q on I_P.

Proof: It is easily shown by using Proposition 3.3.5 that sequences converge in Q if and only if they converge with respect to d_l, and this observation suffices. ∎

We show finally that the immediate consequence operator satisfies the required contractivity conditions for applying the Prieß-Crampe and Ribenboim theorem or the Banach contraction mapping theorem, as appropriate.

5.1.6 Theorem Suppose that P is a normal logic program, and that l is a level mapping. Then the following statements hold.

(a) If P is locally hierarchical with respect to l, then T_P is a strictly contracting.

(b) If P is acyclic with respect to l, then T_P is a contraction.

Furthermore, in both cases, T_P has a unique fixed point, and P has a unique supported model.

Proof: (a) Suppose $I_1, I_2 \in I_P$, and that $d_l(I_1, I_2) = 2^{-\alpha}$ for some ordinal α.

Suppose $\alpha = 0$. Let $A \in T_P(I_1)$ with $l(A) = 0$. Since P is locally hierarchical, A must be the head of a unit clause in $\text{ground}(P)$. From this it follows that $A \in T_P(I_2)$ also. By the same argument, if $A \in T_P(I_2)$ with $l(A) = 0$, then $A \in T_P(I_1)$. Therefore, $T_P(I_1)$ and $T_P(I_2)$ agree on all atoms of level less than 1, and hence we have

$$d_l(T_P(I_1), T_P(I_2)) \le 2^{-1} < 2^{-0} = d_l(I_1, I_2),$$

as required.

Now suppose $\alpha > 0$, so that I_1 and I_2 differ on some element of B_P with level α, but agree on all ground atoms of lower level. Let $A \in T_P(I_1)$

with $l(A) \leq \alpha$. Then there is a clause $A \leftarrow A_1, \ldots, A_{k_1}, \neg B_1, \ldots, \neg B_{l_1}$ in ground(P), where $k_1, l_1 \geq 0$, such that for all k, j we have $A_k \in I_1$ and $B_j \notin I_1$. Since P is locally hierarchical and I_1, I_2 agree on all atoms of level less than α, it follows that for all k, j we have $A_k \in I_2$ and $B_j \notin I_2$. Therefore, $A \in T_P(I_2)$. By the same argument, if $A \in T_P(I_2)$ with $l(A) \leq \alpha$, then $A \in T_P(I_1)$. Hence, we have that $T_P(I_1)$ and $T_P(I_2)$ agree on all atoms of level less than or equal to α, and it follows that

$$d_l(T_P(I_1), T_P(I_2)) \leq 2^{-(\alpha+1)} < 2^{-\alpha} = d_l(I_1, I_2),$$

as required.

Thus, T_P is strictly contracting, and Theorem 4.3.6 yields that T_P has a unique fixed point and therefore that P has a unique supported model.

The proof just given is easily adapted to establish (b). The operator T_P turns out to be contractive with contractivity factor $\frac{1}{2}$, and then Theorem 4.2.3 is applied instead of Theorem 4.3.6. ■

5.1.7 Example Consider the program Tweety1 from Examples 2.1.2 and 2.2.7. Tweety1 is acyclic with level mapping $l(\text{penguin}(X)) = 0, l(\text{bird}(X)) = 1$ and $l(\text{flies}(X)) = 2$ for $X \in \{\text{bob}, \text{tweety}\}$. For $I_0 = \{\text{bird(tweety)}\}$, we obtain

$$I_1 = T_{\text{Tweety1}}(I_0) = \{\text{penguin(tweety)}, \text{bird(bob)}, \text{flies(tweety)}\},$$
$$I_2 = T_{\text{Tweety1}}(I_1) = \{\text{penguin(tweety)}, \text{bird(bob)}, \text{bird(tweety)},$$
$$\text{flies(bob)}\}, \text{ and}$$
$$I_3 = T_{\text{Tweety1}}(I_2) = I_2.$$

Another example is given by the program Even (Program 2.1.3), as discussed at the beginning of Section 5.1.1.

5.1.2   Acceptable Programs

Historically, acyclic programs were introduced in attempts to capture procedural properties, such as termination, under SLDNF-resolution, see [Bezem, 1989, Apt and Bezem, 1990, Cavedon, 1991]. The basic idea behind acyclic programs was extended to take into account the fact that logic programming systems, such as Prolog, evaluate clause bodies from left to right, and this led to the acceptable programs[3] studied in this section. We will focus on declarative aspects of acceptable programs here, generalizing the approach of Section 5.1.1.

---

[3]Acceptable programs were introduced by Apt and Pedreschi in AP94. For further reading concerning termination in resolution-based logic programming, see [Marchiori, 1996, Apt, 1997, Pedreschi et al., 2002].

5.1.8 Definition Let P be a program, and recall from Section 2.5 that an atom $A \in B_P$ *refers to* an atom $B \in B_P$ if B or $\neg B$ occurs as a body literal in a clause $A \leftarrow$ body in P. We say that A *depends on* B if the pair (A, B) is in the transitive closure of the relation *refers to*. We further denote by Neg_P the set of predicate symbols in P which occur in a negative literal in the body of a clause in P, and we set $\text{Neg}_P^* = \text{Neg}_P \cup \mathcal{D}$, where $\mathcal{D}$ is the set of all predicate symbols in P on which the predicate symbols in Neg_P depend. Finally, by P^- we denote the set of clauses in P whose head contains a predicate symbol from Neg_P^*.

Finally, a program P is called *acceptable* with respect to some ω-level mapping $l : B_P \to \omega$ and some interpretation $I \in I_P$ if I is a model for P whose restriction to the predicate symbols in Neg_P^* is a supported model for P^-, and the following condition holds. For each ground instance $A \leftarrow L_1, \ldots, L_n$ of a clause in P and for all $i \in \{1, \ldots, n\}$ we have

$$\text{if} \quad I \models \bigwedge_{j=1}^{i-1} L_j, \quad \text{then} \quad l(A) > l(L_i). \tag{5.1}$$

The following is an example of an acceptable program.

5.1.9 Program Let G be an acyclic finite graph. We define the program *Game* to be the program consisting of the following clauses.[4]

$$\text{win}(X) \leftarrow \text{move}(X, Y), \neg\text{win}(Y).$$
$$\text{move}(a, b) \leftarrow \qquad \text{for all } (a, b) \in G$$

Game is not acyclic. One of the ground instances of the first clause is $\text{win}(a) \leftarrow \text{move}(a, a), \neg\text{win}(a)$, so if Game were acyclic with respect to some level mapping l, we would have $l(\text{win}(a)) < l(\text{win}(a))$, which is impossible. In order to show that Game is acceptable, we need to find a suitable level mapping l and a suitable model I for P. Since G is acyclic and finite, there exists a function f which assigns a natural number to every vertex of G, and such that for each vertex a the following holds.

$$f(a) = \begin{cases} 0 & \text{if there is no } (a, b) \in G, \\ 1 + \max\{f(b) \mid (a, b) \in G\} & \text{otherwise.} \end{cases}$$

We now define l by setting $l(\text{move}(a, b)) = f(a)$ and $l(\text{win}(a)) = f(a) + 1$ for all vertices a, b of G. From acyclicity and finiteness of G, we furthermore obtain that there exists a function g mapping each vertex to $\{0, 1\}$ satisfying the following.

$$g(a) = \begin{cases} 0 & \text{if there is no } (a, b) \in G, \\ 1 - \min\{g(b) \mid (a, b) \in G\} & \text{otherwise.} \end{cases}$$

---

[4]This example is taken from [Apt and Pedreschi, 1994]. For further discussion of programs related to Game, see [Hitzler and Seda, 2003].

Finally, let

$$I = \{\text{move}(a, b) \mid (a, b) \in G\} \cup \{\text{win}(a) \mid g(a) = 1\}.$$

It is straightforward to verify that Game is acceptable with respect to I and l.

We will now show how to construct a complete dislocated metric for any given acceptable program with respect to which the immediate consequence operator associated with the program is a contraction. For this purpose, let P be a program which is acceptable with respect to a level mapping l and an interpretation I. For any $K \in I_P$, we denote by K' the set K restricted to the predicate symbols in Neg_P^*. Next, we define a function $f : I_P \to \mathbb{R}$ by setting $f(K) = 0$ if $K \setminus K' \subseteq I$ and, if $K \setminus K' \not\subseteq I$, by setting $f(K) = 2^{-n}$, where $n \geq 0$ is the smallest integer such that there is an atom $A \in B_P$ with $l(A) = n$, $A \in K \setminus K'$ and $A \notin I$. Now define a function $u : I_P \to \mathbb{R}$ by setting $u(K) = \max\{f(K), d_l(K', I')\}$, where d_l is the generalized ultrametric from Definition 5.1.3.

Finally, for all $J, K \in I_P$, we set[5]

$$\varrho(J, K) = \max\{d_l(J \setminus J', K \setminus K'), u(J), u(K)\}.$$

Thus, for all $J, K \in I_P$, we have

$$\varrho(J, K) = \max\{d_l(J \setminus J', K \setminus K'), f(J), d_l(J', I'), f(K), d_l(K', I')\}.$$

We apply Proposition 4.8.7 in order to show that ϱ is a complete dislocated ultrametric. We will need the following lemma.

5.1.10 Lemma Let $u(K) = \max\{f(K), d_l(K', I')\}$ for $K \in I_P$. Then u is continuous as a function from (I_P, d_l) to $\mathbb{R}$.

Proof: Let K_m be a sequence in I_P which converges in d_l to some $K \in I_P$. We need to show that $d_l(K_m', I')$ converges to $d_l(K', I')$ and that $f(K_m)$ converges to $f(K)$ as $m \to \infty$. Since (K_m) converges to K with respect to the metric d_l, it follows that for each $n \in \mathbb{N}$ there is $m_n \in \mathbb{N}$ such that, for all $m \geq m_n$, K and K_m agree on all atoms of level less than or equal to n. Suppose that $f(K) = 2^{-n_0}$, say, and that $m \geq m_{n_0}$. Then K_m and K agree on all atoms of level less than or equal to n_0, and it follows that K' and K_m' agree on all atoms of level less than or equal to n_0 and, hence, that $K \setminus K'$ and $K_m \setminus K_m'$ agree on all atoms of level less than or equal to n_0. Therefore, we have $f(K_m) = 2^{-n_0} = f(K)$ for all $m \geq m_{n_0}$. Also, if $d_l(K', I') = 2^{-n_0}$, say, then $d_l(K_m', I') = 2^{-n_0} = d_l(K', I')$ for all $m \geq m_{n_0}$.

The result now follows. ∎

It remains to show that T_P is a contraction with respect to ϱ.

---

[5]This approach was inspired by [Fitting, 1994b]. The function u is usually called a *weight function* if it is used for constructing dislocated metrics from metrics, see [Matthews, 1992, Waszkiewicz, 2002]. Here, and in Section 5.1.3, we follow [Seda and Hitzler, 2010].

5.1.11 Theorem Let P be a program which is acceptable with respect to some level mapping l and interpretation I. Then ϱ is a complete dislocated ultrametric, and T_P is a contraction with respect to ϱ. In particular, P has a unique supported model M and $M = \lim T_P^n(I_0)$ for any $I_0 \in I_P$.

Proof: The mapping ϱ is a complete dislocated ultrametric by Lemma 5.1.10 and Proposition 4.8.7. By Matthews' theorem, Theorem 4.4.6, it remains to show that T_P is a contraction with respect to ϱ. The argument for this is essentially the same as the slightly more general one in the proof of Theorem 5.1.14, to be given in the next section, so we omit it here. ∎

5.1.3 Φ^*-Accessible Programs

We have seen in Section 5.1.2 that application of the Banach contraction mapping theorem can be replaced by application of Matthews' theorem when passing from acyclic to acceptable programs. Likewise, the Priess-Crampe and Ribenboim theorem can be used in place of Banach's theorem when passing from acyclic to locally hierarchical programs. Naturally, the question arises as to whether or not a class of programs can be described which generalizes both the acceptable and the locally hierarchical programs such that Theorem 4.5.1, which generalizes both Matthews' theorem and the Priess-Crampe and Ribenboim theorem, can be applied. We will describe such a class of programs in this section.

5.1.12 Definition A program P is called Φ^*-*accessible*[6] if and only if there exists a level mapping l for P and a model I for P whose restriction to Neg_P^* is a supported model for P^- such that the following condition holds. For each clause $A \leftarrow L_1, \ldots, L_n$ in ground(P), either we have $I \models L_1 \wedge \cdots \wedge L_n$ and $l(A) > l(L_i)$ for all $i = 1, \ldots, n$ or there exists $i \in \{1, \ldots, n\}$ such that $I \not\models L_i$ and $l(A) > l(L_i)$.

As an example, we refer again to the generate-and-test scheme described in Program 5.1.2.

5.1.13 Program Assume that the unary predicate symbols `generate` and `test` are defined via acceptable programs P_1 and P_2, and consider the program P which is the union of P_1, P_2 and the following clause.

$$\mathtt{success} \leftarrow \mathtt{generate}(X), \mathtt{test}(X).$$

It is easy to see that P is Φ^*-accessible: first note that P_1 and P_2 are Φ^*-accessible with respect to models I_1 and I_2 and level mappings l_1 and l_2, say, with codomain ω. We can assume without loss of generality that B_{P_1} and B_{P_2}

---

[6]It was shown in [Hitzler and Seda, 2003] that it is possible to compute all partial recursive functions with definite Φ^*-accessible programs using SLD-resolution.

are disjoint and do not contain success. Now define $I = I_1 \cup I_2 \cup \{\text{success}\}$ and define $l : B_P \to \omega + 1$ by $l(A) = l_i(A)$, if $A \in B_{P_i}$, and $l(\text{success}) = \omega$. Then P is easily seen to be Φ^*-accessible with respect to I and l.

We continue to carry over the approach of Section 5.1.2; again, we follow [Seda and Hitzler, 2010]. So let P be a program which is Φ^*-accessible with respect to a level mapping $l : B_P \to \gamma$ and an interpretation I. For any $K \in I_P$, we again denote by K' the set K restricted to the predicate symbols in Neg_P^*. Again, we define a function f on I_P, this time taking values in Γ_l, by setting $f(K) = 0$ if $K \setminus K' \subseteq I$ and, if $K \setminus K' \not\subseteq I$, by setting $f(K) = 2^{-\alpha}$, where α is the smallest ordinal such that there is an atom $A \in B_P$ with $l(A) = \alpha$, $A \in K \setminus K'$ and $A \notin I$. Now define a function $u : I_P \to \Gamma_l$ by again setting $u(K) = \max\{f(K), d_l(K', I')\}$, where d_l is the generalized ultrametric from Definition 5.1.3.

Finally, for all $J, K \in I_P$, we set

$$\varrho(J, K) = \max\{d_l(J \setminus J', K \setminus K'), u(J), u(K)\}$$

as before. Thus, for all $J, K \in I_P$, we have

$$\varrho(J, K) = \max\{d_l(J \setminus J', K \setminus K'), f(J), d_l(J', I'), f(K), d_l(K', I')\}.$$

In fact, the details of the proof of the main result below will be simplified by introducing the functions d_1 and d_2, where, for all $J, K \in I_P$, we set $d_1(J, K) = d_l(J', K')$ and $d_2(J, K) = d_l(J \setminus J', K \setminus K')$. Indeed, in these terms we have

$$\varrho(J, K) = \max\{d_1(J, I), d_1(K, I), d_2(J, K), f(J), f(K)\}$$

for all $J, K \in I_P$.

5.1.14 Theorem Let P be a Φ^*-accessible normal logic program. Then the space (I_P, ϱ) is a spherically complete, dislocated generalized ultrametric space, and T_P is strictly contracting with respect to ϱ. In particular, P has a unique supported model.

Proof: It follows from Proposition 4.8.22 that ϱ is a dislocated generalized ultrametric. For spherical completeness, let $(\mathcal{B}_\alpha)$ be a (decreasing) chain of balls in I_P with centres I_α. Let K be the set of all atoms which are eventually in I_α, that is, the set of all $A \in B_P$ such that there exists some ordinal β with $A \in I_\alpha$ for all $\alpha \geq \beta$. We show that for each ball $B_{2^{-\alpha}}(I_\alpha)$ in the chain, we have $d_l(I_\alpha, I) \leq 2^{-\alpha}$, which suffices to show that K is in the intersection of the chain. Indeed, it is easy to see by the definition of ϱ that all I_β with $\beta > \alpha$ agree on all atoms of level less than α. Hence, by definition of K we obtain that K and I_α agree on all atoms of level less than α, as required.

It remains to show that T_P is strictly contracting with respect to ϱ, for it will then follow from Theorem 4.5.1 that the operator T_P has a unique fixed point, yielding a unique supported model for P. In order to show that T_P is strictly contracting with respect to ϱ, we must show that for all $J, K \in I_P$ with $J \neq K$ we have $\varrho(T_P(J), T_P(K)) < \varrho(J, K)$. In particular, the following results hold.

(a) $d_1(T_P(J), I) < d_1(J, I)$ whenever $d_1(J, I) \neq 0$, and $d_1(T_P(J), I) = 0$ whenever $d_1(J, I) = 0$.

(b) $f(T_P(J)), f(T_P(K)) < \varrho(J, K)$.

(c) $d_2(T_P(J), T_P(K)) < \varrho(J, K)$.

Indeed, it suffices to prove properties (a), (b) and (c), and we proceed to do this next. For convenience, we identify Neg_P^* with the subset of B_P containing predicate symbols from Neg_P^*.

(a) First note that $d_1(T_P(J), I) = d_1(T_{P^-}(J), I)$ since d_1 only depends on the predicate symbols in Neg_P^*. Let $d_l(J, I) = 2^{-\alpha}$. We show that $d_l(T_{P^-}(J), I) \leq 2^{-(\alpha+1)}$. We know that J' and I' agree on all ground atoms of level less than α and differ on an atom of level α. It suffices to show now that $T_{P^-}(J)'$ and I' agree on all ground atoms of level less than or equal to α.

Let A be a ground atom in Neg_P^* with $l(A) \leq \alpha$, and suppose that $T_{P^-}(J)$ and I differ on A. Assume first that $A \in T_{P^-}(J)$ and $A \notin I$. Then there must be a ground instance $A \leftarrow L_1, \ldots, L_m$ of a clause in P^- such that $J \models L_1 \wedge \cdots \wedge L_m$. Since I is a fixed point of T_{P^-}, and using Definition 5.1.12, there must also be a k such that $I \not\models L_k$ and $l(L_k) < \alpha$. Note that the predicate symbol in L_k is contained in Neg_P^*. So we obtain $I \not\models L_k$, $J \models L_k$ and $l(L_k) < \alpha$, which is a contradiction to the assumption that J and I agree on all atoms in Neg_P^* of level less than α. Now assume that $A \in I$ and $A \notin T_{P^-}(J)$. It follows that there is a ground instance $A \leftarrow L_1, \ldots, L_m$ of a clause in P^- such that $I \models L_1 \wedge \cdots \wedge L_m$ and $l(A) > l(L_1), \ldots, l(L_m)$ by Definition 5.1.12. But then $J \models L_1 \wedge \cdots \wedge L_m$ since J and I agree on all atoms of level less than α and consequently $A \in T_{P^-}(J)$. This contradiction establishes the first statement in (a). The second statement in (a) follows by a similar argument, noting that in this case $J' = I'$.

(b) It suffices to show this for K. Assume $\varrho(J, K) = 2^{-\alpha}$. We show that $f(T_P(K)) \leq 2^{-(\alpha+1)}$, for which, in turn, we have to show that, for each $A \in T_P(K)$ not in Neg_P^* with $l(A) \leq \alpha$, we have $A \in I$. Assume that $A \notin I$ for such an A. Since $A \in T_P(K)$, there is a ground instance $A \leftarrow L_1, \ldots, L_m$ of a clause in P with $K \models L_1 \wedge \cdots \wedge L_m$. Since $A \notin I$, there must also be a k with $I \not\models L_k$ and $l(A) > l(L_k)$ by Definition 5.1.12. If the predicate symbol of L_k belongs to Neg_P^*, then, since K and I agree on all atoms in Neg_P^* of level less than α, we obtain $K \not\models L_k$, which contradicts $K \models L_1 \wedge \cdots \wedge L_m$. If the predicate symbol in L_k does not belong to Neg_P^*, then L_k is an atom, and since $f(K) \leq 2^{-\alpha}$, we obtain $I \models L_k$, which is again a contradiction.

(c) Let $\varrho(J, K) = 2^{-\alpha}$, and let A be not in Neg_P^* with $l(A) \leq \alpha$ and $A \in T_P(J)$. By symmetry, it suffices to show that $A \in T_P(K)$. Since $A \in$

$T_P(J)$, we must have a ground instance $A \leftarrow L_1, \ldots, L_m$ of a clause in P with $J \models L_1 \wedge \cdots \wedge L_m$. If $I \models L_1 \wedge \cdots \wedge L_m$, then $l(L_k) < l(A) \leq \alpha$ for all k, and since J and K agree on all atoms of level less than α, we obtain $K \models L_1 \wedge \cdots \wedge L_m$, and hence $A \in T_P(K)$. If there is some L_k such that $I \not\models L_k$, then without loss of generality $l(L_k) < l(A) \leq \alpha$ by Definition 5.1.12. Now, if the predicate symbol of L_k belongs to Neg_P^*, then, since $d_1(J, I) \leq 2^{-\alpha}$, we obtain from $J \models L_k$ that $I \models L_k$, which is a contradiction. Also, if the predicate symbol of L_k does not belong to Neg_P^*, then L_k is an atom, and since $f(J) \leq 2^{-\alpha}$, we obtain $I \models L_k$, again a contradiction. This establishes (c) and completes the proof.   ∎

5.1.4   Φ-Accessible Programs

Definition 5.1.12 of Φ^*-accessibility is obviously related to the level mapping characterization of the Fitting semantics given in Section 2.4. In the present section, we will carry over the approach from Section 5.1.3 to programs with a total Fitting model, and we refer the reader to [Hitzler and Seda, 2003] for further details. The relationships between the different classes of programs studied so far in this chapter will be further clarified in Section 5.2.

5.1.15 Definition A program is called Φ-*accessible* if it has a total Fitting model.

By Corollary 2.4.10, a program P is Φ-accessible if and only if there is a (two-valued) model I and a (total) level mapping l for P such that P satisfies (F) with respect to $I \cup \neg(B_P \setminus I)$ and l. The restriction of I to Neg_P^* is then a supported model for P^-, and it follows easily that every Φ^*-accessible program is Φ-accessible. However, the development of Section 5.1.3 does not generalize without modifications, as the following example shows.

5.1.16 Program Let P be the following program.

$$p\left(s^2(x)\right) \leftarrow p(x)$$
$$p(0) \leftarrow$$
$$p\left(s^4(0)\right) \leftarrow p\left(s^5(0)\right)$$
$$p\left(s^2(0)\right) \leftarrow p\left(s^3(0)\right)$$

The program P is Φ-accessible (and even definite) with respect to the model $B_P = \{p(s^n(0)) \mid n \in \mathbb{N}\}$ and the level mapping $l : B_P \rightarrow \mathbb{N}$ defined by $l(p(s^n(0))) = n$. Using the dislocated generalized ultrametric ϱ from Section 5.1.3, we obtain for $K = \{p(s^5(0))\}$ and $J = \{p(s^3(0))\}$ that $\varrho(K, J) = 2^{-3}$ and $\varrho(T_P(K), T_P(J)) = 2^{-2}$; thus, T_P is not a contraction relative to ϱ.

We will modify the methods used in Section 5.1.3 by means of Proposition 4.8.23.

5.1.17 Theorem Let P be a Φ-accessible program with model I and level mapping l such that P satisfies (F) with respect to $I \cup \neg(B_P \setminus I)$ and l. Then T_P is strictly contracting on the spherically complete dislocated generalized ultrametric space (I_P, ϱ), where for all $J, K \in I_P$ we have $\varrho(J, K) = \max\{d_l(J, I), d_l(I, K)\}$. In particular, P has a unique supported model.

Proof: By Proposition 4.8.23, we have that (I_P, ϱ) is a spherically complete dislocated generalized ultrametric space.

In order to show that T_P is strictly contracting, let $J, K \in I_P$, and assume that $\varrho(J, K) = 2^{-\alpha}$. Then J, K and I agree on all ground atoms of level less than α. We show that $T_P(J)$ and I agree on all ground atoms of level less than or equal to α. A similar argument shows that $T_P(K)$ and I agree on all ground atoms of level less than or equal to α, and this suffices.

Let $A \in T_P(J)$ with $l(A) \leq \alpha$. Then there must be a clause $A \leftarrow L_1, \ldots, L_n$ in ground(P) such that $J \models L_1 \wedge \cdots \wedge L_n$. Since I and J agree on all ground atoms of level less than α, (Fii) cannot hold, because if $I \not\models L_i$ with $l(A) > l(L_i)$, then $J \not\models L_i$ and consequently $J \not\models L_1 \wedge \cdots \wedge L_n$, which is a contradiction. Therefore, (Fi) holds, and so $A \in T_P(I) = I$. Hence, $A \in I$.

Conversely, suppose that $A \in I$. Since $I = T_P(I)$, there must be a clause $A \leftarrow L_1, \ldots, L_n$ in ground(P) such that $I \models L_1 \wedge \cdots \wedge L_n$. Thus, (Fi) must hold, and so we can assume that $A \leftarrow L_1, \ldots, L_n$ also satisfies $l(A) > l(L_i)$ for $i = 1, \ldots, n$. Since I and J agree on all ground atoms of level less than α, we have $J \models L_1 \wedge \cdots \wedge L_n$, and hence $A \in T_P(J)$, as required.

Applying Theorem 4.5.1 now yields a unique fixed point M of the operator T_P, that is, a unique supported model for P. ∎

The proof of Theorem 4.5.1 yields, moreover, that there must be an ordinal α such that $\varrho(M, M) = 0$. Since the only point of X which has non-zero distance from itself is I, we conclude that $I = M$ is the unique supported model for P. This is somewhat unfortunate,[7] since I was needed in order to construct ϱ.

5.2 Three-Valued Supported Models

Recall from Section 2.4 that the three-valued supported models for a program P are exactly the fixed points of the corresponding Fitting operator, while the least fixed point of the operator, that is, the least three-valued supported model for the program, is called its Fitting model. In this section, we will study variants of the Fitting operator and relate them to the classes of programs studied in Section 5.1. Thus, in the present section, unless otherwise

---

[7]We have argued in [Hitzler and Seda, 2003] that self-distance can be understood as a measure of a priori knowledge, but this needs to be substantiated further.

noted, interpretations will be three-valued, and therefore I_P here means $I_{P,3}$ ordered using the knowledge ordering introduced in Section 1.3.2.

5.2.1   Fitting Operators Revisited

We begin with an alternative characterization of the Fitting operator, which is amenable to generalization in various logics. It involves a program transformation which we will introduce next. Later on in Section 5.4, we will consider further generalizations of Fitting operators, called Fitting-style operators, see Definition 5.4.9.

Let P be a program and suppose that $A \in B_P$ is the head of some clause in ground(P). Now let $\{A \leftarrow \text{body}_i \mid i \in \Lambda\}$ be the set of all clauses with head A in ground(P), where Λ is a suitable index set. We call $A \leftarrow \bigvee_{i \in \Lambda} \text{body}_i$ the *pseudo-clause* associated with A, we call $\text{body}_A = \bigvee_{i \in \Lambda} \text{body}_i$ the *body* of the pseudo-clause, and we call A its *head*. As a matter of notation, we may sometimes denote body_i by C_i, and hence we may sometimes denote by $A \leftarrow \bigvee_{i \in \Lambda} C_i$ or even more simply by $A \leftarrow \bigvee C_i$ the pseudo-clause associated with A.

Notice that the family $\{\text{body}_i \mid i \in \Lambda\}$ of bodies may be denumerable and that $\bigvee_{i \in \Lambda} \text{body}_i$ is formal at this stage. Nevertheless, we next assign truth values to bodies of pseudo-clauses with respect to an interpretation in certain three-valued logics[8] and in more generality in Theorem 5.5.1 and in Section 7.6. If $\bigvee_{i \in \Lambda} \text{body}_i$ is such a body, then body_i is a (finite) conjunction for any i and can be evaluated as usual by means of truth tables for conjunction. We will consider three different conjunctions and two different disjunctions, all as given by the truth tables in Table 5.1 on Page 153. Note that $\wedge_1$ and $\vee_1$ are exactly the conjunction and disjunction from Kleene's strong three-valued logic, specified earlier as a sublogic of Belnap's logic in Table 1.1, and already employed in Section 2.4 in evaluating truth values of clause bodies.

With respect to $\vee_1$, a disjunction $p \vee_1 q$ is false if and only if both p and q are false, is true if and only if one of p and q is true, and is undefined otherwise. We use this as a definition of truth values for bodies of pseudo-clauses. Therefore, with respect to $\vee_1$:

> the body $\bigvee_{i \in \Lambda} \text{body}_i$ of a pseudo-clause is *false* if and only if all of the body_i are false, is *true* if and only if one of the body_i is true, and is *undefined* otherwise.

With respect to $\vee_2$, a disjunction $p \vee_2 q$ is false if and only if both p and q are false, is undefined if one of p and q is undefined, and is true otherwise. Therefore, with respect to $\vee_2$:

> the body $\bigvee_{i \in \Lambda} \text{body}_i$ of a pseudo-clause is *false* if and only if

---

[8]Strictly speaking, we discuss different truth tables for logical connectives – or rather different connectives – over three truth values over the same underlying language. It will be convenient to think in terms of different logics, however.

TABLE 5.1: Several truth tables for three-valued logics.

p	q	$p \wedge_1 q$	$p \wedge_2 q$	$p \wedge_3 q$
u	u	u	u	u
u	f	f	u	u
u	t	u	u	u
f	u	f	f	u
f	f	f	f	f
f	t	f	f	f
t	u	u	u	u
t	f	f	f	f
t	t	t	t	t

p	q	$p \vee_1 q$	$p \vee_2 q$
u	u	u	u
u	f	u	u
u	t	t	u
f	u	u	u
f	f	f	f
f	t	t	t
t	u	t	u
t	f	t	t
t	t	t	t

p	$\neg p$
u	u
f	t
t	f

all of the body_i are false, is *undefined* if and only if one of the body_i is undefined, and is *true* otherwise.

Finally, if A is an atom which does not appear as the head of a clause in $\text{ground}(P)$, then we say, by abuse of notation, that $A \leftarrow \bigvee_{i \in \emptyset} \text{body}_i$ is the pseudo-clause associated with A, and we take $\bigvee_{i \in \emptyset} \text{body}_i$ to be false both with respect to $\vee_1$ and with respect to $\vee_2$. Notice now that every element A of B_P is the head of the pseudo-clause associated with A and that this pseudo-clause is uniquely determined by P for a given A.

The following notation will be convenient. Let $A \in B_P$, let body_A be the body of the pseudo-clause associated with A, and let I be a three-valued interpretation. Then write $I_{j,k}(\text{body}_A)$ for the truth value, under I, of body_A with respect to $\wedge_j$ and $\vee_k$, for $j = 1, 2, 3$ and $k = 1, 2$. The following proposition follows easily from the definitions.

5.2.1 Proposition Let P be a program, let I be a three-valued interpretation for P, and let $A \in B_P$. Then $\Phi_P(I)(A) = I_{1,1}(\text{body}_A)$, that is, the truth value of A under $\Phi_P(I)$ is exactly $I_{1,1}(\text{body}_A)$.

The logics from Table 5.1 give rise to different operators.[9]

5.2.2 Definition Let P be a program. For any $j = 1, 2, 3$ and any $k = 1, 2$, we define an operator $\Phi_{P,j,k} : I_{P,3} \to I_{P,3}$ by $\Phi_{P,j,k}(I)(A) = I_{j,k}(\text{body}_A)$.

We can now rephrase Proposition 5.2.1 by saying that the operators $\Phi_{P,1,1}$ and Φ_P coincide. The following proposition lists properties of the $\Phi_{P,j,k}$-operators. We use the notation of three-valued interpretations as signed sets, see Section 1.3.3, and of two-valued interpretations as subsets of B_P.

5.2.3 Proposition Let P be a program, and let $I, J, K \in I_{P,3}$. Then the following hold.

(a) $\Phi_{P,j,k}$ is monotonic for $j = 1, 2, 3$ and $k = 1, 2$.

(b) $\Phi_{P,3,k}(I) \subseteq \Phi_{P,2,k}(J) \subseteq \Phi_{P,1,k}(K)$ for $k = 1, 2$ if $I \subseteq J \subseteq K$.

(c) $\Phi_{P,j,2}(I) \subseteq \Phi_{P,j,1}(I)$ for $j = 1, 2, 3$.

(d) $\Phi_{P,j,2}(I)^- = \Phi_{P,j,1}(I)^-$.

Proof: (a) The proof of this statement is very similar to that of Proposition 2.4.4 and is therefore omitted.

(b) From the truth tables, it follows that for all $A \in B_P$ and each $k \in \{1, 2\}$ we have $I_{3,k}(\text{body}_A) \subseteq J_{2,k}(\text{body}_A) \subseteq K_{1,k}(\text{body}_A)$, and this suffices.

(c) From the truth tables, we obtain $I_{j,2}(\text{body}_A) \subseteq I_{j,1}(\text{body}_A)$ for all $A \in B_P$.

(d) By (c), it suffices to show that $\Phi_{P,j,2}(I)^- \supseteq \Phi_{P,j,1}(I)^-$. So let $A \in B_P$ be such that $I_{j,1}(\text{body}_A) = I_{j,1}\left(\bigvee_{i \in \Lambda} \text{body}_i\right) = \mathbf{f}$. Then $I_{j,1}(\text{body}_i) = \mathbf{f}$ for all i, and hence $I_{j,2}(\text{body}_i) = \mathbf{f}$ for all i. Consequently, $I_{j,2}(\text{body}_A) = \mathbf{f}$, as required. ∎

Proposition 5.2.3 shows that the operators are "nested" and that $\Phi_{P,1,1} = \Phi_P$ is the least sceptical of them. In particular, for each ordinal α and all j and k, the following hold.

$$\Phi_{P,3,k} \uparrow \alpha \subseteq \Phi_{P,2,k} \uparrow \alpha \subseteq \Phi_{P,1,k} \uparrow \alpha$$
$$\Phi_{P,j,2} \uparrow \alpha \subseteq \Phi_{P,j,1} \uparrow \alpha$$

We can also relate Φ_P to the two-valued immediate consequence operator, T_P, thereby extending Proposition 2.4.13.

---

[9] We refer to the papers [Hitzler and Seda, 1999a, Hitzler and Seda, 2002b] for further details concerning the results of this section.

5.2.4 Lemma Let P be a normal logic program, let $I \in I_{P,2}$, and let $K \in I_{P,3}$ be such that $K^+ \subseteq I \subseteq B_P \setminus K^-$. Then $\Phi_P(K)^+ \subseteq T_P(I) \subseteq B_P \setminus \Phi_P(K)^-$. Furthermore, if $K^+ = I = B_P \setminus K^-$, so that K is total, then $\Phi_P(K)^+ = T_P(I) = B_P \setminus \Phi_P(K)^-$.

Proof: Suppose that $A \in \Phi_P(K)^+$. Then A must be the head of a clause $A \leftarrow A_1, \ldots, A_{k_1}, \neg B_1, \ldots, \neg B_{k_2}$ in ground(P) with $A_i \in K^+$ and $B_j \in K^-$ for all $i = 1, \ldots, k_1$ and $j = 1, \ldots, k_2$. By assumption, it follows that for these values of i and j, $A_i \in I$ and $B_j \notin I$, and hence $A \in T_P(I)$.

For the second inclusion, it suffices to show that $\Phi_P(K)^- \subseteq B_P \setminus T_P(I)$. Let $A \in \Phi_P(K)^-$. Then, for every clause of the form $A \leftarrow A_1, \ldots, A_{k_1}, \neg B_1, \ldots, \neg B_{k_2}$ in ground(P), we have some $A_i \in K^-$ or some $B_j \in K^+$. Hence, for every such clause, we have some $A_i \notin I$ or some $B_j \in I$, which implies that $A \notin T_P(I)$.

The final statement was established in Proposition 2.4.13. ∎

The following straightforward corollary provides the essential link between the Φ-operator, the single-step operator T_P, and convergence in Q.

5.2.5 Corollary Let $I_n = T_P^n(I)$ for some $I \in I_{P,2}$, and let $K_n = \Phi_P \uparrow n$. Then, for all $n \in \mathbb{N}$, we obtain $K_n^+ \subseteq I_n \subseteq B_P \setminus K_n^-$.

The following is a direct consequence of Lemma 5.2.4.

5.2.6 Proposition Let P be a normal logic program, and let (I^+, I^-) be a total three-valued interpretation I for P. Then I is a fixed point of Φ_P if and only if I^+ is a fixed point of T_P. Furthermore, if Φ_P has exactly one total fixed point M, then M^+ is the unique fixed point of T_P.

Proof: Let I be a fixed point of Φ_P. Then $I^+ \subseteq I^+ \subseteq B_P \setminus I^-$, and by Lemma 5.2.4 we obtain $I^+ = \Phi_P(I)^+ \subseteq T_P(I^+) \subseteq B_P \setminus \Phi_P(I)^- = B_P \setminus I^- = I^+$. Conversely, let I^+ be a fixed point of T_P. By Lemma 5.2.4, we obtain $\Phi_P(I)^+ = T_P(I^+) = I^+ = B_P \setminus I^- = B_P \setminus \Phi_P(I)^-$, and therefore $\Phi_P(I)^+ = I^+$ and $\Phi_P(I)^- = I^-$. The last statement now follows immediately. ∎

Convergence of iterates with respect to the Cantor topology can now be described, as follows.

5.2.7 Proposition Let P be a normal logic program, and assume that $M = \Phi_P \uparrow \omega$ is total. Then $T_P^n(\emptyset)$ converges in Q to M^+, and M^+ is the unique supported model M_P for P.

Proof: Using the notation from Corollary 5.2.5, we obtain $M^+ = \bigcup K_n^+$ and $M^- = \bigcup K_n^-$. Since M is total, we obtain from Propositions 3.3.5 and 5.2.6 that M^+ is the limit in Q of the sequence I_n. Since totality of $\Phi_P \uparrow \omega$ implies that it is the unique fixed point of Φ_P, it therefore equals (M^+, M^-), so that M^+ is the unique fixed point of T_P by Proposition 5.2.6. ∎

Proposition 5.2.7 allows us to apply Theorem 4.2.5 in the following way. Let P be a normal logic program such that $\Phi_P \uparrow \omega$ is total. Then $T_P^n(I)$ converges in Q to $\Phi_P \uparrow \omega$ for every I, and $\Phi_P \uparrow \omega$ is the unique fixed point of T_P. By Theorem 4.2.5, we can therefore find a metric with respect to which T_P is a contraction. However, this metric does not in general coincide with the metric associated with the dislocated ultrametric ϱ from Theorem 5.1.17, with respect to which T_P is also a contraction under the given condition on P.

The following result is even stronger than Proposition 5.2.7.

5.2.8 Theorem Let P be a normal logic program, let $j \in \{1, 2, 3\}$, let $k \in \{1, 2\}$, and assume that $M = \Phi_{P,j,k} \uparrow \alpha$ is total for some α. Then M^+ is the unique two-valued supported model for P. Furthermore, the transfinite sequence $(\Phi_{P,j,k} \uparrow \beta)_\beta$ converges in the Cantor topology to M^+.

Proof: By totality of M, Propositions 5.2.3 and 5.2.6, we obtain M^+ as a fixed point of T_P. The convergence results follow as in Proposition 5.2.7. ∎

We can extend the treatment of the Fitting operator from Section 2.4 to the operators $\Phi_{P,j,k}$ introduced in Definition 5.2.2. This will, in turn, lead us back to the program classes from Section 5.1. We begin with the $\Phi_{P,3,2}$-operator in the next section.

5.2.2   Acyclic and Locally Hierarchical Programs

We first present conditions analogous to Definition 2.4.8, which was used to characterize the Fitting semantics, beginning with condition (F_{32}) as defined next.

5.2.9 Definition Let P be a normal logic program, let I be a model for P, and let l be an I-partial level mapping for P. We say that P *satisfies* (F_{32}) *with respect to I and l* if for each $A \in \mathrm{dom}(l)$ and for all clauses $A \leftarrow L_1, \ldots, L_n$ in ground(P) we have $L_i \in \mathrm{dom}(l)$ and $l(A) > l(L_i)$ for all $i = 1, \ldots, n$, and furthermore each $A \in \mathrm{dom}(l)$ satisfies one of the following conditions.

(Fi) $A \in I$, and there is a clause $A \leftarrow L_1, \ldots, L_n$ in ground(P) such that $L_i \in I$ and $l(A) > l(L_i)$ for all i.

(Fii) $\neg A \in I$, and for each clause $A \leftarrow L_1, \ldots, L_n$ in ground(P) there exists i with $\neg L_i \in I$ and $l(A) > l(L_i)$.

Conditions (Fi) and (Fii) are identical to those in Definition 2.4.8. The difference between Definitions 2.4.8 and 5.2.9 lies in the additional very strong condition "for each $A \in \mathrm{dom}(l)$ and for all clauses $A \leftarrow L_1, \ldots, L_n$ in ground(P) we have $L_i \in \mathrm{dom}(l)$ and $l(A) > l(L_i)$ for all $i = 1, \ldots, n$". The proof of the following theorem is very similar to the proof of Theorem 2.4.9 and is therefore only sketched.

5.2.10 Theorem Let P be a normal logic program, and let M be the least fixed point of the operator $\Phi_{P,3,2}$. Then, in the knowledge ordering, M is the greatest model among all three-valued models I for which there exists an I-partial level mapping l for P such that P satisfies (F_{32}) with respect to I and l.

Proof: Let M_P be the least fixed point of the operator $\Phi_{P,3,2}$, and define the M_P-partial level mapping l_P as follows: $l_P(A) = \alpha$, where α is the least ordinal such that A is not undefined in $\Phi_P \uparrow (\alpha + 1)$. The proof proceeds by established the following facts. (1) P satisfies (F_{32}) with respect to M and l_P. (2) If I is a three-valued model for P, and l is an I-partial level mapping such that P satisfies (F_{32}) with respect to I and l, then $I \subseteq M_P$.

(1) Let $A \in \text{dom}(l_P)$, and suppose that $l_P(A) = \alpha$. We consider two cases.

Case i. If $A \in M_P$, then Table 5.1 together with the definition of l_P yields that A satisfies (Fi) with respect to M_P and l_P. It also yields that $l(L) < \alpha$ for each literal L in the body of any clause from $\text{ground}(P)$ with head A.

Case ii. If $\neg A \in M_P$, then again Table 5.1 together with the definition of l_P yields that A satisfies (Fii) with respect to M_P and l_P. As before, it also yields $l(L) < \alpha$ for each literal L in the body of any clause from $\text{ground}(P)$ with head A. This completes the proof of (1).

(2) Similarly to the proof of Step (2) in the proof of Theorem 2.4.9, it can be shown via transfinite induction on $\alpha = l(A)$ that: whenever $A \in I$ we have $A \in \Phi_{P,3,2} \uparrow (\alpha + 1)$ and whenever $\neg A \in I$ we have $\neg A \in \Phi_{P,3,2} \uparrow (\alpha + 1)$. This concludes the proof. ∎

5.2.11 Corollary A logic program P is acyclic if and only if $\Phi_{P,3,2} \uparrow \omega$ is total, and is locally hierarchical if and only if $\Phi_{P,3,2} \uparrow \alpha$ is total for some ordinal α.

Proof: Let P be such that $\Phi_{P,3,2} \uparrow \alpha$ is total for some α. Then by Theorem 5.2.10 and Definition 5.2.9 it follows that P is locally hierarchical with respect to the level mapping l_P as defined in the proof of Theorem 5.2.10.

Conversely, let P be locally hierarchical with level mapping l. Then, by Theorem 5.1.6, P has a unique supported model M, that is, M is the unique fixed point of the operator T_P. We show that P satisfies (F_{32}) with respect to $I = M \cup \neg(B_P \setminus M)$ and l. For this it suffices to show that for each $A \in B_P$, conditions (Fi) and (Fii) hold with respect to I. This, however, is an immediate consequence of the fact that M is a fixed point of T_P and that P is locally hierarchical.

The argument to show that P is acyclic if and only if $\Phi_{P,3,2} \uparrow \omega$ is total is similar. ∎

5.2.3   Acceptable Programs

The treatment of Section 5.2.2 carries over to acceptable programs with only minor modifications. Given a program P, an interpretation $I \in I_{P,3}$, and an I-partial level mapping l, we say that a clause $A \leftarrow L_1, \ldots, L_n$ is *k-safe* (with respect to I and l) if either $L_1, \ldots, L_n \in I$ and $l(A) > l(L_i)$ for all $i = 1, \ldots, n$ or $\neg L_k \in I$, $L_1, \ldots, L_{k-1} \in I$ and $l(A) > l(L_i)$ for all $i = 1, \ldots, k$. This notion generalizes condition (5.1) in Definition 5.1.8 in the following sense: a program P is acceptable with respect to some ω-level mapping l and some interpretation $I \in I_{P,2}$ if and only if I is a model for P whose restriction to the predicate symbols in Neg_P^* is a supported model for P^-, and for each clause in ground(P) there exists k such that the clause is k-safe (with respect to $I \cup \neg(B_P \setminus I)$ and l).

5.2.12 Definition Let P be a normal logic program, let I be a model for P, and let l be an I-partial level mapping for P. We say that P *satisfies* (F_{22}) *with respect to I and l* if, for each $A \in \text{dom}(l)$ and for all clauses in ground(P) with head A, there exists k such that the clause is k-safe, and furthermore, each $A \in \text{dom}(l)$ satisfies one of the following conditions.

(Fi) $A \in I$, and there is a clause $A \leftarrow L_1, \ldots, L_n$ in ground(P) such that $L_i \in I$ and $l(A) > l(L_i)$ for all i.

(Fii) $\neg A \in I$, and for each clause $A \leftarrow L_1, \ldots, L_n$ in ground(P) there exists i with $\neg L_i \in I$ and $l(A) > l(L_i)$.

The proof of the following theorem is very similar to the proof of Theorem 5.2.10 and is therefore omitted.

5.2.13 Theorem Let P be a normal logic program and let M be the least fixed point of the operator $\Phi_{P,2,2}$. Then, in the knowledge ordering, M is the greatest model among all three-valued models I for which there exists an I-partial level mapping l for P such that P satisfies (F_{22}) with respect to I and l.

5.2.14 Corollary A normal logic program P is acceptable if and only if $\Phi_{P,2,2} \uparrow \omega$ is total.

Proof: Let P be such that $\Phi_{P,2,2} \uparrow \omega$ is total. From Theorem 5.2.8 we know that P has a unique supported model whose restriction to predicate symbols in Neg_P^* is a supported model for P^-. By Theorem 5.2.10 and Definition 5.2.9, it easily follows that P is acceptable.

The proof of the converse is similar to that of Corollary 5.2.11.   ∎

5.2.4 Φ^*-Accessible Programs

We next give the analogue of Definition 5.2.9 for Φ^*-accessible programs. In order to make it more concise, we have chosen to rearrange the statements of the conditions slightly. The reader will easily identify the parts which correspond to conditions (Fi) and (Fii).

5.2.15 Definition Let P be a normal logic program, let I be a model for P, and let l be an I-partial level mapping for P. We say that P *satisfies* (F$_{12}$) *with respect to I and l* if for each $A \in \mathrm{dom}(l)$ and for all clauses $A \leftarrow L_1, \ldots, L_n$ one of the following conditions (F$_{12}$i), (F$_{12}$ii) holds. Furthermore, if $A \in I$, there must be at least one clause which satisfies (F$_{12}$i), and if $\neg A \in I$, there must be no clauses which satisfy (F$_{12}$i).

(F$_{12}$i) $L_i \in I$ and $l(A) > l(L_i)$ for all i.

(F$_{12}$ii) There exists i with $\neg L_i \in I$ and $l(A) > l(L_i)$.

The proof of the following theorem is very similar to the proof of Theorem 5.2.10 and is therefore omitted.

5.2.16 Theorem Let P be a normal logic program, and let M be the least fixed point of the operator $\Phi_{P,1,2}$. Then, in the knowledge ordering, M is the greatest model among all three-valued models I for which there exists an I-partial level mapping l for P such that P satisfies (F$_{12}$) with respect to I and l.

The proof of the following corollary is similar to the proof of Corollary 5.2.14 and is therefore omitted.

5.2.17 Corollary A normal logic program P is Φ^*-accessible if and only if $\Phi_{P,1,2} \uparrow \alpha$ is total for some ordinal α.

5.2.5 Φ-Accessible Programs

Results for Φ-accessible programs corresponding to those for Φ^*-accessible programs in Section 5.2.4 have already been obtained, and we refrain from repeating them here. Theorem 5.2.16 finds its analogue in Theorem 2.4.9, and the analogue of Corollary 5.2.17 can be found in Definition 5.1.15.

5.3   A Hierarchy of Logic Programs

In Figure 5.1, we present an overview of the relationships between the main classes of normal logic programs discussed in this book. Note that different branches of the graph shown are not necessarily disjoint. For example,

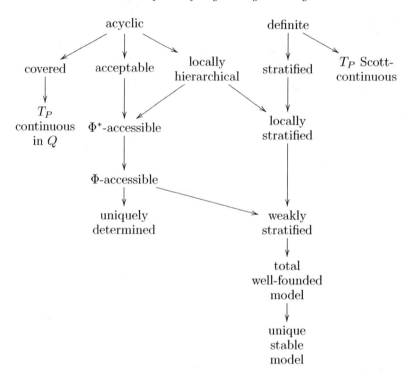

FIGURE 5.1: The main classes of programs discussed in this book. The arrows indicate class inclusion. See the main text of Section 5.3 for further details.

a program can be locally hierarchical without being acyclic, but still have a Q-continuous immediate consequence operator, meaning that its immediate consequence operator is continuous in the topology Q.

Covered programs are defined in Definition 7.5.4. Figure 5.1 indicates that every acyclic program is covered, but note that this is only the case if we assume that the underlying language contains at least one function symbol. Indeed, if this is not the case, then the Herbrand base is finite, and, for example, the program P with the single clause

$$q(a) \leftarrow p(x)$$

is acyclic[10] but not covered. Q-continuity of the immediate consequence operator for covered programs follows from Corollary 5.4.8. Scott continuity of the immediate consequence operator for definite programs follows from Theorem 2.2.3 (it was called *order continuity* there).

The remaining relationships shown in Figure 5.1 follow from results in Chapter 2 and Section 5.2.

---

[10] For example, assume a is the only constant symbol. Then ground(P) is $q(a) \leftarrow p(a)$, and so P is obviously acyclic.

5.4 Consequence Operators and Fitting-Style Operators

We close this section by discussing some natural extensions of certain earlier results. These are obtained by defining a rather general semantic operator T modelled on Fitting operators, but defined over abstract finite logics $\mathcal{T}$ rather than over logics containing two, three, or four elements. We call the resulting operators consequence operators, and an important special case of them we call Fitting-style operators. Our main result here is a careful analysis of the continuity of these operators T in the Cantor topology Q, which yields necessary and sufficient conditions for the continuity in Q of the single-step operator as a special case, see Theorem 5.4.11. Once these results are established, the aforementioned extensions we require are straightforward to present.

Thus, let $\mathcal{T}$ denote a finite set $\{t_1, \ldots, t_n\}$ of truth values containing at least the two distinguished values t_1 and t_n, which are interpreted as being the truth values for "false" and for "true", respectively. We assume that we have truth tables for the usual connectives $\vee$, $\wedge$, $\leftarrow$, and $\neg$. Given a normal logic program P, we denote the set of all (Herbrand) *interpretations* or *valuations* in this logic by $I_{P,n}$; thus, $I_{P,n}$ is the set of all functions $I : B_P \to \mathcal{T}$. If n is clear from the context, we will use the notation I_P instead of $I_{P,n}$, and we note that this usage is consistent with that already established for $n = 2, 3$, and 4. As usual, any interpretation I can be extended, using the truth tables, to give a truth value in $\mathcal{T}$ to any variable-free formula in the language $\mathcal{L}$ underlying P. We assume throughout this section that our underlying language $\mathcal{L}$ contains at least one function symbol, and hence B_P is denumerable. Finally, we endow $I_{P,n}$ with the Cantor topology Q studied in Chapter 3, see Theorem 3.3.1, and recall that this is the product topology of B_P copies of the discrete topology on $\mathcal{T}$. We refer the reader to Theorem 3.3.4 and Proposition 3.3.9 for a summary of the properties of Q. We note that our present assumption that B_P is denumerable and that $\mathcal{T}$ is finite mean that Q is second countable.

We proceed next with introducing a rather general notion of semantic operator T which subsumes many of the particular operators we have encountered in the earlier chapters. As already noted, our main objective here is to study the continuity of T in the topology Q.[11]

5.4.1 Definition An operator T on I_P is called a *consequence operator* for P if for every $I \in I_P$ the following condition holds: for every clause $A \leftarrow$ body in ground(P), where $T(I)(A) = t_i$ and $I(\text{body}) = t_j$, say, we have that the truth table for $\leftarrow$ yields the truth value t_n, that is, true for $t_i \leftarrow t_j$.

---

[11]We refer the reader to [Hitzler et al., 2004] for further details concerning the material of this section.

It turns out that this notion of consequence operator relates nicely to Q, yielding the following result.

5.4.2 Theorem If T is a consequence operator for P and if for any $I \in I_P$ we have that the sequence of iterates $T^m(I)$ converges in Q to some $M \in I_P$, then M is a model for P in the sense that every clause in ground(P) evaluates to t_n under M. Furthermore, continuity of T yields that M is a fixed point of T.

Proof: Suppose that $A \in B_P$ and that $M(A) = t_i$, and let $A \leftarrow$ body belong to ground(P), where body has the form $A_1, \ldots, A_m, \neg B_1, \ldots, \neg B_{m'}$. Then eventually $T(T^k(I))(A) = t_i$. Suppose $M(A_1 \wedge \ldots \wedge A_m \wedge \neg B_1 \wedge \ldots \wedge \neg B_{m'}) = t_j$, say. Taking the sequence $T^k(I)$, we have, by the property stated in the hypothesis (applied to each literal in the conjunction under consideration), that eventually $T^k(I)(A_1 \wedge \ldots \wedge A_m \wedge \neg B_1 \wedge \ldots \wedge \neg B_{m'}) = M(A_1 \wedge \ldots \wedge A_m \wedge \neg B_1 \wedge \ldots \wedge \neg B_{m'}) = t_j$. Since $T(T^k(I))(A) \leftarrow T^k(I)(A_1 \wedge \ldots \wedge A_m \wedge \neg B_1 \wedge \ldots \wedge \neg B_{m'})$ is t_n by the fact that T is a consequence operator, we obtain that $M(A \leftarrow A_1 \wedge \ldots \wedge A_m \wedge \neg B_1 \wedge \ldots \wedge \neg B_{m'}) = t_n$, as required. If T is continuous, then $M = \lim T^{n+1}(I) = T(\lim T^n(I)) = T(M)$.   ∎

Intuitively, consequence operators propagate "truth" along the implication symbols occurring in the program. From this point of view, we would like the outcome of the truth value of such a propagation to be dependent only on the relevant clause bodies. The next definition captures this intuition.

5.4.3 Definition Let $A \in B_P$, and denote by $\mathcal{B}_A$ the set of all body atoms of clauses with head A which occur in ground(P). A consequence operator T is called (*P*-)*local* if for every $A \in B_P$ and any two interpretations $I, K \in I_P$ which agree on all atoms in $\mathcal{B}_A$, we have $T(I)(A) = T(K)(A)$.

It is our desire to study continuity in Q of local consequence operators. Since Q is a product topology, it is reasonable to expect that finiteness conditions will play a role in this context, as already observed in Section 3.3.

5.4.4 Definition Let C be a clause in P, and let $A \in B_P$ be such that A coincides with the head of C. The clause C is said to be of *finite type relative to* A if C has only finitely many different ground instances with head A. The program P will be said to be of *finite type relative to* A if each clause in P is of finite type relative to A, that is, if the set of all clauses in ground(P) with head A is finite. Finally, P will be said to be of *finite type* if P is of finite type relative to A for every $A \in B_P$.

A *local variable* is a variable which appears in a clause body, but not in the corresponding head.[12] It is easy to see that in the context of Herbrand

---

[12]Local variables appear naturally in implementations, but their occurrence is awkward from the point of view of semantics, especially if they occur in negated body literals since this leads to the so-called floundering problem, see [Lloyd, 1987, Apt and Pedreschi, 1994].

interpretations and if function symbols are present, then the absence of local variables is equivalent to a program being of finite type.

5.4.5 Proposition Let P be a normal logic program of finite type, and let T be a local consequence operator for P. Then T is continuous in Q.

Proof: Let $I \in I_P$ be an interpretation, let $G_2 = \mathcal{G}(A, t_i)$ be a subbasic neighbourhood of $T(I)$ in Q, and note that G_2 is the set of all $K \in I_P$ such that $K(A) = t_i$. We need to find a neighbourhood G_1 of I such that $T(G_1) \subseteq G_2$. Since P is of finite type, the set $\mathcal{B}_A$ is finite. Hence, the set $G_1 = \bigcap_{B \in \mathcal{B}_A} \mathcal{G}(B, I(B))$ is a finite intersection of open sets and is therefore open. Since each $K \in G_1$ agrees with I on $\mathcal{B}_A$, we obtain $T(K)(A) = T(I)(A) = t_i$ for each $K \in G_1$ by locality of T. Hence, $T(G_1) \subseteq G_2$. ∎

Now, if P is not of finite type, but we can ensure by some other property of P that the, possibly infinite, intersection $\bigcap_{B \in \mathcal{B}_A} \mathcal{G}(B, I(B))$ is open, then the above proof will carry over to programs which are not of finite type, but satisfy the propert we seek. Alternatively, we would like to be able to disregard the infinite intersection entirely under conditions which ensure that we have to consider finite intersections only, as in the case of a program of finite type. The following definition is, therefore, quite a natural one to make.

5.4.6 Definition Let P be a logic program, and let T be a consequence operator on I_P. We say that T is $(P\text{-})$*locally finite for* $A \in B_P$ *and* $I \in I_P$ if there exists a finite subset $S = S(A, I) \subseteq \mathcal{B}_A$ such that we have $T(J)(A) = T(I)(A)$ for all $J \in I_P$ which agree with I on S. We say that T is $(P\text{-})$*locally finite* if it is locally finite for all $A \in B_P$ and all $I \in I_P$.

Obviously, any locally finite consequence operator is local. Conversely, a local consequence operator for a program of finite type is locally finite. This follows from the observation that, for a program of finite type, the sets $\mathcal{B}_A$, for any $A \in B_P$, are finite. But a much stronger result holds.

5.4.7 Theorem A local consequence operator is locally finite for all $A \in B_P$ and some $I \in I_P$ if and only if it is continuous at I in Q.

Proof: Let T be a locally finite consequence operator, let $I \in I_P$, let $A \in B_P$, and let $G_2 = \mathcal{G}(A, T(I)(A))$ be a subbasic neighbourhood of $T(I)$ in Q. Since T is locally finite, there is a finite set $S \subseteq \mathcal{B}_A$ such that $T(J)(A) = T(I)(A)$ for all $J \in \bigcap_{B \in S} \mathcal{G}(B, I(B))$. By finiteness of S, the set $G_1 = \bigcap_{B \in S} \mathcal{G}(B, I(B))$ is an open neighbourhood of I, and by the choice of S we have $T(G_1) \subseteq G_2$, and this suffices for continuity of T at I.

For the converse, assume that T is continuous at I in Q, and let $A \in B_P$ be chosen arbitrarily. Then $G_2 = \mathcal{G}(A, T(I)(A))$ is a subbasic open neighbourhood of $T(I)$, so that, by continuity of T, there exists a basic open neighbourhood $G_1 = \mathcal{G}(B_1, I(B_1)) \cap \cdots \cap \mathcal{G}(B_k, I(B_k))$ of I with $T(G_1) \subseteq G_2$. In other words, we have $T(J)(A) = T(I)(A)$ for each $J \in \bigcap_{B \in S'} \mathcal{G}(B, I(B))$, where $S' = \{B_1, \ldots, B_k\}$ is a finite set. Since T is local, the value of $T(J)(A)$ depends only on the values $J(A)$ of atoms $A \in \mathcal{B}_A$. So if we set $S = S' \cap \mathcal{B}_A$, then $T(J)(A) = T(I)(A)$ for all $J \in \bigcap_{B \in S} \mathcal{G}(B, I(B))$, which is to say that T is locally finite for A and I. Since A was chosen arbitrarily, we obtain that T is locally finite for I and all $A \in B_P$. ■

The following corollary provides a sufficient condition[13] for continuity in Q.

5.4.8 Corollary Let P be a program, let T be a local consequence operator, and let $l : B_P \to \omega$ be a level mapping for P with the property that $l^{-1}(n)$ is finite for any $n \in \omega$ and such that the following property holds: for each $A \in B_P$ there exists an $n_A \in \omega$ satisfying $l(B) < n_A$ for all $B \in \mathcal{B}_A$. Then T is continuous in Q.

Proof: It follows easily from the given conditions that $\mathcal{B}_A$ is finite for all $A \in B_P$, and hence T is locally-finite. ■

We turn now to the study of a particular type of local consequence operator, which we call a Fitting-style operator, and its continuity. Recall from Section 5.2.1 that bodies of pseudo-clauses may consist of infinite "disjunctions", but this will not pose any particular difficulties with respect to the logics we are going to discuss. We note that a program P is of finite type if and only if all bodies of all pseudo-clauses in P are finite.

Now, if we are given (suitable) truth tables for negation, conjunction, and disjunction, then we are able to evaluate the truth values of bodies of pseudo-clauses relative to given interpretations, as was done in Section 5.2.1.

5.4.9 Definition Let P be a normal logic program. Define the mapping $F_P : I_{P,n} \to I_{P,n}$ relative to a given (suitable) logic with n truth values by $F_P(I) = J$, where J assigns to each $A \in B_P$ the truth value $I(\bigvee C_i)$ of the body $\bigvee C_i$ of the pseudo-clause $A \leftarrow \bigvee C_i$ with head A.

We call operators which satisfy Definition 5.4.9 *Fitting-style operators* or the F_P-operator. If we impose the mild assumption that $t_j \leftarrow t_j$ evaluates to true for every j with respect to the underlying logic, then we immediately obtain that every Fitting-style operator is a local consequence operator. We will impose this condition, namely, that $t_j \leftarrow t_j$ evaluates to true for every j, for the remainder of this section.

If the chosen logic is classical two-valued logic, then the corresponding Fitting-style operator is the immediate consequence operator T_P (for a given program P). Now, if $T_P(I)(A) = \mathbf{t}$, then there exists a clause $A \leftarrow \text{body}$ in ground(P) such that $I(\text{body})$ is true, and we obtain $T_P(J)(A) = \mathbf{t}$ whenever

---

[13] Communicated to us by Howard A. Blair.

$J(\text{body}) = \mathbf{t}$. The observation that bodies of clauses are finite conjunctions leads us to conclude the following lemma.

5.4.10 Lemma If $T_P(I)(A) = \mathbf{t}$, then T_P is locally finite for A and I. Furthermore, T_P is continuous at I if and only if it is locally finite for all A with $T_P(I)(A) = \mathbf{f}$.

A body $\bigvee C_i$ of a pseudo-clause with head A is false in classical logic if and only if all the C_i are false. Since T_P is a Fitting-style operator, we obtain $T_P(I)(A) = \mathbf{f}$ if and only if all the C_i are false. If we require T_P to be locally finite for A and I, then there must be a finite set $S \subseteq \mathcal{B}_A$ such that any $J \in I_P$ which agrees with I on S renders all the C_i false. Conversely, if $S \subseteq \mathcal{B}_A$ is a finite set such that any $J \in I_P$ which agrees with I on S renders all the C_i false, then T is locally finite for A and I. We have just established the following theorem.[14]

5.4.11 Theorem Let P be a normal logic program, and let $I \in I_P$. Then T_P is continuous in Q at I if and only if whenever $T_P(I)(A) = \mathbf{f}$, then either there is no clause with head A or there exists a finite set $S(I, A) = \{A_1, \ldots, A_k, B_1, \ldots, B_m\} \subseteq \mathcal{B}_P$ with the following properties.

(a) $I(A_i) = \mathbf{t}$ and $I(B_j) = \mathbf{f}$ for all i and j.

(b) For every clause $A \leftarrow \text{body}$ in ground(P) at least one $\neg A_i$ or at least one B_j occurs in body.

In the case of Kleene's strong three-valued logic, we obtain the following lemma.

5.4.12 Lemma If $\Phi_P(I)(A) = \mathbf{t}$, then Φ_P is locally finite for A and I. Furthermore, Φ_P is continuous if and only if it is locally finite for all A and I with $\Phi_P(I)(A) \in \{\mathbf{u}, \mathbf{f}\}$.

Similar considerations apply to the Fitting-style operators from Section 5.2.1.[15] We mention in passing that the non-monotonic Gelfond–Lifschitz operator is not a consequence operator in the sense discussed here, and attempts to characterize the continuity of it involve different methods, some of which will be studied in Chapter 6.

We will finally provide a generalization of Theorem 5.1.6 for acyclic programs. So let P be acyclic with level mapping l, and let T be a local consequence operator for P. Again, we define the mapping $d : I_P \times I_P \to \mathbb{R}$ by $d(I, J) = 2^{-n}$, where n is least such that I and J differ on some atom A with $l(A) = n$, see Definition 5.1.3 and the remarks following it. It follows from Propositions 4.3.7 and 5.1.4 that d is a complete ultrametric on I_P, a fact which is easily verified directly.

---

[14] A direct proof without using the notion of local finiteness was given in [Seda, 1995].

[15] The operator Ψ_P defined by means of Belnap's four-valued logic, see [Fitting, 2002, Clifford and Seda, 2000], for example, is also a Fitting-style operator.

5.4.13 Proposition With the hypotheses stated in the previous paragraph, any local consequence operator T is a contraction with respect to d.

Proof: Suppose $d(I, J) = 2^{-n}$. Then I and J coincide on all atoms of level less than n. Now let $A \in B_P$ with $l(A) = n$. Then by acyclicity of P we have that all atoms in the body of the pseudo-clause with head A are of level less than n, and by locality of T we have that $T(I)(A) = T(J)(A)$. So $d(T(I), T(J)) \leq 2^{-(n+1)}$.   ∎

We finally obtain the following theorem.

5.4.14 Theorem Let P be an acyclic program, and let T be a local consequence operator for P. Then, for any $I \in I_P$, we have that $T^n(I)$ converges in Q to the unique fixed point of T.

Proof: Since d is a complete metric, we can apply Proposition 5.4.13 and the Banach contraction mapping theorem. This yields convergence of $T^n(I)$ in d to a unique fixed point M of T. By definition of d, the convergence of the sequence of valuations $T^n(I)$ to M is pointwise and, hence, is also convergence in Q.   ∎

Theorem 5.4.14 is remarkable since the existence of a fixed point of the given semantic operator can be guaranteed without any particular or further knowledge about the underlying multivalued logic.

5.5   Measurability Considerations

As we shall see in Chapter 7, continuity in Q of Fitting-style operators F_P, and T_P in particular, is central in relation to whether or not we can compute them approximately by neural networks. However, in the context of approximate computation by neural networks, the weaker notion of measurability has some interest, although rather less than that of continuity, see [Hornik et al., 1989], for example. Thus, we shall close this chapter by briefly discussing this topic next.[16]

In the previous section, we defined Fitting-style operators over finite truth sets, see Definition 5.4.9. However, unlike the case of the topology Q, finiteness of the truth set $\mathcal{T}$ is not of much importance here. Therefore, we begin by noting that we can, in principle, work over any logic $\mathcal{T}$ in which the truth value in $\mathcal{T}$ of disjunctions of possibly infinite countable collections of elements

---

[16]We do not formally introduce the notion of measurability and refer to [Bartle, 1966] for necessary background. For full details of the results we sketch here, we refer the reader to [Seda and Lane, 2005].

of $\mathcal{T}$ can be evaluated. Given this much and a normal logic program P, one can then easily define a Fitting-style operator as an operator $F_P : I_{P,\mathcal{T}} \to I_{P,\mathcal{T}}$ which satisfies $F_P(I)(A) = I(\bigvee C_i)$ for all $I \in I_{P,\mathcal{T}}$ and all $A \in B_P$. Here, $A \leftarrow \bigvee C_i$ is the pseudo-clause associated with A, and $I_{P,\mathcal{T}}$ denotes the set of all interpretations defined on B_P taking values in $\mathcal{T}$. The question then arises of providing suitable conditions under which possibly infinite countable collections of truth values can be evaluated. This issue is taken up in Section 7.6, where the notion of *finitely determined disjunctions* is given in Definition 7.6.1 and is seen to be adequate for our present purposes. In fact, if disjunctions are finitely determined, then disjunction is idempotent, commutative, and associative. Furthermore, the converse of this last statement holds if $\mathcal{T}$ is finite.

For a collection M of subsets of a set X, we denote by $\sigma(M)$ the smallest σ-algebra containing M, called the *σ-algebra generated by* M. Recall that a function $f : X \to X$ is measurable with respect to $\sigma(M)$ if and only if $f^{-1}(A) \in \sigma(M)$ for each $A \in M$. If β is the subbase of a topology τ and β is countable, then $\sigma(\beta) = \sigma(\tau)$.

It turns out that Fitting-style operators are not always measurable with respect to the σ-algebra $\sigma(Q)$ generated by Q, at least if the underlying truth set is unrestricted. However, under quite mild conditions, Fitting-style operators are always measurable, with no syntactic conditions on the program P whatsoever, as we see next in the following result. (Note also that we make no technical use here of the condition that $t_j \leftarrow t_j$ evaluates to true for each truth value $t_j \in \mathcal{T}$.)

5.5.1 Theorem Suppose $\mathcal{T}$ is a logic in which $\mathcal{T}$ is a countable set and disjunctions are finitely determined. Then for any normal logic program P, the Fitting-style operator F_P determined by P is measurable with respect to the σ-algebra $\sigma(Q)$.

As we shall see in Section 7.6, many logics of interest in logic programming satisfy the requirement that disjunction is finitely determined. Indeed, it is satisfied for Belnap's logic $\mathcal{FOUR}$, and hence T_P, Φ_P, and Ψ_P are all always measurable for any normal logic program P.

Chapter 6

Stable and Perfect Model Semantics

The stable model semantics turns out to be the one which receives the most attention these days. Some of the most popular implementations of non-monotonic reasoning systems are based on it.[1] In this chapter, we provide means to lift our results on the supported model semantics to the stable model semantics. This is done by the so-called fixpoint completion of programs, which we will introduce in Section 6.1. This construction will enable us to draw almost effortlessly a number of corollaries on the stable model semantics, and we will do this in Section 6.2. Finally, in Section 6.3, we will close our discussion with some additional observations on stratification and the perfect model semantics.

6.1 The Fixpoint Completion

The fixpoint completion is a program transformation which is based on the notion of unfolding, meaning the replacement of a body atom A by the body of a clause which also has head A. In essence, the fixpoint completion of a given program is obtained by performing (recursively) a complete unfolding through all positive body atoms and disregarding all clauses which after this process still contain positive body atoms. We will describe this formally in the following definition.

6.1.1 Definition A *quasi-interpretation*[2] is a set of clauses of the form $A \leftarrow \neg B_1, \ldots, \neg B_m$, where A and B_i are ground atoms for all $i = 1, \ldots, m$. Given a normal logic program P and a quasi-interpretation Q, we define $T'_P(Q)$ to be the quasi-interpretation consisting of the set of all clauses $A \leftarrow \text{body}_1, \ldots, \text{body}_n, \neg B_1, \ldots, \neg B_m$ for which there exists a clause $A \leftarrow A_1, \ldots, A_n, \neg B_1, \ldots, \neg B_m$ in $\text{ground}(P)$ and clauses $A_i \leftarrow \text{body}_i$ in Q for all $i = 1, \ldots, n$. We explicitly allow the cases $n = 0$ or $m = 0$ in this definition.

---

[1] See [Leone et al., 2006] for details of the DLV system and [Simons et al., 2002] for details of the smodels system, for example.

[2] This notion is due to [Dung and Kanchanasut, 1989]. We stick to the old terminology, although quasi-interpretations should really be thought of as, and indeed are, programs with negative body literals only.

Note that the set of all quasi-interpretations is a complete partial order with respect to set-inclusion.

6.1.2 Proposition Given a normal logic program P, the operator T'_P is Scott continuous on the set of all quasi-interpretations.

Proof: We show first that T'_P is monotonic. So let $Q \subseteq R$ be quasi-interpretations, and let $A \leftarrow$ body be in $T'_P(Q)$. If $A \leftarrow$ body results from the unfolding of some clause $A \leftarrow$ body$_0$ in P with some clauses $B_i \leftarrow$ body$_i$ in Q, then $B_i \leftarrow$ body$_i$ is contained in R for all i by assumption, and by the existence of the clause $A \leftarrow$ body$_0$ in P we obtain $A \leftarrow$ body in $T'_P(R)$ by unfolding. If $A \leftarrow$ body $\in T'_P(Q)$ does not result from some unfolding, then it is already contained in P and, hence, in $T'_P(R)$. Thus, T'_P is monotonic.

Now let $\mathcal{Q} = \{Q_\lambda \mid \lambda \in \Lambda\}$ be an indexed directed family of quasi-interpretations, and let $Q = \bigsqcup \mathcal{Q} = \bigcup \mathcal{Q}$. Since the order under consideration is set-inclusion and T'_P is monotonic, we immediately have that $T'_P(\mathcal{Q})$ is directed. By the remarks following Definition 1.1.7, it therefore remains to show that $T'_P(Q) \subseteq \bigcup T'_P(\mathcal{Q})$. So suppose that $A \leftarrow$ body belongs to $T'_P(Q)$. If $A \leftarrow$ body does not result from an unfolding, then it is already contained in P, hence also in $T'_P(\mathcal{Q})$. Otherwise, $A \leftarrow$ body results from the unfolding of some $A \leftarrow$ body$_0$ in P with some $B_i \leftarrow$ body$_i$ in Q. But then there is λ such that all $B_i \leftarrow$ body$_i$ are contained in Q_λ; hence, $A \leftarrow$ body is contained in $T'_P(Q_\lambda) \subseteq T'_P(\mathcal{Q})$, as required. ∎

Given a normal logic program P, we define the *fixpoint completion* fix(P) of P by fix$(P) = T'_P \uparrow \omega$.

6.1.3 Example Consider again the example program Tweety2, see Program 2.3.9. We obtain the following.

$T'_{\text{Tweety2}} \uparrow 0 = \emptyset$

$T'_{\text{Tweety2}} \uparrow 1 = \{\texttt{penguin(tweety)} \leftarrow, \texttt{bird(bob)} \leftarrow\}$

$T'_{\text{Tweety2}} \uparrow 2 = T'_{\text{Tweety2}} \uparrow 1 \cup \{\texttt{bird(tweety)}, \texttt{flies(bob)} \leftarrow \neg\texttt{penguin(bob)}\}$

$T'_{\text{Tweety2}} \uparrow 3 = T'_{\text{Tweety2}} \uparrow 2 \cup \{\texttt{flies(tweety)} \leftarrow \neg\texttt{penguin(tweety)}\}$

fix$(\text{Tweety2}) = T'_{\text{Tweety2}} \uparrow 3$.

The importance of the fixpoint completion lies in the fact that the stable models of a given program P are exactly the supported models of fix(P). We can prove an even stronger result.[3]

---

[3]The proof of Theorem 6.1.4 is taken directly from [Wendt, 2002a], which appeared in compressed form as [Wendt, 2002b]. This correspondence can also be carried over to the Fitting/well-founded semantics. More precisely, it was shown in [Wendt, 2002b] that for any normal logic program P and any three-valued interpretation I, we have $\Psi_P(I) = \Phi_{\text{fix}(P)}(I)$, where Ψ_P is the operator due to [Bonnier et al., 1991] used for characterizing three-valued stable models, but is not treated here. A corollary of the result just mentioned is that the well-founded model for a given program P coincides with the Fitting model for fix(P).

6.1.4 Theorem For any normal logic program P and (two-valued) interpretation I, we have

$$\text{GL}_P(I) = T_{\text{fix}(P)}(I).$$

Proof: We show first that for every $A \in \text{GL}_P(I)$ there exists a clause in $\text{fix}(P)$ with head A whose body is true in I, and hence $A \in T_{\text{fix}(P)}(I)$. We show this by induction on the powers of $T_{P/I}$; recall that $\text{GL}_P(I) = T_{P/I} \uparrow \omega$.

For the base case $T_{P/I} \uparrow 0 = \emptyset$, there is nothing to show.

So assume now that for all $A \in T_{P/I} \uparrow n$ there exists a clause in $\text{fix}(P)$ with head A whose body is true in I. For $A \in T_{P/I} \uparrow (n+1)$, there exists a clause $A \leftarrow A_1, \ldots, A_n$ in P/I such that $A_1, \ldots, A_n \in T_{P/I} \uparrow n$, and hence by construction of P/I there is a clause $A \leftarrow A_1, \ldots, A_n, \neg B_1, \ldots, \neg B_m$ in $\text{ground}(P)$ with $B_1, \ldots, B_m \notin I$. By our induction hypothesis, we obtain that for each $i = 1, \ldots, n$ there exists a clause $A_i \leftarrow \text{body}_i$ in $\text{fix}(P)$ with $I \models \text{body}_i$, and hence $A_i \in T_{\text{fix}(P)}(I)$. So by definition of T'_P the clause $A \leftarrow \text{body}_1, \ldots, \text{body}_n, \neg B_1, \ldots, \neg B_m$ is contained in $\text{fix}(P)$. From $I \models \text{body}_i$ and $B_1, \ldots, B_m \notin I$, we obtain $A \in T_{\text{fix}(P)}(I)$, as desired. This finishes the induction argument, and hence $\text{GL}_P(I) \subseteq T_{\text{fix}(P)}(I)$.

Now conversely, assume that $A \in T_{\text{fix}(P)}(I)$. We show that $A \in \text{GL}_P(I)$ by proving inductively on k that $T_{T'_P \uparrow k}(I) \subseteq \text{GL}_P(I)$ for all $k \in \mathbb{N}$.

For the base case, we have $T_{T'_P \uparrow 0}(I) = \emptyset$, so there is nothing to show.

So assume now that $T_{T'_P \uparrow k}(I) \subseteq \text{GL}_P(I)$, and let $A \in T_{T'_P \uparrow (k+1)}(I) \setminus T_{T'_P \uparrow k}(I)$. Then there is a clause $A \leftarrow \text{body}_1, \ldots, \text{body}_n, \neg B_1, \ldots, \neg B_m$ in $T'_P \uparrow (k+1)$ whose body is true in I. Thus, $B_1, \ldots, B_m \notin I$, and for each $i = 1, \ldots, n$ there is a clause $A_i \leftarrow \text{body}_i$ in $T'_P \uparrow k$ with body_i true in I. So $A_i \in T_{T'_P \uparrow k}(I) \subseteq \text{GL}_P(I)$. Furthermore, by definition of T'_P, there exists a clause $A \leftarrow A_1, \ldots, A_n, \neg B_1, \ldots, \neg B_m$ in $\text{ground}(P)$, and since $B_1, \ldots, B_m \notin I$, we obtain $A \leftarrow A_1, \ldots, A_n \in P/I$. Since we know that $A_1, \ldots, A_n \in \text{GL}_P(I)$, we obtain $A \in \text{GL}_P(I)$, and hence $T_{T'_P \uparrow (k+1)}(I) \subseteq \text{GL}_P(I)$. This finishes the induction argument, and we obtain $T_{\text{fix}(P)}(I) \subseteq \text{GL}_P(I)$. ∎

The following corollary is an immediate consequence of Theorem 6.1.4.

6.1.5 Corollary Let P be a normal logic program. Then the stable models of P are exactly the supported models of $\text{fix}(P)$.

6.2 Stable Model Semantics

Theorem 6.1.4 enables us to carry over results on the single-step operator and on the supported model semantics to the Gelfond–Lifschitz operator, respectively, the stable model semantics. We will first consider continuity issues.

The following observation is of technical importance.

6.2.1 Proposition Let P be a definite logic program, let $A \in B_P$, and let $n \in \mathbb{N}$. Then $A \in T_P \uparrow n$ if and only if $A \leftarrow$ is a clause in $T'_P \uparrow n$.

Proof: Let $A \in T_P \uparrow n$ for some $n \in \mathbb{N}$. We proceed by induction on n. If $n = 1$, then there is nothing to show. So assume that $n > 1$. Then there is a clause $A \leftarrow$ body in ground(P) such that all atoms B_i in body are contained in $T_P \uparrow (n-1)$, and by the induction hypothesis there are clauses $B_i \leftarrow$ in $T'_P \uparrow (n-1)$. Unfolding these clauses with $A \leftarrow$ body shows that $A \leftarrow$ is also contained in $T'_P \uparrow n$.

Conversely, assume there is a clause $A \leftarrow$ in $T'_P \uparrow n$. We proceed again by induction. If $n = 1$, there is nothing to show. So let $n > 1$. Then there exists a clause $A \leftarrow A_1, \ldots, A_k$ in ground(P) and clauses $A_i \leftarrow$ in $T'_P \uparrow (n-1)$. By the induction hypothesis, we obtain $A_i \in T_P \uparrow (n-1)$ for all i, and hence $A \in T_P \uparrow n$. $\blacksquare$

Given a program P, we know by Theorem 6.1.4 that GL_P is continuous at some $I \in I_P$ in Q if and only if $T_{\mathrm{fix}(P)}$ is continuous at I. This gives rise to the following theorem.

6.2.2 Theorem Let P be a normal logic program, and let $I \in I_P$. Then GL_P is continuous at I in Q if and only if whenever $\mathrm{GL}_P(I)(A) = \mathbf{f}$, then either there is no clause with head A in ground(P) or there exists a finite set $S(I, A) = \{A_1, \ldots, A_k\} \subseteq B_P$ such that $I(A_i) = \mathbf{t}$ for all i and for every clause $A \leftarrow$ body in ground(P) at least one $\neg A_i$ or some B with $\mathrm{GL}_P(I)(B) = \mathbf{f}$ occurs in body.

Proof: By Theorem 5.4.11 and Theorem 6.1.4, and by observing that there are no positive body atoms occuring in fix(P), we obtain the following.

> GL_P is continuous at I if and only if whenever $\mathrm{GL}_P(I)(A) = \mathbf{f}$, then either there exists no clause with head A in fix(P) or there exists a finite set $S(I, A) = \{A_1, \ldots, A_k\} \subseteq B_P$ such that $I(A_i) = \mathbf{t}$ for all i and for every clause $A \leftarrow$ body in fix(P) at least one $\neg A_i$ occurs in body.

So let P be such that GL_P is continuous at I. If there is no clause with head A in ground(P), then there is nothing to show. So assume that there is a clause with head A in ground(P). Then we already know that there exists a finite set $S(I, A) = \{A_1, \ldots, A_k\} \subseteq B_P$ such that $I(A_i) = \mathbf{t}$ for all i and for every clause $A \leftarrow$ body in fix(P) at least one $\neg A_i$ occurs in body. Now let $A \leftarrow B_1, \ldots, B_k, \neg C_1, \ldots, \neg C_m$ be a clause in ground(P), and assume that no $\neg A_i$ occurs in its body. We show that there is some B_i in body with $\mathrm{GL}_P(I)(B_i) = \mathbf{f}$. Assume the contrary, that is, that $\mathrm{GL}_P(I)(B_i) = \mathbf{t}$ for all i. Then for each B_i we have $B_i \in \mathrm{GL}_P(I) = T_{P/I} \uparrow \omega$. As in the proof of Proposition 6.2.1, we conclude that there is a clause $A \leftarrow \neg D_1, \ldots, \neg D_n, \neg C_1, \ldots, \neg C_m$ in fix(P) with $D_j \notin I$ for all $j = 1, \ldots, n$. Since the clause $A \leftarrow \neg D_1, \ldots, \neg D_n, \neg C_1, \ldots, \neg C_m$ is contained in fix(P), we know that some atom from the set $S(I, A)$ must occur in its body. It cannot occur as any D_i because $I(D_j) = \mathbf{f}$ for all j. It also cannot occur as any C_i by assumption. So we obtain a contradiction, which finishes the argument.

Conversely, let P be such that the condition on GL_P in the statement of the theorem holds. We will again make use of the observation made at the beginning of this proof. So let $A \in B_P$ with $\mathrm{GL}_P(I)(A) = \mathbf{f}$. If there is no clause with head A in $\mathrm{fix}(P)$, then there is nothing to show. So assume there is a clause with head A in $\mathrm{fix}(P)$. Then there is a clause with head A in P, and by assumption we know that there exists a finite set $S(I, A) = \{A_1, \ldots, A_k\} \subseteq B_P$ such that $I(A_i) = \mathbf{t}$ for all i and for every clause $A \leftarrow \mathrm{body}$ in $\mathrm{ground}(P)$ at least one $\neg A_i$ or some B with $\mathrm{GL}_P(I)(B) = \mathbf{f}$ occurs in body. Now let $A \leftarrow \neg B_1, \ldots, \neg B_n$ be a clause in $\mathrm{fix}(P) = T'_P \uparrow \omega$. Then there is $k \in \mathbb{N}$ with $A \leftarrow \neg B_1, \ldots, \neg B_n$ contained in $T'_P \uparrow k$. Note that $n = 0$ is impossible since this would imply $\mathrm{GL}_P(I)(A) = \mathbf{t}$, contradicting the assumption on A. We proceed by induction on k. If $k = 1$, then $A \leftarrow \neg B_1, \ldots, \neg B_n$ is contained in $\mathrm{ground}(P)$; hence, one of the B_j is contained in $S(I, A)$, and this suffices. For $k > 1$, there is a clause $A \leftarrow C_1, \ldots, C_m, \neg D_1, \ldots, \neg D_{m'}$ in $\mathrm{ground}(P)$ and clauses $C_i \leftarrow \mathrm{body}_i$ in $T'_P \uparrow (k - 1)$ which unfold to $A \leftarrow \neg B_1, \ldots, \neg B_n$. By assumption we either have $D_j \in S(I, A)$ for some j, in which case there remains nothing to show, or we have that $\mathrm{GL}_P(I)(C_i) = \mathbf{f}$ for some i. In the latter case we obtain that body_i is non-empty by an argument similar to that of the proof of Proposition 6.2.1. So by assumption there is a (negated) atom B in body_i, and hence B is in $\{B_1, \ldots, B_n\}$. So again one of the B_j is in $S(I, A)$, and this observation finishes the proof. ∎

We also have the following special instance of Theorem 6.2.2.

6.2.3 Corollary Let P be a normal logic program without local variables. Then GL_P is continuous in Q.

Proof: We apply Theorem 6.2.2. Let $I \in I_P$ and $A \in B_P$ be such that $\mathrm{GL}_P(I)(A) = \mathbf{f}$. Since P has no local variables, it is of finite type. Therefore, the set $\mathcal{B}$ of all negated body atoms in clauses with head A is finite. Let $S(I, A) = \{B \in \mathcal{B} \mid I(B) = \mathbf{f}\}$; then $S(I, A)$ is also finite. If each clause with head A contains some negated atom from $S(I, A)$, there is nothing to prove. So assume that there is a clause $A \leftarrow A_1, \ldots, A_n, \neg B_1, \ldots, \neg B_m$ in $\mathrm{ground}(P)$ with $B_j \notin S(I, A)$ for all j, that is, suppose $I(B_j) = \mathbf{t}$ for all j. Then $A \leftarrow A_1, \ldots, A_n$ is a clause in P/I and $A \notin T_{P/I} \uparrow \omega$. It now follows that there is some i with $A_i \notin T_{P/I} \uparrow \omega = \mathrm{GL}_P(I)$, and this observation finishes the argument by Theorem 6.2.2. ∎

Measurability is much simpler to deal with, as we see next.

6.2.4 Theorem Let P be a normal logic program. Then GL_P is measurable with respect to $\sigma(Q)$.

Proof: By Theorem 5.5.1 we obtain that $T_{\mathrm{fix}(P)}$ is measurable with respect to $\sigma(Q)$, and by Theorem 6.1.4 we know that $T_{\mathrm{fix}(P)} = \mathrm{GL}_P$. ∎

The following variant of Theorem 5.4.2 can be proven directly.

6.2.5 Theorem Let P be a normal logic program, and let GL_P be continuous and such that the sequence of iterates $\mathrm{GL}_P^n(I)$ converges in Q to some $M \in I_P$. Then M is a stable model for P.

Proof: By continuity we obtain $M = \lim \mathrm{GL}_P^n(I) = \mathrm{GL}_P(\lim \mathrm{GL}_P^n(I)) = \mathrm{GL}_P(M)$. ∎

We can also exploit our knowledge about the relationships between the single-step operator and the Fitting operator.

6.2.6 Proposition Let P be a normal logic program, and assume that $M = \Phi_{\mathrm{fix}(P)} \uparrow \omega$ is total.[4] Then $\mathrm{GL}_P^n(\emptyset)$ converges in Q to M^+, and M^+ is the unique stable model for P.

Proof: This follows immediately from Proposition 5.2.7 and Theorem 6.1.4. ∎

Metric-based approaches also carry over to our present context; we restrict our discussion to the following corollary of Theorem 5.1.6.

6.2.7 Theorem Let P be a locally stratified normal logic program with corresponding level mapping l. Then GL_P is strictly contracting with respect to d_l. If the codomain of l is ω, then GL_P is a contraction with respect to d_l. Furthermore, in both cases, GL_P has a unique fixed point, and therefore P has a unique stable model.

Proof: If P is locally stratified with respect to l, then $\mathrm{fix}(P)$ is locally hierarchical with respect to l. It thus suffices to apply Theorem 5.1.6 in conjunction with Theorem 6.1.4. ∎

6.2.8 Remark With the comments already made concerning the fact that the well-founded model for a given program P coincides with the Fitting model for $\mathrm{fix}(P)$, for any normal program P, we can also derive the following result.

---

[4]We mentioned earlier in this chapter that $\Phi_{\mathrm{fix}(P)}$ coincides with the operator Ψ_P from [Bonnier et al., 1991] for characterizing three-valued stable models.

Let P be a program with total well-founded model $I \cup \neg(B_P \setminus I)$, where $I \subseteq B_P$. Then GL_P is strictly contracting on the spherically complete dislocated generalized ultrametric space (I_P, ϱ), where we have $\varrho(J, K) = \max\{d_l(J, I), d_l(I, K)\}$ for all $J, K \in I_P$, and l is defined by taking $l(A)$ to be the minimal α such that $\Phi_{\mathrm{fix}(P)} \uparrow (\alpha + 1)(A) = I(A)$.

Indeed, the program P has a total well-founded model in this case, and this implies that $\mathrm{fix}(P)$ has a total Fitting model. So l as just defined is, in fact, well-defined, and $\mathrm{fix}(P)$ satisfies (F) with respect to $I \cup \neg(B_P \setminus I)$ and l. Now apply Theorem 5.1.17.

6.3   Perfect Model Semantics

We return to matters of stratification and the perfect model semantics. More precisely, we will describe an iterative method for obtaining the perfect model for locally stratified programs.[5]

6.3.1 Definition Let P be a normal logic program, and let $l : B_P \to \gamma$ be a level mapping, where $\gamma > 1$. For each n satisfying $0 < n \leq \gamma$, let $P_{[n]}$ denote the set of all clauses in $\mathrm{ground}(P)$ in which only atoms A with $l(A) < n$ occur, and denote by $\mathcal{L}_n$ the set of all atoms A of level $l(A)$ less than n. We define $T_{[n]} : \mathcal{P}(\mathcal{L}_n) \to \mathcal{P}(\mathcal{L}_n)$ by $T_{[n]}(I) = T_{P_{[n]}}(I)$. The mapping $T_{[n]}$ is called the *immediate consequence operator restricted at level n.*

Thus, the idea formalized by this definition is to "cut-off" at level n.

6.3.2 Definition Let P be a locally stratified normal logic program, and let $l : B_P \to \gamma$ be a level mapping, where $\gamma > 1$. We construct the transfinite sequence $(I_n)_{n \in \gamma}$ inductively as follows. For each $m \in \mathbb{N}$, we put $I_{[1,m]} = T_{[1]}^m(\emptyset)$ and set $I_1 = \bigcup_{m=0}^{\infty} I_{[1,m]}$. If $n \in \gamma$, where $n > 1$, is a successor ordinal, then for each $m \in \mathbb{N}$ we put $I_{[n,m]} = T_{[n]}^m(I_{n-1})$ and set $I_n = \bigcup_{m=0}^{\infty} I_{[n,m]}$. If $n \in \gamma$ is a limit ordinal, we put $I_n = \bigcup_{m<n} I_m$. Finally, we put $I_{[P]} = \bigcup_{n<\gamma} I_n$.

6.3.3 Example Consider again the example program Tweety2, Program 2.3.9, where $\mathrm{penguin}(X)$ is assigned level 0, $\mathrm{bird}(X)$ is assigned level 1, and $\mathrm{flies}(X)$ is assigned level 2, for all $X \in \{\mathrm{tweety}, \mathrm{bob}\}$. We obtain the

---

[5]For further details, we refer the reader to the paper [Seda and Hitzler, 1999b].

following.

$$I_1 = \{\texttt{penguin(tweety)}\}$$
$$I_2 = I_1 \cup \{\texttt{bird(bob)}, \texttt{bird(tweety)}\}$$
$$I_3 = I_2 \cup \{\texttt{flies(bob)}\}$$
$$I_{[\text{Tweety2}]} = I_3.$$

The main technical lemma we need is as follows. For its proof, which is by transfinite induction, it will be convenient to put $I_{[n,m]} = I_n$ for all $m \in \mathbb{N}$ whenever n is a limit ordinal; thus, statement (b) in the lemma makes sense for all ordinals n.

6.3.4 Lemma Let P be a normal logic program which is locally stratified with respect to the level mapping $l : B_P \to \gamma$, where $\gamma > 1$. Then the following statements hold.

(a) The sequence $(I_n)_{n \in \gamma}$ is monotonic increasing in n.

(b) For every $n \in \gamma$, where $n \geq 1$, the sequence $(I_{[n,m]})$ is monotonic increasing in m.

(c) For every $n \in \gamma$, where $n \geq 1$, I_n is a fixed point of $T_{[n]}$.

(d) If $l(B) < n$ and $B \notin I_n$, where $B \in B_P$, then for every $m \in \gamma$ with $n < m$ we have $B \notin I_m$ and, hence, $B \notin I_{[P]}$. In particular, if $l(B) < n$ and $B \notin I_{[n+1,m]}$ for some $m \in \mathbb{N}$, then $B \notin I_n$ and, hence, $B \notin I_{[P]}$.

Proof: It is immediate from the construction that the sequence $(I_n)_{n \in \gamma}$ is monotonic increasing in n, and this establishes (a).

The main work is in proving (b) and (c), which we treat simultaneously. To do this, we need to note the technical fact that, for each $n \in \gamma$, we can partition $P_{[n+1]}$ as $P_{[n]} \cup P(n)$, where $P(n)$ denotes the subset of ground(P) consisting of those clauses whose head has level n. Thus, $T_{[n+1]}(I) = T_{[n]}(I) \cup T_{P(n)}(I)$ for any $I \in I_P$; note that if $A \in T_{P(n)}(I)$, then $l(A) = n$.

Let $\mathcal{P}(n)$ be the proposition, depending on the ordinal n, that $(I_{[n,m]})$ is monotonic increasing in m and that I_n is a fixed point of $T_{[n]}$. Suppose that $\mathcal{P}(n)$ holds for all $n < \alpha$, where $\alpha \leq \gamma$ is some ordinal. We must show that $\mathcal{P}(\alpha)$ holds. Indeed, $\mathcal{P}(1)$ holds since $P_{[1]}$ is a definite program and the construction of I_1 is simply the classical construction of the least fixed point of $T_{[1]}$. Therefore, we may assume that $\alpha > 2$. It will be convenient to break up the details of the case when α is a successor ordinal into the four steps (1) to (4) below.

Case i. $\alpha = k + 1$ is a successor ordinal. Thus, $\mathcal{P}(k)$ holds.

(1) We establish the recursion equations[6]:

$$I_{[k+1,0]} = I_k$$
$$I_{[k+1,m+1]} = I_k \cup T_{P(k)}(I_{[k+1,m]})$$

and the first is immediate. Putting $m = 0$, we have $I_{[k+1,1]} = T_{[k+1]}(I_k) = T_{[k]}(I_k) \cup T_{P(k)}(I_k) = I_k \cup T_{P(k)}(I_k) = I_k \cup T_{P(k)}(I_{[k+1,0]})$, using the fact that I_k is a fixed point of $T_{[k]}$. Now suppose that the second of these equations holds for some $m > 0$. Then

$$
\begin{aligned}
I_{[k+1,(m+1)+1]} &= T_{[k+1]}(I_{[k+1,m+1]}) \\
&= T_{[k]}(I_{[k+1,m+1]}) \cup T_{P(k)}(I_{[k+1,m+1]}) \\
&= T_{[k]}(I_k \cup T_{P(k)}(I_{[k+1,m]})) \cup T_{P(k)}(I_{[k+1,m+1]}),
\end{aligned}
$$

and it suffices to show that $T_{[k]}(I_k \cup T_{P(k)}(I_{[k+1,m]})) = I_k$. So suppose that $A \in T_{[k]}(I_k \cup T_{P(k)}(I_{[k+1,m]}))$. Thus, there is a clause in $P_{[k]}$ of the form $A \leftarrow A_1, \ldots, A_{k_1}, \neg B_1, \ldots, \neg B_{l_1}$, where $A_1, \ldots, A_{k_1} \in I_k \cup T_{P(k)}(I_{[k+1,m]})$ and $B_1, \ldots, B_{l_1} \notin I_k \cup T_{P(k)}(I_{[k+1,m]})$. But then level considerations and the hypothesis concerning P imply that $A_1, \ldots, A_{k_1} \in I_k$ and $B_1, \ldots, B_{l_1} \notin I_k$. Therefore, $A \in T_{[k]}(I_k) = I_k$, and the inclusion $T_{[k]}(I_k \cup T_{P(k)}(I_{[k+1,m]})) \subseteq I_k$ holds. The reverse inclusion is demonstrated in like fashion, showing that the second of the recursion equations holds with m replaced by $m+1$ and, hence, by induction on m, that it holds for all m.

(2) We have the inclusions $T_{P(k)}(I_k) \subseteq T_{P(k)}(I_k \cup T_{P(k)}(I_k)) \subseteq T_{P(k)}(I_k \cup T_{P(k)}(I_k \cup T_{P(k)}(I_k))) \ldots$. These inclusions are established by methods similar to those we have just employed, and we omit the details.

It is now clear from this fact and the recursion equations in Step (1) that $(I_{[k+1,m]})$, or $(I_{[\alpha,m]})$, is monotonic increasing in m. Since monotonic increasing sequences converge to their union in Q, and $I_{[k+1,m]}$ is an iterate of I_k, it now follows by Theorem 5.4.2 that I_{k+1} is a model for $P_{[k+1]}$.

(3) If $B \in B_P$ and $l(B) < k$, then $B \in I_{k+1}$ if and only if $B \in I_k$. Indeed, if $B \in I_k$, then it is clear from the recursion equations of Step (1) that $B \in I_{k+1}$. On the other hand, if $B \notin I_k$, then it is equally clear from the recursion equations and level considerations that, for every $m \in \mathbb{N}$, $B \notin I_{[k+1,m]}$ and, hence, that $B \notin I_{k+1}$, as required.

(4) I_{k+1} is a supported model for $P_{[k+1]}$.
To see that this claim holds, suppose that $A \in I_{k+1} = \bigcup_{m=0}^{\infty} I_{[k+1,m]}$. Then there is $m_0 \in \mathbb{N}$ such that $A \in I_{[k+1,m+1]} = T_{[k+1]}^{m+1}(I_k)$ for all $m \geq m_0$. Thus, $A \in T_{[k+1]}(T_{[k+1]}^{m_0}(I_k)) = T_{[k+1]}(I_{[k+1,m_0]})$. Hence, there is a clause $A \leftarrow A_1, \ldots, A_{k_1}, \neg B_1, \ldots, \neg B_{l_1}$ in $P_{[k+1]}$ such that each $A_i \in I_{[k+1,m_0]}$ and no $B_j \in I_{[k+1,m_0]}$. But $l(B_j) < k$ for each j since P is locally stratified. Since

---

[6]As shown here, it results from these equations that the process of constructing $I_{[k+1,m+1]}$ in terms of $I_{[k+1,m]}$ is inflationary, where, formally, an operator G defined on a collection of sets is said to be *inflationary* if $X \subseteq G(X)$ for each set X in the given collection; see also the corresponding recursion equations in Corollary 6.3.5.

$B_j \notin I_{[k+1,m_0]}$, we now see from the recursion equations that $B_j \notin I_k$. From the result in Step (3) we now deduce that, for each j, $B_j \notin I_{k+1}$. Since it is obvious that each A_i belongs to I_{k+1}, we obtain that $A \in T_{[k+1]}(I_{k+1})$. Thus, $I_{k+1} \subseteq T_{[k+1]}(I_{k+1})$, and therefore I_{k+1} is a supported model for $P_{[k+1]}$, or a fixed point of $T_{[k+1]}$, as required.

Thus, $\mathcal{P}(\alpha)$ holds when α is a successor ordinal.

Case ii. α is a limit ordinal.

In this case, it is trivial that $(I_{[\alpha,m]})$ is monotonic increasing in m. Thus, we have only to show that I_α is a fixed point of $T_{[\alpha]}$, that is, a supported model for $P_{[\alpha]}$, and we show first that I_α is a model for $P_{[\alpha]}$. Let $A \in T_{[\alpha]}(I_\alpha)$. Then there is a clause $A \leftarrow A_1, \ldots, A_{k_1}, \neg B_1, \ldots, \neg B_{l_1}$ in $P_{[\alpha]}$ such that $A_1, \ldots, A_{k_1} \in I_\alpha$ and $B_1, \ldots, B_{l_1} \notin I_\alpha$. Indeed, by the definition of $P_{[\alpha]}$ and the hypothesis concerning P, there is $n_0 < \alpha$ such that the clause $A \leftarrow A_1, \ldots, A_{k_1}, \neg B_1, \ldots, \neg B_{l_1}$ belongs to $P_{[n_0]}$. Since the sequence $(I_n)_{n \in \gamma}$ is monotone increasing and $I_\alpha = \bigcup_{n < \alpha} I_n$, there is $n_1 < \alpha$ such that $A_1, \ldots, A_{k_1} \in I_{n_1}$ and $B_1, \ldots, B_{l_1} \notin I_{n_1}$. Choosing $n_2 = \max\{n_0, n_1\}$, we have $A \leftarrow A_1, \ldots, A_{k_1}, \neg B_1, \ldots, \neg B_{l_1} \in P_{[n_2]}$ and also $A_1, \ldots, A_{k_1} \in I_{n_2}$ and $B_1, \ldots, B_{l_1} \notin I_{n_2}$. Therefore, on using the induction hypothesis, we have $A \in T_{[n_2]}(I_{n_2}) = I_{n_2} \subseteq I_\alpha$. Hence, $T_{[\alpha]}(I_\alpha) \subseteq I_\alpha$, as required.

To see that I_α is supported, let $A \in I_\alpha$. By monotonicity of $(I_n)_{n \in \gamma}$ again and the identity $I_\alpha = \bigcup_{n < \alpha} I_n$, there is a successor ordinal $n_0 \geq 1$ such that $A \in I_n$ for all n such that $n_0 \leq n < \alpha$. In particular, we have $A \in I_{n_0} = \bigcup_{m=0}^{\infty} I_{[n_0,m]}$. Therefore, there is $m_1 \in \mathbb{N}$ such that $A \in I_{[n_0,m_1+1]} = T_{[n_0]}(T_{[n_0]}^{m_1}(I_{n_0-1}))$. Consequently, there is a clause $A \leftarrow A_1, \ldots, A_{k_1}, \neg B_1, \ldots, \neg B_{l_1}$ in $P_{[n_0]}$ such that $A_1, \ldots, A_{k_1} \in T_{[n_0]}^{m_1}(I_{n_0-1}) = I_{[n_0,m_1]} \subseteq I_{n_0} \subseteq I_\alpha$ and $B_1, \ldots, B_{k_1} \notin I_{[n_0,m_1]}$. But $l(B_j) < n_0 - 1$ for each j, and so no B_j belongs to I_{n_0-1} by Step (3) of the previous case. Therefore, by this step, no B_j belongs to I_{n_0}, and by iterating this we see that, for every $m \in \mathbb{N}$, no B_j belongs to I_{n_0+m}. Therefore, no B_j belongs to I_α. Hence, we have $A \in T_{[n_0]}(I_\alpha) \subseteq T_{[\alpha]}(I_\alpha)$ or, in other words, that $I_\alpha \subseteq T_{[\alpha]}(I_\alpha)$, as required.

It now follows that $\mathcal{P}(n)$ holds for all ordinals n, and this completes the proof of (b) and (c). In particular, we see that the recursion equations obtained in Step (1) hold for all ordinals k, and we record this fact in the corollary below. Indeed, all that is needed to establish these equations is the fact that each I_k is a fixed point of $T_{[k]}$ and to note that the proof just given shows also that $I_{[P]}$ is a fixed point of T_P. In turn, (d) of the lemma now follows from this observation by iterating Step (3).

The proof of the lemma is therefore complete. ∎

It can be seen here, and it will be seen again later, that the importance of (d) is the control it gives over negation in the manner illustrated in the proof just given that I_{k+1} is a supported model for $P_{[k+1]}$. It is also worth noting that the construction produces a monotonic increasing sequence by means of a non-monotonic operator.[7]

6.3.5 Corollary Suppose the hypothesis of Lemma 6.3.4 holds. Then the following statements hold.

(a) For all ordinals n and all $m \in \mathbb{N}$, we have the recursion equations

$$I_{[n+1,0]} = I_n, \text{ and}$$
$$I_{[n+1,m+1]} = I_n \cup T_{P(n)}(I_{[n+1,m]}).$$

(b) If P is, in fact, locally hierarchical, then for every ordinal $n \geq 1$ we have $I_{[n+1,m]} = I_n \cup T_{P(n)}(I_n)$ for all $m \in \mathbb{N}$, where $P(n)$ is defined as in the proof of Lemma 6.3.4, and therefore the iterates stabilize after one step.

Proof: That (a) holds has already been noted in the proof of Lemma 6.3.4.

For (b), it suffices to prove that $T_{P(n)}(I_n) = T_{P(n)}(I_n \cup T_{P(n)}(I_n))$. So suppose therefore that $A \in T_{P(n)}(I_n \cup T_{P(n)}(I_n))$. Then there is a clause $A \leftarrow A_1, \ldots, A_{k_1}, \neg B_1, \ldots, \neg B_{l_1}$ in $P(n)$ such that $A_1, \ldots, A_{k_1} \in I_n \cup T_{P(n)}(I_n)$ and $B_1, \ldots, B_{k_1} \notin I_n \cup T_{P(n)}(I_n)$. From these statements and by level considerations, we have $A_1, \ldots, A_{k_1} \in I_n$ and $B_1, \ldots, B_{k_1} \notin I_n$. Therefore, $A \in T_{P(n)}(I_n)$, so that $T_{P(n)}(I_n \cup T_{P(n)}(I_n)) \subseteq T_{P(n)}(I_n)$. The reverse inclusion is established similarly to complete the proof. ∎

Statement (b) of this corollary makes the calculation of iterates very easy to perform in the case of locally hierarchical programs.

6.3.6 Theorem Suppose that P is a normal logic program which is locally stratified with respect to the level mapping $l : B_P \to \gamma$. Then $I_{[P]}$ is a minimal supported model for P.

Proof: That $I_{[P]}$ is a supported model for P follows from the proof of Lemma 6.3.4, and so it remains to show that $I_{[P]}$ is minimal. To do this, we establish by transfinite induction the following proposition: "if $J \subseteq I_{[P]}$ and $T_P(J) \subseteq J$, then $I_n \subseteq J$ for all $n \in \gamma$, where $n \geq 1$", and this clearly suffices. Indeed, $T_{[1]}(J) \subseteq T_P(J) \subseteq J$, and therefore J is a model for $P_{[1]}$. But, as already noted in proving Lemma 6.3.4, I_1 is the least model for $P_{[1]}$ by construction, since $P_{[1]}$ is definite. Therefore, $I_1 \subseteq J$, and the proposition holds with $n = 1$.

Now assume that the proposition holds for all ordinals $n < \alpha$ for some ordinal $\alpha \in \gamma$, where $\alpha > 1$; we show that it holds with $n = \alpha$.

Case i. $\alpha = k + 1$ is a successor ordinal, where $k > 0$. We have $I_k \subseteq J$. We show by induction on m that $I_{[k+1,m]} \subseteq J$ for all m. Indeed, with $m = 0$, we have $I_{[k+1,0]} = I_k \subseteq J$. Suppose, therefore, that $I_{[k+1,m_0]} \subseteq J$

---

[7]Lemma 6.3.4 plays a role here similar to that played by [Apt et al., 1988, Lemma 10].

for some $m_0 > 0$. Let $A \in I_{[k+1,m_0+1]} = T_{[k+1]}(T_{[k+1]}^{m_0}(I_k))$. Then there is a clause $A \leftarrow A_1, \ldots, A_{k_1}, \neg B_1, \ldots, \neg B_{l_1}$ in $P_{[k+1]}$ such that $A_1, \ldots, A_{k_1} \in T_{[k+1]}^{m_0}(I_k) = I_{[k+1,m_0]}$ and $B_1, \ldots, B_{l_1} \notin I_{[k+1,m_0]}$. But $l(B_j) < k$ for each j. Applying Lemma 6.3.4 (d) we see that no B_j belongs to $I_{[P]}$, and consequently no B_j belongs to J because $J \subseteq I_{[P]}$. Since $I_{[k+1,m_0]} \subseteq J$ by assumption, we have $A_1, \ldots, A_{k_1} \in J$. Therefore, $A \in T_{[k+1]}(J) \subseteq T_P(J) \subseteq J$, and from this we obtain that $I_{[k+1,m_0+1]} \subseteq J$, as required to complete the proof in this case.

Case ii. α is a limit ordinal. In this case, $I_\alpha = \bigcup_{n<\alpha} I_n$ and $I_n \subseteq J$ for all $n < \alpha$ by hypothesis. Therefore, $I_\alpha \subseteq J$, as required.

Thus, the result follows by transfinite induction. ∎

We can strengthen Theorem 6.3.6.

6.3.7 Theorem Suppose that P is a normal logic program which is locally stratified with respect to a level mapping $l : B_P \to \gamma$, where γ is a countable ordinal. Then $I_{[P]}$ is a perfect model for P.

Proof: Suppose that there is a model N for P which is preferable to $I_{[P]}$ (and therefore distinct from $I_{[P]}$); we will derive a contradiction.

First note that $N \setminus I_{[P]}$ must be non-empty; otherwise, we have $N \subseteq I_{[P]}$. But this inclusion forces equality of N and $I_{[P]}$ since $I_{[P]}$ is a minimal model for P, and therefore N and $I_{[P]}$ are not distinct. This means that there is a ground atom A in $N \setminus I_{[P]}$, which can be chosen so that $l(A)$ has minimum value; let B be a ground atom in $I_{[P]} \setminus N$ corresponding to A in accordance with Definition 2.5.2 and satisfying $l(A) > l(B)$.

Next we note that $T_{[1]}(N) \subseteq T_P(N) \subseteq N$, since N is a model for P. Hence, N is a model for $P_{[1]}$, which implies that $I_1 \subseteq N$ since I_1 is the least model for the definite program $P_{[1]}$. Therefore, B can be chosen so that $B \in I_{n_0} \setminus N$, with minimal $n_0 > 1$. Now n_0 cannot be a limit ordinal; otherwise, we would have $I_{n_0} = \bigcup_{m<n_0} I_m$, from which we would conclude that $B \in I_m \setminus N$ for some $m < n_0$ contrary to the choice of n_0. Thus, n_0 must be a successor ordinal, and therefore B can be chosen so that $B \in I_{[n_0,m_0]} \setminus N$, where m_0 is such that $I_{[n_0,m_1]} \setminus N = \emptyset$ whenever $m_1 < m_0$, ; indeed, since $I_1 \subseteq N$, we must have $n_0 > 1$ and $m_0 \geq 1$ also. Consequently, $B \in T_{[n_0]}(I_{[n_0,m_0-1]}) \setminus N$, showing that there is a clause $B \leftarrow C_1, \ldots, C_{k_1}, \neg D_1, \ldots, \neg D_{l_1}$ in $P_{[n_0]}$ with the property that each $C_i \in I_{[n_0,m_0-1]}$ and no $D_j \in I_{[n_0,m_0-1]}$. Since $l(D_j) < n_0 - 1$ for each j, we see that none of the D_j belong to $I_{[P]}$ by Lemma 6.3.4 (d). But all the C_i, if there are any, must belong to N by the choice of the numbers n_0 and m_0. Moreover, there must be at least one D_j and indeed at least one belonging to N. For if there were no D_j or we had each $D_j \notin N$, then we would have $B \in T_{P_{n_0}}(N) \subseteq T_P(N) \subseteq N$, using again the fact that N is a model for P. But this leads to the conclusion that $B \in N$, which is contrary to $B \in I_{[P]} \setminus N$. Thus, there is a $D = D_j \in N \setminus I_{[P]}$, for some j, satisfying $l(D) < l(B) < l(A)$. Since A was chosen in $N \setminus I_{[P]}$ to have smallest level, we have a contradiction.

This contradiction shows that $I_{[P]}$ must be a perfect model for P, as required. ■

6.3.8 Program Since locally stratified programs are a generalization of locally hierarchical programs, it is clear that each locally hierarchical program has a unique perfect model. This does not hold, however, for Φ^*-accessible programs. Indeed, the program

$$p \leftarrow \neg q$$
$$q \leftarrow r, \neg p$$

is Φ^*-accessible (even acceptable) with respect to the unique supported model $M = \{p\}$. However, $I = \{q\}$ is also a model for this program, and while I is preferable to M, M, in turn, is also preferable to I, so P does not have a perfect model.

We finally return to the special case of stratified programs. We temporarily introduce the *powers of an operator* T mapping a complete lattice to itself:[8]

$$T \uparrow 0(I) = I$$
$$T \uparrow (n+1)(I) = T(T \uparrow n(I)) \cup T \uparrow n(I)$$
$$T \uparrow \omega(I) = \bigcup_{n=0}^{\infty} T \uparrow n(I).$$

Of course, $T \uparrow n(I)$ is *not* equal to $T^n(I)$ unless T happens to be monotonic and $I \subseteq T(I)$. Indeed, the sequence $(T \uparrow n(I))_n$ is always monotonic increasing whether or not T is monotonic. However, this concept can be used to construct an associated model M_P for any stratified program P as follows. We put $M_0 = \emptyset$, $M_1 = T_{P_1} \uparrow \omega(M_0), \ldots, M_m = T_{P_m} \uparrow \omega(M_{m-1})$. Finally, let $M_P = M_m$.

We will show that M_P is the perfect model for P, for stratified P. To do this, it will be convenient to introduce the concept $T \Uparrow n(I)$ for a mapping $T : I_P \rightarrow I_P$ and $I \in I_P$. In fact, $T \Uparrow n(I)$ is defined inductively as follows:

$$T \Uparrow 0(I) = I$$
$$T \Uparrow (n+1)(I) = T(T \Uparrow n(I)) \cup I$$
$$T \Uparrow \omega(I) = \bigcup_{n=0}^{\infty} T \Uparrow n(I).$$

6.3.9 Theorem Let P be a stratified normal logic program. Then $I_{[P]} = M_P$.

Proof: As usual, we take the stratification to be $P = P_1 \cup \ldots \cup P_m$, and we will show by induction that $I_k = M_k$ for $k = 1, \ldots, m$ and that $I_k = M_m$ for $k > m$. From this we clearly have $I_{[P]} = M_m = M_P$, as required.

_____

[8]This and the following construction of M_P was introduced in [Apt et al., 1988].

With the definition of the level mapping we are currently using and with the conventions we have made regarding the stratification, we note first that the equalities $P_{[k]} = \text{ground}(P_1 \cup P_2 \cup \ldots \cup P_k)$ and $P(k-1) = \text{ground}(P_k)$ both hold for $k = 1, \ldots, m$, where $P(k)$ is as defined in the proof of Lemma 6.3.4.

Now $P_{[1]} = \text{ground}(P_1)$ is definite, even if empty, and so it is immediate that $T_{P_1} \Uparrow i(M_0) = T_{P_1} \uparrow i(M_0)$ for all i and that $I_1 = M_1$. So suppose next that $T_{P_{k+1}} \Uparrow i(M_k) = T_{P_{k+1}} \uparrow i(M_k)$ for all i and that $I_{k+1} = M_{k+1}$ for some $k > 0$. Then $T_{P_{k+2}} \Uparrow 0(M_{k+1}) = M_{k+1} = T_{P_{k+2}} \uparrow 0(M_{k+1})$ and also $I_{[k+2,0]} = I_{k+1} = M_{k+1} = T_{P_{k+2}} \uparrow 0(M_{k+1})$. So now suppose that $T_{P_{k+2}} \Uparrow m(M_{k+1}) = T_{P_{k+2}} \uparrow m(M_{k+1})$ and that $I_{[k+2,m]} = T_{P_{k+2}} \uparrow m(M_{k+1})$ for some $m > 0$. Then $T_{P_{k+2}} \Uparrow (m+1)(M_{k+1}) = T_{P_{k+2}}(T_{P_{k+2}} \Uparrow m(M_{k+1})) \cup M_{k+1}$ and $T_{P_{k+2}} \uparrow (m+1)(M_{k+1}) = T_{P_{k+2}}(T_{P_{k+2}} \uparrow m(M_{k+1})) \cup T_{P_{k+2}} \uparrow m(M_{k+1})$, and it is clear that $T_{P_{k+2}} \Uparrow (m+1)(M_{k+1}) \subseteq T_{P_{k+2}} \uparrow (m+1)(M_{k+1})$. For the reverse inclusion, we note that under our present hypotheses we have $T_{P_{k+2}} \uparrow (m+1)(M_{k+1}) = T_{P_{k+2}}(T_{P_{k+2}} \Uparrow m(M_{k+1})) \cup T_{P_{k+2}} \Uparrow m(M_{k+1})$, and so it suffices to show that $T_{P_{k+2}} \Uparrow m(M_{k+1}) \subseteq T_{P_{k+2}}(T_{P_{k+2}} \Uparrow m(M_{k+1})) \cup M_{k+1}$ or, in other words, that $I_{[k+2,m]} \subseteq T_{P(k+1)}(I_{[k+2,m]}) \cup I_{k+1}$. Since this latter set is equal to $I_{[k+2,m+1]}$ by the recursion equations of Corollary 6.3.5, the inclusion we want follows from the monotonicity of the sets $I_{[k+2,m]}$ relative to m. We conclude, therefore, that $T_{P_{k+2}} \Uparrow (m+1)(M_{k+1}) = T_{P_{k+2}} \uparrow (m+1)(M_{k+1})$.

Finally, $I_{[k+2,m+1]} = I_{k+1} \cup T_{P(k+1)}(I_{[k+2,m]}) = M_{k+1} \cup T_{P_{k+2}}(T_{P_{k+2}} \uparrow m(M_{k+1})) = M_{k+1} \cup T_{P_{k+2}}(T_{P_{k+2}} \Uparrow m(M_{k+1})) = T_{P_{k+2}} \Uparrow (m+1)(M_{k+1}) = T_{P_{k+2}} \uparrow (m+1)(M_{k+1})$, by the conclusions of the previous paragraph. Therefore, $I_{[k+2,m+1]} = T_{P_{k+2}} \uparrow (m+1)(M_{k+1})$. From this we obtain, by induction, the equality $I_{[k+2,m]} = T_{P_{k+2}} \uparrow m(M_{k+1})$ for all m and with it the equality $I_{k+2} = M_{k+2}$, as required. ∎

The details of the induction proof just given also establish the following proposition.

6.3.10 Proposition Let $P = P_1 \cup \ldots \cup P_m$ be a stratified normal logic program. Then we have that $T_{P_{k+1}} \Uparrow i(M_k) = T_{P_{k+1}} \uparrow i(M_k)$ for all i and $k = 0, \ldots, m-1$.

Finally, we show that locally stratified programs have a unique perfect model, which is also their total weakly perfect model.

6.3.11 Theorem Let P be locally stratified. Then P has a total weakly perfect model which is a perfect model for P. Furthermore, this model is independent of the choice of level mapping with respect to which P is locally stratified.[9]

Proof: We will employ Theorem 2.5.9 to establish the claim. Let P be locally stratified with respect to some level mapping l'. Consider the equations

---

[9]In fact, it is known that every locally stratified program has a *unique* perfect model, see [Przymusinski, 1988].

established in Corollary 6.3.5 (a) and define the level mapping l mapping to pairs of ordinals as follows. For $A \in I_{[P]}$ let $l(A) = (l'(A), m)$, where m is least such that $A \in I_{[l'(A)+1, m+1]}$. For $A \notin I_{[P]}$ let $l(A) = (l'(A) + 1, 0)$. The recursion equations from Corollary 6.3.5 (a) together with the fact that P is locally stratified thus allow us to conclude that (WSi), (WSiib), or (WSiic) is always satisfied with respect to $I_{[P]}$ and l. Since $I_{[P]}$ is total, we obtain by Theorem 2.5.9 that $I_{[P]} \cup (B_P \setminus I_{[P]})$ is the (total) weakly perfect model for P. Since every program has only one weakly perfect model, and we have just seen that the weakly perfect model for P coincides with $I_{[P]}$, we conclude that the model $I_{[P]}$ as constructed by Theorem 6.3.7 is independent of the choice of level mapping with respect to which P is locally stratified. ∎

6.3.12 Example Consider Tweety2 from Example 2.5.3 again. It is (locally) stratified with respect to the level mapping given in Example 6.3.3. We calculate the perfect model for Tweety2 by employing powers of the operator T_P as discussed just prior to the statement of Theorem 6.3.9. Indeed, with the notation used there, we obtain

$$M_1 = \{\text{penguin}(\text{tweety})\},$$
$$M_2 = \{\text{bird}(\text{bob}), \text{bird}(\text{tweety}), \text{penguin}(\text{tweety})\},$$
$$M_3 = M_{\text{Tweety2}}, \text{and}$$
$$M_4 = M3.$$

As discussed in Example 2.5.3, the latter model is the perfect model for Tweety2.

Chapter 7

Logic Programming and Artificial Neural Networks

Sebastian Bader,[1] *Pascal Hitzler,*[2] *and Anthony Seda*[3]

7.1 Introduction

One of the ultimate goals of artificial intelligence is the creation of agents with human-like intelligence, and many, varied approaches have been made in attempts to realize this goal. Of course, an agent endowed with human-like intelligence should be able to represent and reason with well-structured data and processes, such as those encountered in logic or in mathematics and related subjects, just as human beings can. On the other hand, that same agent should also be able to represent and reason with uncertain, noisy, and incomplete data, again, just as human beings can, at least to a certain extent. Furthermore, the agent should be able to learn by example and refine the reasoning process as a result.

These two aspects of the general process of reasoning and intelligence just considered are complementary and yet are integrated in human intelligence. Thus, their integration within a single artificial computing system is an important objective in the search for true artificial intelligence.[4] Logic-based symbolic systems are good implementations of the first, the formal, style of reasoning, whereas *neural networks* or *connectionist systems* are good implementations of the second, less formal, style. They are therefore good candidates, and indeed are among the most prominent such candidates, for attempting this integration, with each representing one of the two aspects. Certainly, there has been a considerable amount of interest in recent years in exactly this

---

[1]MMIS, Department of Computer Science, University of Rostock, Germany.

[2]Kno.e.sis Center for Knowledge-Enabled Computing, Wright State University, Dayton, Ohio, USA.

[3]Department of Mathematics, University College Cork, Cork, Ireland.

[4]See [Hitzler and Kühnberger, 2009] for a more detailed discussion of this point.

integration, known as *neural-symbolic integration*, with a view to combining the best of both styles of reasoning within a single system.[5]

It will be worth contrasting a little further these two, very different, computing paradigms in order to appreciate better the issues involved in their integration. First, symbolic systems are usually based on a logic of one type or another. They possess a declarative semantics, and knowledge can be modelled in them in a human-like fashion. Thus, their use makes it easy to process knowledge and also to handle structured objects. Unfortunately, such systems are hard to refine from real world data, which usually is noisy, and they are hard to design if no expert knowledge is available. They are essentially discrete models of computation and have been successfully used in many applications. On the other hand, artificial neural networks are a powerful approach to machine learning, inspired by biology and neuroscience. They are trainable from raw data, even if the data is noisy and inconsistent, and thus are capable of adapting to new situations. They are, furthermore, robust in the sense that they degrade gracefully: even if parts of the system fail, the system still works. Unfortunately, they do not possess a declarative semantics and have difficulties in handling structured data. Available (symbolic) background knowledge, which exists in many application domains, is also difficult to use in such systems. Being modelled on natural phenomena, connectionist systems are basically continuous models of computation, and they also have been used successfully in many applications.

Figure 7.1 shows the *Neural-Symbolic Cycle* which depicts, in general terms, our approach to the process of integration followed here. Starting from a symbolic system, which is both readable and writable by humans, we create a neural or connectionist system into which the symbolic knowledge is embedded. The neural system can then be trained using powerful connectionist training methods, which allows modification of the rules by generalization from raw data. If this learned or refined knowledge is later extracted from the neural system, we obtain a readable version of the acquired knowledge.[6] In fact, it is our intention to show in this chapter how to embed knowledge about semantic operators into connectionist systems. More specifically, we show how semantic operators of propositional logic programs P may be computed exactly by neural systems and how these same operators may be approximated in the case of first-order programs. One consequence of this is that a neural system acquires a sort of semantics. Another consequence is that this chapter may be viewed as providing a model of computation for the concepts of the previous chapters, and it deals to a certain extent with the implementation aspects of this model. This chapter therefore is a natural continuation of the earlier ones and gives an example of the use and application of certain of the methods we have developed. Indeed, the notion of approximation just men-

---

[5]See [Bader and Hitzler, 2005, Hammer and Hitzler, 2007] for overviews of the area.

[6]We do not deal with knowledge extraction here, but instead refer the reader to the papers [Jacobsson, 2005, Bader and Hitzler, 2005, Lehmann et al., 2010] for pointers to the literature.

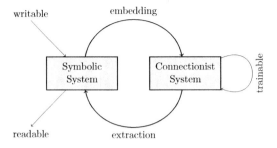

FIGURE 7.1: The neural-symbolic cycle.

tioned occurs in the context of a theorem of Funahashi, see Theorem 7.2.2, and employs the methods of Chapters 3 and 4 in that it casts sets of interpretations into compact metric spaces. This fact permits familiar techniques from analysis to be employed, and their occurrence is to be expected given the continuous nature of neural systems, as already noted. Such methods using approximation are, in fact, forced on us if we wish to employ conventional neural networks having only finitely many neurons because, for first-order programs P, both B_P and ground(P) are infinite sets.

Thus, the main objective of this chapter is to give a detailed account of the foundations of neural-symbolic integration, and the main contents of the chapter are as follows. First, in Section 7.2, we introduce neural networks and the basic definitions and notation we need throughout, including the statement of Funahashi's theorem in the form in which we use it. Next, in Section 7.3, we discuss in some detail the so-called *core method* as a general and well-known approach to neural-symbolic integration. Indeed, it is the method we adopt here, and it is already summarized in the previous paragraph. In Section 7.4, we commence the study of the main topic of the chapter, namely, the process of embedding semantic operators of logic programs into neural networks. Thus, in Section 7.4, we start with a basic result, Theorem 7.4.1, applying to propositional logic programs P and due originally to Hölldobler and Kalinke [Hölldobler and Kalinke, 1994]. This result provides a procedure which, when given a normal propositional logic program P, shows how to construct a neural network which computes the T_P-operator for P. The next section, Section 7.5, is the heart of the chapter and takes up the issue of the approximate computation of the T_P-operator for first-order normal logic programs P. Starting with the propositional approximation of T_P based on the previous section, we go on to study the approximate computation of T_P by sigmoidal networks, radial-basis-function networks, and vector-based networks, in turn, before closing the section with a discussion of the approximate computation of the least fixed point of the T_P-operator for definite normal logic programs P. It should be noted that, thus far, we have concentrated on the T_P-operator, but we take up the study of the computation and the approximate computation of other semantic operators, and their fixed points, in

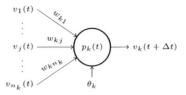

FIGURE 7.2: Unit N_k in a connectionist network.

Sections 7.6 and 7.7. In particular, in Section 7.6, we sketch the construction of neural networks which extend Theorem 7.4.1 to compute the Fitting-style operator F_P for propositional normal logic programs P. Then, in Section 7.7, we consider approximate computation for the operators F_P and GL_P, among others, for first-order normal logic programs P.

At certain places in this chapter, the material we present is just sketched, and detail is provided only to the extent to which it serves to outline the application area under discussion. This is simply because the inclusion of full detail at the places in question would lead us far astray from the main topic of the book. We do give ample references to the literature, however, to facilitate the reader who is interested in studying the relevant matters further.

7.2   Basics of Artificial Neural Networks

We begin by briefly summarizing what we need relating to artificial neural networks or just neural networks for short.[7]

7.2.1 Definition A *neural network* or *connectionist network*[8] is simply a weighted directed graph, or weighted digraph, endowed with extra structure, as follows. A typical *unit* (or *node*) N_k in this digraph is shown in Figure 7.2. We denote by $\mathcal{I}_k = \{1, \ldots, n_k\}$, say, the finite set of indices j for which there is a digraph connection from N_j to N_k, and we let $w_{kj} \in \mathbb{R}$ denote the weight of the digraph connection from a unit N_j to a unit N_k, if there is such a connection, noting that w_{kj} may be 0. Then the unit N_k is characterized, at time t, by the following data: its *input vector* $(i_{k1}(t), \ldots, i_{kn_k}(t))$, where $i_{kj}(t) = w_{kj}v_j(t)$ is the input received by N_k from N_j at time t; its *threshold* $\theta_k \in \mathbb{R}$; its *potential* $p_k(t)$; and its *value* $v_k(t)$. The units are updated synchronously; time becomes $t + \Delta t$; at each update the potential $p_k(t)$ is calculated by means of an *activation function*; and the output value for N_k,

---

[7]Our terminology and notation are fairly standard, and the reader is referred to the papers [Hitzler et al., 2004, Fu, 1994, Hertz et al., 1991] for further details concerning neural networks; in particular, we follow [Hitzler et al., 2004] closely here.

[8]Also called a *connectionist system*.

$v_k(t + \Delta t)$, is calculated by means of an *output function* whose argument is $p_k(t)$. In fact, the activation function we will use most often in our work is the weighted sum of the inputs minus the threshold. In other words, in most of our discussions $p_k(t) = \left(\sum_{j \in I_k} w_{kj} v_j(t) \right) - \theta_k \in \mathbb{R}$. We say that a unit N_k *becomes active at time t* if $p_k(t) \geq 0$. On the other hand, we consider a number of different types of units distinguished mainly by their output function, as follows. A unit is said to be a *binary threshold unit* if its output function is a threshold function or Heaviside function H, so that

$$ v_k(t + \Delta t) = H(p_k(t)) = \left\{ \begin{array}{ll} 1 & \text{if } p_k(t) \geq 0, \\ 0 & \text{otherwise.} \end{array} \right. $$

A unit is said to be a *linear unit* if its output function is the identity as a function of $p_k(t)$ and its threshold θ is 0. A unit is said to be a *sigmoidal unit* or a *squashing unit* if its output function ϕ is non-decreasing and is such that $\lim_{x \to \infty} \phi(x) = 1$ and $\lim_{x \to -\infty} \phi(x) = 0$. Such functions are called *squashing functions*. ∎

We will only consider connectionist networks where the units can be organized in layers, although a variant of this will be encountered in Section 7.6. A *layer* is a vector of units. An *n-layer feedforward network* $\mathcal{F}$ consists of the *input* layer, $n - 2$ *hidden* layers, and the *output* layer, where $n \geq 2$. Each unit occurring in the i-th layer is connected to each unit occurring in the $(i+1)$-st layer, $1 \leq i < n$. Let r and s be the number of units occurring in the input and output layers, respectively. A connectionist network $\mathcal{F}$ is called a *multilayer feedforward network* if it is an n-layer feedforward network for some n. A multilayer feedforward network $\mathcal{F}$ computes a function $f_{\mathcal{F}} : \mathbb{R}^r \to \mathbb{R}^s$, called the *input-output mapping* of $\mathcal{F}$ or the *network function* of $\mathcal{F}$, as follows. The input vector (the argument of $f_{\mathcal{F}}$) is presented to the input layer at time t_0 and propagated through the hidden layers to the output layer. At each time point, all units update their potential and value, as noted above. At time $t_0 + (n - 1)\Delta t$, the output vector (the image under $f_{\mathcal{F}}$ of the input vector) is read off the output layer.

For a 3-layer feedforward network with r linear units in the input layer, squashing units in the hidden layer, and a single linear unit in the output layer, the input-output function of the network as described in the previous paragraph can thus be obtained as a mapping $f : \mathbb{R}^r \to \mathbb{R}$ with

$$ f(x_1, \ldots, x_r) = \sum_j c_j \phi \left(\sum_i w_{ji} x_i - \theta_j \right), $$

where c_j is the weight associated with the connection from the j-th unit of the hidden layer to the single unit in the output layer, ϕ is the squashing output function of the units in the hidden layer, w_{ji} is the weight associated with the connection from the i-th unit of the input layer to the j-th unit of the hidden layer, and θ_j is the threshold of the j-th unit of the hidden layer.

It is our aim to establish results in the following sections on the representation and approximation of various semantic operators, the T_P-operator in particular, by input-output functions of 3-layer feedforward networks. Some of our results rest on the following theorem, which is due to Funahashi, see [Funahashi, 1989].

7.2.2 Theorem (Funahashi) Suppose that $\phi : \mathbb{R} \to \mathbb{R}$ is a non-constant, bounded, monotone increasing and continuous function. Let $K \subseteq \mathbb{R}^n$ be compact, let $f : K \to \mathbb{R}$ be a continuous function, and let $\varepsilon > 0$. Then there exists a 3-layer feedforward network $\mathcal{F}$ with squashing function ϕ whose input-output mapping $f_{\mathcal{F}} : K \to \mathbb{R}$ satisfies $\max_{x \in K} d(f(x), f_{\mathcal{F}}(x)) < \varepsilon$, where d is a metric which induces the natural topology[9] on $\mathbb{R}$.

In other words, each continuous function $f : K \to \mathbb{R}$ can be uniformly approximated by input-output functions of 3-layer (feedforward) networks. Furthermore, on a point of terminology, suppose given $\varepsilon > 0$. We will write *Y approximates X up to ε* if $d(Y, X) < \varepsilon$, where d is some appropriate metric for the objects X, Y in question.[10] There are two cases here where the definition just given will be applied, as follows. In the first case, X is a semantic operator and Y is an operator which we are using to approximate X; d is either the uniform metric used in Theorem 7.2.2 or the metric λ discussed in Section 7.5.2. In the other case, X is a fixed point of a semantic operator and Y is an interpretation which we are using to approximate X; d is the metric d_l determined by a level map (taking values in ω) as in Definition 5.1.3, see again Section 7.5.2 and also Section 7.5.6. We will paraphrase the import of Theorem 7.2.2, noting that it holds for all $\varepsilon > 0$, by writing that *approximating networks exist* for f. Furthermore, for our purposes later, it will suffice to assume that K is a compact subset of the set of real numbers, so that n can be taken to be equal to 1 in the statement of the theorem.

An *n-layer recurrent network* $\mathcal{F}$ consists of an n-layer feedforward network such that the number of units in the input layer is equal to the number of units in the output layer. Furthermore, each unit in the output layer is connected with weight 1 to the unit in the corresponding position in the input layer. Figure 7.3 shows a 3-layer recurrent network. The subnetwork consisting of the three layers and the connections between the input and the hidden layer as well as between the hidden and the output layer is a 3-layer feedforward network called the *kernel* of $\mathcal{F}$.

Notice that any neural network in which the number of units in the input layer is equal to the number of units in the output layer can be *made recurrent* just by adding the necessary obvious connections with weight 1. Notice

---

[9]For example, $d(x, y) = |x - y|$.

[10]The fact that d is symmetric will not render this definition ambiguous, because in practice it will be clear which object is which.

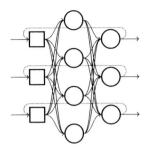

FIGURE 7.3: Sketch of a 3-layer recurrent network containing, from left to right, 3 input, 4 hidden, and 3 output units and showing also the recurrent connections from output layer to input layer.

also that a recurrent network can perform iterated computations because the output values can be returned to the input layer via the connections just described; it can thus perform computation of the iterates $T^k(I)$, $k \in \mathbb{N}$, for example, where I is an interpretation and T is a semantic operator.

7.3 The Core Method as a General Approach to Integration

In this section, we outline the idea underlying the approach presented below. Suppose given a normal logic program P and any one of the semantic operators $\mathcal{T}_P : \mathcal{I}_P \to \mathcal{I}_P$ we have thus far associated with P, using $\mathcal{T}_P$ and $\mathcal{I}_P$ as generic symbols for a semantic operator and its underlying set of interpretations. For simplicity, we assume the interpretations in question are Herbrand interpretations taking values in a truth set $\mathcal{T}$, although the conclusions we make here are valid over any preinterpretation J whose domain D is countable. Can one find, or at least show the existence of, a multilayer feedforward network $\mathcal{F}_P$ which computes $\mathcal{T}_P$ in some sense? Furthermore, can this network $\mathcal{F}_P$, or some other appropriate network, compute the least fixed point of $\mathcal{T}_P$ assuming the least fixed point of $\mathcal{T}_P$ exists?

A few general remarks are in order at this point. To begin with, multilayer feedforward networks, even 3-layer feedforward networks, are known to be extremely powerful computing devices and indeed are known to be universal approximators in the sense made precise in the statement of Funahashi's theorem, Theorem 7.2.2, earlier.[11] Therefore, one might expect them to have the ability to carry out the required computations, and this is so. Indeed, suppose that P is a first-order program and endow $\mathcal{I}_P$ with the Cantor topology,

---

[11]See [Funahashi, 1989, Hornik et al., 1989] for full details.

assuming that the set $\mathcal{T}$ of truth values is finite. Then we obtain a compact Hausdorff space homeomorphic to the Cantor subset of the unit interval in the real line as shown in Theorem 3.3.4. Thus, whenever T_P is continuous in the Cantor topology on $\mathcal{I}_P$ (see Theorem 7.5.3), we can apply Theorem 7.2.2, taking $f = f_{\mathcal{F}_P}$, taking $K = \mathcal{I}_P$, and given a value of $\varepsilon > 0$, to assert the existence of a 3-layer feedforward network satisfying the conclusion of Theorem 7.2.2. Furthermore, by making such a network recurrent, it can also compute iterates of T_P provided that conditions prevail under which the error estimate is uniformly well-behaved relative to ε under iteration. Again, under suitable conditions and with a suitable choice of initial input $I_0 \in \mathcal{I}$ (perhaps the bottom element of $\mathcal{I}$), the iterates $f_{\mathcal{F}_P}^n(I_0)$ will converge to a fixed point (perhaps the least) of T_P, and these observations will be examined in Sections 7.5.2 and 7.5.6, see also Corollary 7.4.3. Finally, as one might expect, if P is actually a propositional program, then the need for approximation disappears, and indeed a 3-layer network can be constructed which actually computes T_P and, again under suitable conditions, computes fixed points of T_P. In fact, in the case of propositional programs, networks of binary threshold units suffice for these purposes, as we shall see. This general method is nowadays known as the *core method*, and a number of instances of it are presented in the following sections.

It is important to note that the proof of Theorem 7.2.2 is non-constructive, and much of our work in the following sections of this chapter is concerned with the problem of constructing suitable approximations to semantic operators in the case of first-order programs.[12] However, we will begin by discussing propositional programs in these terms in the next section.

7.4　Propositional Programs

The previous section delineates the problem we wish to study in this chapter, and we begin by studying the propositional case first relative to the immediate consequence operator. Before doing this however we note that networks yet simpler than those just described, namely, 2-layer feedforward networks of binary threshold units, do not in general suffice to compute the immediate consequence operator for (definite) propositional logic programs, although we give no details of this claim here.[13]

We now present the main result of this section.[14]

---

[12]We know of no constructive proof of Theorem 7.2.2 and refer the reader to the papers [Cybenko, 1989, Funahashi, 1989, Hornik et al., 1989] for well-known versions of the proof.

[13]See [Hitzler et al., 2004] for a discussion of this fact.

[14]This result was first established in [Hölldobler and Kalinke, 1994]; here, and in the rest of this section, we follow [Hitzler et al., 2004].

7.4.1 Theorem For each propositional normal logic program P, a 3-layer feedforward network can be constructed which computes the immediate consequence operator T_P.

Proof: Let m and n be the number of propositional variables and the number of clauses occurring in P, respectively. Without loss of generality, we may assume that the variables are ordered. The network associated with P can now be constructed by the following *translation algorithm*.

(1) Both the input and output layers are vectors of binary threshold units of length m, where the i-th unit in either of these layers represents the i-th variable, $1 \leq i \leq m$. The threshold of each unit occurring in the input or output layer is set to 0.5.

(2) For each clause of the form $A \leftarrow L_1, \ldots, L_k$, $k \geq 0$, occurring in P, do the following.

(2.1) Add a binary threshold unit c to the hidden layer.

(2.2) Connect c to the unit representing A in the output layer with weight 1.

(2.3) For each literal L_j, $1 \leq j \leq k$, connect the unit representing L_j in the input layer to c and, if L_j is an atom, then set the weight to 1; otherwise, set the weight to -1.

(2.4) Set the threshold θ_c of c to $l - 0.5$, where l is the number of positive literals occurring in $L_1, \ldots, L_k$.

Each interpretation I for P can be represented by a binary vector $(v_1, \ldots, v_m)$. Such an interpretation is given as input to the network by externally activating corresponding units of the input layer at time t_0. It remains to show that $T_P(I)(A) = \mathbf{t}$ if and only if the unit representing A in the output layer becomes active at time $t_0 + 2\Delta t$.

If $T_P(I)(A) = \mathbf{t}$, then there is a clause $A \leftarrow L_1, \ldots, L_k$ in P such that for all $1 \leq j \leq k$ we have $I(L_j) = \mathbf{t}$. Let c be the unit in the hidden layer associated with this clause according to (2.1) of the construction. From (2.3) and (2.4) we conclude that c becomes active at time $t_0 + \Delta t$. Consequently, (2.2) and the fact that units occurring in the output layer have a threshold of 0.5 (see Step (1) of the construction) ensure that the unit representing A in the output layer becomes active at time $t_0 + 2\Delta t$.

Conversely, suppose that the unit representing the atom A in the output layer becomes active at time $t_0 + 2\Delta t$. From the construction of the network, we find a unit c in the hidden layer which must have become active at time $t_0 + \Delta t$. This unit is associated with a clause $A \leftarrow L_1, \ldots, L_k$. If $k = 0$, that is, if the body of the clause is empty, then, according to (2.4), c has a threshold of -0.5. Furthermore, according to (2.3), c does not receive any input, that is, $p_c = 0+0.5$, and consequently c will always be active. Otherwise, if $k \geq 1$, then c becomes active only if each unit in the input layer representing

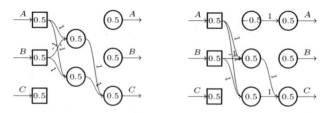

FIGURE 7.4: Two 3-layer feedforward networks of binary threshold units computing T_{P_1} and T_{P_2}, respectively. Only connections with non-zero weight are shown. The numbers occurring within units denote thresholds.

a positive literal and no unit representing a negative literal in the body of the clause is active at time t_0 (see (2.3) and (2.4)). Hence, we have found a clause $A \leftarrow L_1, \ldots, L_k$ such that for all $1 \leq j \leq k$ we have $I(L_j) = \mathbf{t}$, and consequently $T_P(I)(A) = \mathbf{t}$.   ■

7.4.2 Example As an example of Theorem 7.4.1, consider the following two programs P_1 (on the left) and P_2 (on the right):

$$
\begin{array}{ll}
C \leftarrow A, \neg B & A \leftarrow \\
C \leftarrow \neg A, B & C \leftarrow A, \neg B \\
& C \leftarrow \neg A, B
\end{array}
$$

Their corresponding connectionist networks are shown in Figure 7.4. One should observe that P_2 exemplifies the representation of unit clauses in 3-layer feedforward networks.[15]

It is worth noting that the number of units and the number of connections in a network $\mathcal{F}$ corresponding to a program P are bounded by $O(m + n)$ and $O(m \times n)$, respectively, where m is the number of propositional variables and n is the number of clauses occurring in P. Furthermore, $T_P(I)$ is computed in two steps. As the sequential time to compute $T_P(I)$ is bounded by $O(n \times m)$ (assuming that no literal occurs more than once in the conditions of a clause), the parallel computational model is optimal.[16]

We mention in passing and in the context of Theorem 7.4.1 that one can apply the Banach contraction mapping theorem, Theorem 4.2.3, to obtain the following result.

7.4.3 Corollary Let P be a normal propositional logic program such that

---

[15] We can save the unit in the hidden layer corresponding to the unit clause if we change the threshold of the unit representing A in the output layer to -0.5.

[16] A parallel computational model requiring $p(n)$ processors and $t(n)$ time to solve a problem of size n is *optimal* if $p(n) \times t(n) = O(T(n))$, where $T(n)$ is the sequential time to solve this problem, see, for example, [Karp and Ramachandran, 1990].

T_P is a contraction with respect to some (necessarily complete) metric. Then a 3-layer recurrent network can be constructed such that each computation, starting with an arbitrary initial input, converges and yields the unique fixed point of T_P or, in other words, yields the unique supported model for P.

Indeed, there is even a kind of converse of Corollary 7.4.3 also, as follows. Let P be a propositional logic program such that the corresponding network has the property that each computation starting with an arbitrary initial input converges, and in all cases converges to the same state. Then it results that iteration of the T_P-operator exhibits the same behaviour, that is, for each initial interpretation it yields one and the same constant value after a finite number of iterations. This fact suffices to guarantee the existence of a complete metric which renders T_P a contraction, and the claim therefore follows.[17]

Returning to the programs P_1 and P_2 again, we observe that the associated T_P-operators are contractions.[18] Hence, Figure 7.4 shows the kernels of corresponding recurrent networks which compute the least fixed point of T_{P_1} (the interpretation represented by the vector $(0,0,0)$) and of T_{P_2} (the interpretation represented by the vector $(1,0,1)$).

The time needed by the network to settle down into the unique stable state is equal to the time needed by a sequential machine to compute the least fixed point of T_P in the worst case. As an example, consider the definite program P_3 as follows, where $1 \le i < n$

$$A_1 \leftarrow$$
$$A_{i+1} \leftarrow A_i$$

The least fixed point of T_{P_3} is the interpretation which evaluates each A_i, $1 \le i \le n$, to $\mathbf{t}$, and it can be computed in $O(n)$ steps.[19] Obviously, the parallel computational model needs as many steps. More generally, let P be a propositional definite program containing n clauses. The time needed by the network to settle down into the unique stable state is $3n$ in the worst case, and thus, the time is linear with respect to the number of clauses occurring in the program. This comes as no surprise as satisfiability of propositional Horn formulae is P-complete and, thus, is unlikely to be in the class NC.[20] On the other hand, consider the program P_4 containing the following clauses

$$A_i \leftarrow$$
$$A_{i+1} \leftarrow A_i$$

---

[17]See [Hitzler and Seda, 2001, Bessaga, 1959, Jachymski, 2000]; a direct proof of this observation is given in [Hölldobler and Kalinke, 1994].

[18]These programs are actually acceptable, as can be seen by mapping C to 2 and A as well as B, to 1 and considering the model $I(A) = I(C) = \mathbf{t}$ and $I(B) = \mathbf{f}$.

[19]Using techniques described in [Dowling and Gallier, 1984] and [Scutellà, 1990]. To be more precise, the algorithm described in [Dowling and Gallier, 1984] needs $O(n)$ time, where n denotes the total number of occurrences of propositional variables in the formula.

[20]See, for example, [Jones and Laaser, 1977] and [Karp and Ramachandran, 1990].

where $1 \leq i \leq n$ and i is even. The least model for P_4 maps each atom to **t** and is computed in five steps by the recurrent network corresponding to P_4.

We note that the networks constructed by the translation algorithm presented previously cannot be trained by the usual learning methods applied to connectionist systems. It was observed in [d'Avila Garcez et al., 1997] (see also [d'Avila Garcez and Zaverucha, 1999, d'Avila Garcez et al., 2002]) that results similar to Theorem 7.4.1 and Corollary 7.4.3 can be obtained if the binary threshold units occurring in the hidden layer of the feedforward kernels are replaced by sigmoidal units. We omit the technical details here and refer to the above cited literature. Such a move renders the kernels accessible to the backpropagation algorithm, a standard technique for training feedforward networks [Rumelhart et al., 1986].

7.5   First-Order Programs

A central problem for neural-symbolic integration is the determination of a good representation of first-order rules within a connectionist setting. Such a representation would result, at least, in the computation or approximation of the associated semantic operators. That approximating networks exist for the immediate consequence operators of acyclic logic programs was the first result obtained in this regard, see [Hölldobler et al., 1999], but it was shown with the help of Funahashi's theorem, which is non-constructive as we have already observed. In this section, we outline the ideas underlying the general problem and also discuss different constructive approaches to it. But before going into details, we need to answer the following questions.

- Why do we need to approximate operators such as the T_P-operator?

- What does approximation mean in our context?

The first question is easily answered: even a single application of the T_P-operator can lead to infinite results. For example, assume P is a program containing the fact $p(X)$. Applying the T_P-operator once (to an arbitrary interpretation) leads to a result containing infinitely many atoms, namely, all $p(X)$-atoms for every X. In this simple example, we might be able to represent this particular result in a finite way, but things might become arbitrarily complex for other programs using the same or similar representations.[21]

---

[21] Indeed, the so-called rational models were developed to tackle this representational problem for certain programs, see [Bornscheuer, 1996]. Unfortunately, there is no way to compute an upper bound on the size of this rational representation, and hence it does not give us any immediate advantages. Because we are not aware of any other finite representation, we will concentrate here on the standard representation using Herbrand interpretations.

In principle, there are two ways to approximate a given T_P-operator. On the one hand, we can design an approximating function to meet a given level of accuracy. This leads, as accuracy increases, to increasing numbers of units in the hidden layer in the resulting networks, and we call this method *approximation in space*. The approaches presented in this section follow this line of attack. Alternatively, we can construct a system which approximates a single application of the T_P-operator better and better the longer it runs, and we call this method *approximation in time*.[22]

Our discussion here has concentrated on the operator T_P, but all our considerations apply equally well to any of the other semantic operators we have studied, and we will return to this point in Sections 7.6 and 7.7. However, unless stated to the contrary, for a given normal logic program P, we will focus on the operator T_P and the space I_P of two-valued interpretations in Section 7.5.1 through to Section 7.5.6.

7.5.1 Feasibility of the First-Order Approach

As mentioned previously, it is well-known that multilayer feedforward networks are universal approximators for certain real functions and, in particular, for all continuous real functions on compact subsets of $\mathbb{R}^n$. Hence, if we can find a suitable way of representing first-order interpretations by (finite vectors of) real numbers, say, then feedforward networks may be used to approximate the meaning function of suitable programs. It is necessary of course that such representations are compatible with both the logic-programming and the neural-network paradigms.

7.5.1 Program (Even2) We use the following variant of the program Even, Program 2.1.3, as a running example. The equations on the right define a level mapping l assigning odd numbers to $\mathsf{even}(s^i(a))$-atoms and even numbers to $\mathsf{odd}(s^i(a))$-atoms.

$$\mathsf{even}(a) \leftarrow \qquad\qquad l(\mathsf{even}(s^i(a))) := 2i + 1$$
$$\mathsf{even}(s(X)) \leftarrow \mathsf{odd}(X) \qquad\qquad l(\mathsf{odd}(s^i(a))) := 2i + 2$$
$$\mathsf{odd}(X) \leftarrow \neg\mathsf{even}(X)$$

We next define a homeomorphic embedding of the space of interpretations of a given normal logic program into some (compact) subset of the real numbers. In doing this, we use level mappings[23] to realize this embedding. For much of this chapter, although not everywhere, we assume that the level mapping in question is bijective, even though some of the results we discuss can be extended to the case of non-bijective level mappings.[24]

---

[22]This method was employed in [Bader and Hitzler, 2004] and [Bader et al., 2005a].

[23]We are following [Hölldobler et al., 1999] here.

[24]See [Seda, 2006], for example, where the requirement on level mappings $l : B_P \rightarrow \omega$ is the already familiar one that $l^{-1}(n)$ be a finite set for each n.

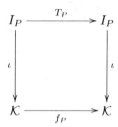

FIGURE 7.5: Transforming T_P into f_P.

7.5.2 Definition Let $l : B_P \to \omega$ be a bijective level mapping defined on the Herbrand base B_P of some normal logic program P, and let b be a natural number such that $b > 2$. We define a function ι on I_P by setting

$$\iota(I) = \sum_{A \in I} b^{-l(A)}$$

for each $I \in I_P$.

In fact, $\iota(I)$ gives a binary representation in the number system with base b to each interpretation I, and moreover ι is an embedding of I_P into the number system with base b. It is straightforward to show that ι is a homeomorphism, and it follows from Theorem 3.3.4 that not only is the set $\mathcal{K} \subset [0,1]$ of all embedded interpretations compact, but that it is also homeomorphic to the Cantor set whenever I_P is endowed with the Cantor topology. Using ι, we can construct the real-valued version $f_P = \iota(T_P)$ of the immediate consequence operator T_P by defining $f_P(x) := \iota(T_P(\iota^{-1}(x)))$ or, in other words, by forcing the diagram in Figure 7.5 to commute.

Furthermore, since ι is a homeomorphism, it follows that f_P is continuous if and only if T_P is continuous in the Cantor topology on I_P. Now, using Funahashi's result, Theorem 7.2.2, we can conclude that approximating networks exist for suitable programs, namely, those for which the immediate consequence operator T_P is continuous in the Cantor topology on I_P.

Conversely, suppose that P is a normal logic program and that approximating networks exist for T_P. Then T_P must be continuous in the Cantor topology on I_P, and we have the following theorem.[25]

7.5.3 Theorem Suppose that P is a normal logic program. Then approximating networks exist for T_P if and only if T_P is continuous in the Cantor topology on I_P.

---

[25]See [Seda, 2006, Theorem 3.24]. In fact, the theorem just cited was established for Fitting-style operators (over finite truth sets, not just for two truth values).

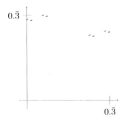

FIGURE 7.6: The embedding of the T_P-operator for Program 7.5.1.

Thus, at this point, we know that approximating networks exist for suitable normal logic programs, but we do not yet know how to construct them. This issue will be taken up in the following sections.

Before discussing the constructions in detail, we will take a closer look at the space of embedded interpretations and at the embedding of the T_P-operator associated with Program 7.5.1. Using the embedding ι defined above with $b = 3$ and taking the level mapping shown in Program 7.5.1, we obtain the embedding of the T_P-operator shown in Figure 7.6. As already mentioned earlier, the space I_P of interpretations is homeomorphic to the Cantor set. This can also be seen by looking at the domain of the graph shown in Figure 7.6.

7.5.2   First-Order Programs by Propositional Approximation

By completely grounding a first-order program P, that is, by forming the set ground(P), we obtain a de facto propositional version of it. In particular, the associated immediate consequence operators of P and of ground(P) are identical. Unfortunately, the ground version of most programs of interest turns out to be an infinite set. Nevertheless, it is a major point to make that we can approximate the immediate consequence operator of P by taking the immediate consequence operator of a subset of ground(P) instead, and we consider this process now.

It will be helpful to say first a few words about the metrics which are useful in the process.[26] Suppose $l : B_P \to \omega$ is a level mapping,[27] and form the metric d_l induced by l, see Definition 5.1.3. Then we can define a metric λ on the set of all mappings from I_P to I_P by[28]

$$\lambda(f, g) = \sup_{I \in I_P} d_l(f(I), g(I)),$$

for $f, g : I_P \to I_P$. Similarly, we write $|\iota(f) - \iota(g)|$ to denote the uniform metric $\sup_{x \in \mathcal{K}} |\iota(f)(x) - \iota(g)(x)|$ defined on the set of all functions mapping $\mathcal{K}$ into itself. Of course, the definition for λ just given can be made generally

---

[26] We refer the reader to [Seda, 2006, Section 3.1] for more details.

[27] It is enough for l to satisfy the property that $l^{-1}(n)$ is finite for each n.

[28] The supremum can be replaced by maximum if f and g are continuous.

and not just for d_l, but this suffices for what we want to say here. Now, given a level n, we form the subset P_n of ground(P) containing all those clauses whose heads have level $\leq n$. Then, for all $A \in B_P$ with $l(A) \leq n$ and for all $I \in I_P$, we have $A \in T_{P_n}(I)$ if and only if $A \in T_P(I)$, or equivalently, by definition of d_l, we have $d_l(T_{P_n}(I), T_P(I)) \leq 2^{-(n+1)}$ for all $I \in I_P$. Hence, $\lambda(T_{P_n}, T_P) \leq 2^{-(n+1)}$. Now suppose that $\varepsilon > 0$ is given. Choose $n \in \mathbb{N}$ so large that $\sum_{i>n} b^{-i} < \varepsilon$, and form P_n. Then for all $I \in I_P$, $T_{P_n}(I)$ and $T_P(I)$ agree on all atoms A with $l(A) \leq n$. Therefore, the expansions $\iota(T_{P_n}(I))$ and $\iota(T_P(I))$ agree in their first n terms. Hence, for all $I \in I_P$ we have, from Figure 7.5, that

$$|f_{P_n}(\iota(I)) - f_P(\iota(I))| = |\iota(T_{P_n}(I)) - \iota(T_P(I))| < \varepsilon.$$

In other words, given any $\varepsilon > 0$, we obtain the approximation $|f_{P_n} - f_P| < \varepsilon$ provided n is sufficiently large. In addition, approximation can be thought of in terms of d_l and λ at the level of interpretations and of T_P itself independently of the embedding ι chosen. We refer to this process of working with P_n as *approximating T_P up to level n*, and we will see shortly that it can be used to show that approximating networks exist for T_P for certain programs P. Indeed, in this terminology the estimates just made show that T_{P_n} approximates T_P up to ε provided T_{P_n} approximates T_P up to level n for large enough n.

Unfortunately, the subsets P_n of ground(P) which, as we have just seen, are appropriate for approximation can be infinitely large. For example, there are infinitely many ground instances of the clause $a \leftarrow p(X)$. Therefore, we consider only so-called covered logic programs in the rest of this section, excluding Section 7.5.6, and we define the notion of a covered program next.

7.5.4 Definition A logic program is called *covered* if it has no local variables, that is, if every variable symbol occurring in the body of a clause also occurs in the head of the same clause.

7.5.5 Proposition Let P be a covered logic program, let l be a bijective level mapping from B_P to ω, and let $n \in \omega$ be fixed. Then the program P_n defined above by

$$P_n := \{C \mid C \in \text{ground}(P) \text{ with } l(H) \leq n, \text{ where } H \text{ is the head of } C\}$$

is finite.

Proof: The finiteness of P_n follows directly from the fact that, for a given level m, there is at most one ground clause C whose head has level m. ∎

Using this finiteness property, we can directly obtain the following theorem showing the existence of approximating networks for a given covered logic program.

7.5.6 Theorem Let P be a covered logic program, and let $n \in \mathbb{N}$. Then we can construct a 3-layer feedforward network whose network function approximates T_P up to level n.

Proof: We can obtain such an approximating network by

(1) Constructing P_n as defined above.

(2) Using the construction presented in the proof of Theorem 7.4.1 to obtain a network computing T_{P_n}.

Since T_{P_n} coincides with T_P for all atoms of level $\leq n$, we conclude that the network we have constructed approximates T_P up to level n, as required. ∎

7.5.7 Example Take P to be Program 7.5.1 introduced earlier. We obtain the corresponding program P_n by means of the level mapping defined in Program 7.5.1. The level of the head atom of the clauses is shown below on the right.

$$
\begin{aligned}
P_1 &= \{\mathsf{even}(a) \leftarrow\} & l(\mathsf{even}(a)) &= 1 \\
P_2 &= \{\mathsf{even}(a) \leftarrow, & l(\mathsf{even}(a)) &= 1 \\
&\quad \mathsf{odd}(a) \leftarrow \neg\mathsf{even}(a)\} & l(\mathsf{odd}(a)) &= 2 \\
P_3 &= \{\mathsf{even}(a) \leftarrow, & l(\mathsf{even}(a)) &= 1 \\
&\quad \mathsf{odd}(a) \leftarrow \neg\mathsf{even}(a), & l(\mathsf{odd}(a)) &= 2 \\
&\quad \mathsf{even}(s(a)) \leftarrow \mathsf{odd}(a)\} & l(\mathsf{even}(s(a))) &= 3
\end{aligned}
$$

The corresponding networks are shown in Figure 7.7.

7.5.3 Approximation by Sigmoidal Networks

In this section, we take a different approach to the approximation of the embedded meaning function. We start by presenting the underlying intuitions and continue with a detailed discussion.[29]

Using the embedding ι defined earlier for $b = 3$ and the level mapping shown in Program 7.5.1, we obtain the embedding of the T_P-operator shown in Figure 7.8 on the left. Under the condition that P is covered and the level mapping l is bijective, we can approximate this graph using a set of appropriately chosen constant pieces. These, in turn, can be computed as a sum of threshold functions, shown in Figure 7.8 in the middle. By replacing the threshold functions by sigmoidals, we obtain an approximation which can directly be implemented within a neural network.

---

[29] The interested reader is referred to [Bader et al., 2005b] and [Bader, 2009] for further details and for implementations.

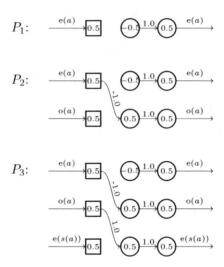

FIGURE 7.7: The networks corresponding to P_1, P_2, and P_3 from Example 7.5.7.

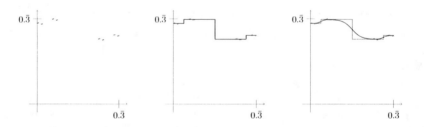

FIGURE 7.8: The embedding of the T_P-operator of Program 7.5.1 is shown on the left. In the middle and on the right, approximations using threshold and sigmoidal functions are depicted.

1. *Approximate the embedded T_P-operator using constant pieces.* As before, we start by constructing P_n for a given level n. After embedding the approximating operator T_{P_n}, we find that the resulting function is a piecewise constant function. Due to the finiteness of the resulting program, we obtain the greatest relevant input level by taking the maximal level of an atom occurring in any of the bodies. Since no atom of a greater level influences the result of the T_P-operator, we see that it is a piecewise constant function.

2. *Approximating the embedded T_P-operator using threshold functions.* Obviously, every piecewise constant function $\mathbb{R} \to \mathbb{R}$ can be represented as a sum of (parametrized) threshold functions. To approximate the embedded T_P-operator of Program 7.5.1 up to level 3, we need the three functions: $H_{0.042}^{0.016}, H_{0.167}^{-0.078}, H_{0.292}^{0.016}$, where $H_p^y(x) := y \cdot H(x - p)$ denotes an h-step at position p.

3. *Approximating the embedded T_P-operator using sigmoidal functions.* To enable the construction of sigmoidal networks, we need to replace the threshold functions with sigmoidal functions. This can be done because (a) we are only interested in the approximation of embedded interpretations, and (b) we can place the threshold functions so that the jumps are located between two embedded interpretations. First, we construct the threshold approximation not for the greatest relevant input level n as introduced earlier, but up to level $n + 1$. Every approximation of this function up to $\varepsilon' := b^{-(n+1)}$ results in a sufficient approximation of the embedded T_P-operator. Under these conditions, we can replace the threshold functions by appropriately set up sigmoidal functions. We just need to make sure that the sigmoidal functions approximate the threshold functions on all embedded interpretations up to ε'. For the example of Program 7.5.1, see also Example 7.5.7, we obtain the following sigmoidal functions: $S_{0.042,135.994}^{0.016}, S_{0.167,53.864}^{-0.078}, S_{0.292,135.994}^{0.016}$, where $S_{p,s}^h(x) := \frac{h}{1+e^{-s(x-p)}}$.

4. *Approximating the embedded T_P-operator using a sigmoidal network.* The approximating sigmoidal functions constructed in Step 3 can easily be embedded into a standard 3-layer sigmoidal network as follows: the input and output layer contain exactly one unit computing the identity function. The hidden layer contains a sigmoidal unit for every sigmoidal function constructed in Step 3. The weights from input to hidden layer are set up such that they represent the steepness of the constructed sigmoidal. The thresholds of the hidden layer correspond to the locations of the sigmoidal functions, and the weights from hidden to output layer coincide with the step width of the underlying threshold functions.

Figure 7.9 shows the resulting network for $\varepsilon = 0.04$ corresponding to an approximation of the T_P-operator up to level 3.

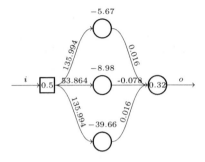

FIGURE 7.9: An approximating sigmoidal network for Program 7.5.1.

We are now in a position to state the following theorem.[30]

7.5.8 Theorem Let P be a covered logic program, let $b > 2$, and let $\varepsilon > 0$. Then we can construct a 3-layer feedforward sigmoidal network whose network function approximates T_P up to ε.

Both approaches presented in the last two sections are based on a subset of ground(P) and embedding the approximated T_P-operator. While the approach presented in Section 7.5.2 creates an input and output unit for every ground atom, we created just a single unit here. Thus, to increase the accuracy of the network we simply have to add a unit to the hidden layer, but the input and output layers can be kept unchanged. Unfortunately, using only a single unit limits the overall accuracy once the network is implemented on a real computer.

7.5.4   Approximation by Radial-Basis-Function Networks

Radial-basis-function (RBF) networks are another common neural network architecture.[31] As in the case of sigmoidal networks, they are known to be universal approximators for continuous functions on compact subsets of $\mathbb{R}^n$. An RBF network consists of three layers: the input, hidden, and output layers. The activation of units in the input layer is set from outside. But in contrast to the networks discussed so far, the hidden units do not compute the weighted sum, but compute the distance between the vector of input unit activations and the weight vector of the corresponding connection. That is, the potential of unit k with n_k incoming connections is computed as $p_k(t) = m(\vec{v}, \vec{w_k})$, with m denoting a metric over n_k-dimensional vectors, $\vec{v}$ denoting the vector of input unit activations, and w_k denoting the vector of weights of the connections to unit k_k. Usually, the Euclidean distance between the two vectors is used as the distance function m.

---

[30]The proof and all details of the construction involved in this result can be found in [Bader, 2009].

[31]Good introductions to them can be found in [Rojas, 1996] and [Bishop, 1995].

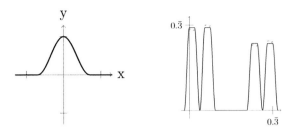

FIGURE 7.10: The raised cosine activation function and an approximation of the embedded T_P-operator of Program 7.5.1 using raised cosine activation functions. Each constant piece is represented using two raised cosines.

In the constructions below, we use the raised cosine function (see Figure 7.10) to compute the activation of the hidden units:

$$\text{rcos}_{p,w}^{h} : \mathbb{R} \to \mathbb{R} : x \mapsto \begin{cases} \frac{h}{2} \cdot \left(1 + \cos\left(\pi \cdot \frac{x-p}{w}\right)\right) & \text{if } |x - p| \leq w, \\ 0 & \text{otherwise.} \end{cases}$$

Note that if two raised cosines $\text{rcos}_{p_1,w}^{h}$ and $\text{rcos}_{p_2,w}^{h}$ with $|p_1 - p_2| = w$ are added, we obtain a function that is constant on the interval $[p_1, p_2]$. Therefore, we can represent each constant piece from above by two raised cosines. Figure 7.10 shows the approximation of the T_P-operator for our running example.

As above, the approximation by raised cosines can easily be implemented using an RBF network. The resulting network contains a single input and output unit serving as interface. Every raised cosine necessary for the approximation is computed by a single hidden unit. The weight between the input and the hidden layer contains the position, and the weight between the hidden and the output unit represents the height of the function. Figure 7.11 shows the RBF network for Program 7.5.1. Using these insights, we can state the following theorem, again without proof.

7.5.9 Theorem Let P be a covered logic program, let $b > 2$, and let $\varepsilon > 0$. Then we can construct an RBF network whose network function approximates T_P up to ε.

Unfortunately, the two approaches discussed in Sections 7.5.3 and 7.5.4 only allow for limited accuracy when implemented on a real computer. This is due to the fact that a single unit is used in the input layer and in the output layer. Even though we can assume unlimited accuracy of real number operations in theory, we cannot assume this when using a computer. To overcome this drawback, we discuss another approach in the following section.

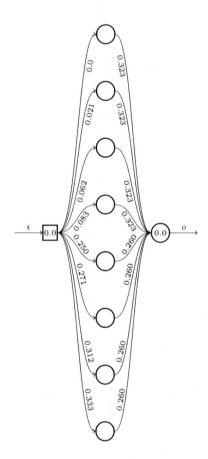

FIGURE 7.11: An RBF network approximating the T_P-operator of Program 7.5.1.

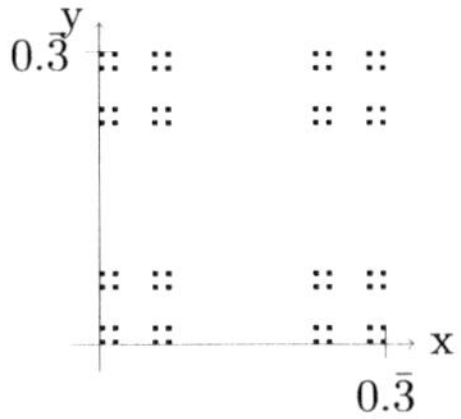

FIGURE 7.12: A two-dimensional version of the Cantor set obtained by embedding all interpretations using a two-dimensional bijective level mapping.

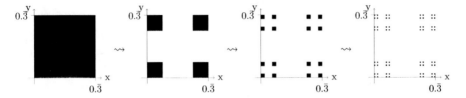

FIGURE 7.13: A construction of the two-dimensional version of the Cantor set.

7.5.5 Approximation by Vector-Based Networks

The approaches presented above are based on level mappings with co-domain ω. Here we extend this approach to multi-dimensional level mappings, which permits the embedding of interpretations into vectors of real numbers. An *n-dimensional level mapping* is a function $L : B_P \to \omega \times \{1, \ldots, n\}$, that is, to each atom A we assign a level $L_l(A) \in \omega$ and some dimension $L_d(A) \in \{1, \ldots, n\}$. As above, we assume a bijective level mapping. On embedding interpretations into n-dimensional real vectors, we obtain an n-dimensional version of the classical Cantor set. A two-dimensional version is shown in Figure 7.12.

Unfortunately, the results obtained so far cannot be extended to the n-dimensional case, at least we do not know how to make such an extension. But nevertheless we can construct approximating networks employing certain knowledge that we have about the set of embedded interpretations. Figure 7.13 shows a possible way of constructing the two-dimensional Cantor set. Starting from a square, in every iteration the current version is copied and scaled down four times. Afterwards, the four copies are placed in the corners. The squares occurring in the n-th step of the construction are referred to below as hypercubes of level n.

As for the one-dimensional case, the T_{P_n}-operator turns out to be a piece-wise constant function. Let P_n be as previously defined, and let $\tilde{n}$ be the maximal level of a body atom in P_n. Then the operator T_{P_n} is constant on all

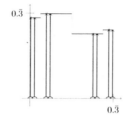

FIGURE 7.14: A depiction of the approximation of the T_P-operator for Program 7.5.1 using a vector-based network.

those interpretations which agree on all atoms up to level $\tilde{n}$, and those areas coincide with the hypercubes of level $\tilde{n}$.[32]

Vector-based networks[33] can be thought of as a generalization of the so-called self-organizing maps.[34] A number of units are distributed over the input space. For every input given to the network, the closest unit is selected as the *winner unit*. The winner's activation is set to 1, and the activation of all other units is set to 0. Thus, only the winner influences the output of the network.

By setting up a network such that there is a unit for every hypercube of level $\tilde{n}$, we can directly embed the T_{P_n}-operator into the weights of the connections from those units to the output units. Figure 7.14 shows what such a network for the one-dimensional case could look like.[35] For every hypercube (coinciding with intervals in the one-dimensional case) a unit is added to the network. The weights between the input and hidden layers define (as for RBF networks) the location of the unit, and the weights between the hidden and output layers define the output, that is, the value of the embedded T_P-operator for an interpretation within the input area of the unit. As before, we are now in a position to state a theorem asserting the existence of approximating vector-based networks, as follows.

7.5.10 Theorem Let P be a covered logic program, let $b > 2$, and let $\varepsilon > 0$. Then we can construct a vector-based network whose network function approximates T_P up to ε.

By using an m-dimensional level mapping, we fix the network to have m input and m output units. That is, we can increase the accuracy of the network by using more units. Unfortunately, the number of hidden units grows exponentially with the dimension of the input layer. Nonetheless, we are now in a position to trade accuracy against space, which has not been possible before.

---

[32]See [Bader, 2009] for details.

[33]See [Martinetz and Schulten, 1991, Fritzke, 1998] for further details.

[34][Kohonen, 1981, Haykin, 1994].

[35]The n-dimensional case for $n > 1$ is hard to depict because the graphics need to be $(n + 1)$-dimensional.

Just as for the network architectures described previously, we can train vector-based networks using a set of input-output pairs. The position of the units, that is, the weights between the input and hidden layer, are modified such that a unit is located in the centre of all the inputs it is responsible for. The output weights are trained such that they represent the average output of all inputs within the unit's responsibility. If, furthermore, two neighbouring units have similar output weights, then one of them can be removed because the other unit will take over in that eventuality. A unit whose accumulated error is very large can be replaced by two units that can be adapted independently, thus allowing the network to refine its input-output function in certain areas.

The first experiments which reported on this approach[36] showed the applicability of this learning method in the area of neural-symbolic integration. A randomly initialized network was trained using the embedded versions of an interpretation I as input values and of $T_P(I)$ as output values for a given program P. The network learned the mapping and could be used iteratively by adding recurrent connections between the output and input layers.

7.5.6 Approximating the (Least) Fixed Point of T_P

Thus far, we have discussed at some length the issue of the approximate computation of the T_P-operator for first-order normal logic programs P. We turn now to discussing, fairly briefly, the question of the approximate computation of its fixed points. One approach is to carry forward the work of the previous sections and employ iterates of (recurrent) neural networks which approximate T_P to approximate iterates of the operator T_P, but, as already noted earlier, the problem then emerges of uniformly controlling the error estimates under iteration.[37]

On the other hand, one can approach the problem of computing the least fixed point of T_P for arbitrary definite logic programs P by a modification of the previous approach employing the subset P_n of ground(P), except that we do not assume that P is covered, and instead we ensure that the appropriate subset of ground(P) is finite by other means.

Thus, let P denote an arbitrary (first-order) definite logic program, and denote by I the least fixed point of T_P. Let $l : B_P \to \omega$ be a level mapping with the property that $l^{-1}(n)$ is a finite set for each $n \in \omega$. We proceed to sketch the details of the construction of a finite subset $\overline{P}_n$ of ground(P), where n is a given natural number, which will play the sort of role here that P_n plays in Proposition 7.5.5 and its companion results.[38] We start with the following claim.

---

[36] See [Bader et al., 2007].

[37] This point is discussed in [Hitzler et al., 2004, Section 4.3], but quite strong conditions, for example, Lipschitz continuity [Hitzler et al., 2004, Theorem 4.19], are required for things to work satisfactorily.

[38] See [Seda, 2006] for full details.

Claim. Suppose that $A \in T_P \uparrow k$. Then there is a clause $A \leftarrow$ body in ground(P) such that A does not occur in body and $T_P \uparrow (k-1) \models$ body.

To establish this claim, we first note that it is clear that $k \geq 1$. Suppose that $A \in T_P \uparrow k_0 = T_P(T_P \uparrow (k_0 - 1))$ and that k_0 is the smallest natural number with this property. Then there is a clause $A \leftarrow$ body in ground(P) such that $T_P \uparrow (k_0 - 1) \models$ body. By definition of k_0, we have $A \notin T_P \uparrow (k_0 - 1)$, and hence A does not occur in body. Finally, by monotonicity, we obtain that $T_P \uparrow (k-1) \models$ body, as required.

Since P is definite, we have

$$T_P \uparrow 0 \subseteq T_P \uparrow 1 \subseteq \cdots \subseteq T_P \uparrow n \subseteq \cdots \subseteq I = \bigcup_{n=1}^{\infty} T_P \uparrow n,$$

where $T_P \uparrow n$ denotes the n-th upward power $T_P^n(\emptyset)$ of T_P, as usual.

Given $n \in \mathbb{N}$, there are only finitely many atoms $A_1, A_2, \ldots, A_m \in I$ with $l(A_i) \leq n$ for $i = 1, \ldots, m$, and, by directedness, there is (a smallest) $k = k_n \in \mathbb{N}$ such that $A_1, A_2, \ldots, A_m \in T_P \uparrow k_n$.[39] Consider the atom A_i, where $1 \leq i \leq m$, and the following three steps.

(1) We have $A_i \in T_P \uparrow k_n = T_P(T_P \uparrow (k_n - 1))$. Therefore, there is a clause

$$A_i \leftarrow A_i^1(1), \ldots, A_i^{m(i)}(1)$$

in ground(P) such that $A_i^1(1), \ldots, A_i^{m(i)}(1) \in T_P \uparrow (k_n - 1)$. Note that this clause may be a unit clause, that is, $m(i) \geq 0$, and there may be many such clauses with head A_i; we choose one of them.

(2) Because $A_i^1(1), \ldots, A_i^{m(i)}(1) \in T_P \uparrow (k_n - 1) = T_P(T_P \uparrow (k_n - 2))$, there are clauses in ground(P) as follows.

$$A_i^1(1) \leftarrow A_{i,1}^1(2), \ldots, A_{i,1}^{m(i,1)}(2)$$
$$A_i^2(1) \leftarrow A_{i,2}^1(2), \ldots, A_{i,2}^{m(i,2)}(2)$$
$$\vdots \quad \leftarrow \quad \vdots$$
$$A_i^{m(i)}(1) \leftarrow A_{i,m(i)}^1(2), \ldots, A_{i,m(i)}^{m(i,m(i))}(2),$$

where each of the atoms $A_{i,j}^r(2)$ in each of the bodies belongs to $T_P \uparrow (k_n - 2)$.

(3) Because each of the $A_{i,j}^r(2)$ in Step (2) belongs to $T_P \uparrow (k_n - 2) = T_P(T_P \uparrow (k_n - 3))$, we have a finite collection of ground clauses (one for each

---

[39] Notice that, depending on l, there may be no atoms A with $l(A) \leq n$; this case is handled by the abuse of notation obtained by allowing m to be 0.

of the $A_{i,j}^r(2)$ in Step (2)) as follows.

$$A_{i,1}^1(2) \leftarrow A_{i,1,1}^1(3), \ldots, A_{i,1,1}^{m(i,1,1)}(3)$$

$$A_{i,1}^2(2) \leftarrow A_{i,1,2}^1(3), \ldots, A_{i,1,2}^{m(i,1,2)}(3)$$

$$\vdots \quad \leftarrow \qquad \vdots$$

$$A_{i,1}^{m(i,1)}(2) \leftarrow A_{i,1,m(i,1)}^1(3), \ldots, A_{i,1,m(i,1)}^{m(i,1,m(i,1))}(3)$$

$$A_{i,2}^1(2) \leftarrow A_{i,2,1}^1(3), \ldots, A_{i,2,1}^{m(i,2,1)}(3)$$

$$A_{i,2}^2(2) \leftarrow A_{i,2,2}^1(3), \ldots, A_{i,2,2}^{m(i,2,2)}(3)$$

$$\vdots \quad \leftarrow \qquad \vdots$$

$$A_{i,2}^{m(i,2)}(2) \leftarrow A_{i,2,m(i,2)}^1(3), \ldots, A_{i,2,m(i,2)}^{m(i,2,m(i,2))}(3)$$

$$\vdots \quad \leftarrow \qquad \vdots$$

$$A_{i,m(i)}^1(2) \leftarrow A_{i,m(i),1}^1(3), \ldots, A_{i,m(i),1}^{m(i,m(i),1)}(3)$$

$$A_{i,m(i)}^2(2) \leftarrow A_{i,m(i),2}^1(3), \ldots, A_{i,m(i),2}^{m(i,m(i),2)}(3)$$

$$\vdots \quad \leftarrow \qquad \vdots$$

$$A_{i,m(i)}^{m(i,m(i))}(2) \leftarrow A_{i,m(i),m(i,m(i))}^1(3), \ldots, A_{i,m(i),m(i,m(i))}^{m(i,m(i),m(i,m(i)))}(3),$$

where each atom in each body belongs to $T_P \uparrow (k_n - 3)$.

Note that at each stage in this process we select a ground clause in which the head of the clause does not occur in the body by means of the claim established earlier.

This process terminates producing unit clauses in its last step. Let $P_{i,n}$ denote the (finite) subset of ground(P) consisting of all the clauses which result; it is clear that $T_{P_{i,n}} \uparrow k_n$ consists of the heads of all the clauses in $P_{i,n}$. We carry out this construction for $i = 1, \ldots, m$ to obtain programs $P_{1,n}, \ldots, P_{m,n}$ such that, for $i = 1, \ldots, m$, $T_{P_{i,n}}(T_{P_{i,n}} \uparrow k_n) = T_{P_{i,n}} \uparrow k_n$ (indeed, $T_{P_{i,n}} \uparrow k_n$ is the least fixed point of $T_{P_{i,n}}$ by Kleene's theorem, Theorem 1.1.9), $A_i \in T_{P_{i,n}} \uparrow k_n$, and $T_{P_{i,n}} \uparrow r \subseteq T_P \uparrow r \subseteq I$ for all $r \in \mathbb{N}$. Let $\overline{P}_n$ denote the program $P_{1,n} \cup \ldots \cup P_{m,n}$. Then $\overline{P}_n$ is a finite subprogram of ground(P), and $T_{P_{i,n}} \uparrow k_n \subseteq T_{\overline{P}_n} \uparrow k_n \subseteq T_P \uparrow k_n \subseteq I$ for $i = 1, \ldots, m$. Furthermore, $A_1, \ldots, A_m \in T_{\overline{P}_n} \uparrow k_n$, and $T_{\overline{P}_n} \uparrow k_n$ is the least fixed point $\overline{I}_n$ of $T_{\overline{P}_n}$.

This completes the construction of the program $\overline{P}_n$.

7.5.11 Example We illustrate the process just described with $k = k_n = 3$. Suppose that $A_1 \in T_P \uparrow 3 = T_P(T_P \uparrow 2)$. Then there is a ground clause $A_1 \leftarrow B_1, B_2$, say, with $B_1, B_2 \in T_P \uparrow 2 = T_P(T_P \uparrow 1)$. Therefore, there exist ground clauses $B_1 \leftarrow C_1, C_2, C_3$ and $B_2 \leftarrow$, say, with $C_1, C_2, C_3 \in T_P \uparrow 1 = T_P(\emptyset)$.

It follows that there are unit clauses $C_1 \leftarrow$, $C_2 \leftarrow$, and $C_3 \leftarrow$ in ground(P). Thus, P_1 is the program

$$C_1 \leftarrow$$
$$C_2 \leftarrow$$
$$C_3 \leftarrow$$
$$B_2 \leftarrow$$
$$B_1 \leftarrow C_1, C_2, C_3$$
$$A_1 \leftarrow B_1, B_2$$

Then we have the following calculations: $T_{P_1} \uparrow 0 = \emptyset$, $T_{P_1} \uparrow 1 = T_{P_1}(\emptyset) = \{B_2, C_1, C_2, C_3\}$, $T_{P_1} \uparrow 2 = T_{P_1}(\{B_2, C_1, C_2, C_3\}) = \{B_1, B_2, C_1, C_2, C_3\}$, $T_{P_1} \uparrow 3 = \{A_1, B_1, B_2, C_1, C_2, C_3\}$, and $T_{P_1} \uparrow 4 = T_{P_1}(T_{P_1} \uparrow 3) = \{A_1, B_1, B_2, C_1, C_2, C_3\} = T_{P_1} \uparrow 3$. Thus, $T_{P_1} \uparrow 3$ is a fixed point of T_{P_1} and indeed is the least such fixed point. Moreover, $A_1 \in T_{P_1} \uparrow 3$.

Further properties of $\overline{P}_n$ can be found in [Seda, 2007].

Now let $\varepsilon > 0$ be given and choose n so large that $2^{-n} < \varepsilon$. Then $d_l(\overline{I}_n, I) \leq 2^{-n} < \varepsilon$, where $\overline{I}_n$ is the least fixed point of $T_{\overline{P}_n}$, I is the least fixed point of T_P, as noted above, and d_l is the metric associated with l. Now apply the algorithm of Theorem 7.4.1 to the propositional program $\overline{P}_n$ and make the resulting network $\mathcal{F}_n$ (which computes $T_{\overline{P}_n}$) recurrent. On inputting the interpretation $\emptyset$ to this network and iterating n times, we obtain $\overline{I}_n$ as output. Thus, $\mathcal{F}_n$ approximates I up to ε, and in this sense the family $\{\mathcal{F}_n \mid n \in \mathbb{N}\}$ *computes I.*

7.5.12 Example Take P to be as in Example 3.2.3, that is, the program

$$p(a) \leftarrow$$
$$p(s(X)) \leftarrow p(X)$$

Applying the procedure above to P, we obtain a sequence $\mathcal{F}_n$ of 3-layer feed-forward recurrent neural networks which computes the least fixed point of T_P and hence computes the set of natural numbers.

7.6 Some Extensions – The Propositional Case

So far in this chapter, we have concentrated on the operator T_P. However, in this section and the next we want to briefly consider extensions of our results to other operators and hence to other semantics. In the present section, we will focus on propositional normal logic programs P and extensions of the results of

Section 7.4. In particular, we consider extensions of Theorem 7.4.1 to Fitting-style operators F_P, including of course the special cases of Φ_P for Kleene's strong three-valued logic and the corresponding operator Ψ_P for Belnap's logic $\mathcal{FOUR}$. In the next section, Section 7.7, we will consider extensions of Section 7.5.2, or in other words we will consider approximations of local consequence operators, including Fitting-style operators, and the Gelfond–Lifschitz operator.

In fact, one can adopt an algebraic approach to the material presented in this section at little extra cost, but with the benefit that the results apply to constraint logic programs (with constraints belonging to a given semiring) and to logic programs involving uncertainty expressed via many-valued logics, as well as to conventional logic programs. We shall not do that, however, as it would take us too far afield, requiring a definition of logic programs allowing elements of an abstract set (the set $\mathcal{C}$ in the next definition) in clause bodies and a corresponding new definition of Fitting-style operators. Instead, we content ourselves with sketching the development for conventional logic programs.[40] Nevertheless, we will present the material in full generality where it helps, ultimately specializing to logics $\mathcal{T}$. Thus, we next present one of the main definitions we need in full generality, as follows.

7.6.1 Definition Suppose that $\mathcal{C}$ is a set equipped with a binary operation $\odot$. We say that $\odot$ is *finitely determined* or that *products (relative to $\odot$) are finitely determined in $\mathcal{C}$* if, for each $c \in \mathcal{C}$, there exists a countable (possibly infinite) collection $\{(R_c^n, E_c^n) \mid n \in \mathcal{J}\}$ of pairs of sets $R_c^n \subseteq \mathcal{C}$ and $E_c^n \subseteq \mathcal{C}$, where each R_c^n is finite, such that a countable (possibly infinite) product $\odot_{i \in M} c_i$ in $\mathcal{C}$ is equal to c if and only if for some $n \in \mathcal{J}$ the following statements hold.

(1) $R_c^n \subseteq \{c_i \mid i \in M\}$.

(2) For all $i \in M$, $c_i \notin E_c^n$, that is, $\{c_i \mid i \in M\} \subseteq (E_c^n)^{co}$, where $(E_c^n)^{co}$ denotes the complement of the set E_c^n.

We call the elements of E_c^n *excluded values* for c, we call the elements of $\mathcal{A}_c^n = (E_c^n)^{co}$ *allowable values* for c, and in particular we call the elements of R_c^n *required values* for c; note that, for each $n \in \mathcal{J}$, we have $R_c^n \subseteq \mathcal{A}_c^n$, so that each required value is also an allowable value (but not conversely). More generally, given $c \in \mathcal{C}$, we call $s \in \mathcal{C}$ an *excluded value for c* if no product $\odot_{i \in M} c_i$ with $\odot_{i \in M} c_i = c$ contains s, that is, in any product $\odot_{i \in M} c_i$ whose value is equal to c, we have $c_i = s$ for no $i \in M$. We let E_c denote the set of all excluded values for c, and let $\mathcal{A}_c$ denote the complement $(E_c)^{co}$ of E_c and call it the set of all *allowable values* for c. Note finally that when confusion might otherwise result, we will superscript each of the sets introduced above

---

[40]For full details of the sketch we present here, the reader should consult the following papers: [Seda and Lane, 2005], [Lane and Seda, 2006], [Komendantskaya et al., 2007] and also [Lane and Seda, 2009].

with the operation in question. Thus, for example, $\mathcal{A}_c^\odot$ denotes the allowable set for c relative to the operation $\odot$. ∎

In particular, we can take $\mathcal{C}$ as a logic $\mathcal{T}$ and $\odot$ as either disjunction or conjunction defined on it. Indeed, the following example and the paragraph following it show the thinking behind Definition 7.6.1, and in fact we shall take $\mathcal{FOUR}$ as a running example throughout this section. Note that, throughout this section, we take $\mathcal{FOUR}$ to be the set $\{\mathbf{u}, \mathbf{f}, \mathbf{t}, \mathbf{b}\}$ with this given listing of its elements, as in Chapter 1.

7.6.2 Example Consider again Belnap's logic $\mathcal{FOUR}$. Taking $\odot$ to be disjunction $\vee$, the sets E and R are as follows.

(1) For $\mathbf{u}$, we have $n = 1$, $E_{\mathbf{u}}^\vee = \{\mathbf{t}, \mathbf{b}\}$, and $R_{\mathbf{u}}^\vee = \{\mathbf{u}\}$.

(2) For $\mathbf{f}$, we have $n = 1$, $E_{\mathbf{f}}^\vee = \{\mathbf{u}, \mathbf{t}, \mathbf{b}\}$, and $R_{\mathbf{f}}^\vee = \{\mathbf{f}\}$.

(3) For $\mathbf{t}$, n takes the values 1 and 2, $E_{\mathbf{t}}^\vee = \emptyset$, $R_{\mathbf{t}}^{\vee,1} = \{\mathbf{t}\}$, and $R_{\mathbf{t}}^{\vee,2} = \{\mathbf{u}, \mathbf{b}\}$.

(4) For $\mathbf{b}$, we have $n = 1$, $E_{\mathbf{b}}^\vee = \{\mathbf{u}, \mathbf{t}\}$, and $R_{\mathbf{b}}^\vee = \{\mathbf{b}\}$.

Thus, for example, a countable disjunction $\bigvee_{i \in M} s_i$ takes value $\mathbf{t}$ if and only if either (i) at least one of the s_i takes value $\mathbf{t}$ or (ii) at least one of the s_i takes value $\mathbf{b}$ and at least one takes value $\mathbf{u}$; no truth value is excluded.

Now taking $\odot$ to be conjunction $\wedge$, the sets E and R are as follows.

(1) For $\mathbf{u}$, we have $n = 1$, $E_{\mathbf{u}}^\wedge = \{\mathbf{f}, \mathbf{b}\}$, and $R_{\mathbf{u}}^\wedge = \{\mathbf{u}\}$.

(2) For $\mathbf{f}$, n takes the values 1 and 2, $E_{\mathbf{f}}^\wedge = \emptyset$, $R_{\mathbf{f}}^{\wedge,1} = \{\mathbf{f}\}$, and $R_{\mathbf{f}}^{\wedge,2} = \{\mathbf{u}, \mathbf{b}\}$.

(3) For $\mathbf{t}$, we have $n = 1$, $E_{\mathbf{t}}^\wedge = \{\mathbf{u}, \mathbf{f}, \mathbf{b}\}$, and $R_{\mathbf{t}}^\wedge = \{\mathbf{t}\}$.

(4) For $\mathbf{b}$, we have $n = 1$, $E_{\mathbf{b}}^\wedge = \{\mathbf{u}, \mathbf{f}\}$, and $R_{\mathbf{b}}^\wedge = \{\mathbf{b}\}$.

In fact, Definition 7.6.1 was motivated by the problem, already mentioned, of defining truth values of bodies of pseudo-clauses over various three-valued logics, see [Hitzler and Seda, 1999b] and Sections 5.2.1 and 5.5 herein. The following facts show how it works, where we take the countable set M to be $\mathbb{N}$ without loss of generality. If $\odot$ is finitely determined, then it is idempotent, commutative, and associative, as already noted in Section 5.5. Furthermore, if $\bigodot_{i \in M} s_i = c$, then the sequence $s_1, s_1 \odot s_2, s_1 \odot s_2 \odot s_3, \ldots$ is eventually constant with value c. In the converse direction, suppose $\mathcal{C}$ is a countable set and $\odot$ is idempotent, commutative, and associative. Suppose further that, for any set $\{s_i \mid i \in M\}$ of elements of $\mathcal{C}$ where M is countable, the sequence $s_1, s_1 \odot s_2, s_1 \odot s_2 \odot s_3, \ldots$ is eventually constant with value c. Then all products in $\mathcal{C}$ are (well-defined and) finitely determined, where we take $\bigodot_{i \in M} s_i = c$ to define $\bigodot_{i \in M} s_i$.

For a finitely determined binary operation $\odot$ on $\mathcal{C}$, we define the partial order $\leq_\odot$ on $\mathcal{C}$ by $s \leq_\odot t$ if and only if $s \odot t = t$. (So that $s \leq_+ t$ if and only if $s + t = t$, and $s \leq_\times t$ if and only if $s \times t = t$, for finitely determined operations $+$ and $\times$, and similarly for finitely determined operations of disjunction $\vee$ and conjunction $\wedge$ in case $\mathcal{C}$ is a logic $\mathcal{T}$.)

7.6.3 Example In $\mathcal{FOUR}$, we have $\mathbf{t} \leq_\wedge \mathbf{u} \leq_\wedge \mathbf{f}$, and $\mathbf{t} \leq_\wedge \mathbf{b} \leq_\wedge \mathbf{f}$. Also, $\mathbf{f} \leq_\vee \mathbf{u} \leq_\vee \mathbf{t}$, and $\mathbf{f} \leq_\vee \mathbf{b} \leq_\vee \mathbf{t}$.

In fact, the allowable and excluded sets for $s \in \mathcal{C}$ can easily be characterized in terms of the partial orders just defined: $s \in \mathcal{A}_t^\odot$ if and only if $s \leq_\odot t$, see [Seda and Lane, 2005, Proposition 3.10]. Because of this fact, we have the following result.

7.6.4 Proposition Suppose that $\odot$ is a finitely determined binary operation on $\mathcal{C}$ and that M is a countable set. Then a product $\bigodot_{i \in M} t_i$ evaluates to the element $s \in \mathcal{C}$, where s is the least element in the ordering $\leq_\odot$ such that $t_i \in \mathcal{A}_s^\odot$ for all $i \in M$.

Having now determined how we evaluate the truth values of the bodies of pseudo-clauses in relation to Fitting-style operators F_P, we move next to consider the computation of these operators by neural networks in the case of propositional normal logic programs P. Indeed, it is shown in [Lane and Seda, 2006] that one can construct conventional 3-layer feedforward networks to compute Φ_P and Ψ_P containing only binary threshold units, in the style of Theorem 7.4.1.[41] However, extending this approach to the general case of F_P is not so simple, as the constructions become overly complicated. Therefore, we will adopt a modular approach in which we construct two types of 2-layer neural networks of binary threshold units. The first of these (the multiplication unit) will compute products or conjunctions of elements of $\mathcal{C}$, and the second of them (the addition unit) will compute sums or disjunctions of elements of $\mathcal{C}$. It then remains to construct 3-layer neural networks to compute F_P in which the hidden layer consists of multiplication units and the output layer consists of addition units; strictly speaking, these networks have five layers of course. In this context, it is worth noting that the partial ordering $\leq_\odot$, defined previously, and Proposition 7.6.4 play a crucial role in establishing the results we discuss here.

For the rest of this section, we shall focus on finite sets $\mathcal{C}$ with n elements listed in some fixed order, $\mathcal{C} = \{c_1, c_2, \ldots, c_n\}$ or $\mathcal{C} = \{t_1, t_2, \ldots, t_n\}$, say. In order to simulate the operations in $\mathcal{C}$ by means of neural networks, we need to represent the elements of $\mathcal{C}$ in a form amenable to their manipulation by neural networks. To do this, we represent elements of $\mathcal{C}$ by vectors of n units, and it is convenient sometimes to view them as column vectors, where the first unit represents c_1, the second unit represents c_2, and so on. Hence, a vector of

---

[41]See the thesis [Kalinke, 1994], where these results are stated. We thank S. Hölldobler for drawing this reference to our attention.

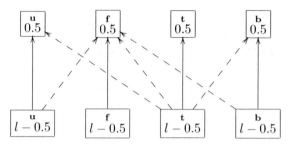

FIGURE 7.15: A conjunction unit for $\mathcal{FOUR}$. The full arrows represent connections with weight 1, and the broken arrows represent connections with weight -1.

units with the first unit activated, or containing 1, represents c_1, a vector with the second unit activated, or containing 1, represents c_2, etc. Indeed, it will sometimes be convenient to denote such vectors by binary strings of length n and to refer to the unit in the i-th position of a string as the i-th unit or the c_i-unit or the unit c_i; as is common, we represent these vectors geometrically by strings of not-necessarily adjacent rectangles. Note that we do not allow more than one unit to be activated at any given time in any of the vectors representing elements of $\mathcal{C}$, and hence all but one of the units in such vectors contain 0. Furthermore, when the input is consistent with this, it turns out from the constructions we make that the output of any network we employ is consistent with it also.

7.6.5 Example Suppose that $\mathcal{C} = \mathcal{FOUR} = \{\mathbf{u}, \mathbf{f}, \mathbf{t}, \mathbf{b}\}$. Then $\mathbf{u}$ is represented by 1000, $\mathbf{f}$ by 0100, $\mathbf{t}$ by 0010, and $\mathbf{b}$ by 0001.

In general, the operations in $\mathcal{C}$ are not linearly separable, and therefore we need two layers to compute addition (or disjunction) and two to compute multiplication (or conjunction). As usual, we take the standard threshold for binary threshold units to be 0.5. This ensures that the Heaviside function H outputs 1 if the input is strictly greater than 0, rather than greater than or equal to 0.

7.6.6 Definition A *multiplication* $(\times)$ *unit* or a *conjunction* $(\wedge)$ *unit* $\mathcal{MU}$ for a given set $\mathcal{C}$ is a 2-layer neural network in which each layer is a vector of n binary threshold units $c_1, c_2, \ldots, c_n$ corresponding to the n elements of $\mathcal{C}$. The units in the input layer have thresholds $l - 0.5$, where l is the number of elements being multiplied or conjoined, and all output units have threshold 0.5. We connect input unit c_i to the output unit c_i with weight 1 and to any unit c_j in the output layer, where $c_i <_\times c_j$, with weight -1.

An input layer representing a product of l elements of $\mathcal{C}$ is connected to a multiplication unit $\mathcal{MU}$ in the following way. For each element c of the product, where c is represented by the n units $c_1, c_2, \ldots, c_n$, the unit c_j is connected, with weight 1, to the c_j-unit in the input layer of $\mathcal{MU}$ and is also connected, with weight 1, to any unit c_k in the input layer of $\mathcal{MU}$ for which $c_j <_\times c_k$. For a negated element $d = \neg c$ in the product, we connect, with weight 1, c_j to the unit representing $\neg c_j$ in the input layer of $\mathcal{MU}$ and also, with weight 1, to any unit c_k in the input layer of $\mathcal{MU}$ for which $\neg c_j <_\times c_k$.

7.6.7 Proposition A multiplication or conjunction unit $\mathcal{MU}$ computes the value of a product of l elements of $\mathcal{C}$ when it is connected to an input layer as just described.

7.6.8 Example Consider again $\mathcal{C} = \mathcal{FOUR}$, and input the two elements **u** and **b** to a multiplication unit $\mathcal{MU}$, where $l = 2$. It is readily checked that the potentials of the units **u**, **t**, and **b** in the input layer of $\mathcal{MU}$ are, respectively, -0.5, -1.5, and -0.5; their outputs are all equal to 0; and the outputs of the units **u**, **t**, and **b** in the output layer of $\mathcal{MU}$ are also all equal to 0. On the other hand, the **f**-unit in the input layer of $\mathcal{MU}$ has potential $1 \times 1 + 1 \times 0 + 1 \times 0 + 1 \times 0 + 1 \times 0 + 1 \times 0 + 1 \times 0 + 1 \times 1 - 1.5 = 0.5$, and therefore the output of this unit is $H(0.5) = 1$. Furthermore, the input to the **f**-unit in the output layer of $\mathcal{MU}$ is $-1 \times 0 + 1 \times 1 - 1 \times 0 - 1 \times 0 = 1$. Hence, the output of this unit is $H(1 - 0.5) = 1$, and so $\mathcal{MU}$ outputs 0100 or **f**, and this indeed is the value of $\mathbf{u} \wedge \mathbf{b}$, as required.

The ideas behind multiplication units work, with minor changes, for addition or disjunction, and we obtain *addition (+)* or *disjunction ($\vee$) units* $\mathcal{AU}$ which compute the sum or disjunction of k, say, elements of $\mathcal{C}$.

We are now in a position to state the main theorem of this section, where we take the set $\mathcal{C}$ to be a logic $\mathcal{T}$ endowed with the operations of disjunction ($\vee$) and conjunction ($\wedge$).

7.6.9 Theorem Suppose that both operations of disjunction and conjunction in $\mathcal{T}$ are finitely determined and that P is a propositional logic program defined over $\mathcal{T}$. Then we can construct a 3-layer feedforward neural network $\mathcal{F}$ which contains multiplication units in its middle layer and addition units in its output layer such that $\mathcal{F}$ computes F_P.

In closing this section, we mention that there is yet another class of logic programs one can consider in our present context of extending Theorem 7.4.1, namely, the class of propositional annotated (bi)lattice-based logic programs. This class is also a very general class of programs capable of handling uncertainty, in this case using lattices and bilattices to model belief estimates for and against a proposition. However, its study would take us too far from our current goal, and instead we refer the reader to [Komendantskaya et al., 2007] again for full details.

7.7   Some Extensions – The First-Order Case

So far, in this chapter we have described how certain methods developed in earlier chapters give rise to approaches to the problem of integrating logic programs and artificial neural networks. The key insight into this integration is the observation that the two paradigms can be formally related by means of functions: on the one hand, semantic operators for logic programs capture the meaning of logic programs; on the other hand, the input-output function of an artificial neural network completely characterizes its functional behaviour. Approaches to neural-symbolic integration thus arise out of methods which allow us to understand semantic operators as I/O functions of artificial neural networks, and vice-versa.

Most of this chapter has focused on the single-step operator in logic programming which, via its fixed points, determines the supported model semantics of logic programs. However, in Section 7.6, we have just seen that some of these methods carry over to other semantics, for propositional programs, via the computation of F_P. In this section, we will now consider the first-order case and extensions of the approximation results we have established for T_P to F_P and other semantic operators. At the same time, we briefly discuss further alternative semantics as treated throughout the book and discuss conclusions which can be drawn concerning neural-symbolic integration in general.

Our conceptual starting point is Theorem 7.5.3, which tells us that approximating networks exist if and only if the single-step operator is continuous in the Cantor topology.[42] We can now use this result to leverage several new results on the relationship between the supported model semantics and other semantics in order to derive similar results for these other semantics.

In Section 5.4, we considered a very general family of semantic operators and also examined the question of how one may characterize Cantor continuity for them. The following result is thus an easy corollary of Theorem 5.4.7.

7.7.1 Theorem Let P be a program with a locally finite local consequence operator T. Then T can be uniformly approximated by 3-layer feedforward networks in the sense of Theorem 7.2.2.

---

[42] We briefly remark that a result established in [Hornik et al., 1989], which states that every measurable function can be approximated almost everywhere by a 3-layer sigmoidal feedforward network, is not necessarily useful for our purposes. This is so despite the fact that it was shown in Theorem 5.5.1 that many semantic operators, including the single-step operator, are always measurable, and hence also the Gelfond–Lifschitz operator, see Theorem 6.2.4. However, it should be noted that the Cantor set is a set of (Lebesgue) measure zero when viewed as a subspace of the reals. Thus, the result just quoted of [Hornik et al., 1989] need not necessarily lead to useful approximation results for these operators. Indeed, such approximations arising from the result of [Hornik et al., 1989] may fail to approximate the operator in question *at every point*. Nevertheless, it remains to be investigated whether non-zero measures exist on the Cantor set, which yield useful approximations in conjunction with the results of [Hornik et al., 1989].

Theorem 7.7.1 covers, among others, all Fitting-style operators from Section 5.2.1.

The fixpoint completion, studied in Section 6.1, also turns out to be very useful, since it allows us to reduce treatments of the Gelfond–Lifschitz operator to the single-step operator. According to Theorem 7.2.2, we are first of all interested in carrying over continuity results with respect to the Cantor topology. From Theorem 6.2.2 we thus obtain the following result.

7.7.2 Theorem Let P be a normal logic program, and let the following condition be satisfied for all $I \in I_P$ and $A \in B_P$: whenever $\mathrm{GL}_P(I)(A) = \mathbf{f}$, then either there is no clause with head A in ground(P) or there exists a finite set $S(I, A) = \{A_1, \ldots, A_k\} \subseteq B_P$ such that $I(A_i) = \mathbf{t}$ for all i, and for every clause $A \leftarrow$ body in ground(P) at least one $\neg A_i$ or some B with $\mathrm{GL}_P(I)(B) = \mathbf{f}$ occurs in body. Then GL_P can be uniformly approximated by 3-layer feedforward networks in the sense of Theorem 7.2.2.

We also obtain the following corollary, taking Corollary 6.2.3 into account.

7.7.3 Corollary Let P be a covered normal logic program. Then GL_P can be uniformly approximated by 3-layer feedforward networks in the sense of Theorem 7.2.2.

Likewise, the remark given in Footnote 3 on page 170 of Chapter 6 together with Lemma 5.4.12 allows us to derive similar characterizations of continuity for the operator characterizing three-valued stable models.

In principle, one can use the results recorded earlier to embark on investigations similar to those undertaken in Sections 7.5.3 to 7.5.5, for example. However, a direct application of the results for the Gelfond–Lifschitz operator is hardly satisfactory since the computation of the fixpoint completion can only be carried out in an approximate manner. How one deals with this problem, and what it entails, remains to be investigated.

It should be clear from Section 7.6 how one carries over the approach using a finite subset of the grounding of a program to other locally finite local consequence operators. For operators like the Gelfond–Lifschitz operator, however, a straightforward approach is rather unsatisfactory due to the fact that one iteration of the Gelfond–Lifschitz operator involves the taking of a limit of the single-step operator for definite programs. As an alternative approach, we could again first compute the fixpoint completion of the program and employ Theorem 6.1.4 in conjunction with the methods from Section 7.6, but alas, we have noted already that computation of the fixpoint completion can only be done in an approximate manner. How to deal with this problem in an appropriate manner again is something which remains to be investigated.

Before closing this chapter, we would like to remark that there is a plethora of work which has been done on the integration of logic and neural networks.[43]

---

[43]See, for example, [Bader and Hitzler, 2005, Hammer and Hitzler, 2007] for overviews.

In particular, the propositional core method (see Section 7.4) has spawned a lot of investigations, including extended semantics for propositional logic programs.[44] But alternative methods are also under investigation which do not connect directly with the investigations into the mathematical foundations of logic programming we have presented in this book.[45]

---

[44] Most notable is the body of work done by Artur d'Avila Garcez of City University London on, for example, modal logic, see [d'Avila Garcez et al., 2007], intuitionistic logic, see [d'Avila Garcez et al., 2006], and epistemic and temporal logic, see, for example, [d'Avila Garcez and Lamb, 2006]. See also [d'Avila Garcez et al., 2009].

[45] For further notable recent work based on methods other than those reported here, the reader should consult the following papers [Gust et al., 2007, Hölldobler and Ramli, 2009, Komendantskaya, 2010, Buillame-Bert et al., 2010].

Chapter 8

Final Thoughts

In this book, we have provided a comprehensive treatment of logic programming semantics from the perspective of fixed-point semantics. In doing so, we have covered a lot of material which also relates to other areas of interest outside the realm of logic programming as such. In this final chapter, we discuss contributions to and relationships between the content of this book and a rather diverse mix of topics, ranging from foundations of computing via artificial intelligence to cognitive science. We do so with the usual understanding that the impact of foundational research is more often than not indirect in nature in providing results, methods, and insights, which can be carried forward by research communities at large until a critical mass is reached, thereby enabling significant or even major advances to take place.

8.1 Foundations of Programming Semantics

The classical semantic analysis of programs in the sense of denotational semantics is based on monotonic, order-continuous operators, via their least fixed points using Theorem 1.1.9 or Theorem 1.1.10. This approach, however, fails for paradigms where the semantics is expressed by fixed points of operators which are not monotonic in general. In particular, it fails for logic programming in several of its variants, as studied throughout this book.

By developing methods for the fixed-point semantic analysis of programs with non-monotonic semantic operators, we therefore widen the scope of applicability of fixed-point semantics. In particular, we provide sufficiency conditions for the existence of fixed points (Chapter 4) and show how they can be applied to various semantics based on non-monotonic operators (Sections 5.1 and 5.4 and Chapter 6).

It seems evident that these methods should carry over to other such paradigms. However, a limitation of some of the work presented in this book is that certain of the fixed-point theorems provided in Chapter 4 always guarantee the existence of a unique fixed point, if there is a fixed point at all, thus rendering the theorems in question of limited applicability to paradigms (or programs) where multiple fixed points are the norm. The latter situation is encountered in the logic programming paradigm in the case of the stable model semantics, for example, and indeed our analysis in Section 6.2 is limited in this respect. Multiple fixed points also arise naturally in the context of disjunctive logic programs, that is, logic programs where additionally disjunctions of atoms are allowed in rule heads as discussed briefly in Section 4.9. The application of fixed-point theorems for multivalued mappings as provided, for example, in Sections 4.9 to 4.13 may provide a remedy when this line of work has been fully worked out. In particular, an approach to this problem based on the Rutten-Smyth theorem and a careful analysis and choice of quasimetrics (perhaps based on level mappings) holds out considerable prospects in this respect, see [Seda, 1997]. In addition, approaches such as the one mentioned in Section 4.14 also overcome this problem to a considerable extent.[1]

8.2   Quantitative Domain Theory

Domain theory,[2] based on order continuity of semantic operators, is the dominant theory underlying the denotational semantics of programming languages. However, an alternative tradition in the semantics of programming languages to that using domains is an approach based on the use of metric spaces, as already mentioned in Chapter 4.[3] A reconciliation of these two approaches is of obvious interest for the theory of programming semantics, and a considerable body of work has been done on this very topic,[4] resulting in the area of *quantitative domain theory*. Indeed, the Rutten-Smyth theorem arose out of precisely these considerations.

In contrast to mainstream work on this reconciliation, which is driven by a mainly conceptual motivation to unite two theories, the work presented in this book is driven by a clear application, namely, the semantic analysis of logic programming. In pursuing this application, we have developed several results which provide conceptual insights into the relationships between domain-theoretic semantics and metric semantics. A key role is played by the Scott and Cantor topologies (Chapter 3) as the underlying spaces. Another key role is played by the relationship between ordered spaces and (generalized) metric spaces (Section 4.8) and by the various fixed-point theorems which can be provided for these spaces (Chapter 4), some of which have been taken directly from work on quantitative domain theory.

A theme which has not been taken up in this book in detail and which provides scope for further work is to investigate more closely how the application-

---

[1]See also [Hitzler and Seda, 1999c, Straccia et al., 2009] for some more investigations into these matters.

[2]See [Scott, 1982a].

[3]See [de Bakker, 2002].

[4]Initiated by work such as [Smyth, 1987].

driven work of quantitative domain theory, as discussed herein, relates to theory-driven advances in the same topic, which were developed in parallel.[5]

8.3   Fixed-Point Theorems for Generalized Metric Spaces

Fixed-point theorems have a rightful place in the core arsenal of mathematical tools applicable to theoretical computer science, with many applications outside this realm of course. The Banach contraction mapping theorem, Theorem 4.2.3, which is the starting point for many of the investigations in this book, is one of the most fundamental of these theorems.

In this book, we have contributed to the study of fixed-point theory by exploring generalized metrics and thereby providing a compilation of extensions of the Banach theorem, together with results concerning their relationships with order-theoretic fixed-point theorems (Chapter 4). We furthermore provide evidence of the usefulness of these theorems by applying them, throughout the book, to the study of the semantics of logic programs.

Another theme which has not been taken up here, and again is scope for further work, is a systematic investigation of the extent to which the Banach theorem, and its relatives, remains valid with respect to generalized distance functions under weaker and weaker conditions. Specifically, how weak can the ambient spaces be and still support a reasonable version of the Banach theorem?

8.4   The Foundations of Knowledge Representation and Reasoning

Knowledge Representation and Reasoning (KR) is one of the classical branches of Artificial Intelligence. Currently, it is experiencing massive renewed interest due to the advent of the Semantic Web.[6] In a nutshell, the Semantic Web strives to improve the World Wide Web by making Web content machine-understandable, and it does so by using KR methods, more precisely, by endowing Web content with additional meta-content in the form of knowledge bases (so-called *ontologies*), which describe the content in a logic-based format.

Several KR languages have been developed and standardized by the World

---

[5]The papers [Waszkiewicz, 2002, Waszkiewicz, 2003, Waszkiewicz, 2006, Krötzsch, 2006, Künzi et al., 2006, Künzi and Kivuvu, 2008], for example, may be consulted.

[6]See [Hitzler et al., 2009b] for an introductory textbook.

Wide Web Consortium[7] for this purpose. One of them, called *RIF*,[8] is essentially a logic programming language, and other ontology languages can also be understood as logic programming variants.[9]

In the light of such recent developments, theoretical investigations into logic programming, as provided in this book, gain further interest. It can be conjectured that the methods developed in this book may be used for design and analysis of new KR languages suitable for application purposes.

Conceptually interesting from this point of view is the observation that the methods of analysis provided herein are close to a denotational semantics approach and thus complement the historically model-theory-driven semantics in KR languages. In particular, there may be scope for the study of decidability and/or semi-decidability of KR languages based on the level-mappings approach discussed in Chapter 2,[10] a topic which has so far been largely neglected for logic programming, although it has played a major role in the development of the currently main ontology language, the Web Ontology Language OWL.[11]

8.5   Clarifying Logic Programming Semantics

In this book, we have covered the most important semantics for normal logic programs. However, many more different semantics for normal logic programs and generalizations of this paradigm have been defined in the literature. The rationale behind these various semantics has been manifold, depending on one's point of view, which may be that of a programmer or inspired by commonsense reasoning. Consequently, the constructions which lead to these semantics are technically very diverse, and the exact relationships between them have not yet been fully understood.

Our work, and in particular the treatment in Chapter 2, but also Section 5.2, provides a uniform perspective of different logic programming semantics, and it should be clear from the proofs that the approach adopted there can be lifted to other fixed-point semantics, in particular to those involving monotonic operators. It thus reconciles these semantics within an overarching framework which can be used for easy comparison of semantics with respect to syntactic structures that can be employed with them, that is, to determine the extent to which a semantics is able to *break up* positive or negative dependencies or loops between atoms in programs.

---

[7]W3C, http://www.w3.org/

[8]See [Boley and Kifer, 2010, Hitzler et al., 2009b].

[9]OWL RL [Hitzler et al., 2009a, Reynolds, 2010], ELP [Krötzsch et al., 2008], or F-Logic [Kifer et al., 1995], for example.

[10]For a preliminary investigation into this, see [Cherchago et al., 2007].

[11]See [Hitzler et al., 2009a, Hitzler et al., 2009b].

It still remains to be seen, however, how far this approach can be carried,[12] and whether or not it is possible to establish a meta-theory which goes beyond mere characterization.[13]

8.6 Symbolic and Subsymbolic Representations

How to overcome the gap between symbolic and subsymbolic representations, and how to integrate them in an efficient and effective manner, is a topic of growing interdisciplinary importance. It is driven by advances in neuroimaging, which call for the modelling of findings in neuroscience on a higher and higher level of abstraction, and by the search in Cognitive Science for suitable cognitive architectures to model complex behaviour. By *symbolic* we mean, of course, knowledge representation formalisms based on logic or similar algebraic structures, while the term *subsymbolic* refers to paradigms such as artificial neural networks, where knowledge is not represented in a crisp, declarative way.

The topology-driven view of logic programming semantics which we pursue herein indirectly embraces this theme by providing a conceptual bridge between the discrete (symbolic) world of logic and the continuous (subsymbolic) world of topology and analysis on the reals.

While, originally, we developed this point of view purely for the purposes of analyzing logic programs and in order to advance quantitative domain theory, it bears, at least conceptually, on the symbolic/subsymbolic issue. However, we have not pursued this in any structured manner, apart from developing neural-symbolic integration (Chapter 7), albeit with a different initial motivation (see Section 8.7). The question remains open to what extent our insights can contribute to the larger quest.

8.7 Neural-Symbolic Integration

Our work on neural-symbolic integration started as a straightforward application of our topological approach to logic programming semantics. The pursuit (Chapter 7) was then driven mainly by an engineering motivation (as

---

[12]Disjunctive well-founded semantics were compared using this approach in the paper [Knorr and Hitzler, 2007], but only with limited success since the characterizations became rather complicated.

[13]In [Cherchago et al., 2007], for example, level mappings were used to study decidability properties.

opposed to a cognitive science motivation as discussed in Section 8.6), that is, by the idea of combining logic programming and artificial neural networks in such a way that the best of both worlds – declarativeness, trainability, robustness, and reasoning capabilities – is retained.

Indeed, this effort has paid off, and while we provide only the theoretical underpinnings in Chapter 7, we are indeed able to show that a declarative, trainable, robust, and reasonable system can be developed on these grounds,[14] although it has to be said that the advance remains conceptual in nature because the system is severely limited in terms of the size of the knowledge base involved. Nevertheless, it is to date one of the two reported systems with these capabilities.[15]

Significant further advances on this front, in particular with respect to the integration of learning and reasoning, would be highly appreciated in practice.[16]

8.8   Topology, Programming, and Artificial Intelligence

It has been argued that there is a strong relationship between topological dynamics (chaos theory), logic programming, neural networks, and other paradigms, and in particular this is so in the context of emergent behaviour as represented by cellular automata, say.[17] Indeed, from a bird's eye perspective each seems to be capable of being mapped onto the others. At the same time, the study in any one of these paradigms seems to pose the same sort of obstacles found in the others, particularly is this so in relation to the handling of chaotic dynamics and emergence.

Some of the work in this book contributes to this discussion, especially with respect to topological dynamics, logic programming, and neural networks, as discussed in Section 7.5.[18] Obviously, this is only a small stepping stone in the pursuit of these issues which, once fully understood, will provide a major

---

[14]See [Bader et al., 2007, Bader et al., 2008, Bader, 2009] for details.

[15]The approach in [Gust et al., 2007] achieves similar results with entirely different methods.

[16]For a discussion of the Semantic Web (see Section 8.4) as a potential test case for neural-symbolic integration, see [Hitzler et al., 2005]. For a general discussion of the need for the integration of learning and reasoning for Semantic Web applications, see [Hitzler, 2009, Hitzler and van Harmelen, 2010].

[17]See, for example, [Blair et al., 1997a, Blair et al., 1999]

[18]In [Bader and Hitzler, 2004], it was shown that there is indeed a tight relationship between logic programs and fractals in the sense in which they arise as attractors of iterated function systems.

advance in our overall understanding of complex phenomena. However, we may not yet have the mathematical tools available to really understand them.[19]

---

[19]This last sentence is a citation from a keynote talk given by Howard A. Blair, of Syracuse University, at the MFCSIT2000 conference in Cork, Ireland.

Appendix

Transfinite Induction and General Topology

In order to help make our discussions relatively self-contained, it will be convenient to collect together in this Appendix the basic facts and notation we need from the theory of ordinals[1] and from the subject of general topology.

A.1   The Principle of Transfinite Induction

We begin with a brief discussion of the theory of ordinals and transfinite induction. In particular, we give a statement of the principle of transfinite induction in the form in which we make use of it on a number of occasions.

A.1.1 Definition A partially ordered set X is *well-ordered* or is a *well-ordering* if each non-empty subset of X has a first or least element.

A.1.2 Example (1) The set $\mathbb{N}$ of natural numbers is well-ordered in the usual ordering $\leq$ on $\mathbb{N}$.

(2) The set $\mathbb{Z}$ of integers is not well-ordered in the usual ordering $\leq$ on $\mathbb{Z}$.

A.1.3 Lemma The following statements hold.

(a) Every well-ordered set is linearly ordered.

(b) No well-ordered set contains an infinite strictly descending sequence.

Proof: (a) Let $(X, \leq_X)$ be a well-ordered set, and let $x, y \in X$. Then the set $\{x, y\}$ is a non-empty subset of X and hence has a least element, x, say. But then $x \leq_X y$, which establishes (a).

For (b), suppose that $(x_n)_{n \in \mathbb{N}}$ is an infinite strictly decreasing sequence in the well-ordered set $(X, \leq_X)$. Then $\{x_n \mid n \in \mathbb{N}\}$ itself is a non-empty subset

---

[1]Our treatment of these matters is informal and non-axiomatic and is in the spirit of the book [Halmos, 1998] to which we refer the reader for further details.

of X which has no least element, contradicting the hypothesis that $(X, \leq_X)$ is well-ordered. ∎

Given two well-ordered sets $(X, \leq_X)$ and $(Y, \leq_Y)$, we call $f : X \to Y$ *monotonic* if $a \leq_X b$ implies $f(a) \leq_Y f(b)$ for all $a, b \in X$. If f is also injective, then f is called an *embedding* of X into Y. If f is both monotonic and bijective, then f is called an *order isomorphism* between X and Y, and in this case the two well-orderings X and Y are called *isomorphic*. Note that all these definitions are consistent with the definitions concerning orderings made in Chapter 1.

A.1.4 Definition Suppose that $(X, \leq_X)$ is a well-ordered set and that $x_0 \in X$. We call the set $I = I(x_0) = \{x \in X \mid x \leq_X x_0\}$ the *initial segment of X determined by x_0*. We call an initial segment I of X a *proper* initial segment if I is a proper subset of X.

A.1.5 Definition Suppose that $(X, \leq_X)$ and $(Y, \leq_Y)$ are two well-ordered sets. Then we write $X \leq Y$ if X is isomorphic to an initial segment of Y. We write $X < Y$ if X is isomorphic to a proper initial segment of Y.

A.1.6 Theorem For any two well-ordered sets X and Y, exactly one of the following statements holds.

(a) $X < Y$.

(b) $X > Y$.

(c) X and Y are isomorphic.

Proof: We first prove the following statement.
(1) No well-ordered set $(Z, \leq_Z)$ is isomorphic to a proper initial segment of itself.

To see this, suppose $f : I \to Z$ is an isomorphism, where I is a proper initial segment of Z. Then we cannot have $f(x) = x$ for all $x \in I$; otherwise, f would not be surjective. Let x_0 be the least element of the set of those elements x of I such that $f(x) \neq x$. Noting in particular that $f(x_0) \neq x_0$, we see that we cannot have $f(x_0) <_Z x_0$ otherwise $f(f(x_0)) = f(x_0)$ by minimality of x_0, and this yields the contradiction that f is not injective. Hence it must be the case that $x_0 <_Z f(x_0)$. Now let $x_1 \in I$ be such that $f(x_1) = x_0$. Then $x_1 \neq x_0$ because $f(x_0) \neq x_0$. If $x_1 <_Z x_0$, then by definition of x_0 again, we obtain $x_0 = f(x_1) = x_1 <_Z x_0$, which is impossible. If $x_0 <_Z x_1$, then $f(x_1) = x_0 <_Z f(x_0)$, which contradicts the monotonicity of f. Hence, Statement (1) holds.

We will also need the following statement.
(2) Suppose the well-ordered sets $(W, \leq_W)$ and $(Z, \leq_Z)$ are isomorphic. Then there is a unique isomorphism $f : (W, \leq_W) \to (Z, \leq_Z)$.

In order to see this, suppose $f, g : W \to Z$ are isomorphisms. We show $f = g$. Assume this is not the case, and let $w_0 \in W$ be the $\leq_W$-least w such that $f(w) \neq g(w)$; suppose in fact that $f(w_0) <_Z g(w_0)$ for the sake of argument. Let $w_1 \in W$ be such that $g(w_1) = f(w_0)$. Then $w_1 \neq w_0$. If $w_1 <_W w_0$, then by minimality of w_0 and monotonicity of f, we obtain $g(w_1) = f(w_1) <_W f(w_0) = g(w_1)$, which is impossible. If $w_0 <_W w_1$, then by monotonicity of g, we have $f(w_0) <_Z g(w_0) <_Z g(w_1) = f(w_0)$, which is also impossible. So Statement (2) holds.

We now turn to the proof of the theorem.

Define the relation R from X to Y by $R(x, y)$ if and only if the initial segments $\{w \in X \mid w \leq_X x\}$ and $\{v \in Y \mid v \leq_Y y\}$ are isomorphic, where $x \in X$ and $y \in Y$. First note that $R(x, y_1)$ and $R(x, y_2)$ implies $y_1 = y_2$ by Statement (1). So R is a partial function. By symmetry, transitivity, and (1) again, R is also injective.

We next show that $\mathrm{dom}(R)$ is an initial segment of X. Suppose $x_2 \in \mathrm{dom}(R)$, say, $R(x_2, y_2)$, and let $x_1 <_X x_2$. Let f be the isomorphism between the initial segments corresponding to x_2 and y_2. Then the initial segments corresponding to x_1 and $f(x_1)$ are also isomorphic, so $R(x_1, f(x_1))$, and hence $x_1 \in \mathrm{dom}(R)$. We have also shown that R is order-preserving.

A similar argument shows that the range of R is an initial segment of Y. Hence, R is an isomorphism from an initial segment $I(x_0)$, say, of X to an initial segment $J(y_0)$, say, of Y; thus, $R(x_0, y_0)$ holds.

Now consider the following cases. If $I(x_0) = X$, but $J(y_0) \neq Y$, then case (a) holds. If $I(x_0) \neq X$, but $J(y_0) = Y$, then case (b) holds. If $I(x_0) = X$ and $J(y_0) = Y$, then case (c) holds. Suppose finally that $I(x_0) \neq X$ and $J(y_0) \neq Y$. Let x_1 be the first element of $X \setminus I(x_0)$ and y_1 be the first element of $Y \setminus J(y_0)$; then x_1 is not in the domain of R (and y_1 is not in the range of R). But clearly $I(x_0) \cup \{x_1\}$ is the initial segment $I(x_1)$ and $J(y_0) \cup \{y_1\}$ is the initial segment $J(y_1)$, and, furthermore, $I(x_1)$ and $J(y_1)$ are clearly isomorphic by an isomorphism which, by (2), must be an extension of R. We therefore obtain the contradiction that x_1 is in the domain of R.

Hence, only one of (a), (b), (c) holds, as required. ∎

Next, we state without proof a well-known theorem usually attributed to E. Zermelo. This theorem has the consequence that any set is a carrier set for some ordinal, see [Halmos, 1998] for details.

A.1.7 Theorem (The Well-Ordering Theorem) Every set can be well-ordered.

A.1.8 Definition An *ordinal* or *ordinal number* is an equivalence class of a well-ordering under the equivalence relation of isomorphism.

The ordinals themselves can be ordered as follows. First, for any well-ordered set A, let $\#A$ denote the equivalence class of A under the equivalence relation of isomorphism. Suppose that $\alpha = \#A$ and $\beta = \#B$ are ordinals. We define the ordering $\leq$ on the ordinals by $\alpha \leq \beta$ if and only if $A \leq B$, and we note that $\leq$ is easily seen to be well-defined on the ordinals. Furthermore, by Theorem A.1.6, the ordering $\leq$ is a partial order and, as we show next, is in fact a well-order.

A.1.9 Lemma Let X be a linearly ordered partially ordered set which is not well-ordered. Then X contains an infinite strictly descending sequence.

Proof: If X is not well-ordered, then there exists a subset X_0 of X which does not contain a least element. Choose some $x_0 \in X_0$, and note that $X_1 = \{y \in X \mid y < x_0\}$ does not contain a least element. Now assume that some $x_i \in X$ has been chosen such that the set $X_{i+1} = \{y \in X \mid y < x_i\}$ does not contain a least element. Then we can choose $x_{i+1} \in X_{i+1}$ arbitrarily and obtain $x_{i+1} < x_i$ and also that $X_{i+2} = \{y \in X \mid y < x_{i+1}\}$ does not contain a least element. By the inductive argument just given, we obtain an infinite strictly descending sequence (x_n), as required. ∎

A.1.10 Proposition Every set of ordinals is itself well-ordered by $\leq$.

Proof: We begin by noting that if α and β are ordinals such that $\alpha \leq \beta$ and $\alpha = \#A$ and $\beta = \#B$, then we can assume without loss of generality that $A \subseteq B$; we will make use of this observation in what follows.

Let X be a set of ordinals which is not well-ordered. Then, by Lemma A.1.9, X contains an infinite descending sequence $\alpha_0 > \alpha_1 > \alpha_2 > \ldots$ of ordinals. For each $i \in \mathbb{N}$, suppose that $\alpha_i = \#A_i$ and that $A_i \supset A_{i+1}$. Then for each $i \in \mathbb{N}$ there exists $a_i \in A_i \setminus A_{i+1}$. Hence, $\{a_i \mid i \in \mathbb{N}\} \subseteq A_0$ is a subset of A_0 without a least element, which is impossible. ∎

It is common practice to identify any ordinal α with the set of all ordinals β such that $\beta < \alpha$; so, in these terms, $\beta < \alpha$ if and only if $\beta \in \alpha$. We will follow this practice in the following. In particular, when we speak of a mapping $f : X \to \alpha$, where α is an ordinal, we mean, in fact, a mapping $f : X \to \{\beta \mid \beta < \alpha\}$.

Ordinals fall into two classes. A *successor ordinal* is an ordinal α such that there is a greatest ordinal β with $\beta < \alpha$. In this case, α is called the *successor* of β and may be denoted by $\beta + 1$; we also call β the *predecessor* of α and may denote it by $\alpha - 1$. Any ordinal which is not a successor ordinal is called a *limit ordinal*.

Any ordinal has a successor. To see this, let α be an ordinal and identify it with the set of ordinals $\{\beta \mid \beta < \alpha\}$. Then $\alpha \cup \{\alpha\}$ is an ordinal above α and indeed is the least ordinal above α and therefore is the successor $\alpha + 1$ of α.

We next give an example containing details of some familiar ordinals.

A.1.11 Example It is easy to see that any finite set $A = \{a_1, \ldots, a_n\}$, containing n elements, can be well-ordered in essentially one way. Thus, if A and B are any well-ordered sets containing n elements, then A and B are isomorphic. Standard notation for the finite ordinals, together with canonical representatives for them, is as follows: $0 = \#\emptyset$, $1 = \#\{\emptyset\}$, $2 = \#\{\emptyset, \{\emptyset\}\}$, $3 = \#\{\emptyset, \{\emptyset\}, \{\emptyset, \{\emptyset\}\}\}$, etc. Thus, we are using the same symbols $0, 1, 2, 3, \ldots$ to denote natural numbers and ordinal numbers (as well as cardinal numbers), but the context in which they occur will determine their meaning. Often, we consider an ordinal to be the set of all its predecessors, as already noted, in which case we view the ordinal n as the set $\{0, 1, \ldots, n-1\}$ for each n. Furthermore, 0 is the least ordinal, 1 is the successor of 0, 2 is the successor of 1, etc. Thus, we have $0 < 1 < 2 < 3 < \cdots$ as ordinals.

Turning now to ordinals determined by infinite sets, we note first that infinite sets can be well-ordered in more than one way. For example, the set $\mathbb{N}$ of natural numbers can be well-ordered by writing it as $\{1, 3, 5, \ldots; 2, 4, 6, \ldots\}$ and ordering it from left to right. The resulting well-order is clearly not isomorphic to $\mathbb{N}$ well-ordered by the usual order on $\mathbb{N}$. Indeed, the *first infinite ordinal* or *least infinite ordinal*, denoted by ω, is the ordinal determined by $\mathbb{N}$ in its usual order, that is, $\omega = \#\mathbb{N}$. Thus, ω is the first limit ordinal. The successor of ω is $\omega + 1 = \{0, 1, 2, \ldots, \omega\}$, the successor of which is $\omega + 2 = (\omega + 1) + 1 = \{0, 1, 2, \ldots, \omega, \omega + 1\}$, etc. The next, or second, limit ordinal is denoted by $\omega 2 = \{0, 1, 2, \ldots, \omega, \omega + 1, \omega + 2, \ldots, \omega + n, \ldots\}$ etc. In this way, the ordinals form a *transfinite sequence*, and indeed any non-finite ordinal is sometimes called a transfinite number. Thus, we have $0 < 1 < 2 < 3 < \cdots < \omega < \omega + 1 < \omega + 2 < \cdots < \omega 2 < \omega 2 + 1 < \omega 2 + 2 < \cdots < \omega 3 < \cdots < \omega n < \cdots < \omega \omega = \omega^2 < \omega^2 + 1 < \omega^2 + 2 < \cdots$ as ordinal numbers. Note also that all the ordinals we have so far displayed in this example are determined by countable sets. The first uncountable ordinal is denoted by ω_1 and as a set is the uncountable well-ordered set containing all the countable ordinals. ∎

We are now in a position to consider the principle of transfinite induction. The reader may note that it is an extension, from $\mathbb{N}$ to arbitrary well-ordered sets, of the well-known strong form[2] of the principle of mathematical induction.

A.1.12 Theorem (Principle of Transfinite Induction) Suppose that A is any well-ordered set and B is a subset of A which satisfies the statement that $a \in B$ whenever $x \in B$ for all $x < a$. Then $B = A$.

Proof: If $B \neq A$, then $A \setminus B \neq \emptyset$. By well-ordering of A and therefore of any subset B of A, $A \setminus B$ has a first element x_0, say. But now we have $x \in B$ for

---

[2]Also known as course of values induction.

all $x < x_0$, and the induction hypothesis leads to the conclusion that x_0 must belong to B. This contradiction shows that $B = A$, as required.   ∎

A.1.13 Corollary Suppose that A is a well-ordered set and $\{p(a) \mid a \in A\}$ is a set of statements indexed by A. Suppose further that for all $b \in A$ it follows that $p(b)$ is true if $p(x)$ is true for all $x < b$. Then $p(a)$ is true for all $a \in A$.

In fact, the form in which we will usually apply the principle of transfinite induction is as follows.

A.1.14 Corollary Suppose that $p(\alpha)$ is a statement depending on the ordinal α. Suppose further that for all ordinals β, $p(\beta)$ is true if $p(\gamma)$ is true for all $\gamma < \beta$. Then $p(\alpha)$ is true for all ordinals α.

When applying the principle of transfinite induction as a proof principle, as formulated in Corollary A.1.14, it is usually convenient to split the argument into two cases. The first of these is when β is assumed to be a successor ordinal, and the second is when β is assumed to be a limit ordinal.

A.2   Basic Concepts from General Topology

We next turn to giving a brief overview of the general topology we need at various points in our discussions.[3] In addition, we include here the proofs of the results we stated without proof in our treatment of the Scott topology in Chapter 3.

A.2.1 Definition A *topology* on a set X is a collection τ of subsets of X, called the *open sets* of τ, satisfying the following properties.

(1) Any union of elements of τ belongs to τ.

(2) Any finite intersection of elements of τ belongs to τ.

(3) $\emptyset$ and X belong to τ.

The pair (X, τ), or simply X by an abuse of notation, is called a *topological space*.

A.2.2 Definition Given two topologies τ_1 and τ_2 on a set X, we say that τ_1 is *weaker* or *coarser* than τ_2, or that τ_2 is *stronger* or *finer* than τ_1, if $\tau_1 \subseteq \tau_2$.

---

[3]Our background references for the material we need from general topology are the books [Kelley, 1975] and [Willard, 1970] to which we refer the reader for proofs of the results we simply state.

Given a set X, the coarsest topology which can be defined on X is the *indiscrete topology* in which the only open sets are $\emptyset$ and X. At the other extreme, the finest topology which can be defined on X is the *discrete topology* in which all subsets of X are taken as open sets.

A.2.3 Definition If X is a topological space and $x \in X$, then a *neighbourhood* of x is a set U containing an open set V containing x, that is, $x \in V \subseteq U$, where V is open. The *neighbourhood system* $\mathcal{U}_x$ of x is the collection of all neighbourhoods of x.

A.2.4 Definition A *neighbourhood base* at x in the topological space X is a subcollection $\mathcal{B}_x \subseteq \mathcal{U}_x$ such that, for each $U \in \mathcal{U}_x$, there exists $V \in \mathcal{B}_x$ satisfying $V \subseteq U$. Thus, $\mathcal{U}_x = \{U \subseteq X \mid V \subseteq U \text{ for some } V \in \mathcal{B}_x\}$. The elements of $\mathcal{B}_x$ are called *basic neighbourhoods* of x.

A.2.5 Theorem Let X be a topological space, and, for each $x \in X$, let $\mathcal{B}_x$ be a neighbourhood base at x. Then the following properties hold.

(a) If $V \in \mathcal{B}_x$, then $x \in V$.

(b) If $V_1, V_2 \in \mathcal{B}_x$, then there is $V_3 \in \mathcal{B}_x$ satisfying $V_3 \subseteq V_1 \cap V_2$.

(c) If $V \in \mathcal{B}_x$, there is some $V_0 \in \mathcal{B}_x$ such that if $y \in V_0$, then there is $W \in \mathcal{B}_y$ satisfying $W \subseteq V$.

(d) $G \subseteq X$ is open if and only if G contains a basic neighbourhood of each of its points.

Conversely, suppose that X is a set and that a collection $\mathcal{B}_x$ of subsets of X, called basic neighbourhoods of x, is assigned to each element $x \in X$ in such a way that (a), (b), and (c) above are satisfied. If we then define a set G to be open if and only if it contains a basic neighbourhood of each of its points, as in (d), we obtain a topology on X in which $\mathcal{B}_x$ is a neighbourhood base at x for each $x \in X$.

A.2.6 Definition In a topological space (X, τ), a *base* for τ (or a base for X by an abuse of terminology) is a collection $\mathcal{B} \subseteq \tau$ of subsets of X such that each element of τ is a union of elements of $\mathcal{B}$. Equivalently, $\mathcal{B}$ is a base for τ if and only if whenever $V \in \tau$ and $x \in V$, there is $U \in \mathcal{B}$ such that $x \in U \subseteq V$. Furthermore, a collection $\mathcal{C} \subseteq \tau$ is called a *subbase* for τ (or a subbase for X) if the collection of all finite intersections of elements of $\mathcal{C}$ forms a base for τ.

A.2.7 Theorem A collection $\mathcal{B}$ of subsets of a set X is a base for a topology on X if and only if the following conditions are satisfied.

(a) $\bigcup_{B \in \mathcal{B}} B = X$.

(b) Whenever $B_1, B_2 \in \mathcal{B}$ and $x \in B_1 \cap B_2$, there is $B_3 \in \mathcal{B}$ satisfying $x \in B_3 \subseteq B_1 \cap B_2$.

Furthermore, any collection $\mathcal{C}$ of subsets of X is a subbase for some topology on X, namely, the topology formed by taking all arbitrary unions of finite intersections of elements of $\mathcal{C}$.

A.2.8 Theorem Suppose that $\mathcal{B}$ is a collection of open sets in a topological space X. Then $\mathcal{B}$ is a base for X if and only if, for each $x \in X$, the collection $\mathcal{B}_x = \{B \in \mathcal{B} \mid x \in B\}$ is a neighbourhood base at x.

As noted in Definition A.2.1, the elements of τ are called the open sets in the given topology on X. By definition, we call a subset F of X *closed* if its complement, $X \setminus F$, is open. It follows immediately that $\emptyset$ and X are closed sets, that any finite union of closed sets is itself closed, and that an arbitrary intersection of closed sets is closed. Therefore, given an arbitrary subset E of X, the intersection $\overline{E}$ of all the closed sets containing E is a closed set, the smallest closed set containing E, and is called the *closure* of E. Clearly, a set F is closed if and only if $F = \overline{F}$. Dually, one defines the *interior* U^o of a subset U of X to be the largest open set contained in U, and it is of course the union of all the open sets contained in U. Moreover, it is also clear that a set O is open if and only if $O = O^o$.

A *closure operator* (also known as a Kuratowski, or topological, closure operator) on a set X is a mapping $^c : \mathcal{P}(X) \to \mathcal{P}(X)$, from the power set $\mathcal{P}(X)$ of X into itself, subject to the following axioms.

(1) $\emptyset^c = \emptyset$.

(2) $A \subseteq A^c$ for all $A \subseteq X$.

(3) $(A \cup B)^c = A^c \cup B^c$ for all $A, B \subseteq X$.

(4) $A^c = (A^c)^c$ for all $A \subseteq X$.

Just as the notion of an open set can be taken as basic in defining topologies, so clearly can the notion of a closed set. More interesting is the fact that closure can be taken as fundamental, and indeed the characteristic properties of closure are precisely the four just stated in defining a closure operator, in the following sense.

A.2.9 Theorem Let X be a non-empty set, and let $^c : \mathcal{P}(X) \to \mathcal{P}(X)$ be a closure operator on X. Then $\tau = \{X \setminus A \mid A \subseteq X, A = A^c\}$ is a topology on X, called the topology *associated with* ^{c}, in which we have $\overline{A} = A^c$ for each subset A of X. Thus, A^c is the topological closure in X of each subset A of X with respect to the topology τ associated with ^{c}.

A.3 Convergence

It is well known, see [Willard, 1970, Chapter 4], that sequences are not adequate to describe all basic notions in topological spaces other than in the class of first countable spaces (a topological space is called first countable if it has a countable neighbourhood base at each of its points). One therefore needs notions more general than that of sequence. Such generalizations are provided by nets and filters, either of which is adequate to describe all topological concepts. Indeed, convergence itself can be taken as the fundamental concept in developing topology, see Theorem 3.1.3, and this is the point of view adopted in Chapter 3. However, we choose to work here only with nets for reasons already mentioned in Chapter 3.

A.3.1 Definition A *net* in a set X is a mapping $s : \mathcal{I} \to X$, where $(\mathcal{I}, \leq)$ or simply $\mathcal{I}$ is a directed set in which the ordering $\leq$ is reflexive and transitive. For each $i \in \mathcal{I}$, we denote $s(i)$ by s_i and denote the net $s : \mathcal{I} \to X$ by $(s_i)_{i \in \mathcal{I}}$ or simply by (s_i) or just by s_i if no confusion results. Similarly, sequences $(s_n)_{n \in \mathbb{N}}$, being special cases of nets, may be denoted simply by (s_n) or s_n. Given a net $(s_i)_{i \in \mathcal{I}}$ in X and an element i_0 of $\mathcal{I}$, we call the set $(s_i)_{i_0 \leq i} = \{s_i \mid i_0 \leq i\}$ a *tail* of $(s_i)_{i \in \mathcal{I}}$. A property will be said to hold *eventually* with respect to a net $(s_i)_{i \in \mathcal{I}}$ if it holds for some tail of the net.

A.3.2 Definition A *subnet* t of a net $s : \mathcal{I} \to X$ is a net $t : \mathcal{J} \to X$ satisfying (i) $t = s \circ \varphi$, where φ is a function mapping $\mathcal{J}$ into $\mathcal{I}$, and (ii) for each $i_0 \in \mathcal{I}$, there exists $j_0 \in \mathcal{J}$ such that $\varphi(j) \geq i_0$ whenever $j \geq j_0$. The point $s \circ \varphi(j)$ is often denoted by s_{i_j}, and we refer to the subnet $(s_{i_j})_{j \in \mathcal{J}}$ of $(s_i)_{i \in \mathcal{I}}$.

A.3.3 Definition Let X be a topological space, and let $x \in X$. A net $(s_i)_{i \in \mathcal{I}}$ in X will be said to *converge* to x, written $s_i \to x$ or $\lim_i s_i = x$, if, for each neighbourhood U of x, there exists $i_0 \in \mathcal{I}$ such that $s_i \in U$ whenever $i_0 \leq i$. If $s_i \to x$, then we call x a *limit* of s_i.

Since the singleton set $\{x\}$ is a neighbourhood of x if X is endowed with the discrete topology, it follows that $s_i \to x$ in the discrete topology if and only if (s_i) is eventually constant.

The notion of continuous function between topological spaces is fundamental in the subject. There are several ways of formulating this concept, but the following is perhaps the most intuitive.

A.3.4 Definition Let X and Y be topological spaces, and suppose that $f : X \to Y$ is a function. Then f is said to be *continuous at* $x \in X$ if, for each neighbourhood V of $f(x)$ in Y, there is a neighbourhood U of x in X such that $f(U) \subseteq V$. We say f is *continuous* if it is continuous at x for each $x \in X$.

The sense, mentioned earlier, in which nets can describe all basic topological notions can now be clarified.

A.3.5 Theorem Let X and Y be topological spaces. Then the following statements hold.

(a) Let $E \subseteq X$. Then $x \in \overline{E}$ if and only if there is a net (s_i) in E such that $s_i \to x$.

(b) A subset O of X is open if and only if, whenever $x \in O$ and (s_i) is a net such that $s_i \to x$, we have that (s_i) is eventually in O.

(c) A subset F of X is closed if and only if, whenever (s_i) is a net in F and $s_i \to x$, we have $x \in F$.

(d) A function $f : X \to Y$ is continuous at $x \in X$ if and only if, whenever $s_i \to x$ in X, we have $f(s_i) \to f(x)$ in Y.

Proof: We include a proof of (b) here since we have specific need of the result. Suppose that O is open, that $x \in O$, and that $s_i \to x$. Then it is clear from the definition of net convergence that (s_i) is eventually in O.

Conversely, assuming the stated condition, we show that O contains a neighbourhood of each of its points and hence is open. Let $x \in O$, and let $\mathcal{U}_x$ be the neighbourhood system of x. Let $\mathcal{I} = \{(y, U) \mid y \in U \in \mathcal{U}_x\}$ ordered by $(y_1, U_1) \leq (y_2, U_2)$ if and only if $U_2 \subseteq U_1$. Then it is easy to see that the ordering $\leq$ directs $\mathcal{I}$ and also that the net $s : \mathcal{I} \to X$ defined by $s(y, U) = y$ converges to x. By our current hypothesis, this net is eventually in O. Let (y_0, U_0) be such that $s_{(y,U)} = y \in O$ whenever $(y_0, U_0) \leq (y, U)$. Since $(y_0, U_0) \leq (y, U_0)$ for all $y \in U_0$, we conclude that $x \in U_0 \subseteq O$, as required. ∎

A.4 Separation Properties and Compactness

It is important to have sufficiently many open sets to be able to distinguish, in some way, between points in a topological space by means of the open sets. This is usually done by means of the following axioms.

A.4.1 Definition Let X be a topological space.

(1) We call X a T_0-*space* if, whenever x and y are distinct points of X, there is an open set containing one but not the other.

(2) We call X a T_1-*space* if, whenever x and y are distinct points of X, there is a neighbourhood of each not containing the other.

(3) We call X a T_2-*space* or a *Hausdorff* space if, whenever x and y are distinct points of X, there are disjoint neighbourhoods of x and y.

One of the important properties of Hausdorff spaces is that stated in the following result.

A.4.2 Theorem A topological space is Hausdorff if and only if every convergent net in X has a unique limit.

On the other hand, it is important that there not be too many open sets in a certain sense.

A.4.3 Definition Let X be a topological space. Then an *open cover* $\{U_i \mid i \in \mathcal{I}\}$ of X is a collection of open sets U_i such that $\bigcup_{i \in \mathcal{I}} U_i = X$. A *subcover* of an open cover $\{U_i \mid i \in \mathcal{I}\}$ is a cover $\{V_j \mid j \in \mathcal{J}\}$, where $\mathcal{J} \subseteq \mathcal{I}$. We call a topological space X *compact* if every open cover of X has a finite subcover.

A.5   Subspaces and Products

There are several ways in which one can create new topological spaces from given ones. We discuss here just two of these, namely, the process of forming subspaces of topological spaces and the process of forming products of families of topological spaces.

A.5.1 Definition Let (X, τ) be a topological space, and let $S \subseteq X$ be a subset of X. Then the collection $\tau_S = \{S \cap O \mid O \in \tau\}$ gives a topology on S, called the *relative topology* or the *subspace topology* for S. The space (S, τ_S) is called a *subspace* of (X, τ) or just a *subspace* of X.

Whenever one has a topological space X and a subset S of X, it will be assumed that S has been endowed with the subspace topology of X unless stated to the contrary. Notice that the sets $S \cap O$, where O is open in X, need not be open in X unless S itself is an open set of X.

Now suppose that X_i is a topological space for each i, where i is an element of some index set $\mathcal{I}$. As usual, we denote the product of the family $\{X_i \mid i \in \mathcal{I}\}$ of sets by $\prod_{i \in \mathcal{I}} X_i = \{f : \mathcal{I} \to \bigcup_{i \in \mathcal{I}} X_i \mid f(i) \in X_i\}$. Associated with any such product are the mappings π_j, $j \in \mathcal{I}$, where $\pi_j : \prod_{i \in \mathcal{I}} X_i \to X_j$ is defined by $\pi_j(f) = f(j)$. Indeed, π_j is termed the *projection on the j-th factor*.

There is a natural topology one can define on $\prod_{i \in \mathcal{I}} X_i$ determined by the projections as follows. Choose any finite set $\{i_1, \ldots, i_n\}$ of elements of $\mathcal{I}$, and choose corresponding open sets U_{i_j} in X_{i_j}, for $j = 1, \ldots, n$. Then we take the collection of sets of the form $\pi_{i_1}^{-1}(U_{i_1}) \cap \ldots \cap \pi_{i_n}^{-1}(U_{i_n})$ as a base for a topology on $\prod_{i \in \mathcal{I}} X_i$ called the *product topology* or the *Tychonoff product topology.* Indeed, the sets $\pi_i^{-1}(U_i)$ form a subbase for this topology, where $i \in \mathcal{I}$ and U_i is an open set in X_i. It is immediate that each of the projections π_i is continuous relative to the product topology and the given topology on the factor X_i.

Subspaces of X and products $\prod_{i \in \mathcal{I}} X_i$ inherit certain properties enjoyed by X and the X_i, respectively, as one would expect. We summarize next the ones relevant to our needs in the following theorem.

A.5.2 Theorem The following statements hold.

(a) Subspaces of T_0 or Hausdorff spaces are T_0 or Hausdorff, respectively.

(b) If X is compact and S is a closed subset of X, then S is compact (as a topological space in its own right). If X is Hausdorff and S is compact, then S is a closed subset of X.

(c) A non-empty product $\prod_{i \in \mathcal{I}} X_i$ is T_0 or Hausdorff if and only if each factor space X_i is T_0 or Hausdorff, respectively.

(d) **(Tychonoff's theorem)** A non-empty product $\prod_{i \in \mathcal{I}} X_i$ is compact if and only if each factor space is compact.

(e) A net (f_λ) in a product space $\prod_{i \in \mathcal{I}} X_i$ converges to f if and only if, for each index $i \in \mathcal{I}$, we have $\pi_i(f_\lambda) \to \pi_i(f)$ in X_i.

A.6   The Scott Topology

We present here the proofs of those results which were simply stated in Chapter 3 concerning the Scott topology. In fact, our development constitutes a treatment of the Scott topology from the point of view of convergence. Unless stated to the contrary, $(D, \sqsubseteq)$ will denote throughout some fixed, but arbitrary, domain with set D_c of compact elements.

A.6.1 Proposition Suppose that $A \subseteq D$ is a directed set. Then A is a net in D, and, as a net, we have that $A \to \bigsqcup A$ in the Scott topology. In particular, for each $s \in D$, approx$(s) \to s$ in the Scott topology.

Proof: Write $A = \{a_i \mid i \in \mathcal{I}\}$ for some index set $\mathcal{I}$, which we identify with A. Then $\mathcal{I}$ is clearly directed by the ordering $\leq$ obtained by restricting $\sqsubseteq$ to A. Therefore, the inclusion map $\mathcal{I} \to D$ is a net in D. Let $\overline{A} = \bigsqcup A$ and suppose that O is a neighbourhood of $\overline{A}$ in the Scott topology. Thus, $\bigsqcup A \in O$, and hence there exists some index i_0 such that $a_{i_0} \in O$. But O is upwards closed, and therefore $a_i \in O$ whenever $i_0 \leq i$. Thus, $A \to \overline{A}$, as required. ∎

A.6.2 Proposition Suppose that $f : D \to E$ is continuous in the Scott topologies on domains D and E. Then whenever $x \in D$, $a \in D_c$, and $a \sqsubseteq x$, we have $f(a) \sqsubseteq f(x)$.

Proof: Let $a \in D_c$. Since f is continuous at a, given any Scott neighbourhood V of $f(a)$, there is a Scott neighbourhood U of a such that $f(U) \subseteq V$. Let $b \in \text{approx}(f(a))$ be arbitrary. Then $V = \uparrow b$ is a Scott neighbourhood of $f(a)$. Furthermore, $\uparrow a$ is a Scott neighbourhood of a contained in any Scott neighbourhood U of a. Therefore, we have $f(\uparrow a) \subseteq \uparrow b$. Thus, if $a \sqsubseteq x$, then $x \in \uparrow a$. Therefore, $f(x) \in \uparrow b$, that is, $b \sqsubseteq f(x)$. But $b \in \text{approx}(f(a))$ is arbitrary. Therefore, $f(a) \sqsubseteq f(x)$, as required. ∎

A.6.3 Proposition Suppose that $f : D \to E$ is continuous in the Scott topologies on domains D and E. Then f is monotonic.

Proof: Suppose that $x \sqsubseteq y$ in D. Note that if $a \in \text{approx}(x)$ is arbitrary, then $a \in D_c$ and $a \sqsubseteq x$, so that $a \sqsubseteq y$. By Proposition A.6.2, we then have $f(a) \sqsubseteq f(y)$. Now, $\text{approx}(x)$ can be thought of as a net $\text{approx}(x) = \{a_i \mid i \in \mathcal{I}\}$, as in Proposition A.6.1, and moreover $a_i \to x$. Therefore, $f(a_i) \to f(x)$. Hence, by Theorem 3.2.4, for each $b \in \text{approx}(f(x))$ there is i_0 such that $b \sqsubseteq f(a_i)$ whenever $i_0 \leq i$. But $a_i \sqsubseteq x \sqsubseteq y$, for each i, and so $a_i \sqsubseteq y$ and hence $f(a_i) \sqsubseteq f(y)$ whenever $i_0 \leq i$ by our first observation. From this we see that $b \sqsubseteq f(y)$. Finally, we now have $f(x) = \bigsqcup\{b \mid b \in \text{approx}(f(x))\} \sqsubseteq f(y)$ so that $f(x) \sqsubseteq f(y)$, as required. ∎

A.6.4 Proposition A function $f : D \to E$, where D and E are domains, is continuous in the Scott topologies on D and E if and only if it is order continuous in the sense of Definition 1.1.7.

Proof: Suppose that f is continuous in the Scott topologies on D and E. Then f is monotonic by Proposition A.6.3. Let $A \subseteq D$ be a directed set, and let $\overline{A} = \bigsqcup A$. By Proposition A.6.1, $A = \{a_i \mid i \in \mathcal{I}\} \to \overline{A}$ as a net, and hence $f(a_i) \to f(\overline{A})$ by our hypothesis concerning f. Therefore, by Theorem 3.2.4, for each $b \in \text{approx}(f(\overline{A}))$, there exists i_0 such that $b \sqsubseteq f(a_i)$ whenever $i_0 \leq i$. From this we obtain $f(\overline{A}) = f(\bigsqcup A) = \bigsqcup\{b \mid b \in \text{approx}(f(\overline{A}))\} \sqsubseteq \bigsqcup\{f(a_i) \mid i \in \mathcal{I}\} = \bigsqcup f(A)$. Thus, $f(\bigsqcup A) \sqsubseteq \bigsqcup f(A)$, and it follows that f is order continuous by the remarks following Definition 1.1.7.

Conversely, suppose that f is order continuous and that $s_i \to s$ in the Scott topology on D. Now, f is monotonic. Therefore, on noting that $\text{approx}(s)$ is directed and thinking of it as the net $\{a_j \mid j \in \mathcal{J}\}$, we have that the set $\{f(a_j) \mid j \in \mathcal{J}\}$ is directed and $f(s) = f(\bigsqcup \text{approx}(s)) = \bigsqcup f(\text{approx}(s)) = \bigsqcup\{f(a_j) \mid j \in \mathcal{J}\}$. Therefore, given any $b \in \text{approx}(f(s))$, there is $j \in \mathcal{J}$ such that $b \sqsubseteq f(a_j)$, where $a_j \in \text{approx}(s)$. Since $s_i \to s$, it follows from Theorem 3.2.4 that there is i_0 such that $a_j \sqsubseteq s_i$ whenever $i_0 \leq i$. Hence, by the monotonicity of f, we have that $b \sqsubseteq f(a_j) \sqsubseteq f(s_i)$ whenever $i_0 \leq i$. Consequently, we have that $f(s_i) \to f(s)$ in the Scott topology on E, and so f is continuous in the Scott topologies, as required. ∎

Finally, we consider briefly the separation and compactness properties of the Scott topology.

A.6.5 Proposition When endowed with the Scott topology, any domain $(D, \sqsubseteq)$ is a compact T_0 topological space, but is not T_1 in general.

Proof: Suppose that $\{U_i \mid i \in \mathcal{I}\}$ is an open cover of D. Then we have $\bot \in U_k$, where U_k is some element of the given cover and $\bot$ denotes the bottom element of D. But $\bot \sqsubseteq x$ for each $x \in D$ and U_k is upwards closed, being Scott open. Therefore, $D \subseteq U_k$, and so $\{U_k\}$ is an open subcover of $\{U_i \mid i \in \mathcal{I}\}$, and hence D is compact.

We show next that D is T_0. Suppose that $x, y \in D$ and $x \neq y$. First, suppose that x and y are comparable, that is, either $x \sqsubseteq y$ or $y \sqsubseteq x$; suppose for the sake of argument that $x \sqsubseteq y$ and, hence, that $x \sqsubset y$ since $x \neq y$. We claim that there is a compact element $a \sqsubseteq y$ such that either $x \sqsubset a \sqsubseteq y$ or x and a are incomparable. If not, then for all compact elements $a \sqsubseteq y$, we have that x and a are comparable and indeed $a \sqsubseteq x$. It follows now that the supremum of such a is less than or equal to x, which is a contradiction since in fact this supremum is y. But then, given the claim, $\uparrow a$ is a Scott neighbourhood of y which does not contain x. Notice that if a is any compact element and $a \sqsubseteq x$, then $a \sqsubseteq y$. So, any Scott neighbourhood of x contains y, and we see that the condition in the definition of T_0 is not symmetric in this case.

Now suppose that x and y are incomparable. We claim this time that there is a compact element $a \in \mathrm{approx}(x)$ such that a and y are incomparable. Suppose that this is not the case, that is, suppose that for each $a \in \mathrm{approx}(x)$, a and y are comparable. Certainly, it cannot be the case that $y \sqsubseteq a$; otherwise, we immediately have $y \sqsubseteq x$. So it must be the case that $a \sqsubseteq y$ for each $a \in \mathrm{approx}(x)$. But then we have $\bigsqcup\{a \mid a \in \mathrm{approx}(x)\} \sqsubseteq y$, that is, $x \sqsubseteq y$, which is again a contradiction. Now, given this claim, $\uparrow a$ is a Scott neighbourhood of x not containing y. Notice that, by symmetry, in this case we also have a Scott neighbourhood of y not containing x; thus, the T_1 property actually applies to some pairs in D (the incomparable pairs), but not to all pairs. In any case, we now see that D is T_0.

Finally, take the two element domain $D = \{\bot, a\}$, where $\bot \sqsubset a$. The Scott topology on D contains $\emptyset$, $\uparrow \bot = D$ and $\uparrow a = \{a\}$ as its open sets (the set $\{\bot\}$ is not Scott open). This space D is not T_1 since any neighbourhood of $\bot$ contains a. ∎

Bibliography

[Abramsky and Jung, 1994] Abramsky, S. and Jung, A. (1994). Domain theory. In Abramsky, S., Gabbay, D. M., and Maibaum, T. S., editors, *Handbook of Logic in Computer Science, Volume 3*, pages 1–168. Oxford University Press, Oxford, UK. An expanded and corrected version is available at http://www.cs.bham.ac.uk/~axj/papers.html.

[Albeverio et al., 1999] Albeverio, S., Khrennikov, A. Y., and Kloeden, P. (1999). Memory retrieval as a p-adic dynamical system. *Biosystems*, 49:105–115.

[Antoniou, 1996] Antoniou, G. (1996). *Non-Monotonic Reasoning*. MIT Press, Cambridge, MA.

[Apt, 1997] Apt, K. R. (1997). *From Logic Programming to Prolog*. International Series in Computer Science. Prentice Hall, Upper Saddle River, NJ.

[Apt and Bezem, 1990] Apt, K. R. and Bezem, M. (1990). Acyclic programs. In Warren, D. H. and Szeredi, P., editors, *Proceedings of the Seventh International Conference on Logic Programming*, pages 617–633. MIT Press, Cambridge, MA.

[Apt and Pedreschi, 1994] Apt, K. R. and Pedreschi, D. (1994). Modular termination proofs for logic and pure Prolog programs. In Levi, G., editor, *Advances in Logic Programming Theory*, pages 183–229. Oxford University Press, Oxford, UK.

[Apt and Wallace, 2007] Apt, K. R. and Wallace, M. (2007). *Constraint Logic Programming Using Eclipse*. Cambridge University Press, London; New York.

[Apt et al., 1988] Apt, K. R., Blair, H. A., and Walker, A. (1988). Towards a theory of declarative knowledge. In Minker, J., editor, *Foundations of Deductive Databases and Logic Programming*, pages 89–148. Morgan Kaufmann Publishers, Los Altos, CA.

[Arnold and Nivat, 1980a] Arnold, A. and Nivat, M. (1980a). Metric interpretations of infinite trees and semantics of non-deterministic recursive programs. *Theoretical Computer Science*, 11:181–205.

[Arnold and Nivat, 1980b] Arnold, A. and Nivat, M. (1980b). The metric space of infinite trees: Algebraic and topological properties. *Fundamenta Informaticae*, 3(4):445–476.

[Bader, 2009] Bader, S. (2009). Neural-Symbolic Integration. PhD thesis, Department of Computer Science, TU Dresden, Dresden, Germany.

[Bader and Hitzler, 2004] Bader, S. and Hitzler, P. (2004). Logic programs, iterated function systems, and recurrent radial basis function networks. *Journal of Applied Logic*, 2(3):273–300.

[Bader and Hitzler, 2005] Bader, S. and Hitzler, P. (2005). Dimensions of neural-symbolic integration — A structured survey. In Artemov, S. N., Barringer, H., d'Avila Garcez, A. S., Lamb, L. C., and Woods, J., editors, *We Will Show Them! Essays in Honour of Dov Gabbay, Volume One*, pages 167–194. College Publications, London, UK.

[Bader et al., 2005a] Bader, S., Hitzler, P., and d'Avila Garcez, A. S. (2005a). Computing first-order logic programs by fibring artificial neural networks. In Russell, I. and Markov, Z., editors, *Proceedings of the 18th International Florida Artificial Intelligence Research Society Conference, FLAIRS05, Clearwater Beach, Florida, May 2005*, pages 314–319. AAAI Press, Menlo Park, CA.

[Bader et al., 2005b] Bader, S., Hitzler, P., and Witzel, A. (2005b). Integrating first-order logic programs and connectionist systems — A constructive approach. In d'Avila Garcez, A., Elman, J., and Hitzler, P., editors, *Proceedings of the IJCAI-05 Workshop on Neural-Symbolic Learning and Reasoning, NeSy'05*, Edinburgh. AAAI Press, Menlo Park, CA.

[Bader et al., 2006] Bader, S., Hitzler, P., and Hölldobler, S. (2006). The integration of connectionism and first-order knowledge representation and reasoning as a challenge for artificial intelligence. *Information*, 9(1):7–20.

[Bader et al., 2007] Bader, S., Hitzler, P., Hölldobler, S., and Witzel, A. (2007). A fully connectionist model generator for covered first-order logic programs. In Veloso, M., editor, *Proceedings of the International Joint Conference on Artificial Intelligence IJCAI07*, pages 666–671, Hyderabad, India. AAAI Press, Menlo Park, CA.

[Bader et al., 2008] Bader, S., Hitzler, P., and Hölldobler, S. (2008). Connectionist model generation: A first-order approach. *Neurocomputing*, 71(13–15):2420–2432.

[Baral, 2003] Baral, C. (2003). *Knowledge Representation, Reasoning and Declarative Problem Solving*. Cambridge University Press, London; New York.

[Bartle, 1966] Bartle, R. G. (1966). *The Elements of Integration*. John Wiley & Sons, New York.

[Batarekh, 1989] Batarekh, A. (1989). Topological Aspects of Logic Programming. PhD thesis, Syracuse University, Syracuse, New York.

[Batarekh and Subrahmanian, 1989a] Batarekh, A. and Subrahmanian, V. S. (1989a). The query topology in logic programming. In Monien, B. and Cori, R., editors, *Proceedings of the 1989 Symposium on Theoretical Aspects of Computer Science, STACS 89, Paderborn, Germany, February, 1989, Lecture Notes in Computer Science*, Volume 349, pages 375–387. Springer, Berlin.

[Batarekh and Subrahmanian, 1989b] Batarekh, A. and Subrahmanian, V. S. (1989b). Topological model set deformations in logic programming. *Fundamenta Informaticae*, 12(3):357–400.

[Belnap, 1977] Belnap, N. D. (1977). A useful four-valued logic. In Dunn, J. M. and Epstein, G., editors, *Modern Uses of Multiple-Valued Logic*, pages 5–37. Reidel, Dordrecht, The Netherlands.

[Berzati, 2007] Berzati, D. (2007). *Non-Monotonic Reasoning: A Unified Framework*. Nova Science Publishers, New York.

[Bessaga, 1959] Bessaga, C. (1959). On the converse of the Banach fixed-point principle. *Colloquium Mathematicum*, 7:41–43.

[Bezem, 1989] Bezem, M. (1989). Characterizing termination of logic programs with level mappings. In Lusk, E. L. and Overbeek, R. A., editors, *Proceedings of the North American Conference on Logic Programming*, pages 69–80. MIT Press, Cambridge, MA.

[Bidoit and Froideveaux, 1991] Bidoit, N. and Froideveaux, C. (1991). Negation by default and unstratifiable logic programs. *Theoretical Computer Science*, 78:85–112.

[Bishop, 1995] Bishop, C. M. (1995). *Neural Networks for Pattern Recognition*. Oxford University Press, Oxford.

[Blair, 2007] Blair, H. A. (2007). Elementary differential calculus on discrete, continuous and hybrid spaces. In Kopperman, R., Panangaden, P., Smyth, M. B., and Spreen, D., editors, *Computational Structures for Modelling Space, Time and Causality, August, 2006*, Volume 06341 of *Dagstuhl Seminar Proceedings*. Internationales Begegnungs- und Forschungszentrum fuer Informatik (IBFI), Schloss Dagstuhl, Germany.

[Blair and Remmel, 2001] Blair, H. A. and Remmel, J. (2001). Hybrid automata: Convergence spaces and continuity. In *Proceedings of the Joint IIIS & IEEE Meeting of the 5th World Multiconference on Systemics,*

Cybernetics and Informatics, SCI2001, and the 7th International Conference on Information Systems Analysis and Synthesis, ISAS2001, Volume XVII, Orlando, Florida, USA, pages 218–222. International Institute of Informatics and Systemics: IIIS, Winter Garden, FL.

[Blair et al., 1997a] Blair, H. A., Chidella, J., Dushin, F., Ferry, A., and Humenn, P. (1997a). A continuum of discrete systems. *Annals of Mathematics and Artificial Intelligence*, 21(2–4):155–185.

[Blair et al., 1997b] Blair, H. A., Dushin, F., and Humenn, P. (1997b). Simulations between programs as cellular automata. In Dix, J., Furbach, U., and Nerode, A., editors, *Logic Programming and Non-Monotonic Reasoning, Proceedings of the 4th International Conference LPNMR97, Dagstuhl, Lecture Notes in Artificial Intelligence*, Volume 1265, pages 115–131. Springer, Berlin.

[Blair et al., 1999] Blair, H. A., Dushin, F., Jakel, D. W., Rivera, A. J., and Sezgin, M. (1999). Continuous models of computation for logic programs. In Apt, K. R., Marek, V. W., Truszczyński, M., and Warren, D. S., editors, *The Logic Programming Paradigm: A 25-Year Persepective*, pages 231–255. Springer, Berlin.

[Blair et al., 2007] Blair, H. A., Jakel, D. W., Irwin, R. J., and Rivera, A. (2007). Elementary differential calculus on discrete and hybrid structures. In Artëmov, S. N. and Nerode, A., editors, *Logical Foundations of Computer Science, International Symposium, LFCS 2007, New York, NY, USA, June 4-7, 2007, Proceedings, Lecture Notes in Computer Science*, Volume 4514, pages 41–53. Springer, Berlin.

[Bochman, 1995] Bochman, A. (1995). Default consequence relations as a logical framework for logic programs. In Marek, V. W. and Nerode, A., editors, *Proceedings of the Third International Conference on Logic Programming and Non-Monotonic Reasoning (LPNMR'95), Lexington, KY, USA, June 26-28, 1995, Lecture Notes in Computer Science*, Volume 928, pages 245–258. Springer-Verlag, Berlin.

[Boley and Kifer, 2010] Boley, H. and Kifer, M., editors (22 June, 2010). *RIF Basic Logic Dialect*. W3C Recommendation. Available from the website http://www.w3.org/TR/rif-bld/.

[Bonnier et al., 1991] Bonnier, S., Nilsson, U., and Näslund, T. (1991). A simple fixed-point characterization of the three-valued stable model semantics. *Information Processing Letters*, 40(2):73–78.

[Bonsangue et al., 1996] Bonsangue, M. M., van Breugel, F., and Rutten, J. J. (1996). Alexandroff and Scott topologies for generalized metric spaces. In Andima, S., Flagg, R., Itzkowitz, G., et al., editors, *Papers on General Topology and Applications: Eleventh Summer Conference on General*

Topology and Applications, University of Southern Maine, Maine, USA, August, 1996, Annals of the New York Academy of Sciences, pages 49–68. New York Academy of Sciences, New York.

[Bornscheuer, 1996] Bornscheuer, S.-E. (1996). Rational models of normal logic programs. In *KI-96: Advances in Artificial Intelligence, Lecture Notes in Artificial Intelligence*, Volume 1137, pages 1–4. Springer, Berlin.

[Bouamama et al., 2000] Bouamama, S., Misane, D., and Priess-Crampe, S. (2000). An application of ultrametric spaces in logic programming. In *Proceedings of the Sixth Maghrebian Conference on Computer Sciences*. Maghrebian Information Processing Society, Fes, Moroco.

[Bramer, 2010] Bramer, M. (2010). *Logic Programming with Prolog*. Springer, Berlin.

[Buillame-Bert et al., 2010] Buillame-Bert, M., Broda, K., and d'Avila Garcez, A. (2010). First-order logic learning in artificial neural networks. In *Proceedings IJCNN 2010*. IEEE. In press.

[Bukatin, 2002] Bukatin, M. A. (2002). Mathematics of Domains. PhD thesis, Brandeis University, Waltham, MA.

[Bukatin and Scott, 1997] Bukatin, M. A. and Scott, J. S. (1997). Towards computing distances between programs via Scott domains. In Adian, S. and Nerode, A., editors, *Logical Foundations of Computer Science, 4th International Symposium, LFCS'97, Yaroslavl, Russia, July, 1997, Proceedings, Lecture Notes in Computer Science*, Volume 1234, pages 33–43. Springer-Verlag, Berlin.

[Castro-Company et al., 2007] Castro-Company, F., Romaguera, S., Sánchez-Álvarez, J., and Tirado, P. (2007). A quasimetric lattice approach for access prediction in replicated database protocols. Technical report, Instituto de Matemática Pura y Aplicada, Universidad Politécnica de Valencia, Spain.

[Cavedon, 1989] Cavedon, L. (1989). Continuity, consistency, and completeness properties for logic programs. In Levi, G. and Martelli, M., editors, *Proceedings of the 6th International Conference on Logic Programming*, pages 571–584. MIT Press, Cambridge, MA.

[Cavedon, 1991] Cavedon, L. (1991). Acyclic programs and the completeness of SLDNF-resolution. *Theoretical Computer Science*, 86:81–92.

[Cherchago et al., 2007] Cherchago, N., Hitzler, P., and Hölldobler, S. (2007). Decidability under the well-founded semantics. In Marchiori, M., Pan, J. Z., and de Sainte Marie, C., editors, *Web Reasoning and Rule Systems, First International Conference, RR 2007, Innsbruck , Austria, June 7-8, 2007, Proceedings, Lecture Notes in Computer Science*, Volume 4524, pages 269–278. Springer, Berlin.

[Clark, 1978] Clark, K. L. (1978). Negation as failure. In Gallaire, H. and Minker, J., editors, *Logic and Data Bases*, pages 293–322. Plenum Press, New York.

[Clifford and Seda, 2000] Clifford, E. and Seda, A. K. (2000). Uniqueness of the fixed points of single-step operators in many-valued logics. *Journal of Electrical Engineering, Slovak Academy of Sciences*, 51(12/s):54–58.

[Colmerauer and Roussel, 1993] Colmerauer, A. and Roussel, P. (1993). The birth of Prolog. In *ACM SIGPLAN Notices*, Volume 28(3), pages 37–52. ACM Press, New York.

[Crazzolara, 1997] Crazzolara, F. (1997). Quasimetric spaces as domains for abstract interpretation. In Falaschi, M., Navarro, M., and Policriti, A., editors, *Proceedings of the 1997 Joint Conference on Declarative Programming, APPIA-GULP-PRODE'97, Grado, Italy, June, 1997*, pages 45–56. University of Udine, Italy.

[Cybenko, 1989] Cybenko, G. (1989). Approximation by superpositions of a sigmoidal function. *Mathematics of Control, Signals, and Systems*, 2:303–314.

[Davey and Priestley, 2002] Davey, B. A. and Priestley, H. A. (2002). *Introduction to Lattices and Order*. Cambridge University Press, Cambridge, UK, second edition.

[d'Avila Garcez and Lamb, 2006] d'Avila Garcez, A. S. and Lamb, L. C. (2006). A connectionist computational model for epistemic and temporal reasoning. *Neural Computation*, 18(7):1711–1738.

[d'Avila Garcez and Zaverucha, 1999] d'Avila Garcez, A. S. and Zaverucha, G. (1999). The connectionist inductive learning and logic programming system. *Applied Intelligence, Special Issue on Neural Networks and Structured Knowledge*, 11(1):59–77.

[d'Avila Garcez et al., 1997] d'Avila Garcez, A. S., Zaverucha, G., and de Carvalho, L. A. (1997). Logical inference and inductive learning in artificial neural networks. In Hermann, C., Reine, F., and Strohmaier, A., editors, *Knowledge Representation in Neural Networks*, pages 33–46. Logos Verlag, Berlin.

[d'Avila Garcez et al., 2002] d'Avila Garcez, A. S., Broda, K. B., and Gabbay, D. M. (2002). Neural-Symbolic Learning Systems — Foundations and Applications. *Perspectives in Neural Computing*. Springer, Berlin.

[d'Avila Garcez et al., 2006] d'Avila Garcez, A. S., Lamb, L. C., and Gabbay, D. M. (2006). Connectionist computations of intuitionistic reasoning. *Theoretical Computer Science*, 358(1):34–55.

[d'Avila Garcez et al., 2007] d'Avila Garcez, A. S., Lamb, L. C., and Gabbay, D. M. (2007). Connectionist modal logic: Representing modalities in neural networks. *Theoretical Computer Science*, 371(1):34–53.

[d'Avila Garcez et al., 2009] d'Avila Garcez, A. S., Lamb, L. C., and Gabbay, D. M. (2009). Neural-Symbolic Cognitive Reasoning. *Cognitive Technologies*. Springer, Berlin.

[de Bakker, 2002] de Bakker, J. W. (2002). Fixed points in metric semantics. *Electronic Notes in Theoretical Computer Science*, 40:70–71.

[de Bakker and de Vink, 1996] de Bakker, J. W. and de Vink, E. P. (1996). *Control Flow Semantics*. Foundations of Computing Series. MIT Press, Cambridge, MA.

[De Raedt et al., 2008] De Raedt, L., Frasconi, P., Kersting, K., and Muggleton, S., editors (2008). *Probabilistic Inductive Logic Programming: Theory and Applications*. Springer-Verlag, Berlin.

[Dowling and Gallier, 1984] Dowling, W. F. and Gallier, J. H. (1984). Linear-time algorithms for testing the satisfiability of propositional Horn formulae. *The Journal of Logic Programming*, 1(3):267–284.

[Dragovich and Dragovich, 2006] Dragovich, B. and Dragovich, A. (2006). A p-adic model of DNA sequence and genetic code. Preprint is available at http://www.arxiv.org/abs/q-bio.GN/0607018.

[Dugundji and Granas, 1982] Dugundji, J. and Granas, A. (1982). *Fixed Point Theory*. Monografie Matematyczne. Polish Scientific Publishers, Warsaw.

[Dung and Kanchanasut, 1989] Dung, P. M. and Kanchanasut, K. (1989). A fixpoint approach to declarative semantics of logic programs. In Lusk, E. L. and Overbeek, R. A., editors, *Logic Programming, Proceedings of the North American Conference 1989, NACLP'89, Cleveland, Ohio*, pages 604–625. MIT Press, Cambridge, MA.

[Edalat and Heckmann, 1998] Edalat, A. and Heckmann, R. (1998). A computational model for metric spaces. *Theoretical Computer Science*, 193:53–73.

[Fages, 1994] Fages, F. (1994). Consistency of Clark's completion and the existence of stable models. *Journal of Methods of Logic in Computer Science*, 1:51–60.

[Ferry, 1994] Ferry, A. P. (1994). Topological Characterizations for Logic Programming Semantics. PhD thesis, University of Michigan, MI.

[Fitting, 1985] Fitting, M. C. (1985). A Kripke-Kleene semantics for general logic programs. *The Journal of Logic Programming*, 2:295–312.

[Fitting, 1991] Fitting, M. C. (1991). Bilattices and the semantics of logic programming. *The Journal of Logic Programming*, 11:91–116.

[Fitting, 1994a] Fitting, M. C. (1994a). Kleene's three-valued logics and their children. *Fundamenta Informaticae*, 20:113–131.

[Fitting, 1994b] Fitting, M. C. (1994b). Metric methods: Three examples and a theorem. *The Journal of Logic Programming*, 21(3):113–127.

[Fitting, 2002] Fitting, M. C. (2002). Fixpoint semantics for logic programming — A survey. *Theoretical Computer Science*, 278(1–2):25–51.

[Fitting and Ben-Jacob, 1990] Fitting, M. C. and Ben-Jacob, M. (1990). Stratified, weak stratified, and three-valued semantics. *Fundamenta Informaticae*, 13:19–33.

[Flagg and Kopperman, 1997] Flagg, B. and Kopperman, R. (1997). Continuity spaces: Reconciling domains and metric spaces. *Theoretical Computer Science*, 177(1):111–138.

[Fritzke, 1998] Fritzke, B. (1998). *Vektorbasierte Neuronale Netze*. Habilitation, Technische Universität Dresden, Germany.

[Fu, 1994] Fu, L. (1994). *Neural Networks in Computer Intelligence*. McGraw-Hill, New York.

[Funahashi, 1989] Funahashi, K.-I. (1989). On the approximate realization of continuous mappings by neural networks. *Neural Networks*, 2:183–192.

[Gabbay et al., 1994] Gabbay, D. M., Hogger, C. J., and Robinson, J. A. (1994). *Non-Monotonic Reasoning and Uncertain Reasoning*, Volume 3 of *Handbook of Logic in Artificial Intelligence and Logic Programming*. Clarendon Press, Oxford University Press, Oxford, UK.

[Ganter and Wille, 1999] Ganter, B. and Wille, R. (1999). *Formal Concept Analysis: Mathematical Foundations*. Springer, Berlin.

[Gelfond and Lifschitz, 1988] Gelfond, M. and Lifschitz, V. (1988). The stable model semantics for logic programming. In Kowalski, R. A. and Bowen, K. A., editors, *Logic Programming. Proceedings of the 5th International Conference and Symposium on Logic Programming*, pages 1070–1080. MIT Press, Cambridge, MA.

[Gelfond and Lifschitz, 1991] Gelfond, M. and Lifschitz, V. (1991). Classical negation in logic programs and disjunctive databases. *New Generation Computing*, 9:365–385.

[Gierz et al., 2003] Gierz, G., Hofmann, K. H., Keimel, K., Lawson, J. D., Mislove, M., and Scott, D. S. (2003). *Continuous Lattices and Domains*, Volume 93 of *Encyclopedia of Mathematics and its Applications*. Cambridge University Press, Cambridge, UK.

[Gust et al., 2007] Gust, H., Kühnberger, K.-U., and Geibel, P. (2007). Learning models of predicate logical theories with neural networks based on topos theory. In Hammer, B. and Hitzler, P., editors, *Perspectives of Neural-Symbolic Integration*, Volume 77 of *Studies in Computational Intelligence*, pages 233–264. Springer, Berlin.

[Halmos, 1998] Halmos, P. R. (1998). *Naive Set Theory*. Undergraduate Texts in Mathematics. Springer-Verlag, Berlin.

[Hammer and Hitzler, 2007] Hammer, B. and Hitzler, P., editors (2007). *Perspectives of Neural-Symbolic Integration*, Volume 77 of *Studies in Computational Intelligence*. Springer, Berlin.

[Haykin, 1994] Haykin, S. (1994). *Neural Networks. A Comprehensive Foundation*. Macmillan College Publishing Company, New York.

[Heckmann, 1999] Heckmann, R. (1999). Approximation of metric spaces by partial metric spaces. *Applied Categorical Structures*, 7:71–83.

[Heckmanns, 1996] Heckmanns, U. (1996). On the topology of ultrametric spaces. In Simon, P., editor, *Proceedings of the 8th Prague Topological Symposium, August 1996, Prague*, pages 149–156. Charles University and Topology Atlas, Prague.

[Heinze, 2003] Heinze, R. (2003). Topological investigations of the operators of the well-founded and alternating fixed-point semantics of normal logic programs. In Hurley, T., MacanAirchinnigh, M., Schellekens, M., and Seda, A. K., editors, *Proceedings of the Second Irish Conference on the Mathematical Foundations of Computer Science and Information Technology (MFCSIT2002), July, 2002, Galway, Ireland*, Volume 74 of *Electronic Notes in Theoretical Computer Science*, pages 51–68. Elsevier Science Publishers, Amsterdam; New York.

[Hertz et al., 1991] Hertz, J., Krogh, A., and Palmer, R. G. (1991). *Introduction to the Theory of Neural Computation*. Addison-Wesley, Reading, MA.

[Hitzler, 2001] Hitzler, P. (2001). Generalized Metrics and Topology in Logic Programming Semantics. PhD thesis, Department of Mathematics, National University of Ireland, University College Cork, Cork, Ireland.

[Hitzler, 2003a] Hitzler, P. (2003a). A resolution theorem for algebraic domains. In Gottlob, G. and Walsh, T., editors, *Proceedings of the 18th International Joint Conference on Artificial Intelligence, Acapulco, Mexico, August, 2003*, pages 1339–1340. Morgan Kaufmann Publishers, San Mateo, CA.

[Hitzler, 2003b] Hitzler, P. (2003b). Towards a systematic account of different logic programming semantics. In Günter, A., Kruse, R., and Neumann,

B., editors, *Proceedings of the 26th German Conference on Artificial Intelligence, KI2003, Hamburg, Germany, September, 2003, Lecture Notes in Artificial Intelligence*, Volume 2821, pages 105–119. Springer, Berlin.

[Hitzler, 2004] Hitzler, P. (2004). Default reasoning over domains and concept hierarchies. In Biundo, S., Frühwirth, T., and Palm, G., editors, *KI2004: Advances in Artificial Intelligence. Proceedings of the 27th Annual German Conference on AI, KI2004, Ulm, Germany, September, 2004, Lecture Notes in Artificial Intelligence*, Volume 3238, pages 351–365. Springer-Verlag, Berlin.

[Hitzler, 2005] Hitzler, P. (2005). Towards a systematic account of different semantics for logic programs. *Journal of Logic and Computation*, 15(3):391–404.

[Hitzler, 2009] Hitzler, P. (2009). Towards reasoning pragmatics. In Janowicz, K., Raubal, M., and Levashkin, S., editors, *GeoSpatial Semantics, Third International Conference, GeoS 2009, Mexico City, Mexico, December 3-4, 2009. Proceedings, Lecture Notes in Computer Science*, Volume 5892, pages 9–25. Springer, Berlin.

[Hitzler and Krötzsch, 2006] Hitzler, P. and Krötzsch, M. (2006). Querying formal contexts with answer set programs. In Schärfe, H., Hitzler, P., and Øhrstrøm, P., editors, *Conceptual Structures: Inspiration and Application, Proceedings of the 14th International Conference on Conceptual Structures, ICCS 2006, Aalborg, Denmark, July, 2006, Lecture Notes in Artificial Intelligence*, Volume 4068, pages 413–426. Springer, Berlin.

[Hitzler and Kühnberger, 2009] Hitzler, P. and Kühnberger, K.-U. (2009). The importance of being neural-symbolic — A wilde position. In Goertzel, B., Hitzler, P., and Hutter, M., editors, *Artificial General Intelligence. Second Conference on Artificial General Intelligence, AGI 2009, Arlington, Virginia, USA, March 6-9, 2009. Proceedings*, pages 208–209. Atlantis Press, Amsterdam; Paris.

[Hitzler and Seda, 1999a] Hitzler, P. and Seda, A. K. (1999a). Acceptable programs revisited. In Etalle, S. and Smaus, J.-G., editors, *Proceedings of the Workshop on Verification in Logic Programming, 16th International Conference on Logic Programming, ICLP'99, Las Cruces, New Mexico, November, 1999, Electronic Notes in Theoretical Computer Science*, Volume 30, pages 59–76. Elsevier Science Publishers, Amsterdam; New York.

[Hitzler and Seda, 1999b] Hitzler, P. and Seda, A. K. (1999b). Characterizations of classes of programs by three-valued operators. In Gelfond, M., Leone, N., and Pfeifer, G., editors, *Logic Programming and Non-Monotonic Reasoning, Proceedings of the 5th International Conference on Logic Programming and Non-Monotonic Reasoning (LPNMR'99), El*

Paso, Texas, USA, December, 1999, Lecture Notes in Artificial Intelligence, Volume 1730, pages 357–371. Springer, Berlin.

[Hitzler and Seda, 1999c] Hitzler, P. and Seda, A. K. (1999c). Some issues concerning fixed points in computational logic: Quasimetrics, multivalued mappings and the Knaster-Tarski theorem. In Comfort, W., Heckmann, R., Kopperman, R., and Narici, L., editors, *Proceedings of the 14th Summer Conference on Topology and Its Applications: Special Session on Topology in Computer Science, Long Island, USA*, Volume 24 of *Topology Proceedings*, pages 223–250.

[Hitzler and Seda, 2000] Hitzler, P. and Seda, A. K. (2000). Dislocated topologies. *Journal of Electrical Engineering, Slovak Academy of Sciences*, 51(12/s):3–7.

[Hitzler and Seda, 2001] Hitzler, P. and Seda, A. K. (2001). A "converse" of the Banach contraction mapping theorem. *Journal of Electrical Engineering, Slovak Academy of Sciences*, 52(10/s):3–6.

[Hitzler and Seda, 2002a] Hitzler, P. and Seda, A. K. (2002a). The fixed-point theorems of Priess-Crampe and Ribenboim in logic programming. In Kuhlmann, F.-V., Kuhlmann, S., and Marshall, M., editors, *Valuation Theory and Its Applications, Proceedings of the International Valuation Theory Conference, University of Saskatchewan in Saskatoon, Canada, July, 1999*, Volume 32 of *Fields Institute Communications Series*, pages 219–235. American Mathematical Society, Providence, RI.

[Hitzler and Seda, 2002b] Hitzler, P. and Seda, A. K. (2002b). On the coincidence of semantics for uniquely determined programs. In Hurley, T., MacanAirchinnigh, M., Schellekens, M., and Seda, A. K., editors, *Proceedings of the First Irish Conference on the Mathematical Foundations of Computer Science and Information Technology (MFCSIT2000), Cork, Ireland, July, 2000, Electronic Notes in Theoretical Computer Science*, Volume 40, pages 189–205. Elsevier Science Publishers, Amsterdam; New York.

[Hitzler and Seda, 2003] Hitzler, P. and Seda, A. K. (2003). Generalized metrics and uniquely determined logic programs. *Theoretical Computer Science*, 305(1–3):187–219.

[Hitzler and van Harmelen, 2010] Hitzler, P. and van Harmelen, F. (2010). A reasonable Semantic Web. *Semantic Web – Interoperability, Usability, Applicability*. In press.

[Hitzler and Wendt, 2002] Hitzler, P. and Wendt, M. (2002). The well-founded semantics is a stratified Fitting semantics. In Jarke, M., Koehler, J., and Lakemeyer, G., editors, *Proceedings of the 25th Annual German Conference on Artificial Intelligence, KI2002, Aachen, Germany,*

September 2002, Lecture Notes in Artificial Intelligence, Volume 2479, pages 205–221. Springer, Berlin.

[Hitzler and Wendt, 2003] Hitzler, P. and Wendt, M. (2003). Formal concept analysis and resolution in algebraic domains. In de Moor, A. and Ganter, B., editors, *Using Conceptual Structures — Contributions to ICCS 2003*, pages 157–170. Shaker Verlag, Aachen.

[Hitzler and Wendt, 2005] Hitzler, P. and Wendt, M. (2005). A uniform approach to logic programming semantics. *Theory and Practice of Logic Programming*, 5(1-2):123–159.

[Hitzler et al., 2004] Hitzler, P., Hölldobler, S., and Seda, A. K. (2004). Logic programs and connectionist networks. *Journal of Applied Logic*, 2(3):245–272.

[Hitzler et al., 2005] Hitzler, P., Bader, S., and d'Avila Garcez, A. (2005). Ontology learning as a use case for neural-symbolic integration. In d'Avila Garcez, A. S., Hitzler, P., and Ellman, J., editors, *Proceedings of the IJCAI-05 Workshop on Neural-Symbolic Learning and Reasoning, NeSy'05*.

[Hitzler et al., 2009a] Hitzler, P., Krötzsch, M., Parsia, B., Patel-Schneider, P., and Rudolph, S., editors (2009a). *OWL 2 Web Ontology Language: Primer*. W3C Recommendation, 27 October 2009. Preprint can be obtained from the website http://www.w3.org/TR/owl-primer.

[Hitzler et al., 2009b] Hitzler, P., Krötzsch, M., and Rudolph, S. (2009b). *Foundations of Semantic Web Technologies*. Chapman & Hall/CRC, Boca Raton, FL.

[Hodel, 1995] Hodel, R. E. (1995). *Introduction to Mathematical Logic*. Thomson Learning PWS, New York.

[Hölldobler and Kalinke, 1994] Hölldobler, S. and Kalinke, Y. (1994). Towards a massively parallel computational model for logic programming. In *Proceedings ECAI94 Workshop on Combining Symbolic and Connectionist Processing, Amsterdam, July, 1994*, pages 68–77. European Coordinating Committee for Artificial Intelligence (ECCAI).

[Hölldobler and Ramli, 2009] Hölldobler, S. and Ramli, C. D. P. K. (2009). Logics and networks for human reasoning. In Alippi, C., Polycarpou, M. M., Panayiotou, C. G., and Ellinas, G., editors, *Artificial Neural Networks (ICANN 2009), 19th International Conference, Limassol, Cyprus, September 14-17, 2009, Proceedings, Lecture Notes in Computer Science*, Volume 5769, pages 85–94. Springer, Berlin.

[Hölldobler et al., 1999] Hölldobler, S., Kalinke, Y., and Störr, H.-P. (1999). Approximating the semantics of logic programs by recurrent neural networks. *Applied Intelligence*, 11:45–58.

[Hornik et al., 1989] Hornik, K., Stinchcombe, M., and White, H. (1989). Multilayer feedforward networks are universal approximators. *Neural Networks*, 2:359–366.

[Istrăţescu, 1981] Istrăţescu, V. I. (1981). *Fixed Point Theory — An Introduction*, Volume 7, *Mathematics and Its Applications*. D. Reidel Publishing Company, Dordrecht, Holland.

[Jachymski, 2000] Jachymski, J. (2000). A short proof of the converse of the contraction principle and some related results. *Topological Methods in Nonlinear Analysis*, 15:179–186.

[Jachymski, 2001] Jachymski, J. (2001). Order-theoretic aspects of metric fixed-point theory. In Kirk, W. A. and Sims, B., editors, *Handbook of Metric Fixed Point Theory*, pages 613–641. Kluwer Academic Publishers, Dordrecht, The Netherlands.

[Jacobsson, 2005] Jacobsson, H. (2005). Rule extraction from recurrent neural networks: A taxonomy and review. *Neural Computation*, 17(6):1223–1263.

[Jones and Laaser, 1977] Jones, N. D. and Laaser, W. T. (1977). Complete problems for deterministic sequential time. *Theoretical Computer Science*, 3:105–117.

[Kalinke, 1994] Kalinke, Y. (1994). *Ein massiv paralleles Berechnungsmodell für normale logische Programme*. PhD thesis, Department of Computer Science, Dresden University of Technology, Dresden, Germany.

[Karp and Ramachandran, 1990] Karp, R. M. and Ramachandran, V. (1990). Parallel algorithms for shared-memory machines. In van Leeuwen, J., editor, *Handbook of Theoretical Computer Science*, Chapter 17, pages 869–941. Elsevier Science Publishers, New York.

[Kelley, 1975] Kelley, J. L. (1975). *General Topology*. Graduate Texts in Mathematics, Volume 27. Springer-Verlag, Berlin.

[Khamsi and Misane, 1998] Khamsi, M. A. and Misane, D. (1997/1998). Disjunctive signed logic programs. *Fundamenta Informaticae*, 32(3–4):349–357.

[Khamsi et al., 1993] Khamsi, M. A., Kreinovich, V., and Misane, D. (1993). A new method of proving the existence of answer sets for disjunctive logic programs: A metric fixed-point theorem for multivalued mappings. In Baral, C. and Gelfond, M., editors, *Proceedings of the Workshop on Logic Programming with Incomplete Information, Vancouver, B.C., Canada*, pages 58–73. University of British Columbia, Vancouver, BC.

[Khrennikov, 1998] Khrennikov, A. Y. (1998). Human subconscious as the p-adic dynamical system. *Journal of Theoretical Biology*, 193:179–196.

[Khrennikov, 2004] Khrennikov, A. Y. (2004). *Information Dynamics in Cognitive, Psychological, Social and Anomalous Phenomena*, Volume 138 of *Fundamental Theories of Physics*. Kluwer Academic Publishers, Dordrecht, Boston, London.

[Khrennikov and Kozyrev, 2007] Khrennikov, A. Y. and Kozyrev, S. V. (2007). Genetic codenext term on the diadic plane. *Physica A: Statistical Mechanics and Its Applications*, 381:265–272.

[Kifer et al., 1995] Kifer, M., Lausen, G., and Wu, J. (1995). Logical foundations of object-oriented and frame-based languages. *Journal of the ACM*, 42(4):741–843.

[Kirk and Sims, 2001] Kirk, W. A. and Sims, B., editors (2001). *Handbook of Metric Fixed Point Theory*. Kluwer Academic Publishers, Dordrecht, The Netherlands.

[Klavins et al., 1998] Klavins, E., Rounds, W. C., and Zhang, G.-Q. (1998). Experimenting with power default reasoning. In *Proceedings of the Fifteenth National Conference on Artificial Intelligence and Tenth Innovative Applications of Artificial Intelligence Conference, AAAI 98, IAAI 98, July, 1998, Madison, Wisconsin, USA*, pages 846–852. AAAI Press/MIT Press.

[Knorr and Hitzler, 2007] Knorr, M. and Hitzler, P. (2007). A comparison of disjunctive well-founded semantics. In Hitzler, P., Roth-Berghofer, T., and Rudolph, S., editors, *Foundations of Artificial Intelligence FAInt 2007, Osnabrück, Germany, September 10, 2007*, Volume 277, *CEUR Workshop Proceedings*.

[Kohonen, 1981] Kohonen, T. (1981). Self-organized formation of topologically correct feature maps. *Biological Cybernetics*, 43(1):59–69.

[Komendantskaya, 2010] Komendantskaya, E. (2010). Unification neural networks: Unification by error-correction learning. *Logic Journal of the IGPL*. In press.

[Komendantskaya et al., 2007] Komendantskaya, E., Lane, M., and Seda, A. K. (2007). Connectionist representation of multivalued logic programs. In Hammer, B. and Hitzler, P., editors, *Perspectives of Neural-Symbolic Integration*, Volume 77 of *Studies in Computational Intelligence*, pages 283–313. Springer, Berlin.

[Kopperman, 1988] Kopperman, R. (1988). All topologies come from generalized metrics. *American Mathematical Monthly*, 95(2):89–97.

[Kowalski, 1974] Kowalski, R. A. (1974). Predicate logic as a programming language. In Rosenfeld, J. L., editor, *Proceedings IFIP'74, Stockholm, Sweden, August, 1974*, pages 569–574. North-Holland, Amsterdam.

[Krötzsch, 2006] Krötzsch, M. (2006). Generalized ultrametric spaces in quantitative domain theory. *Theoretical Computer Science*, 368(1–2):30–49.

[Krötzsch et al., 2008] Krötzsch, M., Rudolph, S., and Hitzler, P. (2008). ELP: Tractable rules for OWL 2. In Sheth, A., Staab, S., Dean, M., Paolucci, M., Maynard, D., Finin, T., and Thirunarayan, K., editors, *Proceedings of the 7th International Semantic Web Conference (ISWC-08)*, *Lecture Notes in Computer Science*, Volume 5318, pages 649–664. Springer, Berlin.

[Kuhlmann, 1999] Kuhlmann, F.-V. (1999). A theorem about maps on spherically complete ultrametric spaces, and its applications. Preprint, Department of Mathematics and Statistics, University of Saskatchewan in Saskatoon, 20 pages.

[Künzi, 2001] Künzi, H.-P. A. (2001). Non-symmetric distances and their associated topologies: About the origins of basic ideas in the area of asymmetric topology. In Aull, C. E. and Lowen, R., editors, *Handbook of the History of General Topology, Volume 3*, pages 853–968. Kluwer Academic Publishers, Dordrecht.

[Künzi and Kivuvu, 2008] Künzi, H.-P. A. and Kivuvu, C. M. (2008). A double completion for an arbitrary T_0-quasimetric space. *Journal of Logic and Algebraic Programming*, 76(2):251–269.

[Künzi et al., 2006] Künzi, H.-P. A., Pajoohesh, H., and Schellekens, M. (2006). Partial quasimetrics. *Theoretical Computer Science*, 365:237–246.

[Lane and Seda, 2006] Lane, M. and Seda, A. K. (2006). Some aspects of the integration of connectionist and logic-based systems. *Information*, 9(4):551–562.

[Lane and Seda, 2009] Lane, M. and Seda, A. K. (2009). Properties of general semantic operators determined by logic-based systems. In Hurley, T., MacanAirchinnigh, M., Schellekens, M., Seda, A. K., and Strong, G., editors, *Proceedings of the Fourth Irish Conference on the Mathematical Foundations of Computer Science and Information Technology (MFC-SIT2006), University College Cork, August, 2006*, *Electronic Notes in Theoretical Computer Science*, Volume 225, pages 181–194. Elsevier Science Publishers, Amsterdam; New York.

[Lassez et al., 1982] Lassez, J.-L., Nguyen, V., and Sonenberg, L. (1982). Fixed-point theorems and semantics: A folk tale. *Information Processing Letters*, 14(3):112–116.

[Lehmann et al., 2010] Lehmann, J., Bader, S., and Hitzler, P. (2010). Extracting reduced logic programs from artificial neural networks. *Applied Intelligence*, 32(3):249–266.

[Leone et al., 2006] Leone, N., Pfeifer, G., Faber, W., Eiter, T., Gottlob, G., Perri, S., and Scarcello, F. (2006). The dlv system for knowledge representation and reasoning. *ACM Transactions on Computational Logic*, 7(3):499–562.

[Lifschitz, 1999] Lifschitz, V. (1999). Answer set planning. In Schreye, D. D., editor, *Logic Programming. Proceedings of the 16th International Conference on Logic Programming, ICLP'99, Las Cruces, New Mexico, November, 1999*, pages 23–37. MIT Press, Cambridge, MA.

[Lifschitz, 2001] Lifschitz, V. (2001). Success of default logic. In Hayes, P., Sandewall, E., Amarel, S., et al., editors, *Logical Foundations for Cognitive Agents: Contributions in Honor of Ray Reiter*, pages 208–212. Springer-Verlag, New York, Secaucus, NJ.

[Lifschitz et al., 1995] Lifschitz, V., McCain, N., Przymusinski, T. C., and Stärk, R. F. (1995). Loop checking and the well-founded semantics. In Marek, V. W. and Nerode, A., editors, *Logic Programming and Non-Monotonic Reasoning, Proceedings of the 3rd International Conference, LPNMR'95, Lexington, KY, USA, June 1995, Lecture Notes in Computer Science*, Volume 928, pages 127–142. Springer, Berlin.

[Lloyd, 1987] Lloyd, J. W. (1987). *Foundations of Logic Programming, Second Edition*. Springer, Berlin.

[Makinson, 2005] Makinson, D. (2005). *Bridges from Classical to Non-Monotonic Logic*. King's College Publications, London.

[Marchiori, 1996] Marchiori, E. (1996). On termination of general logic programs with respect to constructive negation. *The Journal of Logic Programming*, 26(1):69–89.

[Marek and Truszczyński, 1999] Marek, V. W. and Truszczyński, M. (1999). Stable models and an alternative logic programming paradigm. In Apt, K. R., Marek, V. W., Truszczyński, M., and Warren, D. S., editors, *The Logic Programming Paradigm: A 25-Year Perspective*, pages 375–398. Springer, Berlin.

[Markowsky, 1976] Markowsky, G. (1976). Chain-complete posets and directed sets with applications. *Algebra Universalis*, 6:53–68.

[Martin, 2000] Martin, K. (2000). A Foundation for Computation. PhD thesis, Department of Mathematics, Tulane University, New Orleans, LA.

[Martinetz and Schulten, 1991] Martinetz, T. and Schulten, K. (1991). A "Neural-Gas" network learns topologies. *Artificial Neural Networks*, I:397–402.

[Matthews, 1986] Matthews, S. G. (1986). Metric domains for completeness. Technical Report 76, Department of Computer Science, University of Warwick, Coventry, UK. Ph.D. Thesis, 1985.

[Matthews, 1992] Matthews, S. G. (1992). The cycle contraction mapping theorem. Technical Report 228, Department of Computer Science, University of Warwick, Coventry, UK.

[Matthews, 1994] Matthews, S. G. (1994). Partial metric topology. In Andima, S., Itzkowitz, G., Kong, Y., et al., editors, *Proceedings of the Eighth Summer Conference on General Topology and Its Applications, Queens College, CUNY, New York, USA, June, 1992*, Annals of the New York Academy of Sciences, Volume 728, pages 183–197. New York Academy of Sciences, New York.

[McCarthy, 1977] McCarthy, J. (1977). Epistemological problems of artificial intelligence. In *Proceedings of the International Joint Conference on Artificial Intelligence (IJCAI-77)*, pages 1038–1044.

[McCarthy, 1980] McCarthy, J. (1980). Circumscription — A form of non-monotonic reasoning. *Artificial Intelligence*, 13(1):27–39.

[Mendelson, 1987] Mendelson, E. (1987). *Introduction to Mathematical Logic*. Wadsworth & Brooks/Cole Advanced Books and Software, Monterey, CA.

[Moore, 1984] Moore, R. (1984). Possible-worlds semantics for autoepistemic logic. In *Proceedings of the 1984 Non-Monotonic Reasoning Workshop*. AAAI, Menlo Park, CA.

[Moore, 1985] Moore, R. (1985). Semantical considerations on non-monotonic logic. *Artificial Intelligence*, 25(1):75–94.

[Murtagh, 2004] Murtagh, F. (2004). On ultrametricity, data coding, and computation. *Journal of Classification*, 21:167–184.

[Murtagh, 2005] Murtagh, F. (2005). Identifying the ultrametricity of time series. *European Physical Journal*, 43(4):573–579.

[O'Neill, 1996] O'Neill, S. J. (1996). Partial metrics, valuations, and domain theory. In Andima, S., Flagg, R., Itzkowitz, G., et al., editors, *Papers on General Topology and Applications: Eleventh Summer Conference on General Topology and Applications, University of Southern Maine, Maine, August, 1996*, Annals of the New York Academy of Sciences, pages 304–315. New York Academy of Sciences, New York.

[Pedreschi et al., 2002] Pedreschi, D., Ruggieri, S., and Smaus, J.-G. (2002). Classes of terminating logic programs. *Theory and Practice of Logic Programming*, 2(3):369–418.

[Plotkin, 1983] Plotkin, G. D. (1983). *Domains*. Department of Computer Science, University of Edinburgh, Scotland.

[Prieß-Crampe, 1990] Prieß-Crampe, S. (1990). Der Banachsche Fixpunktsatz für ultrametrische Räume. *Results in Mathematics*, 18:178–186.

[Prieß-Crampe and Ribenboim, 1993] Prieß-Crampe, S. and Ribenboim, P. (1993). Fixed points, combs and generalized power series. *Abh. Math. Sem. Univ. Hamburg*, 63:227–244.

[Prieß-Crampe and Ribenboim, 2000a] Prieß-Crampe, S. and Ribenboim, P. (2000a). Fixed-point and attractor theorems for ultrametric spaces. *Forum Mathematicum.*, 12:53–64.

[Prieß-Crampe and Ribenboim, 2000b] Prieß-Crampe, S. and Ribenboim, P. (2000b). Logic programming and ultrametric spaces. *Rendiconti di Mathematica*, VII:1–13.

[Prieß-Crampe and Ribenboim, 2000c] Prieß-Crampe, S. and Ribenboim, P. (2000c). Ultrametric spaces and logic programming. *The Journal of Logic Programming*, 42:59–70.

[Przymusinska and Przymusinski, 1990] Przymusinska, H. and Przymusinski, T. C. (1990). Weakly stratified logic programs. *Fundamenta Informaticae*, 13:51–65.

[Przymusinski, 1988] Przymusinski, T. C. (1988). On the declarative semantics of deductive databases and logic programs. In Minker, J., editor, *Foundations of Deductive Databases and Logic Programming*, pages 193–216. Morgan Kaufmann Publishers, Los Altos, CA.

[Reed et al., 1991] Reed, G. M., Roscoe, A. W., and Wachter, R. F., editors (1991). *Topology and Category Theory in Computer Science*. Oxford University Press, Oxford, UK.

[Reiter, 1980] Reiter, R. (1980). A logic for default reasoning. *Artificial Intelligence*, 13:81–132.

[Reynolds, 2010] Reynolds, D., editor (2010). *OWL 2 RL in RIF*. A W3C Working Group Note. See http://www.w3.org/TR/rif-owl-rl/.

[Ribenboim, 1996] Ribenboim, P. (1996). The new theory of ultrametric spaces. *Periodica Mathematica Hungarica*, 32(1–2):103–111.

[Robinson, 1965] Robinson, J. A. (1965). A machine-oriented logic based on the resolution principle. *Journal of the ACM*, 12(1):23–41.

[Rodríguez-López et al., 2008] Rodríguez-López, J., Romaguera, S., and Valero, O. (2008). Denotational semantics for programming languages, balanced quasimetrics and fixed points. *International Journal of Computer Mathematics*, 85(3):623–630.

[Rojas, 1996] Rojas, R. (1996). *Neural Networks*. Springer, Berlin.

[Romaguera and Schellekens, 2003] Romaguera, S. and Schellekens, M. (2003). Norm-weightable Riesz spaces and the dual complexity space. In Hurley, T., MacanAirchinnigh, M., Schellekens, M., and Seda, A. K., editors, *Proceedings of the Second Irish Conference on the Mathematical Foundations of Computer Science and Information Technology (MFC-SIT2002), Galway, Ireland, July, 2002, Electronic Notes in Theoretical Computer Science*, Volume 74, pages 1–17. Elsevier Science Publishers, Amsterdam; New York.

[Rounds and Zhang, 2001] Rounds, W. C. and Zhang, G.-Q. (2001). Clausal logic and logic programming in algebraic domains. *Information and Computation*, 171(2):156–182.

[Rumelhart et al., 1986] Rumelhart, D. E., Hinton, G. E., and Williams., R. J. (1986). Learning internal representations by error propagation. In McClelland, J. L. and Rumelhart, D. E., editors, *Parallel Distributed Processing*, pages 318–362. MIT Press, Cambridge, MA.

[Rutten, 1995] Rutten, J. J. (1995). Elements of generalized ultrametric domain theory. Technical Report CS-R9507, CWI, Stichting Mathematisch Centrum, Amsterdam, The Netherlands.

[Rutten, 1996] Rutten, J. J. (1996). Elements of generalized ultrametric domain theory. *Theoretical Computer Science*, 170:349–381. Revised version of [Rutten, 1995].

[Scott, 1982a] Scott, D. S. (1982a). Domains for denotational semantics. In Nielsen, M. and Schmidt, E. M., editors, *Automata, Languages and Programming, 9th Colloquium, Aarhus, Denmark, July 12-16, 1982, Proceedings, Lecture Notes in Computer Science*, Volume 140, pages 577–613. Springer, Berlin.

[Scott, 1982b] Scott, D. S. (1982b). Lecture notes on a mathematical theory of computation. In Broy, M. and Schmidt, G., editors, *Theoretical Foundations of Programming Methodology*, pages 145–292. Reidel, Dordrecht.

[Scutellà, 1990] Scutellà, M. G. (1990). A note on Dowling and Gallier's top-down algorithm for propositional Horn satisfiability. *The Journal of Logic Programming*, 8:265–273.

[Seda, 1995] Seda, A. K. (1995). Topology and the semantics of logic programs. *Fundamenta Informaticae*, 24(4):359–386.

[Seda, 1997] Seda, A. K. (1997). Quasimetrics and the semantics of logic programs. *Fundamenta Informaticae*, 29(1):97–117.

[Seda, 2002] Seda, A. K. (2002). Some convergence issues in theoretical computer science. *Information*, 5(4):447–462.

262   Bibliography

[Seda, 2006] Seda, A. K. (2006). On the integration of connectionist and
    logic-based systems. In Hurley, T., MacanAirchinnigh, M., Schellekens,
    M., Seda, A. K., and Strong, G., editors, *Proceedings of the Third Irish
    Conference on the Mathematical Foundations of Computer Science and
    Information Technology (MFCSIT2004), Trinity College Dublin, Ireland,
    July, 2004, Electronic Notes in Theoretical Computer Science*, Volume
    161, pages 109–130. Elsevier Science Publishers, Amsterdam; New York.

[Seda, 2007] Seda, A. K. (2007). Morphisms of ANN and the computation of
    least fixed points of semantic operators. In Mira, J. and Álvarez, J. R.,
    editors, *Proceedings of the Second International Work-Conference on the
    Interplay Between Natural and Artificial Computation (IWINAC2007),
    Murcia, Spain, June, 2007*, Part 1, *Lecture Notes in Computer Science*,
    Volume 4527, pages 224–233. Springer, Berlin.

[Seda and Hitzler, 1999a] Seda, A. K. and Hitzler, P. (1999a). Strictly level-
    decreasing logic programs. In Butterfield, A. and Flynn, S., editors, *Pro-
    ceedings of the Second Irish Workshop on Formal Methods (IWFM'98),
    NUI, Cork, Ireland, July, 1998, Electronic Workshops in Computing*,
    pages 1–18. British Computer Society, Swindon, UK.

[Seda and Hitzler, 1999b] Seda, A. K. and Hitzler, P. (1999b). Topology and
    iterates in computational logic. In Flagg, R., Hart, K., Norden, J., Tym-
    chatyn, E., and Tuncali, M., editors, *Proceedings of the 12th Summer
    Conference on Topology and Its Applications: Special Session on Topol-
    ogy in Computer Science, Ontario, Canada, August, 1997*, Volume 22 of
    Topology Proceedings, pages 427–469.

[Seda and Hitzler, 2010] Seda, A. K. and Hitzler, P. (2010). Generalized dis-
    tance functions in the theory of computation. *The Computer Journal*,
    53(4):443–464.

[Seda and Lane, 2003] Seda, A. K. and Lane, M. (2003). On continuous mod-
    els of computation: Towards computing the distance between (logic) pro-
    grams. In Morris, J., Aziz, B., and Oehl, F., editors, *Proceedings of the
    Sixth International Workshop in Formal Methods (IWFM'03), Dublin
    City University, Dublin, Ireland, July, 2003, Electronic Workshops in
    Computing*, pages 1–15. British Computer Society, Swindon, UK.

[Seda and Lane, 2005] Seda, A. K. and Lane, M. (2005). On the measurability
    of the semantic operators determined by logic programs. *Information*,
    8(1):33–52.

[Seda et al., 2003] Seda, A. K., Heinze, R., and Hitzler, P. (2003). Conver-
    gence classes and spaces of partial functions. In *Domain Theory, Logic
    and Computation. Proceedings of the 2nd International Symposium on*

Domain Theory, ISDT (2001), Sichuan University, Chengdu, China, October, 2001, Semantic Structures in Computation, Volume 3, pages 75–115. Kluwer Academic Publishers, Dordrecht, The Netherlands.

[Simons et al., 2002] Simons, P., Niemelä, I., and Soininen, T. (2002). Extending and implementing the stable model semantics. *Artificial Intelligence*, 138:181–234.

[Smyth, 1987] Smyth, M. B. (1987). Quasi uniformities: Reconciling domains with metric spaces. In Main, M. G., Melton, A., Mislove, M. W., and Schmidt, D. A., editors, *Mathematical Foundations of Programming Language Semantics, Lecture Notes in Computer Science*, Volume 198, pages 236–253. Springer, Berlin.

[Smyth, 1991] Smyth, M. B. (1991). Totally bounded spaces and compact ordered spaces as domains of computation. In Reed, G. M., Roscoe, A. W., and Wachter, R. F., editors, *Topology and Category Theory in Computer Science*, pages 207–229. Oxford University Press, Oxford, UK.

[Smyth, 1992] Smyth, M. B. (1992). Topology. In Abramsky, S., Gabbay, D. M., and Maibaum, T. S., editors, *Handbook of Logic in Computer Science Volume 1*, pages 641–761. Oxford University Press, Oxford, UK.

[Stoltenberg-Hansen et al., 1994] Stoltenberg-Hansen, V., Lindström, I., and Griffor, E. R. (1994). *Mathematical Theory of Domains*. Cambridge Tracts in Theoretical Computer Science No. 22. Cambridge University Press, Cambridge, UK.

[Straccia et al., 2009] Straccia, U., Ojeda-Aciego, M., and Damásio, C. V. (2009). On fixed points of multivalued functions on complete lattices and their application to generalized logic programs. *SIAM Journal of Computing*, 38(5):1881–1911.

[van Emden and Kowalski, 1976] van Emden, M. H. and Kowalski, R. A. (1976). The semantics of predicate logic as a programming language. *Journal of the ACM*, 23(4):733–742.

[Van Gelder et al., 1991] Van Gelder, A., Ross, K. A., and Schlipf, J. S. (1991). The well-founded semantics for general logic programs. *Journal of the ACM*, 38(3):620–650.

[Waszkiewicz, 2002] Waszkiewicz, P. (2002). Quantitative Continuous Domains. PhD thesis, School of Computer Science, The University of Birmingham, Edgbaston, Birmingham, UK.

[Waszkiewicz, 2003] Waszkiewicz, P. (2003). Quantitative continuous domains. *Applied Categorical Structures*, 11(1):41–67.

[Waszkiewicz, 2006] Waszkiewicz, P. (2006). Partial metrizability of continuous posets. *Mathematical Structures in Computer Science*, 16(2):359–372.

[Wendt, 2002a] Wendt, M. (2002a). Unfolding the well-founded semantics. Technical Report WV–02–08, Knowledge Representation and Reasoning Group, Department of Computer Science, Dresden University of Technology.

[Wendt, 2002b] Wendt, M. (2002b). Unfolding the well-founded semantics. *Journal of Electrical Engineering, Slovak Academy of Sciences*, 53(12/s):56–59.

[Willard, 1970] Willard, S. (1970). *General Topology*. Addison-Wesley, Reading, MA.

[Zhang, 1991] Zhang, G.-Q. (1991). *Logic of Domains*. Birkhauser, Boston.

[Zhang and Rounds, 1997a] Zhang, G.-Q. and Rounds, W. C. (1997a). Complexity of power default reasoning. In *Proceedings of the Twelfth Annual IEEE Symposium on Logic in Computer Science, LICS'97, Warsaw, Poland*, pages 328–339. IEEE Computer Society Press.

[Zhang and Rounds, 1997b] Zhang, G.-Q. and Rounds, W. C. (1997b). Reasoning with power defaults (preliminary report). In Dix, J., Furbach, U., and Nerode, A., editors, *Proceedings of the Fourth International Conference on Logic Programming and Non-Monotonic Reasoning (LP-NMR'97), Dagstuhl, Germany, Lecture Notes in Computer Science*, Volume 1265, pages 152–169. Springer, Berlin.

[Zhang and Rounds, 2001] Zhang, Q.-Z. and Rounds, W. C. (2001). Semantics of logic programs and representation of Smyth powerdomains. In Keimel, K. et al., editors, *Domains and Processes*, pages 151–179. Kluwer Academic Publishers, Dordrecht, The Netherlands.

Index